The Domestic Revolution

THE DOMESTIC REVOLUTION

Enlightenment Feminisms
and the Novel

Eve Tavor Bannet

The Johns Hopkins
University Press

Baltimore &
London

9 8 7 6 5 4 3 2 1

A shorter version of Chapter 3 appeared in *Eighteenth-Century Studies* 30, no. 3 (spring 1997): 233–54, and is reprinted by permission. Part of Chapter 2 appeared as "Rewriting the Social Text: The Female *Bildungsroman* in Eighteenth-Century England," in *Reflection and Action: Essays on the Bildungsroman,* ed. James Harden, (Columbia: University of South Carolina Press, 1991) and is reprinted by permission.

The Johns Hopkins University Press
2715 North Charles Street
Baltimore, Maryland 21218-4363
www.press.jhu.edu

Library of Congress Cataloging-in-Publication Data
will be found at the end of this book.

A catalog record for this book is available
from the British Library.

ISBN 0-8018-6416-X
ISBN 0-8018-6417-8 (pbk.)

To my sons,
Jonathan and Alan
Bannet

CONTENTS

Contents

ACKNOWLEDGMENTS

THIS BOOK has been a number of years in the making. It therefore owes an incalculable debt to students who made these eighteenth-century women's writings their own, to the presses that made it possible to bring them into the classroom, to the colleagues who invited me to give lectures and papers about them, and to the anonymous lady at a narrative literature conference in Madison, Wisconsin, one snowy April, who said reprovingly: "I come to your papers every year. When are you going to turn all these bits into a book?"

Earlier versions of part or all of the manuscript were read by Claudia Brodsky-Lacour, Dan Cottom, James Thompson, Jim Harden, Laura Brown, and Ronald Schleifer, and by some general readers who agreed to tell me what was dull or obscure. I thank them all for time taken from other things and for their honesty, good advice, and encouragement. I have been exceptionally fortunate in my editors at the Johns Hopkins University Press, and I thank Jacqueline Wehmuller, Maura Burnett, and Anne Whitmore for their enthusiasm and all their hard work.

This book is dedicated to my sons, Jonathan and Alan, who have become inured to finding their mother's nose in a book and who take lapses of maternal attention in their stride. I hope that they and their future partners will finally be free of the constructions of domesticity they can read about here.

The Domestic Revolution

? not marginal   + cite Hesse on this
                                 issue

domestic rev = 4th revolution
                    scene of the novel.
why family so VIP

INTRODUCTION

Enlightenment Feminisms
and the Domestic Novel

Along side the three revolutions we usually identify with the long eighteenth century — the French Revolution, the American Revolution, and the Glorious Revolution of 1688 — Enlightenment ideology gave rise to a quieter but no less significant revolution in the family and in middle- and upper-class ladies' status and familial roles. This book explores the central and largely forgotten part that the writings of public women played in this domestic revolution, which was later naturalized as the doctrine of "separate spheres."

Women writers of novels, conduct books, and tracts were far from marginal to the eighteenth-century literary scene. Increasing numbers of women entered the literary market place between 1660 and 1800; and between 1750 and the end of the century the sheer numbers of women writing novels, poems, conduct books, and tracts doubled each decade.[1] The novel in particular was so heavily dominated by women writers that men sometimes complained that it was more profitable to publish novels under a woman's name. Although, like the men, these women writers were often forced by the economic exigencies of their personal situations to "live by the pen," they had the courage to "address the major religious, social and political issues of their day"; and after mid century, they acquired extraordinary "literary and extra-literary authority" as guides of public morality.[2]

Public women taught private women[3] to take over government of the family from men and made it, in Hannah More's words, "the profession of ladies to be wives, mothers and mistresses of families." They imagined, proposed, and modeled for their readers an as yet ideal and idealized family in which women "dignified" themselves through their domestic government and through the capacities they demonstrated by their domestic and philanthropic work. Public women used their authority to reconfigure the patriarchal family in ways that precluded ladies from continuing to figure as "upper servants to their husbands" and gave them culturally prized domestic and national roles. They also taught women to manage their sexuality so as to protect themselves from want and fashioned for ladies of superior sense and ability the mask of "Angel in the House." It was these Enlightenment feminists who invented for well-to-do, leisured ladies the purely domestic lifestyle that many women in the late twentieth century fled and to which others desire to return.

Domestic ideal created by ♀♀ not men.

But *why* did these Enlightenment women make the family — rather than, say, women's severe loss of jobs in the economy and their increasing inability to support themselves — the primary issue for both radical and conservative women writers of novels, conduct books, and tracts? Why did they treat these changes in the structure and conduct of the family and in women's proper roles as a central feminist issue with far-reaching social and political implications, as well as practical consequences for the ordinary conduct of women's lives? Should we assume that women writers already derived their authority to speak about the family from the fact of being women — or was it they who constructed the family as a subject about which women might properly and authoritatively speak?

The government and regulation of the family was, as we will see, one of Enlightenment England's major religious, social, and political issues. Throughout the eighteenth century, the family was still a *topos* where different concepts of government, nature, and society; different models of economics, religion, duty, and order; different uses of education, virtue, and power; and different constructions of gender intersected and converged. One might even say that the family was the conceptual and figurative domain par excellence where public moral, social, and political differences were fought out, for the family occupied a different signifying space in eighteenth-century thought than it did later, under nineteenth- and twentieth-century liberalism. Viewed as a microcosm of the state and as the polity's most fundamental component unit, as the guarantor of the nation's peace, order, and prosperity, and as the private origin of the "public good," yet widely held to be in disarray, the family in the eighteenth century was not yet conceived as secondary to the real business of society or to the serious concerns of men.

By entering old texts from a new direction, as Adrienne Rich said, and by allowing women's writings to direct and organize our reading of some of the Enlightenment's major philosophical, political, and legislative texts, we will be able to see how women who wrote novels, conduct books, and tracts challenged and revised public thinking about the family, as well as the traditional patriarchal constructions of the family inscribed in the now "classical" political, philosophical, economic, and legislative writings of public men. This will bring into view a curious and all but forgotten story about a domestic revolution that was largely the fruit of women's imagination and the effect of women's work.

So far doesn't see too original

Matriarchs and Egalitarians

In their novels, conduct books, and tracts, Enlightenment women writers developed and promoted at least two versions of ladies' proper conduct and domestic roles, which I shall refer to as Egalitarian and Matriarchal. Egalitarians from Judith Drake to Charlotte Smith, Mary Hays, and Mary Wollstonecraft argued that "there is no other difference between Men and Us than what their Tyranny has created," and that "we have an equal aptitude to sense and virtue with men."[4] Matriarchs from Mary Astell and Lady Masham to Jane West and Hannah More, by contrast, promoted "Women's Superior Excellence over Men," and held that although "the Men have by fraud and violence gained a superiority of power over us, we still retain our original superiority of sense and virtue over them."[5] Egalitarian and Matriarchal conceptions of the "domestic woman" and of the proper government of the family differed accordingly.

equality/ difference paradigm

While retaining a firm belief in domestic, social, and political hierarchy and appearing more conventional than they were, Matriarchs taught ladies how to obtain and deploy the ascendancy over men, over their families, and over their inferiors, which they thought were the ladies' due. Egalitarians, on the other hand, preached independence from all subordination, both at home and abroad, and sought to level hierarchies both in the family and in the state. Matriarchs imagined a family in which the patriarchal governor of the domestic hierarchy had been surreptitiously supplanted by a wife who understood that she had but to "give the Lords of Creation the appearance of supremacy" to rule them as she would, and who exercised her power over her children and domestics as a capable mother-governess. Egalitarians imagined a family based on consensual relations between parents and children and husbands and wives and on a division of labor between women and men who related to each other as equals and displayed equal softness and equal sense.

That there were, in principle, different strands of feminism during the seventeenth and eighteenth centuries has been clear since Elaine Hobby's and Janet Todd's groundbreaking books: respectively, *Virtue of Necessity* (1988) and *The Sign of Angellica* (1989). Where Hobby described different seventeenth-century feminisms as sequential and generational, however, Todd construed them as "conservative" or "radical/liberal" currents which persisted throughout the long eighteenth century. Todd therefore used the term *conservative* quite broadly to mean "a nostalgic apprehension of a hierarchical and organic past, sometimes including a Christian desire to reassert traditional moral values and sometimes a yearning for external authority," and *liberal* or *radical,* equally broadly, for "a whole spectrum of values from old Whig notions and through Dissenting ones to those reviled by conservatives as 'jacobin.'"[6] These characterizations of Enlightenment women writers proved helpful in a number of ways. Todd's descriptors helped to demonstrate that women authors were "not newborn but already part of culture," by identifying their positions with political platforms familiar from the writings of eighteenth-century men.[7] By using terms that linked feminist debates in the 1970s and 1980s to the early modern period, her division of Enlightenment women writers into conservatives and liberals made visible the extent to which feminist revisionings of history had focused on the liberal tradition. This, in turn, prompted critics like Mitzi Myers, Nicola Watson, and April London to begin to redress the imbalance by reconsidering the impact of "conservative" women writers such as Hannah More, Jane West, and Maria Edgeworth at the turn of the nineteenth century.

But, the binary topography created by the division of Enlightenment women writers into conservatives and liberals or radicals also proved to have disadvantages. It tended to conflate the positions of Enlightenment feminists with those of traditional conservative or liberal patriarchs on the issues of most concern to women, and to do so in such a way as to intimate — almost a priori — that women writers were little more than agents of hegemonic disciplinary practices or complicit with patriarchal domestic agendas. Dividing women into conservative and liberal camps made it harder to flesh out the domestic ideologies of public women as distinct from those of public men, even while it occluded the ground that Enlightenment feminists shared. As Eleanor Ty has pointed out, the misogynist eighteenth-century division of Enlightenment women writers into "sex'd" and "unsex'd" females had much the same effect.[8] These disadvantages of the terms and of the assumptions they carried with them became all the more apparent as feminist scholars like Mitzi Myers, Patricia Myer Spacks, and Anne Mellor began to question and "contest the seamless account of the triumph of domestic ideology in England between 1750 and 1850 put forth in Mary Poovey's *The Proper Lady and the Woman Writer* [1984] and in Nancy Armstrong's *Desire and Domestic Fiction* [1987]"[9] and to argue that Enlightenment feminist writers were "not passively mirroring cultural ascriptions, but . . . purposely appropriating them to serve women-defined ends" and "reshaping ideology closer to their hearts' desire."[10]

Describing Enlightenment women writers as Matriarchs and Egalitarians to distinguish them from their more patriarchal, liberal or conservative, contemporaries is an important step towards complicating the binary view and making it possible to explore the interplay of diverse domestic and political agendas in an environment where, to borrow Margaret Ezell's words, "the patriarch's powers" were still "neither clearly defined nor secure."[11] Exploring this intertexual space makes it apparent that Enlightenment feminist writers inhabited a complex discursive world where diverse feminist and patriarchal agendas were articulated upon one another and where different voices were both joined and divided by the "same" words, the "same" ideals, and the "same" representations, often attaching different meanings to the same lexes.

To speak of the ways in which Matriarchal and Egalitarian feminist writings were joined to and separated from those of conservative and liberal men — as well as from each other — by the same language and the same domestic and political ideologies, one might usefully call on a paradigm of translation which Derrida, among others, has brought back to our attention.[12] In this old-new paradigm of translation, which links what Dryden and Pope called "imitation" to postmodern concepts of "rewriting" and "repetition with difference," translations not only carry ideas, typologies, stories, and ideals across from language to language and from text to text; they also "augment and modify the original" by iterating, transforming, adapting, adding, citing, parodying, selecting, omitting, and displacing its elements at will.[13] Not necessarily equivalent, faithful, or identical to any original, such translations are to be read both for the likenesses and the differences between overlapping and competing texts.

This is useful, because Matriarchal and Egalitarian writers were not only not newborn in cultural terms; they were often learned and thoroughly well-read. When they are understood as translators and transformers of cultural materials, evidence that well-read women authors wove their feminist philosophies and feminist strategies from assumptions or concerns which they shared with their male contemporaries need no longer be construed exclusively as evidence of co-optation or complicity on their part. Indeed, as Elizabeth Grosz has rightly observed, "emersion in patriarchal practices is the condition of effective critique and movement beyond them."[14] By translating hegemonic ideals in their own manner and adapting cultural values to their own ends, Enlightenment women writers both critiqued these values and ideals and moved beyond them. While carrying particular ideas, assumptions, and goals from men's texts into their own, they often analyzed them from a different place and altered, developed, and rewrote them for their own ends. They also inscribed themselves in the lacunae of Enlightenment ideology by indicating — and exploiting or developing — what men's discourses about power, competition, equality, and law, men's representations of the family, and men's expectations of women, willfully or blindly, left unthought. It was precisely by working both inside and outside cultural frames of reference in these ways that Enlightenment feminists took advantage of opportunities and possibilities implicit in the ideology and the culture to reconfigure women's domestic and social lot.

Thus, despite the language and assumptions they shared with their conservative and liberal counterparts, Matriarchal and Egalitarian writers offered visions of the structure and dynamics of the family and of women's domestic roles within it quite different from those of patriarchal ideologues, whether the latter were promoting the "older style patriarchy, with its emphasis on paternal prerogative, hierarchy and the exercise of force" or the more benevolent and paternalistic "new style patriarchy with its appeal to reason . . . and non-coercive exercise of authority," as Elizabeth Kowalski-Wallace puts it.[15] By the second half of the eighteenth century, there were at least four competing patriarchal and feminist constructions of the family, of the domestic woman, and of the relative duties of husbands and wives, parents and children, implicitly or explicitly engaging each other in didactic, fictional, and philosophical texts.

Matriarchal and Egalitarian writers attached different meanings to words like *sense, virtue, God, principle,* and *duty;* they promoted different images of the family , images that corresponded to their different visions and goals for the polity; and their novels offered different emplotments of women's lives. But they joined in confronting the same issues and in a common perception of the problems women faced. Both sought, in their different ways, to raise women from their inferior standing relative to men in the household, in cultural representations and in prescriptive social norms, and to refashion women's manners, women's morals, and women's education to these ends. Both promoted an as yet ideal and idealized division of labour between women and men — later to be dubbed "separate spheres" — which would allow wives to take over the important and culturally valued domestic offices from their husbands and take charge of the governance of children, servants, and dependents in the household themselves. After passage of the Marriage Act in 1753, both analyzed and represented female sexuality as an economic question, not merely a moral question, and revised or critiqued the relations of women within the family to the "friendless and deserted condition" of women without.

Above all, Matriarchs and Egalitarians both understood what Clara Reeve called "the female cause," as a series of issues relating to the government of ladies in the family. For them, the female cause was a question of whether ladies were to govern themselves in their domestic situations or continue to be governed by fathers and husbands playing virtually interchangeable roles. The female cause was a question of whether "the little society of the family" was to be governed by ladies or by their "domestic tyrants." And the female cause was a question of the principles by which both the little society of the family and the greater society of the kingdom were to be structured and ruled.

In defining "the female cause" as a series of issues relating to domestic government, Egalitarians and Matriarchs were engaging men on their own ideological ground. As studies by Lynn Hunt, Eleonor Ty, Caroline Gonda, and Danielle Gobetti have confirmed, what Hunt calls "the family model of politics" was still alive and well at the end of the eighteenth century. In England, men's government of the family remained central to political ideology and public policy, as well as to men's moralized prescriptions for the interpersonal conduct of parents and children, masters and servants, husbands and wives. England was imagined by male ideologues (especially by conservatives) as a hierarchy of propertied families, each with its subordinate women, children, servants, tenants and dependents, and each governed by a humane and beneficent "domestic sovereign" for the public good. Analogies between the way the master of a family governed his wife, children, and domestics and the way the sovereign governed his subjects, and between "the little society of the family" and "the greater society of the kingdom," were still crucial to constructions and representations of both. The public-private divide as liberalism constructed it did not, as feminists argued in the 1970s and 1980s, begin with Locke. As we will see, our key words — *public, private, domestic, family, society, democracy* — occupied different signifying spaces in the eighteenth century than they do now. One of the most important assumptions that Egalitarians and Matriarchs shared with Enlightenment followers of Locke throughout the century — an assumption underlying legislation for the family and patriarchal representations of the family as well as feminist refashionings of ladies' domestic roles — was that the family was both the origin of society and society's most fundamental component unit, and that there was therefore continuity, as well as analogy, between the private and the public good, and between the ordering of private families and the peace, prosperity, and well-being of the state.

In considering the articulations between different constructions and representations of the family and of the public good in the latter half of the eighteenth century, it is important to understand that they were not newly minted and that Egalitarian and Matriarchal domestic agendas already had quite a long genealogy of their own. Feminists in the latter half of the eighteenth century iterated, and translated for their own time, positions developed for women over a century before by those "first feminists" who wrote during and after the English Civil War. Developing out of seventeenth-century women's reactions to debates surrounding religious sectarianism as well as "the family model of politics," Matriarchal and Egalitarian positions grew by accretion, repetition, adaptation, sup-plementation, and dialogue. Egalitarian goals and arguments first articulated in the language of religious sectarianism were translated and transformed by Matriarchal and Egalitarian encounters with Locke and post-Lockean ideology. They were readapted and rearticulated by Egalitarians and Matriarchs in response to the treacherous legal and practical realities created for middle- and upper-class ladies by the 1753 Marriage Act and by the growing shortage of respectable work for ladies without independent means, and they were again reshaped and repositioned by British Enlightenment ideologues' encounters with the leveling principles of the French Revolution.

Throughout the long eighteenth century, Matriarchs and Egalitarians not only repeated themselves a great deal; they also borrowed each others' arguments and built on each other's work. Therefore, despite the Matriarchs' demonization of the leveling Egalitarians at the end of the eighteenth century in the wake of the French Revolution, the relation between these two Enlightenment feminisms was not so much one of mutual opposition as one of intertranslation and mutual articulation. Matriarchs and Egalitarians were articulated onto one another across time and across ideological camps through the migration of particular ideas, arguments, and goals back and forth between them. Particular ideas, arguments, goals, or representations inscribed in the texts of one camp would be incorporated, adapted, and rewritten by the other camp — only, in time, to be taken up by the first camp in their altered form. This is why Hannah More and Mary Wollstonecraft, for instance, echo each other in ways that can be disconcerting and why there are echoes in both of Mary Astell.

The success of the ladies' domestic revolution owed a great deal to this intertranslation, for the Matriarchs, with their studied conventionality and their cautious step-by-step and sphere-by-sphere approach, often succeeded in carrying points which had originated among the more impatient, openly ambitious, and sweeping revolutionary Egalitarians. By the same token, iterations by Egalitarians of positions preached or gained by Matriarchs often enabled them to present some of their own arguments as versions of a wider female consensus and to offer the more far-reaching changes they proposed as corrections, adaptations, or extensions of Matriarchal achievements or goals. It is amusing — and no small tribute to the astuteness of their strategy — that most men should have found Matriarchs so much less threatening than the Egalitarians and that we should be accusing Matriarchs of patriarchalism and conservatism as a result, for it was the Matriarchs — who often disliked or despised men — who in fact carried every feminist point and, step-by-step over the *longue durée,* sucessfully implemented every plank of the seventeenth-century egalitarian platform.

Because Enlightenment feminists reiterated one another and articulated themselves upon one another, across time and across ideological camps, labels like *Matriarch* and *Egalitarian* are more usefully viewed as heuristic devices than as indicators of invariable platforms or of fixed ideological identities. As Anne Phillips has pointed out, "the dominance of a norm can be so powerful that it obscures the startling fact that most people lie outside its boundaries."[16] Exploring "normative" Egalitarian and Matriarchal positions as articulated in conduct books and tracts as well as their fictional exemplifications in literary texts will permit us to understand the extremes of imagined possibility in a particular cultural environment. But, rather than requiring us to assume that every woman necessarily fitted one or other of these norms, this only allows us to see more clearly how particular novels or particular writers — Frances Sheridan, Amelia Opie, the later Burney, or Jane Austen, for instance — constructed their positions, debated the extremes, or negotiated between them. As Alice Browne reminds us, too, there were also those who occupied this middle ground by espousing the sort of "mild instrumental feminism" which sought only to make women better companions for men.[17]

Women's Exemplary Fictions

During the second half of the eighteenth century, Matriarchal and Egalitarian writers of didactic novels tapped into the exemplar tradition, which had, since the Renaissance, conceived of narratives of all sorts as "philosophy teaching by example," to disseminate their different politico-feminist philosophies and to offer their readers altered models of imitation and desire. In making "entertaining examples" the means "of finding him who flees a serious lecture,"[18] women writers were using an already well-established discursive and pedagogical practice, which taught by offering constructed and embodied ideals of conduct for readers' imitation and by persuading them that these ideals were possible and proper, admirable, and entirely worthy of imitation in the state of the current world. Tapping into the exemplar tradition enabled women writers to intervene in social practice by offering their readers alternative models for the conduct of their domestic lives and by moving them to the kinds of domestic and social action they proposed. The exemplary novel therefore put into women's hands a powerful instrument of social change — as everyone well understood. Throughout the century, writers of both sexes pointed out in conduct books, novels, and reviews, and often with marked disapproval, that women were imitating the heroines of the novels they read.

Teaching by literary examples had long been associated with civic education, and claiming that they were making "entertaining stories the vehicle to convey to the young and flexible heart wholesome truths that it refused to receive under the form of precept and instruction"[19] enabled Egalitarian and Matriarchal novelists to construct a respectable public role for themselves as moralists and social reformers. However, appropriation of this public role required Matriarchs and Egalitarians to assume or invent a posture of conventionality, and even of anodyne propriety, which can mislead us into reading the Enlightenment woman writer only as a "proper lady." Certainly, as Mary Poovey has shown, she often portrayed herself as such, but Margaret Ezell and Anne Mellor have both pointed out that proper disclaimers of the desire to appear in print must also be read as a *topos* deriving from an "older attitude about writing, print and readership" which was far from exclusive to women.[20] As we will see, in the latter half of the eighteenth century, Matriarchs and Egalitarians were also using affirmations of propriety and morality as masks for their more innovative or outrageous moves. One might even say that it was precisely because — in the didactic and exemplary novel — women were wielding an instrument of real power and using it to bring about material changes in the conduct of women's social and domestic lives, that Matriarchal and Egalitarian novelists needed to stress the modesty of their pretensions, the morality of their novels, and the utter conventionality of their designs.

It is often in the tension between these not entirely compatible faces of their fictions that much of the literary interest of eighteenth-century women's novels lies. But, to perceive and enjoy this tension, we need to lay bare those now unfamiliar devices of exemplarity which enabled women to use the most proper of fictional representations to disseminate politico-feminist agendas at odds with the dominant patriarchal master-narratives. The use of these devices led Mrs. Barbauld to observe, in her prefatory essay to *The British Novelists* in 1810, that in eighteenth-century novels, the philosophical and ideological "war of systems" had been fought out.

Important new work has been done on Renaissance and seventeenth-century exemplarity by John Lyons and Timothy Hampton, among others, but little or no attention has yet been paid to the deployment of exemplarity by eighteenth-century women writers. During the past ten years, the emphasis in literary studies of eighteenth-century novels has largely been on genre. While exploring alternatives and supplements to Ian Watt's story of the rise of the canonical novel as a prehistory of the realist novel and of our present, a great deal of important work has been done to define (or deconstruct) the differences between novel and romance and between narratives based on fact and fictions, as well as to distinguish male Gothic from female Gothic, male Romanticism from female Romanticism, and male from female novels of sensibility.[21] Yet, these generic questions tend to marginalize or occlude the questions relating to exemplarity which interested eighteenth-century literary theorists and informed the writings of eighteenth-century women novelists. If, as James Thompson has pointed out, "novels are a kind of cultural laboratory or imaginary in which various forms of social evaluation can be modeled and tested," then understanding better how eighteenth-century women deployed exemplarity is key to understanding the ways in which eighteenth-century women's novels "offer models of choice and expectation" and "provide possibilities to imagine, objects to buy and desires to try."[22]

As we will see in Chapters 2 and 5, questions of exemplarity cut across, and in a sense deconstruct, what we conceive to be different genres of narrative and transgress the lines we draw between reality and fiction. One way in which they do so is by iteration of exemplary scenarios and familial problematiques from novel to novel and genre to genre. As Cheryl Turner reminds us, "eighteenth-century women writers were aware of and responsive to each other."[23] Besides being an accepted eighteenth-century method for producing new novels from old fast enough to pay one's bills, narrative "repetition with difference" was how women novelists inscribed their awareness of each other and their responsiveness to one another's work. Matriarchal and Egalitarian novelists conducted their debates with each other by countering each other's examples and rewriting each other's narrative scenarios. The translation of similar plots, the iteration of similar problematiques, the citation of similarly typed characters and situations, and the rewriting of exemplary scenarios from novel to novel and genre to genre were ways for women writers to ally themselves with one of the feminist traditions, to indicate where they disagreed with one another, and to engage in dialogues with their peers.

Matriarchs and Egalitarians both used the conventions of exemplary narratives to critique and castigate whatever they found reprehensible in women's and men's domestic conduct and in the various forms of violence by which women were victimized in patriarchal families, which were still outside the law. Both groups also used the conventions of exemplary narratives to dignify and reward the sorts of conduct in women, the sorts of husband-wife and parent-child relations, and the sorts of solutions to the difficulties facing women that they proposed in their place. As we will see, Egalitarian novels like Fanny Burney's *Evalina* and *Cecilia*, Charlotte Smith's *Emmeline*, Mrs. Inchbald's *A Simple Story*, and Radcliffe's *Romance of the Forest*, and Matriarchal novels like Frances Brooke's *Lady Julia Mandeville*, Sarah Scott's *Cornelia*, Charlotte Lennox's *Sophia*, Eliza Haywood's *Betsy Thoughtless*, and Maria Edgeworth's *Belinda* used the conventions of exemplary narratives in characteristically different ways to disseminate their different feminist philosophies.

Matriarchal and Egalitarian novelists undoubtedly had the cultural impact they did because, beyond and despite their individual differences, each repeated the same arguments (in Milton's sense) and re-presented the same fictional emplotments of family fortunes and of women's lives. Repetition of the same Matriarchal or Egalitarian principles and critiques from novel to novel and from genre to genre was crucial to harnessing exemplarity as a lever for social change. This is nowhere more evident than in Matriarchal and Egalitarian rewritings of Rousseau.

In an important book, Nicola Watson has shown how Saint-Preux and Julie's passion in the first half of *Julie, ou la Nouvelle Héloïse* created a framework for those Matriarchal readings and novelistic rewritings of Rousseau at the turn of the nineteenth century which, like Burke, sought to identify the "plot of revolution" with the Egalitarian cult of "anarchic" private sensibility, in order to suppress both. However, Watson's book, which begins in 1790, leaves at the margins earlier feminist rewritings of Clarens — Rousseau's utopian image in the second half of *Héloïse* of the benevolent patriarchal family on its rural estate governed by a regulating and educating "nursing Father" for the good of all. This image was in many ways more central to the eighteenth-century feminist debate.

Because *Héloïse* and *Emile* were initially read and received in England as fictional translations of Locke's family romance and as redeployments of earlier eighteenth-century British country-house panegyrics, rewritings of Rousseau's image of domestic happiness at Clarens provided both Matriarchs and Egalitarians in the second half of the eighteenth century with a convenient way of challenging and correcting those assumptions about the polity and the family and those traditional patriarchal views of women that Rousseau's novels shared with British male establishment ideologues. Matriarchs, like Frances Brooke in *Lady Julia Mandeville* and *The Excursion*, Sarah Scott in *Millenium Hall* and *Sir George Ellison*, and Lady Mary Hamilton in *Munster Village*, had already subjected Clarens to Matriarchal revision and rewriting during the 1760s and 1770s. Egalitarian rewritings of Rousseau's utopian ideal of domestic government in the 1780s and 1790s — in novels like *Julia*, *The Victim of Prejudice*, *Romance of the Forest*, *Nature and Art*, *Marchmont*, and *Montalbert* — challenged these Matriarchal correctives of Clarens as much as they challenged Rousseau. As we will see, the curious transformation of Rousseau in England from establishment patriarch in the 1760s to dangerous leveler of hierarchies and persons in the 1790s owes more than we now remember to these debating women's novels and to the impact of Egalitarian novelists like Mary Hays, Maria Helen Williams, Eliza Fenwick, Ann Radcliffe, and Charlotte Smith, who rewrote Rousseau as an Egalitarian and whose positions came to be mistaken for his.

Some Questions of History and Time

Precept and example were the two pillars of Enlightenment pedagogy, and in their conduct books and novels, Enlightenment women writers used both. This book consequently juxtaposes each with the other and places them in dialogue. Each chapter also focuses on an important area of difference or dispute between Egalitarians and Matriarchs and relates their positions to those of their male contemporaries.

Chapter 1, "The Question of Domestic Government," considers how the Egalitarians' and Matriarchs' rival leveling or hierarchical visions of "societies great and small" played out in their respective constructions of the nonpatriarchal family, in the changes they envisioned in women's relative place in the domestic hierarchy, in their arguments for women's agency (which they called self-government), and in their demands for extension of education to women and of law into the home. In the process, this chapter discusses how Matriarchal and Egalitarian precepts during the second half of the eighteenth century repeated and revised precepts inscribed a century before by those "first feminists" writing during and after the Civil War and how Matriarchal and Egalitarian platforms developed as alternative feminist responses to Locke and to other key philosophical and political Enlightenment texts that assumed analogy between the public and the private and between the family and the state.

Chapter 2, "Domestic Fictions and the Pedagogy of Example," lays bare the mechanisms and conventions of fictional exemplification. It shows how the Matriarchal and Egalitarian precepts delineated in Chapter 1 were exemplified, fleshed out, and complicated in novels from mid century on and how Matriarchs and Egalitarians used morality in their novels as masks, to make themselves seem more proper than they were. The novels discussed in some detail are Frances Brooke's *Lady Julia Mandeville,* Fanny Burney's *Evalina* and *Cecilia,* Charlotte Smith's *Emmeline,* Mrs. Inchbald's *A Simple Story,* Eliza Haywood's *Betsy Thoughtless,* Charlotte Lennox's *Sophia,* Sarah Scott's *Cornelia,* Sarah Fielding's *Cleopatra and Octavia,* Maria Edgeworth's *Belinda,* and Mary Brunton's *Self-Control.*

Chapter 3, "Sexual Revolution and the Hardwicke Marriage Act," explains why the Marriage Act of 1753, which introduced marriage as we know it — with banns or a licence, parental permission for minors, before witnesses and an authorized clergyman, and by recording the event in a marriage register — demanded a revolution in women's sexual practices and in traditional forms of marriage which materially altered middle- and upper-class women's lives. Egalitarians and Matriarchs both saw it as a dramatic turning point, and this chapter shows how they developed precepts which offered women alternative responses to the strictures of the act and how they represented, explored, and debated the act's problematical principles and unexpected consequences for people and population in novels like Frances Sheridan's *Sidney Bidulph,* Eliza Fenwick's *Secresy,* and Amelia Opie's *Adeline Mowbray* into the first decades of the nineteenth century.

In Chapter 4, "The Public Uses of Private Families," the focus is on how Matriarchs and Egalitarians constructed the family as a sphere of properly female action and imagined women and men governing separate spheres after passage of the Marriage Act — when political economists were representing children as "a source of wealth" to the nation, and when public policy was urging private men to abandon their dissipations, to develop a taste for "domestic happiness," and to act as "nursing Fathers" for the public good. The chapter shows how male ideologues conceived of the "public uses of private families" and where Matriarchs and Egalitarians shared assumptions and reshaped them to make government of the family women's work. Recovering a forgotten argument between Matriarchs and Egalitarians about how the domestic revolution was to come about, this chapter also indicates why women by and large chose to follow the Matriarchs and to abandon the Egalitarian path.

Chapter 5, "Governing Utopias and the Feminist Rousseau," considers how Matriarchs and Egalitarians used rewritings of Rousseau's novels to exemplify or contest the public uses of private families and to compare or put in question the effectiveness of men's patriarchal and ladies' matriarchal domestic government. It shows how Matriarchs and Egalitarians used rewritings of Rousseau to critique conventional representations of the "benevolent" patriarchal family, as well as to debate differences between them bearing both on women's lives and on the "public Good."

The concluding chapter, "The Domestic Revolution," recovers a forgotten debate between Egalitarians and Matriarchs about power and competition with men in the domestic arena, which lays bare the strategies Matriarchs used to take over government of the family from men and the Egalitarian critiques of their methods and goals. This chapter also considers how Matriarchal strategy all but required Matriarchs to participate in erasing all memory of the Enlightenment feminist debate and of their own central role in the domestic revolution.

The story emerging from these chapters inhabits and supports a recent revision of the historical timeline assumed during the 1970s and 1980s by feminist critiques of what Jean Bethke Elshtain called "Private (moral) Woman" and "Public (immoral) Man." Following historians of the family, like Stone, Trumbach, Schochet, and Laslett, these critiques assumed that the public-private divide began with Locke at the end of the seventeenth century and that by the second half of the eighteenth century the economic and cultural shift from the household mode of production to separation of the workplace from home, from arranged marriages to the "affective individualism" of "companionate marriages," and from extended families to the modern nuclear family was already firmly in place. These assumptions suggested that the private woman had been left behind in the household when men, money, and workplaces migrated elsewhere. It led to the argument that domestic women were bracketed with nature, nurture, and the family in a space divided off from the public sphere and construed as marginal to the Enlightenment polity's civic concerns. It also made the domestic woman a victim or agent of a construction in which she had played no formative part.

The timeline underlying this representation of the domestic woman has been revised by recent historians of the family, like Leonore Davidoff and Catherine Hall, Bridget Hill, John Gillis, and F. M. L. Thompson. These historians have shown that *in practice* the separation of household from workplace probably did not occur before the second or third quarters of the *nineteenth* century. Their work shows that during the eighteenth century the family household still remained the primary economic and social unit for both men and women in most classes. It statistically documents the instabilities of eighteenth-century family life which contemporaries complained about and sought to correct through the Marriage Act and through family ideologies of different kinds, and it shows that the cult of domesticity did not become normative even for the middle classes until the second or third decades of the nineteenth century.

This revision of the historical timeline makes better sense of eighteenth-century texts, since these repeatedly underline the difference between whatever they describe as "natural" to family life and actual family life in the society around them. Eighteenth-century philosophies, parliamentary debates, sermons, tracts, and canonical novels may valorize paternalistic benevolence towards dependents, the pleasures of domesticity, obedience to husbands and fathers, parental care of children, marriage choices based on moral and intellectual compatibilities, blandly virtuous daughters, innocuously deferential wives, and stable, harmonious families whose members conscientiously perform their relative duties each to each, but they describe the reality of marriage and family life in almost opposite terms. They say that wives instead of being submissive, rule; that spouses are more interested in "licentiousness" and "dissipation" than in each other; that marriage choices are based on money or interest, rather than on affection and compatibility; that men are deserting wives and children (often to destitution and prostitution) and moving on; that bastardy, bigamy, and even polygamy are rampant — abortion and infanticide too; that parents are abandoning their children or neglecting to give them proper care; and that nothing could be less stable, harmonious, or happy than most peoples' family lives.

On the old timeline, which placed "affective individualism" and separate spheres in the eighteenth century because people were talking about them then, we erased this distance and this difference. As Houlbrooke, Laslett, and Wall put it, we "confuse[d] prescription with practice" and supposed that "ideology and behavior were entirely congruent."[24] The revised timeline better respects the distance and the difference between prescription and practice indicated in Enlightenment texts. Even more interesting perhaps, it enables us to construct this distance and this difference as delay and to consider later nineteenth-century family practices as imitations or adaptations of models of family life and of female "virtue" imagined, debated, and exemplified by women in late eighteenth-century and earlier nineteenth-century texts.

The lag between fictioned models of family life and actual changes in domestic and sexual conduct thus becomes the time of (re)education and reorientation of imitation and desire. The space between prescription and practice re-presents the time it took for women's domestic novels and conduct books to do their work. While putting in question poststructuralist and postmarxist assumptions about the automatism and immediacy of the effect of language, recognition of the lag between words and words' "creation of reality" makes better sense of Enlightenment feminists' preoccupation with precept and example as instruments of public pedagogy and of domestic change. It also requires us to pay due attention to the sorts of literary and cultural repetition which were inseparable from their effect.

The deferred timeline adopted by recent historians of the family has been underwritten by neo-Tory historians like John Cannon, Jonathan Clark, James Sack, and Dustin Griffin who argue — against the Whig (liberal or marxist) historians of the 1960s, 1970s, and early 1980s — that Britain's monarchical and aristocratic *ancien régime* persisted well into the second half of the nineteenth century. These historians argue that, far from being the Age of Reason, of democratic revolutions and the rising bourgoisie, the long eighteenth century was an age in which "gentlemen, the Church of England and the Crown commanded an intellectual and social hegemony."[25] The landed aristocracy continued to dominate government, society, and literary as well as political and ecclesiastical patronage throughout the century, comfortably ensconced at the apex of a vast patriarchal "system of authority and subordination which formed the context of men's lives."[26] And far from bucking the system, the new men who made their fortunes in trade sought only to rise to the top of it, to become gentlemen themselves. According to this Burkean view of history, then, Britain in the eighteenth century was still an almost entirely traditional society governed by a small, aristocratic or gentrified patriarchal elite. "The normal units of economic as well as political continuity were families,"[27] and because the household remained the primary unit of production in commercial houses as well as on the land, well over half the male population were "servants" or "domestics," under the same domestic, patriarchal rule as women and children.

This representation of the period may be as one-sided in its way as the Whig or left-wing histories it contests, especially when it returns us to the old historical practice of focusing on monarchs, ministers, and (male) aristocratic magnates at the expense of everyone else or evades all mention of those ideas, situations, and movements that do not fit into this mold. But, as Robert Shoemaker has said, it does make "arguments linking changes in gender roles specifically to a narrative of class development, arguments which were common to the period when Feminist history and Marxist history were closely linked . . . difficult to sustain."[28] This helps put in question any too-facile identification of Enlightenment feminisms with the middle class. This is important, for there is, as we will see, little evidence in their texts that Matriarchal and Egalitarian issues, strategies, and concerns related exclusively to women of the middle class or that their writings were addressed primarily to them. Indeed, the nineteenth-century concept of class may not, ultimately, be very illuminating for women's situation in the eighteenth century, when, as Harold Perkin noted, Blackstone could still distinguish forty different social levels or ranks, each proclaiming its differential status through every outward sign — from manner, speech, and deportment to size of house and household, dress, and food.[29]

Neo-Tory historians' conservative vision of eighteenth-century England as an intensely hierarchical, patriarchal domestic and social order, sustained by a confessional state that taught the duty of submission and obedience to masters, husbands, governors, and sovereigns from every pulpit in the land, is helpful in another way too. As we will see, it corresponds more closely to what both Matriarchal and Egalitarian writers said women were up against than does the "progressive" Whig story of enlightenment, increasing democratization, and incipient modernity.

Before labeling any feminist position "conservative" or "progressive," Naomi Schor advises us, we should bear in mind that "context here is everything."[30] For Enlightenment feminist writers, two different temporal and cultural contexts intersect: the already complex context of the political, economic, and ideological debates in which they engaged during their own time, in which Matriarchs can figure as unexpectedly progressive, and the changing contemporary contexts in which Enlightenment women's representations of the family have subsequently been read.

In the context of women's struggle to enter the public sphere and the work-a-day world as equals, Second Wave feminists in the 1970s and early 1980s critiqued all those "enlightened" male philosophers and political theorists, from Locke and Rousseau on, who claimed equality, citizenship, and self-government for men while arguing that hierarchy, submission, and patriarchal rule were a "law of nature" for the home. Assuming an "obvious split between the two spheres of family and personal life on the one hand and public life on the other,"[31] Second Wave feminists saw feminism proper as beginning with the Wollstonecraft who, in *Vindication of the Rights of Woman*, "questions the male bias of concepts of rationality and citizenship and seeks to open this world of industrious, useful, active persons to women by extending equality of opportunity to them."[32] In this context, when visible at all, Enlightenment women writers' representations in novels, conduct books, and tracts of women's domestic roles, and the language of morality, religion, virtue, duty, and principle in which they spoke, seemed not only conservative and unprogressive but blinkered and unfeminist as well.

More recently, however, as Rosalind Coward says, "the family has swung back into fashion"[33] in the wake of the conservative backlash and of working mothers' increasing dissatisfaction with the double shift. This has been accompanied by a revalorization of motherhood and of women's difference from men in surprisingly diverse sectors of feminist thought, as Judith Evans has shown,[34] as well as by a rewriting of women's history as a history of the rivalry between women's arguments that we are equal or different, "unsex'd" or "sex'd," and therefore belong primarily in the workforce or primarily in the home.[35] As increasing numbers of successful and well-to-do professional women have sought at least partial retreat from the workplace in order to balance careers with the care of children, while less well-to-do families have largely become economically dependent on women's continued work outside the home, contemporary public women, like Carol Lee Bacchi, Constance Buchanan, and Betty Friedan, have begun to argue that the family must take center stage as a focal public, civic and economic, problem of childrens' care and education, which needs to be addressed by both women and men.[36]

One might say that the wheel has come full circle and that the family has been moving back into the public sphere as an issue bearing on larger economic, social, and political concerns. The analysis in this book suggests, however, that it is more the case that none of our contemporary contexts have fully broken out of the circle of assumptions — or, indeed, of economic, social, and religious argument and Egalitarian or Matriarchal counterargument — established by long-forgotten Enlightenment debates. They still ventriloquize through us. It is to be hoped that viewing these spectres of another time and place in contexts and connections so different from our own will help to lay at least some of them to rest.

1

The Question of Domestic Government

Is it not then partial in Men to the Last Degree, to contend for, and practise that Arbitrary Dominion in their Families, which they abhor and exclaim against in the State? — MARY ASTELL

ONCE IDENTIFIED by scholars with the very inception of modernity, Locke's *Two Treatises on Government* link debates surrounding the Glorious Revolution of 1688 to debates surrounding the French Revolution of 1789, and they link arguments made by women like Damaris Masham, Mary Astell, and Judith Drake at the end of the seventeenth century to Matriarchal and Egalitarian arguments a hundred years later. Locke's association with the Glorious Revolution and with the inception of modernity was, as Martyn Thompson has shown, itself an eighteenth-century phenomenon.[1] Locke was singled out from among other late seventeenth-century political theorists only in the middle of the eighteenth century, and once constructed by eighteenth-century ideologues as one of the polity's founding texts, Locke's *Treatises* inscribed assumptions about government, education, liberty, and law and about the relation of the family to the state that were repeated, with variations, into the early decades of the nineteenth century, in women's arguments as well as men's.

At the same time, as we have come to understand, Locke's text was not particularly original or new even when it first appeared; from this point of view, it links the Glorious Revolution back to men's and women's debates that were going on during and after the Civil War. Viewed as a *summum* of the past, Locke's *Treatises* can be read as combining and holding in balance the views of battling Civil War factions in order to promote peaceful settlement by establishing a middle ground on which most Englishmen might agree. Locke's *Treatises* could be read — and indeed were read by men and women both in England and in France during the eighteenth century — in almost opposite ways, depending on whether they highlighted the text's leveling-egalitarian or feudal-hierarchical face.

Throughout the long eighteenth century, as we will see below, Matriarchs and Egalitarians fashioned their domestic agendas on opposite sides of the egalitarian-feudal divide precariously balanced in Locke. At the same time, at the end of the seventeenth century and again in the latter half of the eighteenth, Enlightenment feminists both challenged and used Lockean assumptions about the family and the state, and about government, society, education, liberty, and the law. They read Locke's *Treatises* both as re-presenting the old patriarchal and the new "benevolent" paternalistic doctrines, which kept women in subjection to their fathers and husbands, and as offering ladies openings for autonomy and self-government and for changes in "the proper government of our families" which were not readily available elsewhere.

For these reasons, and because his text is such a compendium of borrowed and incommensurable elements, Locke's *Treatises* can serve as a matrix in which men and women's different positions at different historical times reveal their articulations each upon the others. The focus, however, will be on reading Locke and other male ideologues through Enlightenment feminist texts, in order to delineate the continuity of Matriarchal and Egalitarian arguments over time, their fundamental differences from each other, and the interfaces between their arguments for women's "self-government" and the changes in the structure, dynamics, and government of the family that those arguments entailed. Mary Astell's critique of Locke is a convenient point of entry into the recurrent issues women raised.

Astell on Locke's Family-State Analogy

At the end of the seventeenth century, Mary Astell complained that Locke was using a double standard to claim equality, independence, and freedom for men in society while insisting that hierarchy, submission, and patriarchal rule remain a law of nature for women in the home.[2] Astell took issue with Locke's rationale for male government of the family in some short but pithy passages of *Some Reflections on Marriage*. Locke had argued in his *Treatises* that husbands and wives, though sharing the same interests and concerns, have "different understandings" and thus, unavoidably, "different wills," and that "it therefore being necessary that the last Determination, i.e. the Rule, should be placed somewhere, it naturally falls to the Man's share, as the abler and stronger."[3]

Astell sarcastically recast this argument to show its inconsistencies:

> Reason, or that which stands for it, the Will and Pleasure of the Governor, is to be the Reason of those who will not be guided by their own . . . Nor can there be any Society, great or little, from Empires down to private Families, without a last Resort, to determine the Affairs of that Society as an irresistible Sentence. Now unless this Supremacy be fixed somewhere, there will be a perpetual Contention about it . . . So that since Women are acknowledged to have least bodily Strength, their being commanded to Obey is pure Kindness to them, and for Quiet and Security as well as for the Exercise of their Vertue. But does it follow, that Domestick Governors have more sense than their Subjects, any more than other Governors have? We do not find that any Man thinks the worse of his own Understanding because another has superior Power . . . Indeed, Government would be much more desirable than it is, did it invest the Possessor with a superior Understanding, as well as Power.[4]

On one level, Astell's response to Locke's argument that men naturally rule the family because their reason is naturally abler and stronger than women's is that Locke was confusing superior sense and understanding with superior physical strength and political power and assuming that men have the one because they have the other. Man's supposedly superior reason, she is saying, is a function of superior power and bodily strength, not the other way around. If Locke were to start from the assumption that there is no more "Natural Inferiority" in women's understanding because they are subordinate to men than there is in the understanding of men because they have to submit to more powerful men, then the argument that men are naturally abler than women to govern domestic society would fall to the ground.

On another level, however, Astell is invoking a familiar analogy between the family and the state to indicate that Locke was also applying a double standard in other respects. In the "little society" of the family, Astell was saying, Locke had argued that contention could only be avoided and order, quiet, security, and virtue secured by women's obedience to the will and pleasure of a husband-governor. But, in society at large, he had argued, order, quiet, and virtue could only be secured by *freeing* subjects from such passive obedience. In the little society of the family, Locke had made a single man the governor, and that governor "the last Resort, to determine the Affairs of that Society by an irresistible Sentence." In empires, however, and in the great society of the kingdom, he had made *subjects* "the last Resort," by insisting that the people retain the right and power to resist the sentences of governors who abuse their lives, liberty, and property.

By making a difference between the family and the state, Locke had limited the power of domestic governors. He had distinguished the little society, which consists of "a *Master of a Family* with all these subordinate Relations of *Wife, Children, Servants,* and *Slaves* united under the Domestick Rule of a Family,"[5] from the larger society of the kingdom, by arguing that the master of a family does not have the civil governor's power over life and death or his power to make laws, and he curtailed the duration of a father's power over his male children (at least in theory) to the period of their minority. But, as Astell points out, these restrictions did not protect women in the household, for they left the master of a family free to be a perfect domestic tyrant still: "What though a Husband can't deprive a Wife of Life, without being responsible to the Law, he may, however, do what is much more grievous to a generous Mind, render Life miserable for which she has no Redress, scarce Pity, which is afforded to every other Complainant, it being thought a Wife's Duty to suffer everything without Complaint."[6]

Civil law offered a wife no redress for abuses of *her* life, liberty, or property; it assumed that it was the wife's duty to suffer without complaint whatever cruelties her husband subjected her to, short of actually killing her.[7] Domestic society remained outside or before the law, and women continued to be subject to the arbitrary humors of men; but, as Astell underlined, "being subjected to the inconstant, uncertain, unknown, arbitrary Will of Men" is — by Locke's own definition — "*the perfect Condition of Slavery.*"[8]

For Astell, then, Locke's double standard manifested itself as a failure to develop the analogy between government of a family and government of the kingdom as consistently as he should. In the kingdom, men had freed themselves from slavery by instituting a social compact that limited the sovereign's exercise of arbitrary power and made men "equally Subjects to the same Law together." Astell argued that since the marriage contract was analogous to the social contract, the "domestick Sovereign's" power ought to be limited in a similar way:

> If the Authority of the Husband, so far as it extends, is sacred and inalienable, why not that of the Prince? The Domestic Sovereign is, without dispute elected, and the Stipulations and Contract mutual; is it not then partial in Men to the Last Degree, to contend for, and practise that Arbitrary Dominion in their Families, which they abhor and exclaim against in the State? For if Arbitrary Power is evil in it self, and an improper Method for governing rational and Free Agents, it ought not to be practis'd any where.[9]

Translating into the domestic arena arguments that men had used against absolute monarchy in the political arena, Astell was challenging Locke on his own ground and using him against himself. For, contrary to what we once thought, the family-state analogy, so prevalent in the political debates of the Civil War, was central to Locke's argument too. As Armstrong and Tennenhouse have pointed out, "Locke's model did mount a powerful argument against absolute monarchy, but it also kept the patriarchal family at the center of the political arena."[10] Locke's rhetorico-political move against Filmer did not consist in dividing the family from the state and the public from the private domain, as we assumed when our readings focused only on the differences he inscribed between them. In traditional rhetoric and thought, analogy was a figure marking *both* the differences and the likenesses between the terms or entities it linked. And Locke's rhetorico-political move against Filmer consisted of replacing what Daniella Gobetti has called Filmer's "assimilation" of the paterfamilias to the monarch by an "analogy" between the good monarch and the benevolent father and between the virtuous family and right government which remained operative — and fundamental to policy and ideology — throughout the eighteenth century.[11]

Astell had challenged Locke on his own ground, but her double-standard argument — that men claimed liberty and equality for themselves in the public sphere while imposing subordination on women in the home — would not hold, because in Locke's *Treatises,* the family and the state were in fact absolutely analogical in the traditional rhetorical sense.

As Peter Laslett and Gordon Schochet have pointed out, in the political arena Locke "divides off the process of compact, which creates a community, from the further process by which the community entrusts political power to a government."[12] Men are joined together laterally into a community or society, for the purpose of preserving their life, liberty, and property, by a voluntary "compact," "agreement," or "contract"; and they are linked vertically to those who govern them, not by a contract, but by a "Trust." Political authority is "held as a sacred trust for the Publick Good and Safety," and "when rulers fail to act 'for the Public Good,' the bonds of political obligation are dissolved, and power potentially reverts to the people."[13]

Locke structures "family society" in the same double way. "Conjugal Society is made by a voluntary Compact between Man and Woman" for the purpose of procreation and mutual assistance, just as civil society is made by a voluntary "Compact . . . agreeing together mutually to enter into one Community" for the purpose of preserving life, liberty, and property.[14] Conjugal society and civil society are both consensual, contractual relationships that are brought into being for a specific purpose and can, in principle, be dissolved by mutual consent.[15] For Locke (who perhaps remembered that the social contract had been modeled on the marriage contract, not the other way around), the difference lay only in the "Endes, Tyes and Bounds" of each: the end of conjugal society being procreation and mutual assistance in the upbringing of children, while the end of civil society is the preservation of life, liberty, and property.

Paternal or parental power over children, on the other hand, is held as a trust. As Laslett says, Locke "tends to use the language of trust whenever he talks of the power of one man over another, even for fathers and children."[16] Paternal authority to govern children is "designed to the Children's Good"[17] and dissolves where this condition is not fulfilled, just as political authority is designed to serve the public good and dissolves where it is not doing its job. Locke insists that the power to govern his children "so little belongs to the Father by any particular right of nature, but only as he is Guardian of his Children, that when he quits his Care of them, he loses his power over them, which goes along with their Nourishment and Education, to which it is inseparably annexed, and it belongs as much to the *Foster-Father* of an exposed Child as to the Natural Father of another."[18] Although the "Endes, Tyes and Bounds" of paternal and political authority differ, in both cases a man is entrusted with the clearly delimited power to govern others for their "good"; and in both cases, he holds his title to authority only insofar, and as long, as he fulfils this trust.

But *trust* is a feudal word, implying fealty and obedience, and so is Locke's social and domestic imaginary. Locke assumed a hierarchical society. He assumed that there were going to be differences in "Precedency" on the basis of "Age, Birth and Parts and Merits" in civil society, just as there were going to be differences in precedency based on age, birth (male) and "Parts and Merits" (superior male) in domestic society. As Burke pointed out a century later, the 1688 Revolutionary Settlement did not, like the French Revolution, confiscate property or abolish ranks; Locke's doctrine likewise protected property and the social inequality it inevitably entailed. And in England throughout the eighteenth century, arguing for "natural equality" or for "popular equality" did not at all mean that one was arguing to abolish rank, precedency, privilege, and differences in wealth. "Popular equality" meant "that Subjection by which all are equally Subject to Law." "Popular government" meant government "in which the People have a Share, as they have in ours of Great Britain, by their Representatives."[19] In other words, equality was conceived as the rational and voluntary foundation of social hierarchy and proper subordination to one's legal governors and social superiors.

From this point of view, it is interesting to observe that Locke's argument for man's rule over women — that the husband governed because he was "abler and stronger" — came to be used to justify the rule of some men over others in society at large. Hutcheson, for instance, argued that because "some of our species are manifestly superior in wisdom to the vulgar, as the vulgar are often sensible," the original "covenant" to enter into society had always been a covenant to enter into "a firm society, to be regulated by the counsel of the wiser few, in all matters relating to the safety and advantage either of individuals or of the whole body."[20] Indeed, one of the benefits for men of entering into the social compact was that men "of superior capacity" would "point out more effective methods for each individual to promote his own interests, if his direction is complied with."[21] In society, men voluntarily chose, or tacitly consented, to subordinate themselves to men "abler and stronger" than they.

One could not, therefore, argue very effectively that the family and civil society were based on opposite principles: the family on the obedience, dependence, and inequality of its members and civil society on the freedom, independence, and equality of its members; for, while men, as Astell says, might not have thought the worse of their own understandings because another man had superior power, in civil and political society, men did acknowledge other men's superior power, did subordinate themselves to other men, did depend on other men and obey their commands. The family and the polity were absolutely analogical, inasmuch as they were both conceived as hierarchical institutions in which relations of dependence and proper subordination prevailed. Reading both the social contract and the marriage contract as voluntary agreements to live in a pecking order, Englishmen celebrated their equality while reinstituting precedency and subordination everywhere.

Enlightenment feminists in the latter half of the eighteenth century returned to all the points that Astell had made against Locke, with the exception of one. They argued that women are rational agents, in no way naturally inferior to men, that some law applicable in domestic society was needed to protect women from the violence and arbitrary will of men, and that order and virtue required a different disposition of power and governance in the family than that assumed either by the old absolutist and "tyrannical" patriarchs or by the newer, more benevolent, paternalistic, and "enlightened" Lockean patriarchs. They dropped Astell's argument that men were using different standards for civil and domestic government, preferring to substitute family-state analogies of their own.

Ladies' Self-government: Education and the Law

Enlightenment feminists lived in hierarchical families and in a hierarchical culture, where the hegemonic ideology constructed women as men's "natural" and divinely appointed inferiors and declared it women's duty — as mothers, wives, and daughters — to be "governed" by their fathers, husbands, and guardians "in all things."[22] In law, as Lawrence Stone explains, echoing Astell, "a married woman was the nearest approximation in a free society to a slave. Her person, her property, both real and personal, her earnings and her children all passed on marriage into the absolute control of her husband. The latter could use her sexually as he wished, and beat her (within reason) or confine her for disobedience of any orders. The children were entirely at the disposal of the father."[23] Men were likely to be told, in conduct books like *The Art of Governing a Wife with Rules for Batchelors* (1747), that the husband "must govern with absolute power" and that it was the duty of the wife "not to understand but to obey." Women were, after all, as Lord Chesterfield put it in 1774, "only children of a larger growth."[24]

Neither Matriarchs nor Egalitarians accepted that adult ladies must remain inferior to anyone and be subordinate and obedient to men for all of their lives, nor did they agree that in the marriage contract women "abdicated all right to be their own governor." A primary, and perhaps most fundamental, "freedom" that both of these Enlightenment feminisms sought for women was the freedom to govern themselves. Throughout the long eighteenth century, both feminisms countered analogically grounded patriarchal arguments that it was a woman's duty to entirely subordinate her will and reason to the wishes and commands of her "domestic governor"; they did so by demanding, modeling, or engineering domestic spaces where ladies could govern their own consciences, their own conduct, and their own lives.

Besides helping to transpose feminist arguments from the church to the polis and from the language of religion to that of contemporary political debates, feminist encounters with Locke at the end of the seventeenth century and again in the eighteenth linked Matriarchal and Egalitarian struggles for women's self-government to questions of education and to questions of law. It is important to notice, therefore, not only where Locke re-presented conventional patriarchal impediments to women's autonomous moral, spiritual, and intellectual agency, but also where seventeenth- and eighteenth-century feminists read his *Treatises* as offering women opportunities and openings not readily available elsewhere.

One such opening occurs in the now much maligned chapter on "Paternal Power." Here Locke argues that children are subject to parental "Rule and Jurisdiction" during their minority because they are born "ignorant and without the use of Reason." As long as a child lacks the understanding to direct his actions rationally to his own proper interest, "he that *understands* for him, must *will* for him too; he must prescribe to his will, and regulate his Actions." When "Age and Education" have brought him "Reason and Ability to govern himself and others," however, the bonds of subjection drop off. When "he comes to the Estate that made his *Father* a *Freeman,* the *Son is a Freeman* too." Reason and education are the conditions for self-government, as well as for liberty, for equality, and for full adult citizenship. "Lunaticks, Ideots, Innocents, Children and Madmen" are "never capable of being a freeman" because they do not possess "such a degree of Reason."[25]

Contemporary feminist scholars have noted that earlier in the *Treatises* Locke insisted that Reason, Revelation, Nature and the Right of Generation all gave mothers an "equal Title" to power over their children with fathers, whereas in this part of his argument he spoke only of father and son. But this is not Locke's only resounding silence. The other is the absence of women on Locke's list of those who are never capable of becoming freemen. Locke does not mention women along with lunatics, idiots, innocents, children, and madmen, *even though* the de facto civil and domestic status of women as perpetual minors should have put them there. Locke had also insisted that "all that share in the same common Nature, Faculty and Powers, are in Nature equal, and ought to partake in the same common Rights and Privileges."[26]

Enlightenment feminists treated this as a window of opportunity. From Judith Drake and Damaris Masham at the end of the seventeenth century to Mary Hays and Hannah More at the end of the eighteenth, Enlightenment feminists asserted and tried to demonstrate that "we use all our Natural Faculties as well as Men, nay and our Rational too," and that "there is no difference in Sense, or understanding, between Males and Females."[27] The only difference between the sexes that Enlightenment feminists admitted lay in "the advantages Men have over us by their Education."[28] If ladies seemed frivolous, flighty, and foolish — as men and both Enlightenment feminisms agreed they did — it was only because they had not been given the opportunity to exercise their reason and to acquire the knowledge they needed to demonstrate their equality, or superiority, of Sense with men. "Most in this deprived later Age," said Hannah Woolley, "think a woman learned and wise enough if she can distinguish her Husband's Bed from another."[29]

Enlightenment feminists urged ladies to expect more of themselves. In their novels, conduct books, and tracts, they criticized frivolous, flighty, and foolish women — those who failed to exercise their reason or set aside time each day for acquiring the education they lacked — by representing them as "imbecile coquettes," whose vain and thoughtless conduct made them unworthy of imitation or respect. Reading nineteenth-century class divisions back into the eighteenth century, contemporary marxist critics like Gary Kelly have identified this figure with the aristocratic lady in order to argue that women writers were promoting "professional middle class" values against the aristocracy. It should be noted, however, that reason and education were central feminist issues throughout our period, primarily because both Enlightenment feminisms viewed the educational lacks and foolish, unmeaning character of women both in the middling *and* upper ranks as at once the result, the instrument, and the *sine qua non* of women's domestic and civil subjection.

Egalitarians marshaled evidence from nature, reason, and revelation to show that "the abilities and capacities of the sexes are so nearly alike that, with the same advantages, it were difficult to determine to whom the palm were due" and to argue that there is therefore no justification for a subjection of women to men which "keeps women in a perpetual state of babyism."[30] Men would not have to understand for women, will for women, prescribe to women, or govern them "in all things" if women had as much education as men. If women had as much education, it would be clear that men were not "fitter to govern women, than women are to govern themselves."[31] When Egalitarians argued that women should be given "an education equally rational in itself, equally improving to the mind, and equally consequential to the happiness of the individual, as that which [men] think it proper to bestow upon themselves,"[32] they were arguing that, with the proper education, women could meet both Locke's conditions for liberty, equality, and full adult status. With the same rational, civil, and secular education as men, women would be men's equals.

Matriarchs were more concerned about the role of education in the hierarchy of power between men and women. They argued that men kept women "ignorant and without the use of reason" to deprive them of power. Keeping women foolish and ignorant, they said, protected male supremacy. "Why," asked Eliza Haywood, "do they call us *silly women*, and not endeavour to make us otherwise?" Because, she replied, "men say" that making women otherwise "would destroy that implicit obedience which it is necessary the women should pay to our commands. If once they have the capacity of arguing with us, where would be our authority?"[33] An intelligent, a principled, an educated woman would think for herself. She would answer back. She would not be as inclined to obey a husband or father or be as easily ruled. Keeping women foolish and ignorant justified men in neglecting, ignoring, or ill-treating them — as one of Lady Chudleigh's male characters points out in *The Ladies' Defence:* "Yes, as we please, we may our Wives chastise, / 'Tis the Prerogative of being wise; / They are but Fools, and as such must be us'd."[34] A husband could treat a foolish, frivolous, and ignorant wife as badly as could be and feel that it was all she deserved.

Damaris Masham made the even more telling point that gentlemen wanted to exclude women from knowledge, which confers superiority, because they themselves had so little knowledge, and thus real superiority: "Thus wretchedly destitute of all that Knowledge which they ought to have, are our English Gentlemen: And being so, what wonder can it be, if they like not that Women should have Knowledge; for this is a quality that will give a sort of Superiority even to those who care not to have it."[35] It was by keeping knowledge and education to themselves that men secured their purely artificial preeminence over women, as another of Lady Chudleigh's male characters agrees: "Then blame us not if we our interest mind, / And would have knowledge to ourselves confin'd, / Since that alone Preeminence does give . . . / While you are ignorant, we are secure."[36] Or, as Mary Wollstonecraft put it nearly a century later when she borrowed this Matriarchal argument: "Strengthen the female mind by enlarging it, and there will be an end to blind obedience; but as blind obedience is ever sought for by power, tyrants and sensualists are in the right when they endeavour to keep women in the dark, because the former only want slaves, the latter a plaything."[37]

If knowledge conferred superiority in the hierarchy between men and women, then knowledge was definitely something for Matriarchs — who preached women's "Superiority of Sense and Virtue over Men" — to secure for themselves. Matriarchal writers were therefore often "learned ladies." They were often "blue-stockings" long before and long after the ladies in the Montagu circle came to be identified by that name.[38]

While Egalitarians demanded for women the same secular education as men — "mankind should all be educated after the same model, or the intercourse of the sexes will never deserve the name of fellowship"[39] — Matriarchs paid greater attention to the kind of education men were said to need to govern themselves and others. Locke's condition for assuming the freedom to govern oneself and to dispose of one's own life and property was the possession of such reason and education as enabled a man to understand the natural, moral, and positive laws by which he must govern himself and others: "The *Freedom* then of Man and Liberty of acting according to his own Will, is *grounded* on his having *Reason* which is able to instruct him in that Law he is to govern himself by, and makes him know how far he is left to the Freedom of his own Will."[40] In other words, the freedom of the freeman was not, as we now tend to think, the freedom to do whatever one pleased; it was a man's freedom to govern himself by his own reason in light of the relevant laws.[41] The freedom to do whatever one pleased belonged to the state of nature, not to the social compact, which basically constituted an agreement with others to abide by the same law. The reason which the son had to demonstrate to become a freeman like his father was, therefore, such reason and discretion as would enable him to know "how far this Law is to be his Guide, and how far he may make use of his Freedom."[42]

To demonstrate that men are not fitter to govern women than women are to govern themselves, Matriarchs sought to demonstrate that women knew the positive, moral, and religious laws which bore on their conduct — and that they understood better than men when and how far to be guided by them. Self-righteous though they appear to us today, each demonstration that Matriarchs or their exemplary heroines *could* rationally govern themselves by moral, positive, or religious laws to which men were in principle equally subject made the point that women attain "the State of Maturity" just as men do. And, as we will see in the next chapter, each demonstration that Matriarchs or their exemplary heroines know *better* than their domestic governors how to direct their conduct by the appropriate rule or law made the point that women are *fitter* to govern themselves than men are to govern them.

Following Foucault and Lacan, we might say that the freedom that Matriarchs sought was only the freedom to become "the principle of their own subjection" and that they were simply internalizing the "Law of the Father." But we can also hear them with another ear if we remind ourselves that the ladies' immediate problem was not domination and subjection by anonymous systems of subjectivation in an impersonal, technocratic society; it was to free some people from being dominated and subjected by other people. This had been Locke's problem too. For Locke and for the ladies, power and domination still wore the all-too-human face of a particular governor — a tyrannical king or lord, a domineering father or husband. It was the enforcible whim of people one knew.[43]

Hence the appeal of, and to, law. As Locke said, "Where there is no law, there is no freedom," for "who could be free when every other Man's Humour might domineer over him?" In the public sphere, the revolutionaries of 1688 substituted rational and voluntary obedience to natural, moral, and positive law for passive obedience to the unreasonable humors of particular men. Locke too looked to law to "preserve" freedom from "restraint and violence from others" and from all "subject[ion] to the arbitrary will of another."[44] And his eighteenth-century followers did too. As Hutcheson said, "Laws are so far from excluding liberty that they are its natural and surest defence . . . a people is denominated free when their important interests are well secured against any rapacious or capricious wills of those in power."[45] Ferguson, too, stressed that "liberty is opposed to injustice, not to restraint; for liberty cannot subsist without the supposition of every just restraint.[46]

Enlightenment thinkers conceived of law as an "enlargement" of freedom, inasmuch as it enabled each rational being to govern his own conduct and order his own life "within the Allowance of the Law" without the interference or mediation of anyone else.[47] Our modern term *negative liberty* fails to capture this sense of enlargement.

It was this sort of enlargement of freedom that Matriarchs sought for ladies in their domestic situations too. They sought to release ladies from their "subjection to the inconstant, uncertain, unknown, arbitrary Will of Men" through their own rational and voluntary government of themselves by a higher law. As Astell put it, "if the Essence of Freedom consists, as our Masters say it does, in having a Standing Rule to live by," women should live by a standing rule and have such freedom too;[48] for, as Jane West said almost a century later, the liberty ladies sought was "not the power of doing what you please, for that is licentiousness, but the security that others shall not do what they please to you."[49]

Matriarchs insisted throughout the long eighteenth century that the most important education for ladies to receive is a virtuous Christian education, because they thought that only appeal to the law of God would give women this "security that others shall not do as they please to you," by extending to women in their domestic situations that which civil law denied them: what Hume called "the government of laws, not men." In their novels, Matriarchs taught ladies how to deploy the law of God to their own advantage in the household, where civil law left them without redress.

In their tracts, they taught ladies that "the female cause is the cause of virtue"[50] and followed Damaris Masham in urging ladies to champion a virtue underwritten by the law of God against all the values and practices imposed by what Locke had called the "Law of Fashion or Opinion."[51] The latter, they said, required ladies to live empty, dissipated lives and encouraged gentlemen to pride themselves on socially condoned vices — like debauchery, gambling, and heavy drinking — which rebounded on women to their hurt. The law of fashion or opinion offered ladies no protection from the restraint or violence of others, but with a little help from the ladies, the law of God would.[52]

Matriarchs taught ladies that by adhering to the law of God, they would also be able to demonstrate their natural superiority to men in sense and virtue and to realize their very highest ambitions. "Every one," said Mary Astell, "is desirous of advancing"; and should not women then advance and demonstrate their superiority "in the best things rather than in mere Dress, Intrigue and Coquetry?"[53] "Christianity," said Hannah More, "has exalted Women to true and undisputed Dignity; in Jesus Christ, as there is neither Rich nor Poor, Bond nor Free, so there is neither Male nor Female. In the view of that Immortality which is brought to light in the Gospel, she has no Superior. Here her highest claims are allowed."[54] Here there was no glass ceiling. In Christianity, there was scope for women's moral, spiritual, and intellectual advancement and for demonstrable female superiority and respect-ability. There was scope for reading and writing, for missionary and charitable work, and for the ladies' highest claims to value and importance. As the eighteenth century wore on, and like their dissenting predecessors, established Anglican churchmen increasingly "allowed" the Matriarchs' claims, in the hope that the ladies would prove conformable allies against husbands and brothers who seemed to be abandoning the church in droves for "Infidelity, Atheism and Immorality."

Many of these Enlightenment feminist arguments relating to women's rationality, equality, and education and to women's relation to civil law have since been naturalized by repetition. It is therefore doubly important to remember as we read their work that, during the Enlightenment, Matriarchal and Egalitarian struggles for women's self-government — and later for women's government of their families — and the steps they took to achieve their goals, brought them up against established hierarchies and put them at odds with the "relative duties" prescribed to women as men's inferiors at home and abroad. In women's novels, it was still a significant feminist act to portray a heroine as a rational and educated woman who governed herself by moral and religious laws, determined her own conduct against the commands or advice of a parent or guardian, and was proved right by events.

Both Enlightenment feminisms saw hierarchy as more fundamental and more ubiquitous than the nineteenth-century concept of class, which obscured the pervasiveness of hierarchy to later critics, until Foucault rendered hierarchy visible to us again. They saw that hierarchy not only structured the relations among ranks or classes of society; even more insidiously and all-pervasively, it structured the relations each to each among members of the same family, the same household, and the same class. Differences of privilege and precedency were lived, both in the little society of the family and in the larger society of the polis, as a series of hierarchical interpersonal relationships in which people were positioned as inferior or superior in relation to one another and placed in diverse relations of domination and subjection each to each. This is why so much moral and social prescription during the eighteenth century, as well as so much feminist argument, took the form of conduct books discussing the "relative duties" of superiors and inferiors: masters and servants, governors and subjects, husbands and wives, fathers and children, mothers and daughters, and friends of different ages or ranks.

To distinguish Matriarchal and Egalitarian positions from each other, one might relate them to twentieth-century feminist debates by presenting Matriarchs as "sex'd" females who argued for women's superiority and "difference" from men and Egalitarians as "unsex'd" females who argued that women were equal to men, because the same. But the evidence suggests that for Enlightenment feminists such arguments were only instrumental and secondary to their real obsession: the question of precedency as it bore on women's relative place in the domestic hierarchy. And since, in common with their male counterparts, Enlightenment feminists saw the little society of the family as analogous to the greater society of the state, their arguments for changes in women's position relative to men in the family drew on, and were imbricated with, contemporary arguments about men's positions relative to one another in the state.

The Issue of Relative Place

For Enlightenment feminists, patriarchal ideology's dangerous line of fracture fell, not between the public and the private spheres as we long assumed, but between the fundamentally incommensurable presumptions of hierarchy and equality which were precariously joined together in Locke. In the seventeenth century and again in the eighteenth, Matriarchs and Egalitarians positioned themselves on either side of this ideological line of fracture, shaping their domestic agendas, their re-visions of the family, and their arguments for changing women's place relative to men in the domestic order to reflect their fundamentally egalitarian or hierarchical sociopolitical imaginaries.

G. T. A. Pocock has shown that during the long eighteenth century, "Whiggism" denoted "a diversity of realities" and that arguments migrated between factions — arguments which were "Tory" in one generation became "Whig" in the next, or vice versa — and that at any given time the same arguments might be deployed both by Tories and by particular factions among the Whigs.[55] Enlightenment feminists too have been identified with such political factions (Dissenter, Old Whig, Jacobin, etc.), and arguments migrated amongst women also. But for our purpose here — which is to sketch out their rival domestic agendas and to demonstrate continuities across faction and the persistence of their arguments across time — it will be more useful, even at the risk of appearing a little schematic, to represent Matriarchal and Egalitarian visions of the family and of women's relative place in the domestic hierarchy in less factional and more fundamental terms.

Montesquieu pointed out that equality and hierarchy entail different social and political systems, which he dubbed "democracy" and "aristocracy" respectively. What Montesquieu, in common with eighteenth-century Englishmen, called democracy was an absolutely egalitarian system of government in which discrepancies of power and wealth are leveled and "the people in themselves, and by themselves, perform all that belongs to government."[56] Democracy was what the nineteenth century identified with the ideals of communism. What Montesquieu called aristocracy, on the other hand, was an essentially hierarchical system of government which places sovereign power, wealth, and privilege in the hands of a relatively small number of people, who make and execute decisions for or in the name of the people, while the rest of the people "relate to them as subjects to a monarch."[57] This aristocracy is what came to be called democracy in the nineteenth century. Democracy in the eighteenth-century sense placed people on the same level, laterally and horizontally; while aristocracy disposed them vertically, one above the other, in unequal relations of power and dependence.

Effects of the geometric imagination, aristocracy and democracy were not logically compatible, but Locke had tried to make them so. Locke's *Treatises* attempted to cobble together an ideological settlement that would prove acceptable to both parties to the Civil War: the feudal-traditionalists, who wanted to preserve monarchy and aristocratic hierarchies of power and privilege, and the more egalitarian and leveling or democratic Dissenters.[58] Consequently, the *Treatises* borrowed arguments from each camp. Like Lilburne and Winstanley, Locke restated the principal leveling arguments: that the fruits of the earth had originally been given to all men equally, for the purpose of their preservation; that power was entrusted to governors and magistrates for the good of the people and for the protection of their just rights and liberties; and that if rulers did not fulfil their trust, the people could reassume their power and reconstitute authority anew.[59]

On the other hand, Locke also argued, as did Filmer, the political patriarch, that society could be reconstructed and legitimized in the present by returning to its pattern and origin in the patriarchal family and to an order founded on the subordination of one person to another — on condition that it was patterned after a kinder, gentler patriarchal family than that imagined by Filmer.[60] Fathers, says Locke, were made rulers in the "infancy of Commonwealths" precisely because of their natural "tenderness and affection" for their children and because "without such nursing Fathers, tender and carefull of the Public Weale, all Governments would have sunk under the Weakness and Infirmity of their Infancy."[61] Or, as Ferguson put it nearly a century later, "The affections of good magistrates should resemble those of parents, in pursuing constantly the good of their subjects; hence such governors obtain the most honourable name of *fathers of their people*."[62] King William, "our great Preserver," and his heirs were to be just such fathers of the people.

In Locke, therefore, men were both equal and unequal, both freemen and bound to obedience and due subordination to a hereditary monarchy and nobility. The *Treatises* were "an unstable blend of conservative and radical elements,"[63] and from the first, people in England and France could, and did, read them in different ways, according to their political preference.

Giving the lie to eighteenth-century arguments that such discrepancies had been reconciled by Britain's famed system of "mixed government," the aristocratic-democratic, feudal-egalitarian divide was reinscribed in culture and thought during the last decade of the eighteenth century under the impact of the French Revolution, which many in England saw as an embodiment of pure democracy and of the leveling philosophy. It was reinscribed, moreover, in and through Locke. For in England, both the radical egalitarian supporters and the conservative feudal-traditionalist opponents of the French Revolution claimed the Revolutionary Settlement and Locke's writings as their precedent and source.[64] As Stephen Prickett points out, "the connection between the events in France of 1788-89 and the English Revolution of 1688 was given immediate and powerful rhetorical sanction by Richard Price, a leading nonconformist minister of the day who, on 4 November 1789, delivered a *Discourse on the Love of Our Country* . . . to the Society for Commemorating the Revolution in Great Britain."[65] Invoking Milton and Locke in England and Montesquieu and Turgot in France, Price made Astell's point. The major principle underlying the Revolution of 1688, as well as the French Revolution of 1789, he said, was Locke's principle that the people had the "right to resist power when abused" and that "civil authority is a delegation from the people," which they have "a right to take back and reconstitute otherwise."[66] The difference between the two revolutions, Price said, was that the English revolution of 1688 had been "imperfect," because it had failed to extend the franchise and to ensure equal representation to all. Here, as Bridget Hill has shown, Price was echoing Catherine Macauley and the "Old Whig" position she pioneered during the 1760s and 1770s.[67] What Price was hearing and re-presenting, in other words, was the tamer Old Whig version of the leveling principles in Locke.

Burke's argument against Price in his *Reflections on the Revolution in France* was that Price was confusing three revolutions — the Republican Revolution of 1640, the Glorious Revolution of 1688, and the French Revolution of 1789 — in order to disseminate "democratic and levelling principles" which the English people "have no share of" and which they had in fact "disclaimed" in 1688.[68] The Revolutionary Settlement of 1688 was, Burke said, a return to the feudal past, to Britain's "*antient* laws and liberties" and to the gothic (i.e., medieval), hierarchical verities of the "Great Chain of Being." It was to be read as "a clause in the great primeval contract of eternal society, linking the lower with the higher natures, connecting the visible and invisible world, according to a fixed compact sanctioned by the inviolable oath which holds all physical and all moral natures, each in their appointed place."[69]

Burke insisted that, in the social contract of which Locke spoke, man "abdicates all right to be his own governor." He transfers his right to self-determination to governors and superiors, who "act in trust" not to man, but to God, "the one great master, author and founder of society."[70] This is essential, Burke insisted, because without "external restraints" on men's passions imposed by the laws and by due subordination to their legal governors and social superiors, all societies must, like revolutionary France, return to anarchy. What the leveling philosophy of the French Revolution had failed to grasp was that "men cannot enjoy the rights of an uncivil and civil state together" and that the civil state begins when, to "secure some liberty," man "makes a surrender in trust of the whole of it."[71] No wonder Catherine Macauley accused Burke of "Aristocratic Faction and Party."[72] Like Bolingbroke, in his *Idea of a Patriot King* at mid century, what Burke was hearing and re-presenting was the Filmer in Locke.[73]

We have tended to relate the work of late-eighteenth-century feminists like Wollstonecraft and More almost exclusively to this debate in England about the French Revolution, placing More on Burke's side of the debate and Wollstonecraft on Price's.[74] But Wollstonecraft and More were already writing within quite a longstanding feminist tradition, which also had other ends in view, and their differences are more fruitfully understood in terms of a tradition of gender politics which re-presented through the long eighteenth century that divide between the feudal-hierarchical traditionalists and the leveling democrats so unstably blended in the political culture, which Pocock (who only reads the men) argued became all but invisible between what he called "the first Eighteenth Century" of Harrington and Locke and "the second Eighteenth Century" of democratic revolutions.[75]

Egalitarian feminists were democrats in Montesquieu's sense. As "Sophia" put it in 1751, they held that "there is no other difference between

Men and Us than what their Tyranny has created" and that "we have an equal aptitude to Sense and Virtue with men."[76] Egalitarian feminists insisted that saying that women and men are equal means that they are, and ought to be treated, the same. Women were as capable of rational thought and virtuous action as men, and consent and reciprocity should characterize all their domestic interactions. Although eighteenth-century Egalitarians used the moral, philosophical, and spiritual language of Enlighteners, like Shaftesbury, Hutcheson, and Adam Smith, sociopolitically they were levelers, as these writers were not. That is to say, they were heirs of that seventeenth-century Dissenter tradition which not only razed hierarchies of rank and class and sought to extend the franchise to all (as the French Revolution was later to do) but also leveled all hierarchy between the genders (as the French Revolution did not).[77] In the middle of the nineteenth century, long after they had joined forces with Owenite socialists, Egalitarian feminists were still being identified with the "leveling vision" of "the early communitarian sects."[78]

The Matriarchs, on the other hand, were female supremacists, and sometimes female separatists too. They promoted "Woman's Superior Excellence over Man" and held that although "the MEN have by fraud and violence gained a superiority of power over us, we still retain our original Superiority of Sense and Virtue over them."[79] As we will see, Astell's breathtaking image of the Shunamite towering over men in a woman-centered world recurs throughout the century in their work:

> Whether it as not the Custom in *Shunam* for the Husband to dictate, or whether her's was conscious of her superior Vertue, or whatever was the Reason, we find it is she who governs, *dwelling* with great Honour *among her own People* . . . The text calls her a *Great Woman,* while her Husband is hardly taken Notice of . . . It is *her* Piety and Hospitality that are recorded. *She* invites the Prophet to *her House;* who converses with and is entertained by *her.* She gives her Husband no Account of *her* Afairs any further than to tell him *her* Designs, that he may see them executed. When he desires to know the Reason of her Conduct, all the Answer she affords is *Well,* or as the margin has it from the Hebrew, *Peace.* Nor can this be thought assuming, since it is no more than what the Prophet encourages, for all his addresses are to *her,* he takes no Notice of her Husband. His Benefits are conferr'd on *her,* 'tis *she* and *her Household* whom he warns of a Famine, and 'tis

she who appeals to the King for the Restitution of *her House and Land.* (Astell's emphases)[80]

The Shunamite is surrounded by men: a husband, a prophet, a king. But *she* is the "Great Woman," the embodiment of her people and governor of her household; and their stature shrinks beside hers to the point were no "Notice" need be taken even of their proper names. The presence of husband, prophet, and king is necessary to her greatness only as its measuring stick: while she governs, they must be present to do her honor and to do her will. But it is *her* virtue and *her* designs, *her* piety and *her* hospitality, *her* conversation and the benefits *she* brings to *her* household and *her* people that occupy center stage and carry everything and everyone before them. For they are the foundation of her enormous power, a power capable even of subordinating men who have a legal and official title to rule.

Matriarchs were strong believers in hierarchy and proper subordination. They used the philosophical and spiritual language of the established church, and sociopolitically they were aristocrats in Montesquieu's sense; as a result, they are often accused of patriarchalism now.[81] But it was Matriarchs who put ladies on that pedestal and invented what Virginia Woolf called "the Angel in the House." And, as we will have many occasions to observe, their talk of obedience and due subordination masked a gender politics anchored in the will to power and designed to invert the extant hierarchy between women and men.

Although the gender politics of the Egalitarians and that of the Matriarchs were inscribed on opposite sides of the feudal-egalitarian divide, it is important to understand that they did not merely follow parallel paths. Ideas, goals, and arguments migrated back and forth between them. They translated ideas and arguments across camps, and indeed across time, by adapting them to their own hierarchical or egalitarian templates and to the particular political and ideological debates of the times. Identifying a particular novel, tract, or woman writer as Matriarch or Egalitarian therefore often depends on recognizing some of each camp's more characteristic moves.

Egalitarians reasoned from the middle of the seventeenth century that it followed from the proofs they advanced that women are by nature men's equals, that women ought to be positioned more as men's equals in all the different departments of life: in family, church, and state. Egalitarian women demanded freedom of the city, freedom of the pulpit, and freedom to govern their own conduct, from the 1640s and 1650s when the argument for women's moral and spiritual equality with men was still a cutting-edge, sectarian, leveling argument. Often supported by Dissenting ministers,[82] female Quakers and Levellers deconstructed established and authoritative readings of the Scriptures to show that "God hath put no such difference between Male and Female as men would make."[83] And they supplied alternative readings of their own to argue that men and women are equal in Christ; that women, like men, can be inspired to preach or "speak;" and that men and women both have the same path to salvation and consequently, the same moral and religious duties and rewards. These early Egalitarians argued that, though a husband might have de facto authority over his wife "in bodily and civil respects," he is by no means "lord of her conscience."[84] They argued likewise that women have equal concern in the polity with men and should have the same liberties and securities too: "Have we not an equal interest with the men of this Nation, in those Liberties and Securities contained in the Petition of Right and other good laws of this land?" asked a group of Leveller women in a petition to the Government.[85]

By the end of the seventeenth century, Egalitarian arguments for women's spiritual equality and freedom of conscience had migrated to the Matriarchs.[86] Matriarchs like Mary Astell and Damaris Masham insisted that women could certainly be inspired to preach, and they did so themselves in a host of religious tracts. Astell used the same methods of scriptural deconstruction and re-exegesis as her Egalitarian forebears to show that "the Bible is for, not against us, and cannot without great Violence done to it, be urged to our prejudice." Like their leveling Egalitarian predecessors, too, Masham insisted that women could be expected to be Christians just like men, and Astell declared that, with respect to religion, women and men were "in all things co-equal." "There is no sex in souls," she said. God gave women and men equal souls and equal sense, and "God has [therefore] not only allowed, but required us to judge for ourselves."[87] No man was to be "lord of her conscience."

As adapted by Matriarchs, however, these Egalitarian arguments received two characteristic supplementary spins. The first is that, unlike the Egalitarians, Matriarchs proceeded on Bathsua Makin's principle that "to ask too much is to be denied all."[88] The Matriarchs put forward only one limited and carefully defined goal at a time. Where Egalitarians had argued from the seventeenth century that women should participate in the polity with men, Matriarchs only took up such questions in the latter half of the nineteenth century when they fought for the vote. At the end of the eighteenth century, their primary goal was to take over government of the family from men. At the end of the seventeenth century, it was to give women government of their own conduct by entitling them to think, judge, and decide for themselves. As Lady Chudleigh's feminist character Melissa put it in *The Ladies' Defence:* "You shall be Chief, and still yourselves admire: / The Tyrant Man may still possess the Throne; / 'Tis in our Minds that we would rule alone."[89]

While pursuing only one limited and carefully defined goal at a time, Matriarchs always sought to make themselves appear more conventional than they were. Consider their strategy in contesting the idea that an adult woman must be obedient to men "in all things" and subordinate her mind, will, and conscience to the pleasure of her domestic governor. On the one hand, Matriarchs calmly urged women to govern their own minds, their own consciences, and their own conduct, and to cease to "pay too great a deference to other Peoples' Judgement and too little to our own."[90] When told to do something opposed to their conscience, they said, women should not consult the wishes or satisfaction of others, "but having rightly informed themselves what ought to be done on each Emergency, go steadily on, without being disturbed either at Unkindness, Reproaches, Affronts or Disappointments; that all who see them have have just cause to conclude . . . that they are infinitely better pleased with the secret Plaudits of their own Consciences, than they would be with the flattering Acclamations of a deceitful world."[91]

On the other hand, at the same time, they were careful to emphasize how conformable they were. They were, they said, true daughters of the church and the most *abject* believers in obedience and due subordination. They had, they insisted, the greatest *possible* respect for authority — the authority of Scripture, the authority of the church, the authority of monarchs and the authority of husbands. Allowed to rule in their own minds, and to act according to their own consciences, they would prove: "humble, mild, forgiving, just and true, / Sincere to all, respectful unto you." What more could any man want? Was it not evident that women's moral and spiritual self-government would threaten neither the status quo nor the relative duties of husbands and wives, parents and children, governors and governed? Self-government for women would leave everything *just as it ought to be:* "With want of duty, none shall us upbraid; / Where e'er 'tis due, it shall be nicely pay'd."[92]

The second spin that Matriarchs gave to Egalitarian doctrine was to back their claims by appealing to the very Highest Power and authority. One reason that Matriarchs saw no contradiction between championing women's spiritual, moral, and intellectual self-government and affirming their commitment to proper subordination, as well as to authority, hierarchy, and church doctrine was that they found that the latter could very conveniently be used to guarantee and underwrite the former.

Mary Astell illustrates this technique nicely. Against the widespread argument that "St Paul, by declaring that [women] are the weaker vessel, does confirm common experience that their judgements are not so fixed, nor their Reason so elated as that sex which is the *Glory of God;* though their other accomplishments sufficiently answer the ends of their Creation to be the *Glory of Man.*"[93] Astell replied:

> 'tis no Arrogance in a Woman to conclude that she was made for the service of God, and this is her End. Because God hath made all things for Himself and a rational Mind is too noble a Being to be made for the Sake and Service of any Creature. The Service she at any time becomes oblig'd to pay to a Man is only a Business by the Bye, just as it may be any Man's Business and Duty to keep Hogs; he is not made for this, but if he Hires out to such an Employment, he ought conscientiously to perform it.[94]

Women are not, as men argued, created to be "the Glory of Man" rather than "the Glory of God." They are not "made for the sake and service of men" and they are not the "upper servants" of their husbands. They are servants of God.[95] If it has pleased God to send women into this world to serve hogs — or if women have hired themselves out to do so by being foolish or heroic enough to marry — they have a duty to do their job; but women's primary duty is to God, not to man. It is therefore women's duty to obey God *over* man. As Elizabeth Carter put it, "Our duty to the Supreme Being is infinitely superior to all human authority, however great."[96] Or, as Jane West said, Christianity "founds [even] obedience to kings on submission to the Most High;" it teaches that (like the hogs), Caesar must be given his due, *not* that Caesar must be unconditionally obeyed. This enabled West and other Matriarchs to "plead against the justice of absolute passive obedience in a wife" that when a husband disobeys God's law in any way, a wife unquestionably "has the right to lift her voice against the absolute authority of husbands."[97]

The shaky premise underlying churchmen's injunction that wives were to obey their husbands as the Lord — which was that there could be no difference between God's will and a husband's — was thus exposed; and the absolute authority of husbands was displaced and subordinated to the absolute authority of God.

For Matriarchs, then, the fact that the world was a great hierarchy with God at its head meant that the authority and power of God's moral and spiritual law could always be appealed to against the lesser power and authority of man, on behalf of whatever extension of freedom they sought for women: "God hath not only allowed, but required us, to judge for ourselves." "Whereever he is concerned" — and of course, for the pious, He is concerned in *all* our thoughts, conduct, duties, and life choices — "our inquiries must be personal and will admit of no representation."[98] Authority, hierarchy, and religious doctrine thus underwrote women's moral, intellectual, and spiritual autonomy, their independence from men who claimed that "the extent of wives' subjection doth stretch very farre, even to *all things*."[99]

The fact that God's moral and spiritual law had come down to women through a male tradition only made this strategy more delicious, as becomes apparent when Melissa's promise of duty, quoted earlier, is fully contextualized: "*While* as becomes you, sacred truths you teach, / And live those Sermons you to others preach, / With want of duty, none shall us upbraid; / *Where e'er 'tis due,* it shall be nicely pay'd" (emphases added).

Matriarchs hoisted men on their own petard by making women's obedience to men conditional on men's obedience to the sacred truths they themselves taught. While affirming that a single set of divine laws applied to both sexes, the Matriarchs' appeal to a law men taught was higher than that of mere men gave women a laudable pretext for escaping passive obedience to men and for governing themselves. Stressing and magnifying their all but angelic virtue also enabled these latter-day Shunamites to signal their towering superiority to men.

By the latter half of the eighteenth century, these Matriarchal spins on Egalitarian ideas had migrated back to the Egalitarians. Catherine Macauley and Mary Wollstonecraft are echoing Matriarchs when they say, for instance, that "women must rise above opinion and feel the dignity of a rational will that bows only to God" and that "there can be but one rule of right, if morality has an eternal foundation" or that "it is a farce to call any being virtuous whose virtues do not result from the exercise of its own reason" and that "the untutored and undisciplined mind is totally incapacitated for self-government."[100]

Egalitarians gave Matriarchal arguments characteristic spins of their own. Two such spins are evident in Wollstonecraft's version of the Matriarchal argument that woman's primary duty is to God *over* man: "I love man as my fellow; but his scepter, real or usurped, extends not to me, unless the reason of an individual demands my homage; and even then, the submission is to reason and not to man."[101]

The first characteristic spin here is to put the law of reason in the place occupied by the law of God in Matriarchal thinking: women should govern themselves by reason and obey reason over man. Eighteenth-century Egalitarians secularized the religious discourse of the Matriarchs and of their mid-seventeenth-century Egalitarian forebears by appealing to Enlightenment reason rather than to religion as the ultimate governor of human conduct. Consequently, although Egalitarians and Matriarchs used the same words in their arguments — *God, principle, virtue, duty* — they used them with different meanings. When eighteenth-century Egalitarians spoke of God, they meant Newton's God, who governed the world through laws accessible to reason, and who could be contemplated and adored in the sublimity of His creation; Matriarchs meant Christ as revealed through the Scriptures. When Egalitarians spoke of principle and duty, they meant the principles of justice, equality, and human nature and the reciprocal duties of human beings towards one another; Matriarchs meant the principles of Christianity and the "relative duties" of inferiors to superiors. When Egalitarians spoke of virtue, they meant the Enlightenment virtues of sympathy and benevolence; Matriarchs meant the Christian virtues of patience, charity, and chastity. Egalitarians and Matriarchs were joined and separated by the same words.

The Egalitarians' second characteristic spin was to level hierarchies that Matriarchs preserved and acknowledged: "I love man as my fellow." The Matriarchal imaginary always placed people above or below one another in a hierarchy of relative superiority or inferiority. The Egalitarian imaginary,

on the other hand, put everyone on a par. "The sexual should not destroy the human character," Wollstonecraft insisted, for it was through their common human character that men and women were equal, because the same. Men and women were "fellows" inasmuch as they had the same human nature; and inasmuch as they had the same human nature, they had the same reason, the same set of virtues, the same law, and the same demands on their conduct. As Catherine Macauley put it: "There is but one rule of right for the conduct of rational beings; consequently, true virtue in one sex must be equally so in the other."[102] For Egalitarians, there must be no difference between men and women where reason, education, right, and duty were concerned. Mary Hays, echoing Wollstonecraft, said that there must therefore also be no "disgusting contention between them for superiority: on occasions of importance, both [must] yield to reason."[103]

Feminist Revisionings of the Patriarchal Family

Changes in the patriarchal family were essential if self-governing women were to take their proper — Egalitarian or Matriarchal — place in the domestic arena. Indeed, projecting changes in the structure, dynamics, and government of the patriarchal family was logically inseparable from projecting changes in women's education and conduct, changes in the terms governing women's interactions with men, and changes in their relative place in the domestic hierarchy. To represent a self-governing woman who had cultivated her own mind and heart, whether in Egalitarian or Matriarchal style, was also to represent her in an altered domestic situation. From the 1750s on, Enlightenment feminists therefore developed exemplary, and highly idealized, images of the family in their novels, conduct books, and tracts, which accommodated whichever "revolution in female manners" they recommended. Figured forth as fictioned images of the ways in which "virtuous" parents and children and husbands and wives might interact, the radical changes they proposed in "conjugal society" and patriarchal government are easily overlooked.

To explain these changes, one might say that Enlightenment feminists modeled what Lyotard would call their "desirevolution" in the little society of the family on their visions of the polis, rather than justifying the political order by analogical sketches of the "natural family," as patriarchal theorists like Filmer, Locke, Bolingbroke, and Burke tended to do. Re-marking the feudal-egalitarian divide, Matriarchs and Egalitarians constructed

use of postmodernism often seems like a rude intrusion

their alternative visions of the family with different analogies in mind: "A man has been termed a microcosm; and every family might also be called a state," said Egalitarian Mary Wollstonecraft; Jane West, the Matriarch, spoke of "the little Monarchy of our own households."[104]

In their novels, conduct books, and tracts, Egalitarians sought to re-model the little society of the family according to the same principles of liberty, equality, and independence which, they argued, should revolution-ize the kingdom and turn it into a nonmonarchical and nonhierarchical republic. For them, the most important things about the social contract, which supposedly instituted society as such, were that it was a voluntary compact between people of equal worth to enter into one community for mutual assistance and the good of all and that its governors might only gov-ern with the consent of the ruled and for as long as they fulfilled their trust.

In the Egalitarian imaginary of the family, therefore, marital partners make their contract freely and as a result of rational choice — thus expressly not at the command of parents, guardians, or kin who have some social or economic interest in forcing the match. Parents or guardians govern chil-dren not by virtue of their authority, for their own advantage, or to grow a family estate, but "to their Children's Good", and children defer to parents or guardians and consent to be ruled by them because they respect their elders' reason and recognize that they have only their best interests at heart.

In the Egalitarian imaginary of the family, men and women live to-gether as persons of equal sense, who have the same right and authority to direct each other's conduct. Both sexes exhibit the same human nature — a compound of "masculine reason" and "feminine softness" — and obey the same models of conduct. Egalitarians argued that "attention to children and family . . . ought to be a prominent feature in the character and em-ployment of every woman who has children and families to attend to,"[105] and they insisted that mothers ought to teach and nurse their own chil-dren; but they valorized the father or male guardian too. In Egalitarian representations of the family, the father or guardian is generally present as a "nursing Father" who educates his children, tenderly and carefully guides his nurselings to rational independence, and demonstrates through his treatment of his daughters how "men in the character of fathers" can be "infinitely more amiable, and do more justice to the [female] sex, than in any other character whatever."[106]

In this way, although we usually regard them as more subversive of patriarchy than the Matriarchs, Egalitarians supported the new patriarchy over the old. To make his political points against Filmer, Locke had stressed the father's natural "tenderness and affection" towards his sons and natural desire to use his trust to the children's Good; and, like the Levellers before him, he had argued that government both in the family and in the state is only legitimized by what feminist scholars now call an ethics of care, which they attribute exclusively to women.[107] This image of the "nursing Father" proliferated in the eighteenth century. It was taken up and fleshed out in idealized typologies of "the good-natured man," "the man of feeling," and the "benevolent patriarch,"[108] who cared for his dependent children, felt for the suffering of others, helped his poor or unfortunate neighbours and friends, and governed his social and domestic inferiors with justice mitigated by compassion.[109]

Eighteenth-century Egalitarian feminists almost invariably valorized men in this new, more nurturing paternal role. In their fictional representations of the "good father" — one has only to think of Mr. Villars in Burney's *Evalina*, Mr. Raymond in Hays's *The Victim of Prejudice*, Sandiforth in the second half of Inchbald's *A Simple Story*, or M. Le Luc in Radcliffe's *Romance of the Forest* — they also often exemplified Locke's argument that paternal power belongs to the father not by virtue of "any particular right of nature, but only as he is Guardian of his Children" and governs them to their good. They did so by underlining the difference between the heroine's natural father — who abandons her and is shown to have little or no title to her duty — and nursing "Foster-Fathers," like Villars, Raymond, Sandiforth, and Le Luc, who act as the heroine's guardian and earn her love and duty by supplying her natural father's place and giving her nourishment, education, and care.[110]

The Matriarchs took a different line. They accepted and endorsed the primarily hierarchical character of British society under constitutional monarchy. What they found particularly instructive about the new social contract was the way the Revolutionary Settlement had dealt with the abusive power of absolute monarchs: it had formally left the sovereign in place at the top of the sociopolitical hierarchy, while gradually transferring increasingly significant portions of his power, and of the actual government of the country, to his parliamentary vice-regents.

In rewriting the little society of the family, the Matriarchs did much the same thing. They left fathers and husbands as nominal sovereigns at the top of the domestic hierarchy, while transferring increasingly significant portions of their power and of the actual government of the family to mothers and wives. The Matriarchs taught ladies how to govern "the little kingdom over which we exert vice-regal dignity," and they taught them how to do so while exercising "that intermediate power which should always subsist between the sovereign and the subject" in such a way as to make it the lynchpin that "harmonizes the whole system"[111] — and controls it. Matriarchs appropriated for ladies in the role of domestic "vice-regent" all those functions of domestic order and good government, domestic economy, and domestic education which patriarchal family ideology in the latter half of the eighteenth century called on gentlemen to perform, thus continuing to give women powerful images of themselves as capable and virtuous Shunamites.

Fathers and husbands are therefore not a strong presence in the Matriarchal vision of the family; their functions are severely curtailed and marginalized, for while Matriarchs permitted husbands and fathers to "retain / The name and all th'addition to a king," they ensured that wives and mothers took over "the sway, the revenue and the execution of the rest."[112] As Jane West said, "Give the Lords of Creation but the appearance of supremacy, and they are contented to obey."[113]

Matriarchs thus preserved the appearance of the patriarchal family, while seeking to displace the actual seat of its power from the paterfamilias to the materfamilias. Preservation of the forms enabled Matriarchs to appear more conventional and less threatening to men than they were, but their empowerment of women, their inversion of the power relationship between husbands and wives, and their changes in family dynamics made their image of the family markedly different from that of their male contemporaries — including the Evangelicals, with whom they are often identified.

Throughout the long eighteenth century, most male conduct book writers repeated Locke's analogical argument for the subordination of women in a family conceived as a hierarchy in which the Master of the Family ruled supreme.[114] Here, for instance, is Fleetwood in 1705:

> All Inferiours are commanded to be *subject* to higher Powers, and Children to their Parents, and Servants to their Masters, and Men to one another, as well as Wives to their Husbands . . . It is impossible for any Company of

People to subsist any while together, without a Subordination of one to the other . . . The Father is the Superiour Authority and must be obeyed because both the Laws of God and of Man have subjected the Wife to the Husband; she is not presumed to have a will contrary to her Husband, and therefore the Child disobeys not his Mother who obeys his Father's Command, because the Mother is to be obedient also.[115]

Here is the Evangelical Gisbourne in 1797:

As the burden of the most laborious offices in life, of those offices which require the greatest exertions, the deepest and most comprehensive judgement, is devolved upon Men; and as man, that he may be qualified for the discharge of those offices, has been furnished by his Creator with powers of investigation and foresight in a somewhat greater measure than the other sex . . . it seems an appointment both reasonable in its nature and most conducive to the happiness not only of man himself, but also of his wife and children, and of all his connections, that he should be the person to whom the Superiority should be committed.[116]

Without such superiority in the man, Gisbourne continues, repeating both Filmer and Locke, there would be only bickering, conflicts, and pertinacious contrariety between husband and wife, and confusion in families.

Finally, here is Paley, whose influence stretches to mid nineteenth century, sounding a slightly more conciliatory, but not essentially different, note:

The wife promises *obedience* to her husband. Nature may have left the sexes of the human species nearly equal in their faculties and perfectly so in their rights; but to guard against those competitions which equality or contested superiority is almost sure to produce, the Christian Scriptures enjoin upon the wife that obedience that she here promises in terms so peremptory and absolute that it seems to extend to everything not criminal or entirely inconsistent with a woman's happiness. "Let the wife," says St. Paul, "be subject to her husband in every thing."[117]

As Jane West commented drily more than a century after Astell: "the greatest sticklers for public freedom have been the veriest domestick bashaws . . . In their precincts, *freedom* is always considered to be of the masculine gender."[118]

These rival domestic agendas, which Matriarchs and Egalitarians offered ladies of the middling and upper ranks in their novels, conduct
books, and tracts from the 1750s on, challenged both the old "tyrannical"
patriarchal family and its new more "benevolent" paternalistic incarnation,
both of which were represented in eighteenth-century essays, novels, and
conduct books by men. But Matriarchs and Egalitarians also had in the
novel a powerful instrument of social change, and they deployed a well-
tried narrative pedagogy of example to ensure that their fictioned images
of ladies in their domestic situations would have the required transfor-
mative social effect.

2

Domestic Fictions and the
Pedagogy of Example

Let me make the novels of a country and let who will make the
systems. — MRS. BARBAULD

THE EIGHTEENTH CENTURY was no stranger to the supposedly
postmodern assumption that "our life comes from books" and that
"to change the book is to change life itself."[1] Lady novelists, literary theorists, reviewers, essayists, moralists, and educators well understood the
power that fictions exercise over life. It was because they held that fictional
narratives have the power to "excite the actions they describe"[2] and
thought their influence "likely to be considerable both on the Morals and
the Taste of a nation,"[3] that they paid so much attention to the principles
governing fictional actions and to the potentially beneficial or harmful effects of the novels they discussed. As Catharine Macauley said, fictions
were *pharmakons*, which could imprint people's minds for good or ill: "If
the arts have the power of softening and increasing the delicacy of the human mind, they must have the power of engraving on it mischievous as
well as useful impressions, and deluding us as well as pleasing the imagination . . . Let us endeavour to take from them the poisons which lie min-
gled in their sweets . . . to the nobler purpose of the general good."[4]
It was because they believed that books had the power to fashion the
manners, morals, and sentiments of the reading public that eighteenth-
century clergymen, conduct book writers, and educators either proscribed
novel reading altogether or insisted that parents carefully select the novels
their daughters read. And, as Clara Reeve and Maria Edgeworth tell us, it
was precisely because they considered that women readers were already
modeling their lives, conduct, expectations, and values on the mischievous,
shoddy, and fantastic romances they borrowed from the circulating li-

braries that from mid century on, Egalitarian and Matriarchal novelists set out to change the books that women were imitating in order to change their very lives.

If "the virtues of the people depend on the nature of the instruction they receive," using the novel as a vehicle of public instruction and as a means of reeducating their largely female readership enabled Egalitarian and Matriarchal authors to construct for themselves a public role as moralists and social reformers that was far more respectable than the role of earlier women writers, like Behn and Manley, or Haywood in her younger years. Through popular fictions, which "open[ed] a door of civilization to the meanest ranks of the people,"[5] Enlightenment feminists could reach all those women who devoured novels but fled — or lacked access to — any course of serious reading or study, for as Jane Barker said, "a pleasant story may find him who flies a serious lecture."[6] Making "works of fancy . . . subservient to the improvement of the rising generation,"[7] they could work for whichever "revolution in female manners" they sought by impressing upon their readers the truth, desirability, and practical benefits of their own domestic agendas and politico-feminist philosophies.

As a result, as Mrs. Barbauld said: "No small proportion of modern novels have been devoted to recommending or to marking with reprobation, those systems of philosophy which have raised so much ferment in late years."[8] It was in the novel, a genre still dominated in the eighteenth century by female authors, that what she called "the war of systems" was fought out. The popular novel was where different ideas about the polity, different models of domestic life, and different norms of conduct were presented, contrasted, and contested. At the end of the eighteenth century, Matriarchs complained that other women's novels had become "alarmingly democratical" and were being "employed to diffuse destructive Politics, deplorable Profligacy and impudent Infidelity;"[9] and they justified their own compositions in the genre by explaining that they themselves wrote "only as an antidote to the bad effects of them, though under the guise and names of novels."[10] But Matriarchs had been infusing their politico-feminist positions into novels and into periodicals for women from the early 1740s and 1750s — and into poems and romances before that — and they may well have been the original provocateurs. Whoever started the war of systems, the effect, as Jane West said, was to inject "prejudice and party" into every novel, and to "turn . . . us into a nation of disputants and censors."[11]

To disseminate their domestic agendas and politico-feminist platforms while constructing themselves as moral educators and social reformers, Egalitarian and Matriarchal novelists tapped into the exemplar tradition, which had, since the Renaissance, conceived of narratives of all sorts as "philosophy teaching by example."[12] They tell us so. They say that they were making "entertaining stories the vehicle to convey to the young and flexible heart wholesome truths that it refused to receive under the form of precept and instructions," or "temper[ing] the *utile* with the *dulce,* and under the guise of Novels, giv[ing] examples of virtue rewarded and vice punished."[13] They advise each other to convey their principles and precepts through "some striking exemplification . . . something that shall illustrate your instruction, shall realize your position, shall embody your idea and give shape and form and colour to your precept."[14] And they indicate, both in the prefaces to their novels and in the body of their texts, that their fictional characters and actions are to be read as examples.

This does not mean that their exemplary narratives necessarily reflected universal, typical, or even widely held beliefs and practices, as we often assume when we speak of their compositions as didactic, ideological, or proto-realist novels. It means that they were employing a traditional rhetoric to persuade their readers that acting on particular principles in the current state of society was possible and proper, admirable, and entirely worthy of imitation. For conduct to qualify as exemplary, it had to be uncommon, exceptional, or rare. To read them again today, therefore, we need to complicate our picture of women's exemplary fictions by considering both how they were supposed to work and how they played with their own conventions to construct and deconstruct themselves.

"Example is a Duty which we owe all the World"

In the eighteenth century, exemplary narratives came in all shapes and forms and colors, crossing what we now consider established generic boundaries.[15] History and fiction, periodicals and "lives," romance and the novel, the epistolary novel, the Gothic novel, and the novel of sensibility were all, in principle, exemplary narratives. In the eighteenth century, when "history" still meant both story and history, as the French word *histoire* does today, novels were a kind of history. Like romances, they were "imagined" or "fictitious histories"; and unlike romances, they were "familiar histories," because they dealt with such familiar situations as everyone met with in the course of common life. But, whether "true" or "fictitious," "romantic" or "familiar," it was the proper function of a history to teach some moralized political philosophy by example. Said Hugh Blair, "It is not every record of fact, however true, that is entitled to the name of History, but such record as enables us to apply the transactions of former ages to our own instruction."[16] Or, as Manley very properly reminds her readers in the preface to one of her naughty romances, "the chief end of history is to instruct and inspire into men the love of virtue and the abhorrence of vice, by the examples proposed to them; therefore the conclusion of a story ought to have some tract of morality which may engage virtue."[17]

Renaissance humanists had looked to true history for their exemplary models of character, conduct, and virtue and had presented the male heroes of the past as patterns for men's imitation in the present. Augustan poets still did. And women writers never entirely gave up the practice either. Eliza Haywood said of the fictitious "little histories" that she inserted in *The Female Spectator*, "Whenever I find any example among the antients, which may serve to illustrate the topic I shall happen to be upon, I shall make no scruple to insert it," for "an instance of shining virtue of any age, can never be too often proposed as a pattern, nor the fatality of misconduct too much impressed on the minds of our youth of both sexes."[18]

However, there was also a growing sense, especially among women writers, that true history presented only "a terrible list of crimes and calamities, treachery, fraud and barbarity"[19] and that, in any case, the public acts of great men recorded by true history were of little value to women. Rather than take true history for their pattern, therefore, women writers would project the mores, values, and concerns of their own contemporaries onto an imagined ancient or Gothic past or clothe their examples in the eighteenth-century dress of "familiar histories."

They reasoned that if ladies were to change their family situations as daughters, wives, mothers, and mistresses of the family, they needed to be "furnished with a stock of ideas and principles and qualifications and habits ready to be applied and appropriated as occasions may demand to each of these respective situations."[20] What better instrument to furnish them with such ideas than narratives that portrayed them in their familiar situations as daughters, wives, mothers, and mistresses of the family and which showed them contending with the sort of issues and choices they would, in all probability, have to confront themselves? "Familiar histories" offered women more useful examples than "true histories," both because they were familiar, in the sense of dealing with situations with which women were well acquainted, and because they were familiar in the older, eighteenth-century sense of "pertaining to the family" and to the behavior due among members of a family or household.[21] As Sarah Fielding says, in the voice of a "Lady of the House" who is distinguished for having "bred up three sons and three daughters who do honour to her Education of them": "I really think the penetrating into the motives that actuate the persons in a private Family, of much more general use to be known, than those concerning the Management of any Kingdom or Empire whatsoever: the latter, Princes, Governors and Politicians only can be the better for, whilst every Parent, every Child, every Sister and every Brother, are concerned in the former, and may take Example by such as are in the same situation as themselves."[22]

Eighteenth-century women writers did not construct their exemplary narratives around heroic deeds or the individual and society. They conceived of the social world as constituted by a multitude of families, and by a multitude of diverse but analogical family relationships. Their orphaned heroines travel through a series of familial and social situations, meeting a variety of what Greimas would call "helpers" and "opponents," and conquering — or falling victim to — all those features of character, conduct, and society which the novels they inhabit construct as obstacles to the sort of family society and the sort of interpersonal relationships they mark as virtuous.

The fact that women's exemplary fictions were familiar in these senses does not at all mean that they purported to reflect reality. There was a clear conviction among women writers that society was unjust (Egalitarians) or dissipated and immoral (Matriarchs) and that exemplary patterns for imitation simply could not be derived from people's real conduct in the world: "In the world, few people act from principle; present feelings and early habits are the grand springs: but how would the former be deadened, and the latter rendered corroding fetters, if the world were shown to young people as it is."[23]

No one pretended that people were actually behaving like the heroines and heroes in exemplary fictions or that narratives which showed virtue rewarded and vice punished reflected life. They said instead that such narratives "supply the defects of experience" or "supply the want of experience" and that they "accommodate the appearances of things to the desires of the mind."[24] Exemplary fictions were designed to give women "ideas of delicacy and refinement which were not, perhaps, to be gained by any society she had access to" and to inculcate sentiments which "served to counteract the spirit of the world, where selfish considerations always have more than their due weight."[25] The function of exemplary narratives, in the Enlightenment as in the Renaissance, was not to reflect social practices but to intervene in practice by offering a constructed and embodied ideal — in the eighteenth-century sense of "mental idea" or "archetype" or "pattern of excellence" — as a model for readers' imitation, as a motive for their actions, and as an object of their desire. Exemplary narratives were rhetorical and pedagogical devices designed, as Timothy Hampton has said, "to move readers to various kinds of moral and political behavior" by "provid[ing] the reader with a variety of options for possible action in the world."[26]

This is also why, for much of the century, "mixed character" was viewed with such suspicion. Mixed characters could certainly be justified on the grounds of probability, verisimilitude, or realism, as Johnson said, for even the good people in our families and social lives are likely to have some admixture of faults. But could they be justified pedagogically if familiar histories were "written chiefly to the young, the ignorant and the idle, to whom they serve as lectures of conduct and instructions into life?" Dr. Johnson thought not, for "as we accompany them through their adventures with delight, and are led by degrees to interest ourselves in their favour, we lose the abhorrence of their faults, because they do not hinder our pleasure, or perhaps regard them with some kindness for being united with so much merit." There must be no mixing of poison, he insisted, in their sweets. To serve as "lectures of conduct and instructions into life," familiar histories had to ensure that their chief protagonists exhibited "the most perfect idea of virtue" and showed vice in such a way that it "should always disgust."[27] These sentiments were widely repeated by later reviewers and theorists of the novel, and those eighteenth-century women writers who were cited for being "sollicitous of the morals of their readers" accordingly tended to center their narratives on characters who exemplified whatever their domestic agendas designated as the most perfect idea of virtue or of vice.

Novels did not have to reflect reality to achieve their moralized political and pedagogical aims, for, according to eighteenth-century theorists, it made no difference to their effect on the reader whether examples were true or fictitious. Fictitious examples could educate, motivate, and awaken a desire of imitation in the reader as well as true ones; as everyone from Montaigne to Clara Reeve said, "the effects of Romance and true History are not very different — when the imagination is raised, men do not stand to inquire whether the motive be true or false."[28] It also followed from post-Lockean semiology, where words stood not for things but for ideas in the mind, that language had the same effect on the mind whether it described a material reality or an invented archetype. Language communicated ideas from mind to mind, more or less vividly depending on the writer's abilities, regardless of whether those ideas were of real or fictitious things. Kames explained:

> Ideal presence supplies the want of real presence, and in idea we perceive persons acting and suffering precisely as in an original survey . . . If in reading, ideal presence be the means by which our passions are moved, it makes no difference whether the subject be a fable or a true history. Even general history has no command over our passions but by an ideal presence only . . . in this respect, it stands upon the same footing as fable.[29]

Words had always already murdered the thing; words had always already replaced real presence with the ideal presence of things, that is, with their presence in, as, and for idea. Language was idea-logy or ideal-ogy. But for eighteenth-century theorists, this was not a defect of language; it was what permitted language to "accommodate the appearances of things to the desires of the mind," and to create fictions where ideal (mental, archetypal) patterns of excellence were perceived to be "acting and suffering precisely as in an original survey." If the effect of language depended on its ability to summon up ideas (or images or emotions) in the reader's mind, then the writer of exemplary novels could "gain his end not by imitating nature, but by assuming her power, and causing the same effect upon the imagination which her charms produce on the senses."[30]

By the same token, there was thought to be little or no difference between teaching politico-moral precepts through the example of real people, and teaching them through historical or fictional exemplars. Examples would be imitated whether they were embodied in human beings or fictional characters, inscribed in physical bodies or in written texts.

This was why children's governors and tutors were advised *both* to exemplify their precepts in some lively anecdote or (hi)story *and* to construct themselves as examples by modeling and embodying the precepts they taught. Paternal governors and tutors were warned to do nothing before children which they would not have them imitate and to be extremely careful of the company they kept:

> Let them have what Instructions you will, and ever so learned lectures of Breeding daily inculcated into them, that which will most influence their Carriage, will be the Company they converse with and the fashion of those around them. Children (nay Men too) do most by Example. We are all a sort of Camelions that still take a Tincture from those near us.[31]

> The example [of governors and governesses] ought to be such as to enforce their precepts, and by shewing the beauty of a regular life in themselves, make their pupils fall in love with it and endeavour an imitation.[32]

It was for this reason, too, that Matriarchs told ladies that they could change the conduct and the principles of all those in their "sphere of influence" by constructing themselves as examples in all the relative duties of their everyday lives. Educators taught that from our earliest childhood, it was easiest and most natural for us to learn by imitating the example of others; and people or classes of people like women and the lower orders — who had little or no formal education and were not accustomed to learning by abstracting or applying general principles — continued to do so all their lives. They learned not only whatever skill, art, or trade they practised by following someone else's example (repeating and trying to copy as closely as they could what they had seen someone else do before them) but also how to conduct themselves in societies, great and small. And at a time when every rank was trying to raise itself by imitating the behavior, lifestyle, and values of the rank or ranks above it, Matriarchs reasoned, ladies in the higher or more affluent ranks of society were models whose example would be copied. As objects of imitation to their children, to their servants, to young people, to ladies in neighboring families, and to the lower orders, every lady had the power to "benefit society" by her exemplary conduct as daughter, wife, mother, mistress of the family, economist, and friend:

> If women who derive authority from their rank or talents did but reflect how their sentiments are repeated, and how their authority is quoted, they

would be so on their guard that general society might become the scene of profitable communication and common improvement; and the young, who are looking for models on which to fashion themselves, would be ashamed and afraid to exhibit anything like levity or scepticism or prophaneness.[33]

In vain shall we preach economy and prosperity, if we show those who look up to us for example, the method of being extravagant and ridiculous. Thus, as in all authoritative situations, example closes the circle of prescribed duties, and its influence on subordinate stations is almost invincible.[34]

If everyone was thought to imitate the example of those above them, it also makes sense that in eighteenth-century women's novels, what Gary Kelly has called "professional middle-class" values should so frequently have been exemplified through the lives and conduct of genteel or aristocratic characters in high life.[35] It was clearly as desirable for both fictitious and real ladies to use their social authority to fire others to imitate their example as it was for women writers to use the authority of language to fire their readers to emulate them. Example was a duty that real ladies, fictitious ladies, and lady novelists owed all the world.

In the latter half of the eighteenth century, there was also a sense that much of the force and invincibility of the power of example derived from its ability to circumvent reason and the will. Johnson, for instance, said that "the power of example is so great as to take possession of the memory by a kind of violence and produce effects almost without the interaction of the will." Dodsley argued that fables give the precept "birth in the mind of the person for whom it is intended" by making us "*feel* our duties at the very instant we comprehend them."[36] And Lord Kames explained that the characteristic that "bestows upon good example the utmost influence, in prompting us to imitate what we admire"[37] is that it has an immediate impact on sympathy and the emotions. Enlightenment feminists, too, saw that "there is a kind of Contagion in Minds, as well as Bodies," for "what we admire we fondly wish to imitate" and "from admiring to adopting, the step is short and the progress rapid."[38] And in their novels, they sought to use "the Contagion of Examples" to "fire the mind to emulation" and "excite the reader to the practice of" those precepts they exemplified.[39] From this point of view, the novel of sensibility and the later Gothic romance — with their emphases on awakening strong emotions of pity and horror in the reader — can be viewed as attempts to heighten example's emotive and firing power in order to exploit narrative fiction's ability to take possession of the reader's mind and imprint ideas and values "almost without the interaction of the will."[40]

Freeing language from real presence and from the burden of past precedent meant that the power of example could begin to promote the different and the novel. Women novelists now had a theory of language and of reader reception that allowed exemplarity to move into "the boundless regions of possibility which fiction claims for her domain."[41] Women novelists could exemplify their ideas about other possible characters for women and other possible lives, and rewrite familiar relations in accordance with their desire, by giving the possible a local habitation and a name. By clothing the precept in the example and the constructed ideal in the real, women novelists could make their ideas "perceptible as in an original survey" and prove that acting on certain principles in the current state of society was possible. "Examples," as Sarah Fielding said, "are so much the more powerful to persuade as they prove the possibility of following them."[42] By giving fiction the concreteness and familiarity of fact and accommodating the "real" appearances of things to the purposes of a narrative "argument" (in Milton's sense), they could demonstrate the probability that acting on particular "virtuous" or "vicious" principles would have particular happy or unhappy outcomes in the real world. And by surrounding their exemplary characters with a number of wholly or partially idealized mentors and friends, and with a wide variety of nonidealized characters who displayed humankind's more vicious practices — all of whom were disposed according to what the century called "a general plan" of parallel and contrasting virtues and vices — they could also make their patterns of excellence serve as a standard against which the failings of society and of family life were judged.

However, exemplary narratives were not the fail-safe, monological, or authoritarian fictions we sometimes suppose. As John Lyons and Susan Suleiman have both shown, example teaches by induction: the meaning of an example lies outside itself in its relation to that general idea (philosophy, idealogy, agenda, or politico-moral system) of which it is a particular, local instance, and the reader is left to discover the implicit relation of the particular to the general for herself through inference and interpretation. Consequently, the meaning of an example is notably unstable, for the same illustrative event can illustrate a variety of different ideas: "The death of

Socrates can be used to show that death holds no fear for a good man, since he drank the hemlock so cheerfully; but also to show that virtue is prey to ill-will and far from safe amidst a swarm of evils; or again that the study of philosophy is useless or even harmful unless you conform to general patterns of behavior."[43] The illustrative event therefore depends for stabilization of its meaning on the intratextual context of the narrative which either repeats or moralizes it in an attempt to pin it down.

The meaning of an example can, however, become more, not less, unstable in narratives like eighteenth-century women's novels, where the significance of each character and event grows out of its diverse relations to analogical characters and events which not only repeat but also vary, contradict, negate, affirm, or develop one or more of its features. In this sort of text, the reader is expected to "collect the moral" by considering what Locke called "the agreement and disagreement of ideas" among the analogical features of the text. For considering the agreement and disagreement of ideas was how the mind was thought to reason and know.[44] And as Fielding illustrates in the incident in *Tom Jones* where the servant girl concludes from the puppet show she has been watching that "a great lady can be a whore, as well as we," there was no telling where such analogical reasoning might lead.

This was a matter of some anxiety to eighteenth-century purists. On the one hand, they understood the importance of leaving the reader to make her own inferences from the agreement and disagreement of ideas. As Dodsley says, when discussing fable's ability to "teach and imprint some Truth": "'Tis the particular excellence of Fable to waive the air of superiority: it leaves the *reader* to collect the moral; who by thus discovering more than is shown to him, finds his principle of self-love *gratified*, instead of being disgusted . . . Strictly speaking, one should render needless any *detached* or *explicit* moral . . . otherwise the precept is *direct* which is contrary to the nature and end" of this species of composition.[45]

If the purpose of telling an exemplary story is to convey wholesome truths that people "refuse to receive under the form of moral precept and instructions," it makes no sense to court this refusal — this perennial resistance to theory — by offering the precept direct and abandoning fable for injunction and example for philosophy. Hannah More's *Coelebs in Search of a Wife* is readable today only as an "Awful Warning" of what can happen to a story when example is not trusted to convey the author's precept or idea. On the other hand, she was not alone in distrusting example and in thinking that it was safer for the idea and the moral to be expressly introduced. Dodsley and others thought so, too. And the desire for unmixed characters, as well as for examples capable of circumventing reason by appealing directly to sympathy and the emotions betrays the same fear of contamination and anxiety of proper moral influence.

This anxiety was not misplaced, for one of the most unexpected things about Egalitarian and Matriarchal novels is that the moral can be as unstable as the example — and not only for the obvious reason that the perfect pattern of domestic virtue and of the good society had become culturally plural and contested space. The moral, even detached and explicit, was unstable because it often served women writers as a mask to conceal their designs.

Stephen Greenblatt has argued that individuals like More or Tyndale who opposed the community and resisted power in the Renaissance always did so in obedience to another, "higher" power and that their resistance was always an inverted mirror image of the authoritarian "disciplinary paradigm" they were resisting.[46] The same might be said of the characters and authors of eighteenth-century women's novels, but to leave the argument here is to overlook the extent to which, at least in the eighteenth century, innovations were masked as tradition and political revolutions were justified by appeal to authority, and it is to confuse function and form. Presenting the new as "what oft was thought but ne'er so well exemplified," and justifying social change by appeals to moral authority were two of the Egalitarian novelist's most successful strategies for opposing the power of social norms and practices and for making radical alternatives seem acceptable — as everyone well understood. Eighteenth-century readers and reviewers did not take such an extraordinary interest in the morality of novels because they found morality less boring than we do but because that was where the real political action lay, and, invoking morality in their turn, readers and reviewers were quick to point out when a novel's "morality" masked political innovations with which they disagreed. Here, for instance, is a reviewer of Charlotte Smith's *Emmeline* (1788):

> Is it the business of the moral writer, who should strengthen the young mind in habits of virtue, to invent situations where every event is supposed to concur in making such temptation [Adelina's] irresistible, and such

breach of engagement [Emmeline's] excusable; to draw the characters eminently virtuous, yet contrive to make them err without incurring our blame for it — to make adultery amiable and perfidy meritorious, and dismiss the perpetrators of both to honour and to happiness?[47]

What this reviewer was objecting to was Smith's use of the language of virtue to extend the idea of social contracts as consensual relationships to a woman's right to leave a man — fiancé or husband — who has proved himself unworthy of her love or respect. The standard Matriarchal complaint about Egalitarian novels was precisely this, that they used the language of virtue to mask an agenda too radical (and therefore "vicious") for their taste: "vices are made to look like virtues," by being "dressed in the engaging shape of amiable indiscretions and venial errors, or perhaps in the bolder attire of those frailties which *honour* the heart."[48] Egalitarian novelists had, Matriarchs complained, adopted Rousseau's technique of "seduc[ing] the affections . . . through the medium of the principles" and of "allur[ing] the warm-hearted to embrace vice, not because they prefer vice, but because vice is given so natural an air of virtue."[49] Today, we often need the help of eighteenth-century commentators of one sort or another to recognize where virtue is being used as a mask in Egalitarian novels to extend society's tolerance or women's freedom in non-normative ways.

Matriarchs tended to go about things differently: they would allow the play of possible meanings arising from "the agreement and disagreement of ideas" to exceed any moral or interpretation offered in the story. In this way, the most proper of exemplary narratives could be written double-voiced, to disprove the evidence of its own example and seem more conventional than it was.[50]

Consider a relatively simple narrative by that most proper of proper ladies, Frances Brooke.[51] In its time, *Lady Julia Mandeville*, an epistolary novel published in 1762, was one of the most popular and most praised of the many eighteenth-century British rewrites of Rousseau's *Julie, ou La Nouvelle Héloïse*. Lord Belmont is Baron L'Etange and Wolmar rolled into one: like Wolmar he presides over an ideal society on his country estate, and like Baron L'Etange, he has an unshakable prejudice against his daughter's marrying beneath her class. Like Rousseau's Julie, Julia, his daughter, is a beautiful heiress, well educated and sensible to the "finer impressions" of pity and tenderness. And like Saint-Preux, Julia's cousin

Henry Mandeville is an impoverished but otherwise altogether admirable young man, who comes to stay in the Belmont household. As in *Héloïse*, too, Henry and Julia fall in love and want to marry; but knowing that Lord Belmont will never consent to such an unequal match, they keep their relationship secret while Henry goes out into the world to make his fortune. As Henry says, echoing the picture of England that Rousseau gives through his British Lord B——: "I have many powerful friends; we have a Prince in the early prime of life, the season of generous virtue; a Prince to whom the patriot glow, and that disinterested loyalty which is almost my whole inheritance, cannot but be the strongest recommendation."

Lord Belmont's government of his estate, Belmont, to which much of the novel is devoted, corrects the cold, rational, rather Prussian domestic ordering of Rousseau's Clarens, by embodying the mid-century British Enlightenment ideal of benevolent patriarchal government. Henry underlines the political correctness of Belmont's "perfectly domestic" idyll:

> His estate conveys the strongest idea of patriarchal government: he seems a beneficent father surrounded by children, over whom reverence and gratitude and love give him an absolute authority, which he never exerts but for their good: every eye shines with transport at his sight; parents point him out to their children . . . and age supported by his bounteous hand, pours out the fervent prayer to Heaven for its benefactor.[52]

Lord Belmont is a re-presentation of Hume's "humane and beneficent man," who was to be the enlightened moral and political mainstay of a kingdom composed of little domestic sovereignties (one hesitates to say which is more fictional):

> His children never feel his authority, but when employed to their advantage. With him, the ties of love are consolidated by beneficence and friendship. The ties of friendship approach, in a fond observance of each obliging office, to those of love and inclination. His domestics and dependents have in him a sure resource . . . From him, the hungry receive food, the naked clothing, the ignorant and slothful, skill and industry. Like the sun, an inferior minister of Providence, he cheers, invigorates and sustains the surrounding world.[53]

As a pattern of beneficent patriarchal excellence, Lord Belmont uses his fortune and his influence to encourage industry and relieve poverty and

suffering among his tenants, and to preserve and maintain the social hierarchy. He ensures that his tenants do not "rise to exorbitant wealth"
(though their industry increases the value of his estate), and when "due to
a misfortune and too careless oeconomy," a neighboring gentleman is
forced to sell his estate, Lord Belmont comes to his rescue with an inter-
est-free loan and a plan of economy which will put him straight, because
he regards "the independent country gentlemen as the strength and support of this kingdom, and the best supports of our excellent constitution."
All this public beneficence is possible because, unlike his peers in the fashionable world, Lord Belmont stays at home on his estate to seek his personal happiness "in the sweets of dear domestic life" and "in the tender and
pleasant duties of husband and father." As he tells Henry, personal happiness is not possible without a "fortunate choice" in marriage and a "soft
union of hearts," and his own happiness with Lady Belmont has been kept
alive for thirty years by her "angel purity" and "delicacy of behaviour."
These are demonstrated in the novel by Lady Belmont's unfailing attend-
ance at church and noninterference in Lord Belmont's government of all
his domestics, including her daughter. In these respects, as in all others,
the Belmonts are repeatedly and heavily marked as exemplary: "How forcible, how irresistible, are such examples in superior life! Who can know
Lord and Lady Belmont without endeavouring to imitate them? and who
can imitate them without becoming all that is amiable and praiseworthy?"

Unaccountably, the novel has a tragic ending. Lord Belmont and
Henry's father had educated Julia and Henry for each other, like Emile
and Sophie, because Lord Belmont intends their marriage to unite his
branch of the family, which has no male heir, to the senior branch of the
family represented by Henry and his father, which had lost the Belmont
title and fortune after supporting the Stuarts during the Civil War. Lord
Belmont's beneficence thus also extends to Henry. But Henry and Julia do
not know it. Under the false impression that Julia is destined by Lord Belmont to marry Lord Melvyn, Henry fights a duel with him, during which
he is killed; and Julia dies of a broken heart.

The "detached and explicit" moral at the end of the story interprets this
catastrophe in perfectly proper ways: Belmont has "defeated [his] own
purpose" by an "over-solicitude" for the continuity of his family and the
happiness of his child; Henry was jealous and rash in duelling Melvyn; Julia was at fault for "distrusting the indulgence of the best of parents" and

for forgetting her duty to her father; and "virtue alone bids defiance to the grave." The *Critical Review* regretted Mrs. Brooke's "introducing any politics at all," but had to grant that it was "done with great propriety."[54] The *Monthly Review* described the "catastrophe" as "highly affecting and exemplary."[55] But it made them both uncomfortable, and they wished the novel had not ended this way.

And no wonder, for the moral explanations are unsatisfying: trite, trivial, purely personal, and incommensurate with the larger political concerns of the novel. As Henry indicates on his deathbed, if Belmont's "gay structure of ideal happiness has fallen in a moment to the ground," we would do better to consider "the many accidents" which have conspired to bring this about — and just how accidental the novel indicates they are. The immediate cause of Henry's own downfall — the duel with Melvyn — was his failure to receive a crucial letter from Lord Belmont, due to a Lord Belmont–like act of beneficence to George Mordaunt, who was to be his factor. And Mordaunt is analogous to Henry in several ways. In one respect, he represents Henry's future with Julia should they marry without Belmont's consent; for Mordaunt is a penniless young gentleman, married to the best of women for that "union of hearts" that Lord Belmont recommends, but living with her in desperate poverty because he lacks a paternal inheritance and depends on his independent efforts as a clergyman to provide for his family. But in another respect, Mordaunt's experience of the world has been the same as Henry's, for both have found it impossible to earn a respectable living independently despite their merit and education. Lord T——, who represents "the world as it is" in relation to both these men, tells Henry that his hope of serving his prince as a patriot is "romantic for a man with no party connexions." And while Henry's father and Lord Belmont continue to recommend to Henry "such active pursuits as may make you a useful member of society and contribute to raise your own fortune and consequence in the world, as well as secure the esteem of your fellow citizens, and the approbation of your prince," it rapidly becomes apparent that the only way Henry could follow this advice would be to leave England and support his wife on an army salary — as John Brooke, Frances's husband, was obliged to do.

The novel's heavily underscored exemplary representation of benevolent patriarchal government, headed by a "Prince to whom the patriot glow" and supported by little domestic sovereigns on their paternal estates, thus figures as a mere citation of a common patriarchal political ideal, which is shown up for the empty rhetoric it is by repeated demonstrations that there is no room in England for gentlemen without a paternal fortune and prior "interest" with the ruling patriarchal elite.

The analogies between Julia and Lady Ann Wilmot (a visitor at Belmont) work in the same sort of way to unmask Lord Belmont's "over-solïcitude" for his daughter's happiness. Lady Wilmot was first married to a rich country gentleman by her father, who "could not refuse his daughter to a jointure of £3,000 a year." She was "forced by a tyrannic father to the insupportable yoke," and, as she says, "with the man to whom I was a victim, my life was one continued misery." Now that she is widowed and "relieved from those gall-chains," she is prevented from marrying Colonel Belville, whom she loves, by the way her husband has willed his money. The disposal of paternal estates determines the feasibility of both marriages in her case — as it does in Julia's, whose father intends to marry her to Henry to continue the Belmont family and name.[56] Julia's situation differs from Lady Wilmot's first marriage only by the fortunate "accident" of falling in love with the man her father chose. Lady Wilmot's tyrannical father and Julia's benevolent father conduct themselves in the same way towards their daughters, domestics, and dependents, for the same selfish motives of grandeur and wealth; and behind the benevolent face of Lord Belmont's ideal pattern of patriarchal government, with its "solicitude" for everyone's happiness, lurks the iron fist of Lady Wilmot's "tyrannic father" governing others just as he wills, "in all things," for what *he* determines to be society's good.[57]

By putting the evidence of its own exemplarity in question, Brooke's novel shows that the ideal of benevolent patriarchal government which Belmont represents, and which all the men in the Belmont family buy into, is a sham. If they do not see it, it is, as Lady Ann says, because "men are ever dupes of their own vanity . . . and self-complacency." Frances Brooke, and Mrs. Barbauld after her, were content for men to continue dupes. In her preface to *Lady Julia Mandeville,* and contrary to her usual practice, Mrs. Barbauld described the novel in one short sentence — "It is a forcible appeal to the feelings against the savage practice of duelling"[58] — an allusion to the only moral perceived and unctuously praised by the *Monthly Review.* One can almost see her proper, thin-lipped little smile. For those accustomed to being dismissed as mere women by "the lords of creation," less could often, quite deliciously, be more. And the understated morals and "modest" disclaimers of ladies of "Superior Sense and Virtue" do not always check out.

Montaigne rightly said of reading exemplary fictions that inevitably "we fasten together our comparisons by some corner." In what follows, Egalitarian and Matriarchal novels will be fastened into groups by the ways they used the formulae and conventions of exemplary narratives to rewrite family society and alter the social text.

Exemplary Egalitarian Novels

Egalitarian writers tended to center their narratives on characters who portrayed what Mary Hays described as "a sort of ideal perfection, in which nature and passion are melted away and jarring attributes wonderfully combined."[59] Egalitarian heroines like Evalina, Cecilia, Emmeline, and Mary in *The Victim of Prejudice,* Adeline in *Romance of the Forest,* and Matilda in Mrs. Inchbald's *A Simple Story* demonstrate a wide variety of social, domestic, and intellectual perfections: they have benevolent and feeling hearts; they are dutiful and patient under adversity; they are capable of close and loyal friendships; they are innocent, pure, artless, chaste, and beautiful; they are gentle, amiable, accomplished, and reasonable; they delight in reading and writing and often have considerable formal education as well. And, since in almost all respects they are already all that they ought to be, they do not develop as a heroine in a nineteenth-century realist novel would.

Egalitarian heroines were allowed only one flaw — ignorance of the ways of the world. But this one flaw makes them interesting, by giving them a double, Janus-faced, function in the Egalitarian novel's general plan of contrasting virtues and vices. On the one hand, it enabled the heroine's exposures to society to serve as "instructions into life" both for herself and for young women readers who, it was argued, could attain "knowledge of the world" with "more ease" and "less danger" by reading such novels than by "mixing in real life."[60] Ignorant of the world, the Egalitarian's heroine could be allowed to make the worldly errors it was hoped her example would help other young women to avoid, and she could be shown learning the prudence or judgment necessary to guard herself from disaster in domestic and social life. Yet, because ignorance of the world was her only flaw, she could — at the same time and in the same process — serve as a standard against which the conduct and households she encountered were judged. The more she was victimized by unjust or avaricious guardians, by false and disloyal friends, by devious or predatory libertines, or by selfish, greedy, or indelicate persons of all sorts, the more the world was shown not to be made to her measure and the more forcible the novel's critique of domestic practices becomes. The more the Egalitarian's heroine suffered emotionally and economically at the hands of those who ought to be her "natural protectors"; the more difficulty she had in escaping the violence, traps, impediments, abductions, rapes, or imprisonments that threatened her on every side; and the more desperate her situation became, the more vividly she illustrated the ills to which women were heir through no fault of their own.[61] The repeated victimization of the exemplary heroine in Egalitarian novels served both to point up her virtues and to make the reader "feel" the evil of a wide variety of domestic practices. The exemplary Egalitarian heroine, therefore, made novels doubly "instructions into life." From the point of view of the Janus-faced formula, the difference between *Evalina, Romance of the Forest,* and *The Victim of Prejudice* lies only in the relative proportions given to these two faces of the heroine's text and in the extent to which the heroine defeated — or was defeated by — the violence and evils to which she was exposed.

The Egalitarian heroine was generally an orphan, and this figure had its own Janus-faced and heavily overdetermined qualities. From one point of view, the orphan represented a reality — and indeed a danger — to which all young people were prone since, according to demographers and historians of the family, a very large proportion of young people in the eighteenth century lost one or both parents before they reached marriageable age. In this respect, the female orphan also represented the precariousness of women's family situations in perhaps its most acute form. Situated at once inside and outside the families of her relatives or guardians, the orphan was, if anything, an even more liminal figure than the marriageable young girl who might or might not "fall" and be "ruined" while she was revolving from one family society to another, because the orphan might find herself exposed not only to the violence or seduction of suitors, but also to the lust, selfishness, cruelty, or greed of those who stood to her *in loco parentis.* And since her position inside the families of others depended largely on their benevolence, friendship, and good will, it might as easily be lost by a misstep, by envy, by a family member's schemes, or by misunderstandings as by any of the more dramatic forms of evil. In one of her embodiments at least, the orphan was the helpless victim par excellence.

From another point of view, the orphan represented an extremely fruitful opportunity to rewrite family society, for the orphan was also a heroine who was free from many of the bonds and dependencies that would normally curtail a young woman's freedom of choice and freedom of action. As long as a young woman was constrained, like Richardson's Clarissa, by the sacred authority of parents and by filial duty, there was virtually nothing she could do of herself. By eliminating the heroine's parents, and often by giving her not "a room of her own," but money of her own, Egalitarian novelists like Fanny Burney and Charlotte Smith could not only significantly increase her freedom of choice and action; they could also show that a young woman could govern her life and her conduct for herself, and they could delineate alternative modes of relation between the generations.

Her mother dead, deserted by her father and by all her relations, the heroine of Burney's *Evalina* (1778) is brought up by her mother's old tutor, Mr. Villars, who represents the parental ideal. Evalina addresses him as "my most reverenced, most beloved father," saying, "by what other name can I call you!" The pattern of authority and subjection of absolutist, tyrannical patriarchs is represented in this novel by Mme. Duval, Evalina's grandmother — not an isolated example in Egalitarian novels of women occupying this position.[62] Using the figure to do double duty was one way for Egalitarians to strike a glancing blow at Matriarchs, by dramatizing what they also said: that men and women had the same fundamental nature and that there was no difference between the tyranny of patriarchs and that of matriarchs who appropriated for themselves the patriarch's domineering function and governing place.

In accordance with the formula's "general plan" of parallel but contrasting characterizations of virtues and vices, Mr. Villars's and Mme. Duval's modes of parenting are opposed throughout the novel. Mme. Duval had "tyrannically endeavoured to effect a union" between her own daughter and her husband's nephew, and then, "when she found her power inadequate to the attempt, enraged at her non-compliance, she treated her with the grossest unkindnesss," and abandoned her to "poverty and ruin." But Mr. Villars leaves Evalina to make her own choice of partner, is never enraged or unkind, and determines to leave Evalina "a modest fortune" (which is all he has) when he dies. Mme. Duval refuses to let anyone "dispute her authority to guide [Evalina] by her own pleasure," but Mr. Villars "aims not at an authority which deprives her of liberty," and in his wishes for Evalina he is guided not, like Mme. Duval, by "ambition" and "her own pleasure" but by a concern for Evalina's happiness. Mme. Duval has shown herself completely uninterested in Evalina's early education, but she thinks that the blood tie now gives her the right to command; Mr. Villars, on the other hand, has taken charge of Evalina's early education. He has "cherished, succoured and supported her from her earliest infancy to her sixteenth year" and now continues his care by acting as her guide and counselor. Where Mme. Duval is "violent," obstinate, "uneducated and unprincipled," Mr. Villars is a nursing father — gentle, persuadable, principled, and wise. Evalina obeys Mr. Villars not because she has to but voluntarily, because she loves him and respects his reasoning and his judgment; and she flees Mme. Duval.

In *Evalina*, then, Fanny Burney subjects "tyrannical" patriarchal family patterns to a critique — a critique reinforced by the constant satirizing and humiliation of Mme. Duval — and she delineates a radical alternative. One of the most revolutionary moments in the book occurs when Mr. Villars — speaking, as always, in the voice of morality and righteousness — tells Evalina that while she must outwardly show Mme. Duval "all the respect and deference due to so near a relation," she need not in fact obey her, because of "the independence I assure you of." By assuring Evalina an independence (the "moderate fortune" he will leave her), Mr. Villars makes her economically independent of Mme. Duval's fortune, and he frees her from all subjection to her natural family. This freedom is confirmed at the end of the novel by the self-confessed "humiliation" of Evalina's natural father, by his consequent abdication of paternal authority, and by Mr. Villars's retention of the parental role. In displacing and replacing her natural family, Mr. Villars displaces parental authority based on the tie of blood and on a parent's absolute and supposedly God-given right to dispose of the life he has given. In Mr. Villars, parental authority derives instead from parental care and support, from superior wisdom and understanding, and from the affection and respect he inspires, so that if Mr. Villars governs Evalina, he does so with her consent. Iterating the principles that inspired the Glorious Revolution in the microcosm of the family, Fanny Burney exemplifies an alternative to authoritarian relations between the generations in which paternal power plays no part and voluntary relationship is all.[63]

Cecilia (1782) opens with a repetition of Mr. Villars' gesture and with the issue of voluntary relationship. An heiress and orphan who has been brought up by "an aged and maternal counsellor, whom she loves as her mother," Cecilia sets off for London to choose which of the three trustees to her fortune she will live with until she attains her majority. Accordingly, she visits each of her trustees to "observe their manners and way of life, and then, to the best of her judgement, decide with which she would be most contented." "Rich without connections, powerful without wants," Cecilia need submit to no one's authority. When Mr. Harrel, for instance, tries to play the heavy-handed guardian, she is "amazed by his author-itative speech" and removes herself to Mrs. Delvile's house. Showing the respect and deference due her hosts, Cecilia obeys only those who can win her affections or her respect. Consequently, of her three sets of guardians, only Mrs. Delvile can occupy the parental position. Like Mr. Villars, she governs Cecilia by her qualities and influence, not by authority: "You will not, I think, act materially without consulting me, and for your thoughts — it were tyranny, not friendship, to investigate them more narrowly." But, unlike Mr. Villars, Mrs. Delvile is not an exemplary character; for all her sense, her accomplishments, and her seductiveness, she is afflicted with family pride and ambition and with a "want of that lenity which is the milk of human kindness and the bond of society." Consequently, she can never assume that ascendancy over Cecilia's mind and heart which Mr. Villars exercised over Evalina's, and Cecilia remains free to judge, decide, and act for herself.

In deciding and acting for herself, Cecilia gives the lie to Belfield's as-sertion that "man is brought up, not as if he were the noblest work of God, but as a mere ductile machine of human formation." She gives the lie to the assertion that a human being, and most particularly a woman, is nec-essarily nothing but a "docile body" or "ductile machine" formed by what Foucault calls "disciplinary practices" and Fanny Burney "the tyranny of perpetual restraint." Cecilia shows herself immensely capable of following her own understanding and her own inclinations and of using her riches and power for her own benefit and that of others. She avoids all the snares that are laid for her, refuses unsuitable matches, goes to money lenders herself, efficiently assists the needy, manages everything when Mr. Harrel commits suicide at Vauxhall, and like a country gentleman, with one week of her minority left, "take[s] possession of a large house that belonged to her uncle . . . and employ[s] herself in giving orders for fitting it up, and in hearing complaints, and promising indulgences to various of her tenants."

Her behavior, which is unconventional for a woman — Mortimer Delvile calls her "exceptional," and Lady Honoraria "odd" — also gives the lie to Mr. Monckton's assertion that "the opposition of an individual to a community is always dangerous in the operation, and seldom successful in the event." Cecilia is, on the whole, enormously successful — until she loses her fortune and her independence by marrying. The plot, as Terry Castle says, turns (at least temporarily) into "a plot of female subjugation," as Lady Delvile, heretofore her friend and ally, "sacrifices Cecilia in the face of Delvile Senior's outrage" at her marriage to his son, by becoming "an apologist for patriarchal principle" and abandoning Cecilia to humiliation and want.[64] At the mercy of this conventional patriarchal family while her husband is abroad, Cecilia loses her identity as an heiress, loses her freedom of action, loses control of events, and goes symbolically mad.

In many respects, Charlotte Smith's *Emmeline* can be described as a dialogical response to *Cecilia,* which is actually read aloud to Emmeline and her mentor and friend, Mrs. Stafford, in the course of the book. Charlotte Smith uses methods similar to those of Fanny Burney to discredit relations of authority and force between the generations and to stress the importance of voluntary relationship. She orphans Emmeline at birth and surrounds her with a variety of parental figures disposed according to the usual plan of analogical forms of parenting. She displaces the blood tie to the patriarchal family (here represented by Emmeline's uncle and aunt, Lord and Lady Montreville) and replaces it with two Mr. Villars–type figures (first Mrs. Carey, the housekeeper who brings up Emmeline at Mowbray Castle, and then Mrs. Stafford). And she shows Emmeline resisting Lady Montreville and voluntarily submitting to Mrs. Stafford — "referring herself entirely to Mrs. Stafford" — to the point where even the otherwise unperceptive Delamere is "well aware of the power a woman of her understanding must have over a heart like Emmeline's."

But Smith also critiques Burney's solution to the shortcomings of the patriarchal family. She does not deny that a woman can govern herself by her own understanding; she gives Emmeline not only intelligence but also "a native firmness in a degree very unusual to her age and sex" and shows her using both quite independently of Mrs. Stafford — and she does not deny that a woman can use her riches and time to worthwhile public ends. But she does deny that the miraculous acquisition of a financial independence is likely to be a universally applicable panacea, and she refutes the scenario according to which women without financial independence abandon each other and resign themselves to the patriarchal status quo.

Charlotte Smith looks instead to what women can do by simply helping each other. In *Emmeline,* Mrs. Stafford, Emmeline, and Adelina are constantly helping each other in every way they can — by lending each other countenance and counsel, by giving material and mental support, by speaking for each other, and by promoting each other's interests. It is as a direct or indirect result of this reciprocal help that Mrs. Stafford is able to leave her awful husband, that Emmeline is able to break her unwilling engagement to Delamere and marry Adelina's brother, Godolphin, instead, and that Adelina is not only reconciled first to Godolphin and then to the father of her illegitimately and adulterously conceived child but also enabled to marry him in the end. In *Emmeline,* then, the bond of friendship, support, and assistance among women who are not related to each other by family ties all but replaces family and makes it possible for Emmeline, Adelina, and Mrs. Stafford to live outside the confines of their own proper family societies when they must.[65]

One way the Egalitarian novel exploited the possibilities of exemplary narratives to rewrite domestic government, then, was by orphaning the idealized heroine, displacing normal family constraints, and replacing them with alternative forms of family relationship based on care, support, and consent.

Another way was by using the exemplary narrative's requirement that virtue be rewarded and vice punished to rewrite relations between women and men. Together with the establishment of a general plan of parallel but contrasting man-woman relationships, this moralizing convention provided Egalitarian novelists with a convenient way of marking what they found vicious in relations between men and women and what they considered conducive to happiness.

Mrs. Inchbald's *A Simple Story* (1791) provides a particularly telling statement about what Egalitarians perceived to be vicious in relations between men and women, because the statement is made in the framework of a love match. Miss Milner and Dorriforth, to whom the first half of the novel is dedicated, have to love each other long and overcome enormous

obstacles before they can confess their love and get married, if only because Dorriforth begins the novel as a Catholic priest and as Miss Milner's
guardian and foster father. Since Miss Milner is both an orphan and an
heiress, and since Dorriforth eventually inherits a title and an estate, both
are free to marry whom they will. There is no question but that their relationship is voluntary and based on love, but it is marred, almost from the
first, by what the narrator describes as "the various, though delicate struggles for power between Miss Milner and her guardian." No sooner are they
engaged, for instance, than Miss Milner determines to get the upper hand
in the relationship by exploiting Dorriforth's love for her: "I will do something that no prudent man *ought* to forgive; and yet with all his vast share
of prudence, *he* shall forgive it, and make a sacrifice of just resentment to
partial affection." If she can get Dorriforth to love and give way to her no
matter what she does, if she can exploit her power over him, then she has
him in the palm of her hand. Dorriforth, however, is not going to play.
Stubborn and willful in his turn, he expects to keep the authority of the
parent and guardian even when he becomes the lover and husband. As
Miss Woodley tells Miss Milner: "He will not indulge you with any power
before marriage, to which he does not intend to submit hereafter." The
struggle for power between Dorriforth and Miss Milner almost breaks
their engagement; it eventually does break up their marriage, leaving both
with broken lives and hearts.

The point here is not merely that Dorriforth's and Miss Milner's struggle for power was unconducive to their happiness together but also that,
from the beginning, each was seeking the wrong thing. With Miss Milner
using her sexual power to try to rule him and Dorriforth (con)fusing the
power and roles of husband, lover, and father and insisting on his patriarchal right to rule her, each sought an unequal relationship, a relationship in
which he or she had the ascendancy.[66] Matilda, their daughter, will do
better, despite having the tyrannical Dorriforth for a natural father, for she
desires no ascendancy; and the character of Rushbrook, her prospective
husband, is distinct from both her tyrannical natural father and Sandiford,
who serves as her nursing foster father throughout the book.[67]

In *Emmeline,* too, marriages in which one partner has the ascendancy
are invariably shown to come to a bad end — and there are again quite as
many examples of women having the ascendancy as men. "Accustomed to
undisputed power in her own family," Lady Montreville "intimidates" her

husband not only into preventing Emmeline's marriage to her son but also into actions to which "he could not entirely reconcile his heart." Her willful government of her family leads to her son's death, to her husband's broken heart, and to the destruction of their "house," while her lack of government of herself is fittingly punished by a burst blood vessel in the brain, which kills her. Her daughter, Lady Frances, also has the ascendancy in her marriage, but this time in part because she has married beneath her and her husband defers to her so that her family will not withhold her fortune. Contemptuous of her husband, Lady Frances sets up a separate establishment and flaunts a lover, whom she eventually follows to France. Here she is finally incarcerated in a convent by a *lettre de cachet* taken out against her by her husband. Adelina and Mrs. Stafford also have the ascendancy in their marriages, but in the sense that both are married to men who are their moral and intellectual inferiors and whose careless or irresponsible mismanagement of family finances bankrupts them. This makes Adelina dependent on Fitz-Edward, whose child she eventually bears after her husband deserts her, and it leaves Mrs. Stafford to see the officers of the law, the tradesmen, and the moneylenders and to do what she can to buy time to retrieve her children's fortunes. As Mrs. Stafford says, "Where others have in their husbands protectors and friends; mine, not only throws on me the burthen of affairs which he himself has embroiled, but adds to their weight by cruelty and oppression." Here, too, inequality leads to the break-up of both marriages.[68]

By contrast with such unequal matches, the relationships rewarded with happiness could be said to demonstrate what Mill described as "a principle of perfect equality, admitting no power or privilege on the one side, nor disability on the other."[69] In the idealized relationships rewarded with happiness, both partners are given power over each other's minds and hearts. When Delvile learned that Cecilia loved him, he "became acquainted with his power, and knew himself to be the master of her destiny." But he, in turn, immediately tells Cecilia: "I give you the direction of my conduct, I entreat you to become my counsellor and guide." And when their fortunes are restored by an unexpected bequest from Delvile's aunt, he underlines the fact that this reciprocity extends to their finances too. Far from rendering her dependent upon him, as a wife would normally have been to a husband, he tells her that, as she has lost her fortune by marrying him, so the bequest represents an opportunity to "restore to her through his own family, any part of that power and independence of which her generous and pure regard for himself had deprived her."[70] Similarly, Godolphin tells Emmeline that her "power over his heart . . . is absolute and fixed," and he promises to be "guided wholly" by her, while Emmeline confesses to him "his power over her mind" and the fact that she has made him "in the same measure the director of her actions."

In the idealized relationships that Egalitarian novelists rewarded with happiness, both partners are also given the same disabilities. Where male moralists and conduct book writers were preaching the *difference* between the sexes and condemning those who transgressed gender boundaries — "a masculine woman . . . that throws off all the lovely softness of her nature" or "an effeminate fellow, that, destitute of every manly sentiment, copies the inverted ambition of your sex" — Egalitarian novelists were basing happy relationships on a transgressive, composite, hermaphrodite ideal.[71] They were giving both partners in the happy relationship both "masculine sense" and "feminine softness" and showing that women could have "manly sentiments" of honor, courage, and determination, while men could both fulfil a nurturing role and devote themselves to the well-being of others. Evalina praises Lord Orville in both masculine and feminine terms: "So steady did I think his honour, so *feminine* his delicacy, and so amiable his nature! I have a thousand times imagined that the whole study of his life, and whole purport of his reflections, tended solely to the good and happiness of others." Lord Orville, in turn, praises Evalina both because "she is gentle and amiable, a truly *feminine* character" and because she is, like a man, "informed, sensible and intelligent." The problem with Mrs. Selwyn, who serves as a contrast to *both* Evalina and Lord Orville, is that while "her understanding, indeed, may be called *masculine*," she "has lost all the softness" and "gentleness" of the "female character" which ought to accompany it both in women and in men.[72] Godolphin, too, has both the masculine and the feminine virtues. He had many times demonstrated in the service of his country "a courage undaunted by danger . . . *sans peur et sans reproche*," and his sense of honor is irreproachable; but he also "possesses a softness of heart," which the sight of Adelina and her infant son "melted into more than feminine tenderness," and he spends much of the novel nursing and nurturing both, while Emmeline wanders the world, proving in her relationships with Delvile and Lord Montreville that she has a sense of honor as nice as his own. Along with the requisite softness, Emmeline shows physical courage and competence — "to personal inconvenience she was always indifferent when the service of those she loved engaged her to brave fatigue and cold."

Using exemplar conventions to rewrite domestic relations and the social text, therefore, Egalitarian novels punished relations between men and women based on subjection and on inequalities of power, character, delicacy, or honor; and they rewarded relationships based on a principle of equality in which both partners have equal power over each other, equal softness, and equal sense.

Exemplary Matriarchal Novels

In Matriarchal novels, the exemplary heroine is not a wonderful combination of "jarring attributes"; she is a full-blown Shunamite. Astell's image of the Shunamite towering over men in a woman-centered world haunts the Matriarchal novel from Sarah Scott's *The History of Cornelia* (1750) to Mary Brunton's *Self-Control* (1810), reaching its apotheosis — and total humiliation — in Jane Austen's *Emma*.[73] Set in narrative motion as a young heroine exposed to the rigors of life, the Matriarch's budding Shunamite is not victimized by the evils of the world she travels through. She rises triumphant above all reverses of fortune — as well as above all the ploys of lustful or avaricious guardians, all the seductions of devious or violent libertines, and all the schemes of false or disloyal friends — to become a towering pattern and example to everyone else in her novel. The Matriarch's heroine teaches and governs others; they rarely teach or govern her. The perfect incarnation of virtue and sense, often also markedly a Christian, she never falters. There is *nothing* she cannot do, and governing her conduct by divine and moral law, she never fails to know and to do what is right.

Consequently, where the Egalitarian heroine voluntarily submits to mentoring foster parents who demonstrate their wisdom and care, the Matriarchal heroine often inverts the hierarchy between the generations: it is she who mentors, reforms, and corrects those whom age, rank, care, or circumstance have placed *in loco parentis*. In Matriarchal novels, those in the parental position voluntarily submit to the heroine, from a recognition of her superiority to them in sense and virtue. For however young or poor or untried she may be, the Matriarchal heroine is herself a better parent, guardian, and governor than any she may encounter: she is her own — and everyone else's — parent, guardian, and governess.

The History of Cornelia, for instance, opens with Sarah Scott's orphaned heroine having to flee her home to escape attempts by her uncle and guardian to seduce her and then to abduct her. As a result, "young, unused to the world, never exposed to any hardships, [she is] forced to encounter all the difficulties that attend poverty, perhaps indigence, in those who have been bred up to ease and plenty."

But Cornelia is not afraid of work, and she uses her exceptional abilities to gain the ascendancy in other women's households. When she lives with Mme. Miteau, she works nineteen hours a day to support herself by her sewing (while reading in her spare time!) and takes over the instruction of that lady's children; and when there is an action out against Mme. Miteau for debt, she also takes over "the regulation of her affairs." Mme. Miteau is a milliner, and though Cornelia has no previous experience of trade, she immediately succeeds in managing everything in the most exemplary Matriarchal fashion:

> By the regularity Cornelia introduced into the whole, the new branches which her ingenuity enabled her to extend their trade; and the industry by which she set an example to all that were concerned in the shop, and took care to have followed by them, soon brought in more business to it than ever. As some of the children were old enough to be of great use, and all of them some; she ordered it so that each should contribute with their services as far as they were able. The eldest daughter she taught book-keeping, and the management of their little family, and all the oeconomy that could be useful to them.

Impressed by this performance, Mme. du Maine, a rich and elderly woman who has quarreled with her entire family, asks Cornelia to "manage her affairs with the oeconomy she so well [understands]," and tells her that if she agrees to live in her household, "she [will] be on an equal footing with herself and be welcome in all her company." But the balance tips almost at once, for though Mme. du Maine assumes the parental position by offering to make Cornelia her heir, on condition she "make her old age happy by her conversation and friendship," her parental functions are strictly limited to teaching Cornelia "the customs of the world" and to supplying Cornelia with all the money she needs. Also, being "a woman of learning, sense and taste, sufficient to relish Cornelia's understanding," Mme. du Maine soon "[owns] herself, however advanced in years, not too old to receive instruction from her." Once she has gained the ascendancy, Cornelia uses it not only to govern Mme. du Maine and her household better than they have ever been governed before but also to reconcile Mme. du Maine to her estranged family and bring them all back together under one roof on a harmonious domestic footing. Mme. du Maine declares Cornelia's "behaviour . . . in every particular a worthy pattern for that of every other woman."[74] As Cornelia goes on to flee seducers and outsmart a series of powerful and violent men from whom even Mme. du Maine cannot offer her protection, the latter's comments also identify the source of Cornelia's moral and intellectual independence and of her "visible Superiority": "All that you have gone through served only to exalt your virtue . . . [your] triumphant virtue . . . Consider that these sufferings have been necessary to shew, that as much as they exceed what are commonly undergone, so far you exceed your own species."

The same reversal occurs in Charlotte Lennox's *Sophia* (1762), which is an early version of Jane Austen's *Sense and Sensibility*, but this time in a daughter's relation to a natural parent.[75] Mrs. Darnley, Sophia's widowed mother, is (like Mrs. Dashwood in *Sense and Sensibility*) an impoverished gentlewoman of "great beauty and no merit, with a taste for luxury and expense," who desires, above all, that her daughters marry well. Like Marianne, Harriot is the more beautiful and frivolous daughter; Sophia, like Eleanor, is the daughter with more sense than beauty. Unlike her mother and her sister, Sophia has a "dignity which she derived from innate virtue and exalted understanding," and which she has improved by constant reflection and reading, and this has already, when the novel opens, given her de facto management of the family economy and ascendancy over her mother: "Nature here had transferred the parent's rights to the child, and the gay, imprudent, ambitious mother stood awed and abashed in the presence of her worthier daughter."

As the novel proceeds, Sophia's judgment of character and her sense of the conduct which will best serve herself and her mother and sister in any given situation are constantly juxtaposed with those of her mother. While her mother's folly is exposed, Sophia's judgment and conduct are repeatedly marked as "right," both by the outcome of events, and by the confirmation and support of her father's old friend, Mr. Herbert, whose role is to mitigate the impropriety of Sophia's independence by supporting her against her mother and insisting on the superiority of her views.

This drama of inversion of the parent-child relationship was still being played out in Matriarchal novels more than half a century later. Belinda, in Maria Edgeworth's novel of that name (1801), has two parental figures: Mrs. Stanhope, a notable matchmaker whose particular area of expertise lies in enabling young ladies with small fortunes, like Belinda, to "rise in the world" by getting them well married; and Lady Delacour, a "woman of fashion" who devotes her time to amusements, frivolities, flirtations, and dress, and who courts nothing more than the envy and admiration of the world. From the beginning of the novel, the common expectations of Belinda — given her inferior place in the social and generational hierarchy and in Lady Delacour's household — are made clear by Mrs. Stanhope:

> From her ladyship's situation and knowledge of the world, it will always be proper, upon all subjects of conversation, for her to lead and you to follow: it would be very unfit for a young woman like you to suffer yourself to stand in competition with Lady Delacour, whose high pretensions to wit and beauty are *indisputable* . . . Even with your limited experience, you must have observed how foolish young people offend those who are most necessary to their interests, by an imprudent indulgence in their vanity.

Rather than following Lady Delacour's lead, however, Belinda teaches Lady Delacour to follow *hers* and to govern herself by the entirely different set of principles which Belinda exemplifies. Inversion of the parent-child, mentor-mentoree relationship, here leads to the complete reformation and transformation of Lady Delacourt's life. Belinda cures Lady Delacour of the cancer of which she fears she is dying — which also symbolizes the evil and corruption underlying her frivolous and worldly existence and the domestic misery concealed behind her gaiety and painted public face — and Belinda "domesticates" Lady Delacour by teaching her the value of "domestic pleasures" and the importance of her domestic role. Like Cornelia, Belinda reconciles Lady Delacour to her family and brings them all back together under the same roof as "a happy family party." Also like Cornelia, Belinda makes a woman who is her domestic, economic, and social superior and to whom she is very much obliged, obliged to her, reaping her reward in universal "admiration" and "respect."[76]

In Mary Brunton's *Self-Control*, the inverting mechanism is laid bare: exemplary control of self — the rigid governance of oneself by the laws of religion and morality — is the key to control over others.[77] Brunton's heroine, nineteen-year-old Laura, carefully regulates her conduct by principle, prudence, duty, and religion; and the awe this inspires gives her the ascendancy over her very difficult aunt, even though her aunt is in every other respect (domestic, social, economic, generational) her hierarchical superior: "Notwithstanding her youth and her almost dependent situation, Laura inspired Lady Pelham with involuntary awe. Her dignified manners, her vigorous understanding, the inflexible integrity which descended even to the regulation of her forms of speech, extorted some degree of respectful caution from one not usually over careful of giving offence." Laura's self-control and habitual virtue also make her her father's parent: when he displays "a total want of fortitude and self-command" at the increasingly desperate state of their fortunes and allows himself to sink into despair and melancholy, it is Laura — whose habitual self-command has taught her to fight melancholy and given her "the habit of meeting and overcoming adverse circumstances" — who shields him from reality and finds solutions to their immediate difficulties. While showing proper filial deference throughout, Laura takes over the parental role of counsel, guidance, governance, and support from her maudlin and ineffectual parent.

The Matriarchal heroine has her principles, her superior sense and virtue, and her God, and she follows these as more constant and reliable guides than any mere person. As Sarah Scott says in *Cornelia*, "a woman of Sense and Virtue, however great her ignorance or innocence may be, will always know how to repel vice as soon as she sees it." And by repelling vice and practising virtue in the name of the highest principle, she becomes superior to any of her superiors in the domestic and social hierarchy and obtains all the deference, respect, control over others, and freedom from control by others that she could possibly want.

Consequently, while the Matriarchal heroine is often an orphan, she does not have to be orphaned to gain the power and freedom to govern herself and others which she seeks. Though Matriarchal novelists often stacked the deck in her favor by giving her a parent who was seriously flawed — blind, foolish, vain, ineffectual, worldly, or vicious — no parent ever rivals her qualities or supplies the place of her understanding; and should her parent have any shred of sense or virtue, it only enables him or her to recognize that the daughter's following her own reason and conscience over any parental command has proved the right course in the end.

Matriarchal rewritings of the relation between women and men were more ambivalent, conflicted, and problematized. Ideally, in the Matriarchal imaginary, there is the same sort of inversion of the patriarchal hierarchy between women and men as in parent-child relations. Like the Shunamite, the principled and virtuous Matriarchal heroine triumphs over suitors and husbands by means of her superior virtue and sense. And she marries only after her suitor has been taught that the proper posture for "the lords of creation" is on their knees at her feet, looking up at her example with admiration and wonder, while promising to submit themselves to her in all things.

In *Cornelia*, for instance, Bernardo (the "one" man Cornelia says she can love and marry) shows that he is worthy of her when he says that "nature when it made her had given her a right to command, and mankind a sufficient reward in the pleasure of obeying her." Unlike the Egalitarian heroine, who at this point would allow him to direct her too, Cornelia decides what is best for both of them to do and "inclines him to submit patiently to her, whose will he could on no other occasion have contradicted." Like the Shunamite, Cornelia eventually dominates in the same way every other man she encounters, including her uncle, who is also her guardian, and the king of France. By the same token, Belinda shows herself a more competent teacher and domestic governor than Clarence Hervey, who becomes worthy of her when he confesses his own "presumption and imprudence" in trying to fashion a woman (Virginia) in his own patriarchal image and recognizes Belinda's superiority in sense and virtue to anything he could create or control. They marry only when Clarence has finally joined all the other characters in acknowledging that "Miss Belinda Portman's character for prudence and propriety stands so high, and is fixed so firmly, that she may venture to let us cling to it."[78]

To persuade their readers that it was possible as well as proper for ladies of superior sense and virtue to become the governors of men, Matriarchs used the exemplar convention of punishing vice and rewarding virtue to defeat their one serious rival for the mastery they desired: the "imbecile coquette." The coquette was the superior lady's rival because, like the superior lady, her design was to captivate, to conquer, and to bend men to her will. Like the superior lady, the coquette ruled over men by using her beauty and sexuality to arouse and manipulate admiration and desire. Like the superior lady, too, the coquette needed to marry, and to marry well. The two were, moreover, competing for the same well-to-do and titled men. But the coquette often had more immediately visible power over men than did the superior lady, as well as more evident success.[79]

Sarah Fielding's *The Lives of Cleopatra and Octavia* (1757) illustrates the problem this presented for Matriarchs. Octavia is described in Fielding's Preface as "an example of all those Graces and Embellishments worthy of the most refined female Character and Dignity." She proves in the course of the narrative to be a lady of superior sense and virtue, as well as a model, obedient, long-suffering, and "self-sacrificing" wife. But Octavia does keep losing those husbands to Cleopatra — "an haughty, false and intriguing woman, whose Views were to exercise her Charms and prostitute her Power to the Gratification of a boundless Vanity."[80] And for all her vaunted private and public virtues, Octavia is shown living a lonely, unappreciated, deserted, and manless life. She is a patient Griselda awaiting her reward in the afterlife while the coquette, Cleopatra, indulges her private and public vices and enjoys all the power, attention, and pleasures in the world. As Jane West bitterly said, "Men are ever the most easily vanquished by the *meanest* antagonists. An artful woman is a despicable creature . . . Yet I hardly know a proficient in deception who did not govern all her male connections and moreover persuade them that she was the most amiable of creatures."[81]

What the Matriarchal heroine has to demonstrate, therefore, to persuade her readers to emulate her example rather than that of the coquette, is that her sense and virtue ultimately give her more real power over men — and more domestic, social, and economic success — than the coquette can attain merely by exploiting her sexual capital and "playing off those contemptible infantile airs that undermine esteem even while they excite desire."[82]

In *Sophia* and *Betsy Thoughtless*, Charlotte Lennox and Eliza Haywood use the distribution of rewards and punishments to show that, however much they seem to suffer in the short term, in the long run ladies of superior sense and virtue prevail over the transitory and merely external charms of the imbecile coquette. In these novels, Lennox and Haywood approached this narrative argument from opposite standpoints, while also exemplifying precepts and warnings that Haywood first gave her readers in

The Female Spectator.[83] Focusing on the triumphs of the superior lady over the foolish coquette, Lennox's *Sophia* exemplifies Haywood's optimistic dictum that "she who has not the least pretence to beauty has it in her power, would she but once be prevailed upon to exert it, to awe the boldest or most affectedly nice libertine into submission, and force him to confess her worthy of serious attachment."[84] Focusing on the trials of the unsuccessful coquette, the narrative argument of Haywood's *History of Betsy Thoughtless* (1751) is that "we can impute all those mistakes, miscarriages, those cruelties, oppressions, unnatural actions and innumerable train of mischiefs which we either bring upon ourselves or inflict on others, to the want of thought or to thought misapplied,"[85] and that the coquette who thoughtlessly "sports with the affections of a man of sense," will forfeit his respect, lose him to a woman of sense, and have to watch her more virtuous rival become his happy wife.[86]

The History of Betsy Thoughtless uses the old plot of the reformed coquette to fictitiously prove that Betsy's thoughtless life as a coquette leads to suffering and misadventures and that she can triumph only when she develops enough sense and virtue to become a matriarchal lady of superior sense and virtue.[87] At the beginning of her story, Betsy imagines that beauty, charm, and caprice will subordinate men to her will: "'As the barometer,' said she to herself 'is governed by the weather, so is the man in love governed by the woman he admires; he is a mere machine — acts nothing of himself — has no will or power of his own, but is lifted up or depressed, just as the charmer of his heart is in the humour.'" But in the event, Betsy's "wanton vanity of attracting universal admiration" leads her to conduct which exposes her to "perpetual dangers." Subject to sexual advances, villainy, violence, and defamation, and narrowly escaping rape, she is all too easily mistaken for her friend, Miss Forward, a wanton and a whore. Mr. Trueworth (whom she realizes too late is her true love) compares "the capricious turns, the pride, the giddy lightness he had observed in the behaviour of Miss Betsy," with "the steady temper, the affability, the ease, unaffected chearfulness, mixed with a becoming reserve" of the sensible and virtuous Miss Harriot; and abandoning his courtship of Betsy, he marries Harriot instead. Her reputation in shreds, Betsy is then forced by her brothers to marry Mr. Munden, who almost immediately "throws off the lover, and exerts the husband;" and she learns the hard way that beauty and caprice do not give her the ascendancy when her husband refuses to be "contradicted" in anything: "'Is this to be a wife! — Is this the state of wedlock! Call it rather Egyptian bondage . . . Ungrateful man!' pursued she, bursting into tears, 'is this the love, the tenderness, you vowed?'"

Betsy's suffering at Mr. Munden's hands illustrates Haywood's dicta in *The Female Spectator* that "many women have been deceived by the show of obsequiousness in those who have afterwards become their tyrants" and that, joined to "a man of mean capacity" who abuses a husband's power, a woman of sense has no option but to avoid arousing his ill-humor, "bear with him as much as possible" and remember: "There is no virtue that more truly demonstrates a noble soul than fortitude. It is indeed the utmost dignity of human nature and brings it very near to the angelic."[88] Betsy's sufferings do teach her fortitude, as well as "command over herself," compassion for the suffering of others, and the paltry value of those "external charms" on which she had once prided herself, compared to the importance of guarding her virtue and developing "those perfections of the mind which she was sensible could alone entitle her to the esteem of the virtuous and the wise." She learns these Matriarchal lessons so well that at length, even Trueworth comes to "behold her . . . with a silent admiration," and promises to "obey" her commands, because, as he tells her: "you are all angel." Once she has acquired the Matriarchal virtues and become an example to others, she is fit to become Mrs. Trueworth. Released from Munden by his fortunate demise, Betsy is allowed to find the same happiness in marriage with Trueworth as did the virtuous and sensible Miss Harriot before her equally convenient death.

In *Sophia* the same triumph of the lady of superior sense and virtue over the coquette is played out by juxtaposing the fate of two sisters. A coquette like her mother, Harriot is her mother's favorite child, because she has inherited Mrs. Darnley's beauty and love of dress and amusements. Mrs. Darnley expects Harriot to captivate and capture Sir Charles Stanley, a rich baronet and a libertine, and she teaches her daughters that "when a man of rank and fortune makes his addresses to a woman who is inferior to him in both, he expects a thousand complacencies and attentions from her, which, without wounding her honour, may convince him that it is not to his riches she sacrifices herself." Harriot follows her mother's advice. Sophia, on the other hand, does not, for she realizes: "That is a snare which has been fatal to many young women in my circumstances. Who sees not the advantages this gives a man whose aim is to seduce?" Sophia always pursues the more difficult and less immediately gratifying course of protecting her "honour" and doing what sense and virtue dictate.

At first, Harriot enjoys all the power, social success, and pleasure that Sophia lacks. But Sir Charles eventually shifts his attentions from Harriot to Sophia, and when he tries to seduce her by every possible means — from courtship to bribing her mother with money and a house in London — Sophia resists Mrs. Darnley's folly in believing he means marriage. She flees her mother's home where she is in constant danger of capitulating to Sir Charles, whom, by now, she also loves. And the distribution of rewards and punishments confirms Sophia's wisdom in following her own counsel, by witholding sexual favors and resisting both her mother and her own heart. By dint of "complacencies and attentions" to men of rank and fortune, Harriot ends up as a kept woman in a fancy London house, while Sophia conquers the libertine Sir Charles and makes him confess her worthy of a serious attachment: "I lay myself and fortune at her feet." As Sir Charles prepares to shower settlements on Sophia and her mother, he confirms that Sophia's "exalted merit makes her fortune" and that for him, sense and virtue supply the place of her missing dowry: "Miss Sophia, in virtue, wit, good sense and every female excellence, brings me an immense portion."

As Mrs. Stanhope tells Belinda, young ladies of small fortunes do need to marry to "rise in the world"; but Matriarchal heroines mark their difference from fools and coquettes — like Betsy, Mrs. Darnley, and Mrs. Stanhope, who think that rising is all and that any man of rank and fortune will do — by showing that they understand the dangers of wedding a man who has even the faintest inclination to dissipation, gambling, improvidence, tyranny, or vice. Like Belinda who belies the men's expectations that no woman would avoid getting married if she could, Matriarchal heroines like Cornelia, Laura, and Sophia demonstrate that it is always better to "endure the short-lived pangs of combatting an unhappy inclination than by yielding to it, run the hazard of miseries to which death alone can put a period."[89] The Matriarchal heroine demonstrates her willingness to avoid risky marriages by refusing matches that others would regard as advantageous, by refusing to marry a flawed man even when she is *both* in love with him *and* economically desperate, or by holding off until she is convinced that her lover is fully reformed and has acquired "all the virtues."

As Matriarchal novels often indicate, a man lacking in virtue and sense cannot be counted upon to be awed, impressed, and governed by either quality in a wife. He is more likely, like Mr. Munden, to require her to demonstrate *all* her Christian principles under the crosses he gives her to bear. The dangers, constrictions, and miseries of subordination to a foolish and vicious man in the married state are therefore always present to the heroine's mind, and she would rather undergo the suffering of parting from her lover than allow love for any man to triumph over her good sense.

Matriarchs recognized that marriage was an important public duty, especially after the discussions of the population question which surrounded the Marriage Act of 1753; but marriage was a duty which, on the whole, they and their heroines preferred to leave to others. As Mrs. Morgan says in Sarah Scott's *Millenium Hall* (1763):

> We consider matrimony to be absolutely necessary to the good of society; it is a general duty; but as, according to all antient tenures, those obligated to perform knight's service might, if they chose to enjoy their own firesides, be excused by sending deputies to supply their places; so we, using the same privilege, substitute many others, and certainly much more promote wedlock, than we could do by entering it ourselves.

Envisioning only two alternatives in marriage — dominate or be cruelly subjected, govern or be abused — and recognizing that women do not, in practice, always succeed in getting the upper hand, Matriarchs had a lively fear of marriage. Their familiar histories demonstrate more clearly than Egalitarian novels that for women, marriage was "a kind of precipice which, when once leaped, there is no possibility of reclimbing — and wary ought the person who stands on it to be."[90]

3

Sexual Revolution and the Hardwicke Marriage Act

> The most respectable women are the most oppressed.
> — MARY WOLLSTONECRAFT

I F ANY EVENT in the eighteenth century qualifies as a watershed for sexual politics and family life, it is the 1753 Hardwicke Marriage Act. The Marriage Act demanded and accomplished a sexual revolution that materially changed women's lives, redefined the family, and almost alone created those modern categories the "unmarried mother" and the "fatherless child" as outlaws condemned to pay the social and economic price for intercourse not regulated by law and registered with the state. Enlightenment feminisms were still honing their responses to the act's strictures in the first decade of the nineteenth century, and women's novels and tracts diverge according to whether they were written before or after the Marriage Act.

The Hardwicke Marriage Bill was presented to the House of Commons by Mr. Attorney General Ryder in such a way as to appeal to the private interest of every gentleman present. The government called it a "Bill for the Better Preventing of Clandestine Marriages," and emphasized that it was designed to prevent rich heirs and heiresses of good family from being seduced into clandestine or runaway marriages with their social or economic inferiors. Modern historians of the family have accepted this as truth, rather than as an attempt by the government to get the bill passed with a minimum of fuss. They have therefore largely ignored the Marriage Act in their evolutionary or counterevolutionary theories about the emergence of the modern family.[1] After all, the bill only required that people get married in what we now take to be the normal and natural way: with banns or a licence and parental permission for minors, before witnesses and an authorized clergyman, and by recording the event in a marriage register. And hadn't the church been trying to impose many of these prescriptions on an unwilling populace for centuries?

For eighteenth-century Englishmen and Englishwomen, however, there was nothing normal or natural about the Marriage Bill's prescriptions. Both inside and outside the House, opponents of the bill protested that the government was giving "the word Marriage . . . a different signification from what it had before." It was making those "Circumstances" prescribed by the bill (banns, witnesses, the register) "part of the idea of marriage" for the first time; and it was voiding all unions "not performed in the Manner and Form, with all those Circumstances and Ceremonies which the Law hath appointed."[2] The government, they said, had changed the meaning of marriage by making the existence of marriage depend entirely on the couple's public observance of some purely ceremonial and procedural forms.

Before the Marriage Act, marriages had been based on the proposition that "what creates the married state and constitutes the contract" is "that FAITH by which the Man and Woman *bind themselves* to each other to live as Man and Wife."[3] If expressed in words of the present tense (*spousalia per verba de praesenti*), the couple's promises to live together as man and wife created a binding marriage, even when unconsummated and without the presence of any witnesses; if the couple's promises were expressed in words of the future tense (*spousalia per verba de futuro*), the marriage became binding as soon as consummation had occurred. In either case, the marriage would in principle be sustained by the courts against any subsequent marriage — even if the latter had been celebrated publicly according to church ritual and was followed by years of married bliss — because it was the private exchange of promises between a man and a woman to live together as man and wife which actually brought the marriage into being.[4] The public ceremony in church or before witnesses was only viewed as a public repetition and solemnization of that primary promissory and contractual act.[5]

It was therefore perfectly acceptable in many classes for a couple to exchange promises, go to bed and start a family before going to church, or even to skip the church ceremony altogether. Church courts and justices of the peace would uphold the claim of a pregnant woman that she had been "debauched under promise of marriage," and if necessary compel the man in question to perform his promise. Seductions, as well as abductions and clandestine marriages, were for "all intents and purposes" real marriages.

Once the Marriage Act became law, however, a woman who yielded to her lover and was with child after exchanging promises of undying fidelity and devotion no longer had any recourse if he left her. The man who debauched her under promise of marriage could no longer be compelled to perform his promise. The Marriage Act meant, in effect, that the couple's private verbal promises to live together as man and wife no longer had any force in law, as Blackstone explains: "Any contract made, *per verba de praesenti* or in words of the present tense, and in case of cohabitation *per verba de futuro* also, between persons able to contract was before the late Act deemed a valid marriage to many purposes; and the parties might be compelled in the spiritual courts to celebrate it *in facie ecclesiae*. But these verbal contracts are now of no force to compel a future marriage."[6]

The Gentleman's Magazine describes the magnitude of the change here when it writes that "a contract which before was deemed marriage is now declared to be otherwise."[7] After the Marriage Act became law, a woman who contracted to live with a man in the old way, without all the precise ceremonial forms required by the act, was no longer legally a wife. All traditional "bargains of cohabitation," all the old local marriage rites, all seductions, abductions, and clandestine marriages — and indeed, all intercourse outside the state of marriage as demarcated by the act — now made a woman a whore and her children bastards and meant that she was no longer entitled to any maintenance or financial support from the father of her children.[8]

This had, and indeed was intended to have, real consequences for the conduct of women's lives, as Mr. Solicitor General Murray makes clear during debate of the Marriage Bill in the House: "As the law stands at present, a young girl may trust to a promise of marriage, because she may have hopes of being able to compel the man to fulfil his promise . . . but when it is declared by a positive law, that no such promise will be binding, no young girl will trust to him."[9] Opponents of the bill in the House objected that women would no more change their sexual practices in light of Parliament's laws about marriage than they had changed their purchasing habits in light of Parliament's laws about cambric and that young women would be entrapped into now ruinous sexual relationships by trusting to promises of marriage which were — suddenly — no longer legally binding. The Marriage Bill was, they said, "one of the most cruel enterprises against the fair sex that ever entered into the heart of man," for it would be "the ruin of a multitude of young women."[10]

The questions to be addressed, therefore, are why men passed the act despite its cruelty to the fair sex and how Matriarchs and Egalitarians responded to the strictures of the act in their tracts and explored its unforeseen practical effects in their novels.

Political Economy, Public Policy, and the Family

The Marriage Bill of 1753 was one of the first fruits of the burgeoning discipline of political economy. It represented the best contemporary thinking about how to manage population in order to increase Britain's wealth. For eighteenth-century political economists, the connections among marriage, population, and wealth were quite simply this: "without marriages, the population would every year decrease; and agriculture, trade and manufactures could not be carried on."[11] It was the population's industry and skill that enriched the nation by supplying its wants more abundantly and by producing a surplus of commodities with which to bring in wealth from foreign trade. Labor or "industry" was now, according to Adam Smith, "the real measure of value," and what mattered about people (especially before the Industrial Revolution) was that they had — or in the metonomy characteristic of political economy, that they *were* — "hands." The more hands, the more industry, the more wealth for the nation. And the more children, the more hands.[12] As Adam Smith said, "the most decisive mark of the prosperity of any country is the increase in the number of its inhabitants."[13] Or, as Ferguson put it, "the state of a nation's wealth is not to be estimated from the state of its coffers . . . but from the numbers, frugality, industry and skill of its people.[14]

Marriages had become the nation's "Manufactory for making Children," and children had become "a source of wealth." But there was a rider to this. For just as a difference was made between productive (wealth-making) labor and its unproductive other, so a difference was made between the "real" productive multiplication of the population and *its* unproductive other. As James Steuart explains: "Children produced from parents who are able to maintain them and bring them up to a way of getting bread for themselves, do really multiply and serve the State . . . When marriage is contracted without these requisites for multiplication, it produces

[mere] procreation."[15] Or, as the Earl of Hillsborough put it in the House, when he was defending the Marriage Bill against the charge that it would have a negative impact on the growth of population: "The happiness and prosperity of a country does not depend on having a great number of children born, but on having always a great number well brought up and inured from their infancy to labour and industry."[16]

Children born to parents who could not support them, or brought up without the skills to support themselves, did not "really multiply" the population. They either died of starvation or became an economic burden to the parish and the nation. Children represented "a source of wealth" only if they were raised to adulthood and educated to labor and industry in some publicly useful art, skill, or profession. Paley said: "In civilized life, everything is affected by art and skill. Whence a person who is provided with neither (and neither can be acquired without exercise and instruction) will be useless; and he that is useless will be at the same time mischievous to the community. So that to send an uneducated child into the world is injurious to the rest of mankind."[17] England's wealth and prosperity depended on increasing the supply of children who survived to adulthood and on ensuring that they were educated to become industrious, and therefore "useful Commonwealthsmen."[18]

This sheds rather disturbing light on the "sentimental" cult of the child in the second half of the eighteenth century and beginning of the nineteenth, as well as on the shift from female midwives to male obstetricians during this period. Scholars have treated the late-eighteenth-century "invention" of childhood as a state separate from adulthood and deserving of special care and attention as evidence of mankind's growing "enlightenment." They have also viewed the transition from female midwives to male obstetricians as a moment in the triumphant advance of science, or more recently as an instance of logocentrism and patriarchal control supplying the place of the wisdom and herbal remedies of the traditional wise woman or witch. But this emphasis in eighteenth-century political economy and public policy on the importance of "really" multiplying the population suggests that children became important ideologically and scientifically — that is, important enough for concentrated male attention — only when they also became "a source of wealth."

With very few exceptions, historians of the family have tended to give us delightfully tidy pictures of the eighteenth-century patriarchal family and of historical shifts supposedly occurring during this period — from extended kinship systems to the modern nuclear family, from household-based systems of production to a manufacture-based system centered outside the home, from marriages of convenience to companionate marriages, or from one system of childbearing or childrearing to another. More recently, they have given us Burkean pictures of an orderly land where the traditional seventeenth-century household, with its wife, children, and servants and its patriarchal governor, continued to go about its business, virtually unchanged, in the shadow of the parochial Anglican church.[19] What struck eighteenth-century observers, by contrast, was the general *lack* of stability in conjugal and family relationships, the extent to which parents preferred their "dissipations" to the troubles of the nursery, and the numbers of children born or raised outside of families willing or able to maintain and educate them to useful adulthood.

Eighteenth-century writers say that desertions were frequent, polygamy and bastardy rampant, and "licentiousness" the rule rather than the exception. They flesh out these general observations with particular instances, or in the case of women writers addressing a primarily female readership, with "examples of such events as there is a possibility may happen to herself or to those persons for whom she has the most tender concern."[20]

The case which was said to have led to the Marriage Bill of 1753, for instance, involved a "clandestine marriage set up after a man's death which was never heard of in his lifetime." The man's "innocent offspring" were "cut off from succession" by the children of a woman no one had ever heard of before, who suddenly appeared out of nowhere with "an incontestable proof, which may by ways and means be obtained" that she had privately married that man before his marriage to the woman who now thought herself his widow. The fact that the latter had actually lived with him publicly as his wife for many years was set aside by the true or trumped up evidence of his earlier contract to another woman, for it meant that the woman who thought herself his widow had been married to him bigamously and that her children were in fact illegitimate. "His whole effects" were "carried away from his relations by the children of a woman whom he had never acknowledged as his wife," because the woman he had acknowledged as his wife could not prove the legitimacy of her children.[21]

Henry Gally, who wrote a tract in support of the Marriage Bill, recounts a similar case.[22] He tells of a Miss Warnsford who married a Mr. Cresswell in good faith and bore him several children, only to discover after many years not only that prior to their marriage, Mr. Cresswell had already been the husband of a Miss Scrope but also that Mr. Cresswell had embarked on a marriage prior even to that, with yet another woman who was still living and whom he had likewise abandoned. Mr. Cresswell was therefore a polygamist, who, in the absence of any real possibility of divorce, simply deserted wives and children when he grew tired of them, and moved on. The problem for Gally is that the accidental discovery of this polygamy also transformed the children of two marriages from legitimate to illegitimate offspring.

Gally also gives an example of another kind of polygamy, the whole purpose of which *was* to marry someone who was already married. Here a Mrs. Philips married M. De La Field, knowing full well that he was already married, in order to screen herself from debt (the creditors being unable, by law, to proceed against her until the marriage was proved null and void). Mrs. Philips then married a Mr. Muilman, with whom she actually proceeded to live. But the legality of her marriage to Mr. Muilman depended on M. De La Field's being married to another woman when Mrs. Philips married him, and since there was some difficulty proving that point, the legitimacy of the children Mrs. Philips had born to Mr. Muilman remained in suspense.

Women writers like Delariviere Manley and Eliza Haywood focus less on the legality of the children in such cases than on the unenviable fate of the abandoned wife. The sort of example they choose to highlight usually involves an inequality of power. Although virtuous and well-educated, the wife is her husband's social or economic inferior and thus essentially "unprotected." She marries privately *per verba* in good faith to gratify a mutual passion, or if there is also a ceremony, she is enjoined by her husband to keep the marriage secret until he comes into his inheritance or until he can persuade his parent or guardian to accept the match. When she is with child, however, her husband abandons her for a more advantageous marriage to a woman of rank and fortune. This leaves the abandoned wife and her young child to poverty and destitution, as well as to contempt and abuse, since for one reason or another "she cannot prove herself a wife."[23] Censuses of the poor show that in some towns, abandoned wives had long been a major problem.[24]

The government too pointed out in the House that the frequency of such cases of polygamy was one reason for the bill: "At present a man may have privately a wife in every corner of this city or in every town he has been in, without it being possible for them to know one another, or for the next woman to whom he makes his addresses, to discover his being a married man."[25] Thanks to Defoe and the New Critics, we probably associate this cavalier treatment of still living spouses with Moll Flanders, a woman and a whore; but for the gentlemen of the House, the main offenders were men.

Defoe blames men for a different kind of abandonment of wives, and here Eliza Haywood concurs with him. These are wives who are forced or seduced into marriages designed to rob them of their fortunes, and then deserted by husbands who disappear without a trace. In *Conjugal Lewdness* (1727) for instance, Defoe describes how a young lady of fortune is

> snatch'd up, seized upon, hurry'd up into a coach and six, a Fellow dressed up in a Clergyman's Habit to perform the Ceremony, and a Pistol clapt to her Breast to make her consent to be marry'd, and thus the work was done. She was then carry'd to a private Lodging, put to Bed under the same Awe of Swords and Pistols; and a Fellow she never saw before in her Life, and knows nothing of, comes to Bed with her, deflowers her or as may well be said, ravishes her, and the next Day she is called Wife, and her Fortune seized upon in the Name of the Husband; and perhaps in a few Days more, play'd all away at the Box and the Dice, and the Lady sent home again naked, and a Beggar.[26]

Eliza Haywood also warns her gentle readers not to follow the example of Samantha, who was courted by a personable young man, and persuaded into a private marriage, only to discover the morning after the night before that "the villain had drawn her whole fortune out of the Bank, robbed her of all her jewels and the best of her apparel, had skipped everything off, and was himself embarked they knew not to what place."[27] Once a young lady of fashion and fortune, Samantha subsequently became the humble dependent of whoever was willing to take her in, and her husband was heard of no more. Eighteenth-century writers seem to have made little distinction between rapes of seduction and rapes by force. If there was *rap-ere* (i.e., seizure of the woman), the assumption appears to have been that the outcome was likely to be the same: abandonment of the woman and her children to poverty and want.[28]

The difficulties of proving one's marital status or of tracking down a mislaid spouse were multiplied by the proliferation of marriages conducted at cheap wedding factories like Keith's Chapel in the Fleet, which, according to Sir Robert Nugent, conducted six thousand marriages a year, while St. Anne's Church, in a populous parish, conducted only about fifty.[29] At such wedding factories, clergy could be trusted to turn a blind eye to the age of the bride, to the length of time the couple had known one another, and to whether the couple exchanging vows was quite sober. Witnesses could also be bribed to deny a marriage that had taken place or to affirm that one had taken place when it had not, and for a fee, certificates of marriage could be forged, antedated, or removed from the register.

It was the design of the Marriage Bill to promote more stable unions, and to hinder the contracting of marriages in circumstances that would preclude the proper multiplication of children. As a defender of the bill put it: "The Compact of Marriage being of no Utility unless the Conditions are fulfilled, Public Wisdom should try to hinder the contracting of this Alliance under such Circumstances as preclude all reasonable chance of Domestic Comfort, and of the Propagation and Care of the Issue."[30] In the Marriage Bill, public wisdom set about ensuring the socioeconomic utility of marriages in a number of ways.

First, the bill sought to prevent "rash" marriages, which would bring "want and misery" on the couple and its children, by using the reading of banns, a particular form of public ceremony, and for minors, parental consent, to introduce a delay between desire and its consummation, during which each potential coupling would necessarily be exposed to the scrutiny of others (parents and peers). This immediately eliminated a variety of marriages likely to be abandoned after consummation and possible pregnancy: drunken marriages, impulsive marriages contracted in a moment of passion, marriages entered into for the immediate gratification of greed or lust, clandestine runaway marriages, and forced marriages subsequent to abduction. It was argued, too, that the deferment of the union, together with all the formal and ceremonial obstacles to wedlock imposed by the bill, would discourage the poor from thoughtlessly marrying and producing children they could not afford and would prevent the wealthy from being seduced into "unequal Matches," which likewise tended to terminate in beggary and want.

Secondly, the bill sought to eliminate "the frequency of polygamy" — in its eighteenth-century version, where men married several times, abandoning wives and children as they went along — by insisting that marriages be publicly performed and officially registered. Polygamy was a recurrent topic in the discussion of population, because some people argued that each man would be able to produce more children if he had more wives. Paley neatly summarizes the position on polygamy embodied in the Marriage Bill and expounded by most of the Enlighteners when he says:

> The question is not whether one man will have more children by five or more wives than one; but whether these five wives would not bear the same or a greater number of children to five separate husbands; and as to the care of children when produced, and the sending them into the world in situations in which they may be likely to form and bring up families of their own . . . this is provided for and less practicable where twenty or thirty children are to be supported by the attention and fortunes of one father than if they were divided into five or six families, to each of which were assigned the industry and inheritance of two parents.[31]

Political economy decided that monogamous unions were most likely to propagate and raise children who would grow up to produce wealth in both its contemporary forms: children and industry. Marriage therefore had to be "done publicly" and officially registered to prevent men from marrying polygamously, abandoning wives and children to penury as they went along. From this point of view, the marriage register acted very much like copyright, which had been introduced shortly before: as copyright ensured that texts could be attached and attributed to their authors, the marriage register ensured that women could be attached and attributed to a husband, and their children to a father, who was in the language of the time, "the Author" of a child's "Being."[32] By removing extant difficulties in proving the existence and legitimacy of a marriage, the register ensured that men could be held responsible for the support of their wives and for the maintenance and education of their children. As Blackstone put it:

"The main end and design of marriage [is] to ascertain and fix upon some certain person to whom the care, the protection, the maintenance and the education of the Children should belong."[33]

Thirdly, the Marriage Bill sought to "restrain all Commerce between the sexes except in Marriage"[34] by declaring null and void all unions that had not been performed with all the "Circumstances" required by the law and registered with the state. It was argued that restricting sex to marriage would force men to marry: "Promiscuous concubinage discourages marriage, by abating the chief temptation to it. The male part of the species will not undertake the encumbrance, expense and restraint of married life, if they can gratify their passions at a cheaper price."[35] Eighteenth-century observers feared that marriage was "stagnating" because it had become fashionable for men to mock and duck "wedlock-fetlock" and to obtain their pleasures "licentiously" outside the married state. But the public had an interest in promoting marriages, to multiply the population and to manufacture "useful Commonwealthsmen." By penalizing "concubinage" and seeking to restrict all "Commerce" between men and women to marriage, the Marriage Bill sought to reduce the supply of sex on the open market and thus to increase men's demand for marriage. It sought to ensure that marriage and "the care, the protection, the maintenance and the education of children" would be the price that men had to pay to purchase sex.

Restriction of sex to marriage was also thought to be conducive to fathers' caring for their children in another way: "The Engagement of mutual Constancy as to the Woman's Part is evidently meant to be a Security to the Man, that her Children are his Offspring, by which Means the Father becomes interested with the Mother in a Joint Care of their Issue."[36] Here, the function of female chastity was not so much to ensure the proper succession of inheritance and circulation of property, as Dr. Johnson said; it was to ensure that a man's "natural affection" for his children was allowed to kick in. A man had to be sure that the children his wife bore were his, in order to feel that "natural affection" which would make him attend to "the care, protection, maintenance and education of children." For if they were uncertain of their paternity, as Hutcheson said, men would "have no other incitement to any cares about them than the general Tye of humanity, which we know not to be sufficient," and mothers would be left with the burden of raising and educating their children alone.[37]

Finally, the Marriage Act served "the political Endes of Public Wisdom" by encouraging labor or "industry." Marriage was thought to increase men's industry, and with it, the wealth of the nation. In the minds of the Enlighteners, marriage, industry, and the multiplication of the population were linked by the eternal return of the same analogical economic mechanism. In the state, the fruits of industry and labor (wages, profit, affluence) encouraged marriage and propagation, made it possible for men to support their children to adulthood, and led to the "multiplication of labourers." The multiplication of laborers, in turn, served as "a remedy against sloth" by increasing the demand, and thus the price, of necessaries, and forcing men to work harder to obtain them. By the same token, in the family, the fruits of industry and labor permitted a man to marry and procreate; and the multiplication of mouths to feed forced the husband and father to work harder to obtain the means of subsistence for his family. This was important, because men were thought "naturally" to prefer ease to work; they worked only to provide for their needs. Having to provide for the needs of an entire family would therefore make men more industrious than they would be if they worked only to provide for themselves. Married men would supply the nation with a surplus of labor, for "if the married man succeeds in business, he has the pleasure to reflect that by the blessing of God upon his industry and prudence, a whole family are made happy."[38]

It was therefore to force *men* to marry and support their offspring that the Marriage Act punished *women* for "fornication" outside registered and now clearly demarcated marriages, by declaring null and void all traditional "bargains of cohabitation," and leaving such women without any possible recourse if their lovers left them with child. It was to make *men* "really multiply" the population by caring for their children and manufacturing "useful Commonwealthsmen" that the Marriage Act "ruined" *women* who yielded to their lover in the old way upon a promise, and freed men from the consequences of their acts by voiding their verbal promises of marriage in law.

This was cruel to the fair sex, no doubt, but male ideologues argued that it was "fair" and "reasonable" too, because "the mother without the aid of the father is not at all sufficient" for "the preservation of human offspring and the giving it the education necessary for the higher purposes of a rational life."[39] Men said that women's inability to support their offspring was "the natural origin of the superior disgrace which attends a breach of chastity in women rather than in men." They said that men might rationally "agree to punish" a woman who "was connected with a man, who had entered into no compact to maintain her children," because "it could not be expected that women should have resources sufficient to support their own children" and because without a man to maintain them, "these children must necessarily fall for support on society or starve."[40]

The Marriage Act required an extraordinary sea change in longstanding, customary sexual and marital practices, to ensure that children were raised and educated in such a way as to "really multiply" the population and increase Britain's wealth. To force the change, it made women and their children into whores and bastards and justified making them pay the full social and economic price for any infraction of the law. Illegitimate births more than doubled between the 1750s and 1800. This suggests how steep that price was and how long actual sexual practices lagged behind the prescriptions of the law.[41]

"The female cause is the cause of Virtue"

Egalitarians in the latter part of the eighteenth century insisted, against the men, that the real reason that women did not have sufficient "resources" to support themselves and their children was that women — especially well-bred ladies of the middling and upper ranks without independent means, like themselves — were finding it increasingly difficult to get remunerative work. There was, they argued, no inherent "insufficiency" in women, no fundamental inability on their part to support and educate their own children. The real reason that women often found themselves in penury and want when they did not have a man to support them was that *men* had increasingly appropriated to themselves what had once been considered women's jobs in the economy at large.[42]

At the same time, because the Marriage Act meant that women could be entrapped into ruinous sexual relationships by promises of marriage which no longer had contractual force, sex before marriage and sex outside marriage became important feminist issues. Enlightenment feminists understood that the Marriage Act inserted itself into women's everyday lives through the discipline and punishment of their sexual conduct, and therefore that "the female cause [was] the cause of virtue."[43] They also understood that the Marriage Act had problematized female "virtue" and women's sexual conduct by creating a disjunction between the morality or "troth" of sexual unions and their legality. For what had been declared null and void by the Marriage Act was not the moral validity of the promise plighted by a man and a woman as they hopped into bed — only its legal consequences. This meant that people could now be "morally" married, or married "in conscience" and "before God," by virtue of exchanging promises and/or consummating their union, without being legally married. Lord Barrington made this quite clear in the House:

> As to the moral obligation of the marriage vow, it is certainly in conscience as binding when made before a ploughman in a barn or between two parties without the presence of any witness whatsoever, as when made in a parish Church, before a parson and in the face of a congregation. This vow, as it is a moral obligation, we do not pretend to declare void: we are only in this Bill to declare that it shall have no legal effects, unless made in a legal manner.[44]

And this point was widely publicized. For instance, in its response to "objections against the late Act to prevent clandestine marriages" in October 1753 and again in March 1754 *The Gentleman's Magazine* reiterated the government's argument:

> The legislature assumes no power to dispense with the *moral* obligation of solemn vows and engagements, but only determines to what contract it will give the sanction of marriage for political and civil purposes.

> In this controversy, it should be remembered that, by annulling a marriage, the legislature does not dispense with the moral obligation between the parties to keep a solemn and deliberate vow made to each other, the object of which was not evil in itself, and that every legislature has a right to determine the particular mode and conditions of that engagement to which the civil advantages of marriage shall be annexed, the right of maintenance and the legitimacy of children.[45]

Couples married in the old way by exchanging promises in private were married in conscience and morally obligated to each other, but without the legalizing ceremonial forms required by the Marriage Act, they were no longer legally man and wife. She no longer had the right to be supported by her husband, and her children became illegitimate. Under the act, couples married only "morally" were "oblige[d], if they live[d] together, not to live together as husband and wife, but as whore and rogue . . . and to be actually treated as such by law."[46]

Egalitarians, like Wollstonecraft and Hays, responded by arguing that the female cause, "the cause of virtue," still lay on the side of conscience and morality rather than on that of legality. A woman was not a whore because she had children in a sexual union based on a purely private consensual arrangement with her partner. What really counted was still the truth and troth of the union, not observance of the legal procedural forms. Even after the Marriage Act, a woman was not to be punished and ostracized because she had yielded upon her lover's promise; she was a victim of injustices done to women by men and by society, as well as a victim of her own too-loving heart. Instead of agreeing that women must be disgraced and punished for not binding a man legally to support them and their children, Egalitarians argued, women should fight to restore their right to remunerative work. What women really needed was to regain their economic independence.

Matriarchs, like Hannah More, Jane West, and Maria Edgeworth, on the other hand, insisted that the female cause, "the cause of virtue" and good sense, now lay on the side of legality. They tried to get other women to understand that, after the Marriage Act, a legally solemnized contract of marriage was the only way to transfer the "Property of one's Person" to the "Possession" of another, which assured ladies of a financial "Maintenance" in return. Ladies who could not get remunerative work, they said, must get a husband who was able and legally bound to support them. But this did not mean that they must abjure work. On the contrary, as we will see in the next chapter, Matriarchs advised ladies to work in and on the family — "it is the profession of ladies," said Hannah More, "to be wives, mothers and mistresses of families."

Looking around them, it must have been obvious to Enlightenment feminists that women's sexuality was an economic issue to different ranks in different ways. In the ranks of the propertied, where marriages were designed to join two fortunes or estates, what was primarily at stake was right of access to a lady's wealth, rather than to her sexuality.[47] Here the physical conveyance of a girl from one household to another represented a conveyance of funds, rather than of exclusive property in her person. As a result, ladies of fortune could afford to take their pleasures where they would: their husbands would politely bring up other gentlemen's children as their own, and plant their own issue in other gentlemen's nurseries. In the lower ranks, as Gillis has recently shown, what was sexually permissible changed according to what was economically viable.[48] At times and in parts of the country where families required every working hand to subsist, girls were positively encouraged to "bundle" with their suitors and to go on living with their families of origin as unmarried mothers, rather than to marry and take their labor and their children's labor elsewhere. Similarly, where women could support themselves independently of their families (through work in manufacture, for instance) unmarried girls enjoyed sexual freedom and no social stigma attached to their having children out of wedlock. But at other times, *in the same communities,* when women were unable to support themselves or when unmarried mothers became an economic burden to their families, sexual norms became restrictive and unmarried mothers were abandoned to their fate. Both in the wealthy upper ranks and in the lower ranks, women's sexual freedom was linked to their economic independence.

From this point of view, the Egalitarians were quite right in insisting that ladies of the middle and upper ranks who were without independent means had to regain their economic independence. They were quite right in thinking that such women would only be able to circumvent the Marriage Act's restrictive sexual norms, and nullify the punishments it imposed on women who had children outside registered marriages, if they could regain the power to support themselves and their children through their work.[49]

The Matriarchs were right too, though, and perhaps rather more immediately practical, for they understood that ladies who were unable to cut any figure in the marriage mart as ambulatory cheques and who could not get remunerative work had little *immediate* alternative but to offer the only property they had — the property which natural law said all people possessed in their own body — in exchange for their "Maintenance." As Jane West put it:

> The manner of the times, and the prevailing style of education, render women at once extravagant and dependent: girls can do nothing to maintain themselves; they must therefore at all events *get husbands.* Formerly, they were not reduced to such a style of helplessness . . . In that contest be-

tween the sexes, which consists of the lady's endeavour to entrap a wealthy partner who will let her dash, and the gentleman's wishing to seize upon some pretty girl who will look smart in his phaeton, success (as it is called) generally crowns the hero. Let not this combat of artifice be rendered even more unequal on the heroine's side by her being pre-assured that *to yield is to conquer.*[50]

West is saying that girls must use their sexuality to get a husband who is able to maintain them. A woman could no longer afford to yield and *not* conquer. Conquering a suitor and yielding to him only to get the money to live or the means to cut a dash, Matriarchs insisted long before Marx, made marriage little more than a form of "legal prostitution."[51] But given the strictures of the Marriage Act, yielding *without* conquering spelled economic ruin besides. This is why the "death" that generally comes to "fallen" ladies in Matriarchal tracts and novels in this period is primarily a symbolic, economic death: death in destitution and despair, in some miserable room with no fire in the grate or food in the cupboard; death from regret for an act of "imprudence" and "folly," which is only felt or understood as such when successive desertions by family, friends, and lover have translated into loss of all means of subsistence; death as the symbolic expression of the financial inability to sustain life.

Matriarchs understood that after the Marriage Act, a woman's "Maintenance" by a man turned entirely on just *how* she conveyed her person to his possession, and that, under the Marriage Act, only a designated set of formalities distinguished legal from illegal "bargains of cohabitation." What distinguished the virtuous from the fallen, the young lady who married for money or a maintenance from a common prostitute, and the young lady who conquered and then yielded from the one who yielded in the hope or belief that she would conquer, was only whether she had done the thing in due form. This is why Matriarchs presented "fallen" women as an "Awful Warning" of what happened to women who yielded to their lovers *without* ceremony, and why they insisted that the difference between "virtuous" and "fallen" women be marked — marked in the sense of emphasized and magnified and marked in the sense of represented and made noticeable — by the establishment of an unmistakable physical, social, and moral distance. Matriarchs magnified the distance between different ways of offering a man "Possession of one's Person" precisely because they understood the proximity of each to each and understood the poor opinion a young woman was likely to have of the importance of "Ceremony and Circumstance" when her heart was fixed on a suitor's love or on his bankroll and when she falsely imagined that she need pay no more attention to Parliament's new laws about marriage than she did to its new laws about cambric.[52]

We tend to think of Egalitarians like Wollstonecraft and Hays as avant-garde and of Matriarchs like More and West as old-fashioned in their concepts of virtue and in their sexual prescriptions, but in fact, it was the Egalitarians who were old-fashioned. The "free love" they championed was only a new name for the old way of doing things: it was a new name for a sexual union based on a purely private, consensual agreement that derived its "troth" not from its legality or its public solemnization but from that faith by which a man and woman bind themselves to each other. It was the Matriarchs who were actually moving with the times, who really understood that, in the wake of the Marriage Act, "free love" was also something quite new, something created by the formal legal demarcations of marriage in the Marriage Act as its outlawed, nonbinding, and illicit other. In the presence of rising numbers of illegitimate births and large numbers of women who had been "ruined" by yielding to their lovers upon a promise, it was the Matriarchs who tried to make women understand that, repositioned in this way, "free love" came with a devastating price tag for women and that continuing to yield upon a promise would only turn more and more of the population into bastards and whores.[53] What the Matriarchs called virtue — a woman's exchange of "Possession of her Person" for a legally binding compact to support her and her children — was the only defence Matriarchs could fashion for ladies without means, who had been replaced in the workforce by men, against the Marriage Act's "cruelty to the fair sex."

Legal and Amatory Fictions

The Marriage Act left its traces in innumerable novels, which exemplify the diverse concepts of virtue outlined above or show women paying the price for sexual conduct incompatible with the strictures of the act. Some of the most interesting of these novels also use their exemplary narratives and general plan of analogical virtues and vices to unmask the false expectations and more complex ramifications of the act. Three novels from different moments conveniently illustrate both the range of these ramifications and the persistence of women's concern with issues raised by the Marriage Act into the first decade of the nineteenth century.

Frances Sheridan's *Memoirs of Miss Sidney Bidulph* (1761) has been described as a study of the devasting effects of a daughter's passive obedience to her mother and as an instance of the "institutionalized self-suppression of the [virtuous] female."[54] It is that too. What has been overlooked, however, is the issue on which Sidney's obedience and self-effacement turn: a fundamental difference of opinion between two generations and two genders, separated by the Marriage Act, about whether a man who has gotten one woman with child should be free to marry another.

Lady Bidulph, a woman of "exemplary piety" with a "rigid conception of virtue," forbids her daughter Sidney's marriage to Falkland only when she discovers that Falkland has already enjoyed a sexual union with a girl of good family whom he has gotten with child. Her "partiality to her own sex" makes her "throw the whole blame on the man's side" and assume that Falkland has seduced and deceived Miss Burchell. Even more to the point, Lady Bidulph considers Sidney's situation absolutely "parallel" to her own, when, at 21, her affianced husband recused himself on their wedding day on the grounds that he had "formerly been engaged to a young lady by the most solemn vows" — a fact that he had conveniently ignored upon seeing her and falling in love. Because she thinks the two cases are alike, Lady Bidulph wants Sidney to "imitate [her] example" by overcoming her love for Falkland and marrying another man picked out for her; and she wants Falkland to behave as her own fiancé had done all those years before, by recognizing that he is not free to marry Sidney and returning to fulfill his obligations to Miss Burchell. Though Falkland insists "I am under no promises, no ties, no engagements whatsoever to the lady," Lady Bidulph tries, like a justice of the peace before the Marriage Act, to make Falkland "repair the mischief" he has done Miss Burchell, rather than embark on what she clearly views as a career of serial polygamy:

> No ties, Sir! Is your own honour no tie upon you, supposing you free from any other obligation? You see the consequence of this fatal error, as you call it: here is a young person, of fashion perhaps, (I don't enquire who she is, but she seems to have had no mean education) who is likely to bring a child into the world, to the disgrace of herself and her family. On you, Sir, she charges her dishonour, and mentions your marrying another, as the blow which is to

complete her ruin . . . I will never bring down the curses of an injured maid upon my daughter's head, nor purchase her worldly prosperity at the expence of the shame and sorrow of another woman, for aught I know, as well born, as tenderly bred, and till she knew you, perhaps as innocent as herself . . . What reason can you urge in your conscience for not doing her justice? None — but your own inconstant inclinations, which happen now to be better pleased with another woman, whom, perhaps, you might foresake in a few months.

Sidney, who has been well taught by her mother, concurs: "Miss Burchell deserves your love and has a just right to your hand. She throws herself upon your honour, without pretending to have any lawful claim."[55]

In the contest between a pregnant woman's moral right to marriage and her legal and civil entitlement, Sidney and her mother affirm the importance of ensuring that men honor the moral obligation to marry the mother of their child, as the law used to require them to do. They support the "female cause" by helping the abandoned mother, by refusing to benefit from another woman's ruin, and by insisting that virtue is a matter of honor, conscience, and morality rather than of mere legality.

Sidney's brother, Sir George, who has traveled abroad and knows the world as it is now rather than as it was when his mother was twenty-one, says that this is folly and "romantic" (i.e., bizarre and eccentric) nonsense. He knew about Miss Burchell when he promoted the match between Falkland and his sister but thought it a "trivial matter." Miss Burchell yielded to Falkland on the advice of the "vile designing woman who had care of her" only to entrap him into marriage. Falkland has been decent enough to pay for her lying in, and as far as Sir George is concerned, he has discharged his obligations; he is certainly not bound to her in any way. After the Marriage Act, of course, Sir George is absolutely right: Falkland is perfectly free to marry his sister even if Miss Burchell is carrying his child. Sir George repeatedly tries to convince Sidney and her mother that Lady Bidulph's "unseasonable scruples" are outdated and misplaced: "If you knew the world as well as *I* do, you would think that Mr. Falkland is one of the best." His uncle, another man of the world, confirms Sir George's masculine judgment of the situation: "Our sex have no such *chimaera* notions as you women have."

Sidney's life is ruined because she obeys her mother's directives rather than her brother's. It is ruined by Lady Bidulph's obstinate championship of the cause of "virtue" and of women in the person of Miss Burchell and by her ruthless silencing of the men. And it is ruined because Sidney accepts the sexual attitudes and moral judgments of her mother's generation, while ignoring her brother's more informed, worldly, and contemporary advice. Sidney demonstrates — as Miss Burchell also does in another way by following her aunt's advice to yield in order to conquer Falkland — that after the Marriage Act, a girl could no longer profitably follow her mother's example or do as her mother had done.

It is not clear from the novel, however, just what else she might have done. Frances Sheridan uses each position to show up the shortcomings of the other and complicates the issues to the point where it becomes apparent that no simple or single, one-time answer will serve. Falkland and Sir George clearly fail to measure up to Lady Bidulph's standard of morality, which holds that a man should be held as accountable as the woman for the life they both propagate, whether or not the thing has been done in due form. The novel also unmasks the government's claim that redefining the conditions under which a marriage is recognized in law would not render null and void the moral obligation between the parties, by showing that this was precisely its practical effect. On the other hand, Lady Bidulph's system of values and governance of her daughter clearly fail Sir George's and his uncle's reality test, by failing to take either the way of the world or particular and palliating circumstances into account. As Miss Burchell's real character emerges in the course of the novel, it becomes apparent that her "artfulness," deceitfulness, and promiscuity make her unworthy both of Lady Bidolph's championship and of Sidney's sacrifice.

If the purpose of the Marriage Act was to prevent a man's estate from being carried away from his actual relations, to ensure the proper care and education of children, and to preclude the possibility of bigamous marriages, the novel indicates that it failed on all these counts. When Sidney, after becoming Mrs. Arnold, is herself a widow and mother, the estate which Mr. Arnold inherited from his brother and bequeathed to her children is carried away from them in a curious reprise of the case which led to the Marriage Act. This time, however, it is not an unknown woman, but the woman legally married to Mr. Arnold's brother who gets the estate for a love child. She does so by swearing and adducing corrupt witnesses to confirm that, although she and her husband had lived separately for over two years before his death, they had come together for one night; and Sidney and her children are left destitute. Falkland in turn refuses to maintain his son by Miss Burchell, who relies on Lady Bidulph's charity, until Sidney finally forces him to marry Miss Burchell; only then does that child's existence and education become a matter of any moment to him. And later, convinced that Miss Burchell is dead, Sidney marries Falkland herself — in a full-blown public ceremony, in the presence of her brother and uncle — only to discover that, unknown even to Falkland, Miss Burchell is still alive after all. Despite the publicity of the marriage, and indeed of the whole train of events, Sidney therefore finds herself in a bigamous marriage, with no possible claim to her spouse.

If the virtue of the old law of marriage lay in compelling a man to perform his promise, whether implicit or explicit, as Sidney and Lady Bidulph seem to think, then the novel shows that this approach to marriage had its shortcomings too. At the end of the novel, the tables are turned on Sidney, who promises to marry Falkland in a moment of weakness, love, and compassion for his despair (he has just killed his wife's lover and has to flee the country). Sidney almost immediately regrets her promise, because she is reluctant to be a party to what is going to look like the (not unheard of) situation of a man murdering his wife to be able to marry another woman. This time, however, her uncle, Sir George, and Falkland all cooperate to compel *her* to perform her promise. The point here, I think, is not merely that what is sauce for the goose is rarely sauce for the gander, or that even when Sidney does finally try to assert herself against the will of others, they conspire to make her submit. The point is also that it *is* possible to make a promise of marriage without having thought it through, to regret the promise one has given, and to be quite right in doing so — as Sidney is proved right when her marriage to Falkland turns out to be bigamous. If Sheridan demonstrates anything unequivocally, therefore, it is that, given the dangerous shoals and complex moral and legal situations they have to navigate, it does women no service to teach them that submission to the will of a mother, a husband, or an uncle is the standard of virtue and right.

Eliza Fenwick's *Secresy: or Ruin on the Rock* (1795) might be described as a rewrite of *Sidney Bidulph* from the point of view of an innocent and virtuous Miss Burchell, who truly believes that marriages still work, as Lady Bidulph thinks they ought to work, according to the pre–Marriage Act

principles of natural law.[56] Fenwick explores many of the same oppositions, but this time in such a way as to lay the blame on the economic de-
terminations of social relations.

Like Emile and Sophie (and indeed Sidney in her way), Sibella and
Clement are educated outside of society by a tyrannical parent-governor,
Valmont, who hates the world and thinks that children have nothing to do
but obey. In an act of disobedience, justified as an attempt to save Clement
from despair and identified with the innocence and virtue of a Rousseauesque state of nature, Sibella "marries" Clement in the old way, by exchanging promises and consummating the union: "I am about to do nothing rash . . . 'tis our hearts alone that can bind the vow." In a letter to her
friend and confidante, Carolyn, subsequent to their union, Sibella echoes
some of the arguments made by opponents to the Marriage Act over forty
years earlier, while demonstrating her own ignorance of how the difference
between the older, divinely sanctioned, "natural" way of marrying and the
new legally and socially sanctioned ceremonial form of marriage is going
to decide her fate:

> What is new in my destiny is delightful to remembrance: it is the sacred
> union plighted by our willing hearts in the sight of heaven, the confirmation
> of the everlasting bond of affection, which renders every blessing in this life
> subordinate, from which no change of circumstance could release us, nor
> not even death itself shall cancel. I heard Clement speak one day of some
> ceremonials which would be deemed necessary to the ratification of this
> covenant, when we should enter the world. — Methinks I shall be loath to
> submit to them. The vow of the heart is of sacred dignity. Forms and cere-
> monies seem too trifling for its nature. But of the customs of your world,
> Carolyn, I am ignorant.[57]

Like Falkland, Clement has already traveled the world and tasted its
fruits and temptations, and he is not ignorant. He writes his friend Murden of "the secret of that contract": "Clement has been admitted to her
embraces. For I am her husband. She never heard of ties more holy, more
binding than those of the heart. Custom has not placed its sordid restraints upon her feelings. Nature forms her impulses." Once back in London, however, Clement resumes his usual dissipations and disowns his
marriage to Sibella: "She may call the early union of our affections a marriage, for *I know of none other.*"[58] And then, fearing that Valmont has dis-

inherited him, he marries Carolyn's mother — a foolish woman twice his age who has nothing to recommend her but a large fortune — with all the publicity and ceremony required by the Marriage Act.

The relative value of the two women and of the two marriages is dramatized at the end of the novel, when Sibella is brought to London, ill and pregnant with Clement's child. Standing beside his new but aging bride, who is piquing herself on having acquired a young, handsome, and engaging husband, Clement cruelly informs Sibella that he "can now give her no protection" because he "is married." Sibella is bewildered:

> "Are *we* not both married?" said she, with an emphasis that thrilled [i.e., pierced] him. — What is this? — speak Clement."

> "Nay, now, Miss Valmont, you are childish," said Mrs. Ashburn [Clement's new bride]. "What man of taste marries a woman after an affair with her?"[59]

Society is judged by this judgment of Sibella's "contract" with Clement, by its cruelty to the pregnant woman, and by the respectability it refuses her but accords to a rich, vain old woman who has married her gigolo "with all those Circumstances and Ceremonies which the Law has appointed."

Clement proves as unworthy of Sibella's love and troth as Miss Burchell proved of Falkland's, but as Fenwick demonstrates through the analogical episode of Davenport, who has also gotten Arabella with child and been separated from her by a tyrannical father, the problem is less a matter of character than of economics. Where Clement is only interested in his own economic survival, Davenport earlier determines to marry Carolyn's mother for her money only as a "resource against the worst evils" of watching Arabella and his child die of want; and once Carolyn has assured him of a "yearly income," he returns to Arabella. If Davenport is more worthy than Clement in one respect, they are absolutely alike in another: *both* refuse to work at any trade or profession which would enable them to support a wife and child. Both prefer to acquire money by taking it from others: by accepting a yearly income, by coming into an inheritance, or by marrying a fortune. The novel therefore indicates what political economists had overlooked when they argued that the way to get men to increase their industry was to ensure that they had more mouths to feed: the world might be driven by money, but gentlemen were not yet willing to work for it.

If the purpose of the Marriage Act was to make sexual unions more stable and enduring by using the publicity of private engagements to restrict sex to marriage and prevent men from abandoning women and moving on, *Secrecy* indicates that it failed on these counts too. The act does not prevent Clement from having sexual relations in secret, both with Sibella and with Janette Laundy (a mistress he acquired in Paris), outside the legal demarcations of marriage. And while the two women and the two affairs are different — Clement has never pretended to be Janette's "husband" in the old pre–Marriage Act way, and unlike Sibella, Janette is an "abandoned woman" and a woman of the world — the outcome of both unions is the same. Clement abandons Sibella, as he abandons Janette, when he moves on to marry Mrs. Ashburn with all the necessary public ceremonial forms. Moreover, even the public ceremonial forms required by the act do not prevent him from abandoning a wife — as Mrs. Ashburn discovers shortly after their marriage, when Clement ups and leaves her too. Serial polygamy has not been abolished by the act, and the novel suggests that women are as likely to be deserted by a selfish and ambitious man whether they are married in the old way or in the new and whether they are married or not.

The question is how women are to deal with their loss. And here Janette, the abandoned woman, comes closest to Carolyn, the novel's model of female rationality, when — learning that she is to be "sacrificed to some rival" — she tells Clement: "Be it so. I am content to resign you . . . I have but one request to make; and that, Sir, is a last request. Remember that I am friendless and dependent. Be generously silent . . . Guard carefully a secret that would ruin me in my situation." While the overt moral of the novel condemns secrecy in all its forms, Janette recognizes that keeping the existence of sexual relationships secret and being "content to resign" men who do not work out, may still be the most politick course for those who are economically dependent on others. Sibella, by contrast, refuses to keep her "marriage" to Clement secret, as he repeatedly urges her to do; she would rather die than resign him to Mrs. Ashburn and build a life for herself and her child with Murden, who loves her to distraction. Mrs. Ashburn is little better, blaming Carolyn for Clement's desertion, and making her refusal to resign Clement embarrassingly public by having fits. Carolyn differs from Janette and Sibella by not yielding to a man she cannot conquer; but like Janette, she is wise enough keeps her affairs secret and to give Murden up with good grace when she realizes he is in love with Sibella: "I could have loved him, if he would let me. But 'tis past;

'twas a trace on the sands. Love shall never write its lasting character on my mind, till my reason invites it; and where hope rests not, reason cannot abide." For a woman, then, sexual acts and desires which cannot be given public sanction had best remain clandestine.

If the purpose of the Marriage Act was to "really multiply" the industrious population, by drawing a clear line of demarcation between legitimate and illegitimate births to ensure that men supported and educated their children, then *Secrecy* shows it has failed in this respect also. Valmont brought up Clement alongside Sibella, his brother's child, with the idea of marrying them to each other, if Clement obeyed him and turned out as he hoped. But Clement is Valmont's illegitimate child, and Valmont's purpose in marrying Clement to Sibella was to enable Clement to take his name, inherit the Valmont family fortune, and "bury the disgrace of [his] birth in the nobleness of [Valmont's] possessions." Valmont's purpose, then, was to circumvent society's sentence of illegitimacy on his son. But here, as elsewhere, the design of the father fails to bear fruit. Economic imperatives drive both Clement and Davenport away from what should have been their natural families and legitimate issue. The child Sibella bears is still-born, and Clement's marriage to Mrs. Ashburn is barren. Only Carolyn lives on, to symbolize, through her lifelong spinsterhood, the deadening effect of the government's legislation to "truly multiply" the population.

Amelia Opie's *Adeline Mowbray, or The Mother and Daughter* (1804) combines elements of both these novels into a stinging indictment of women's "no-exit" situation in the wake of the Marriage Act. Opie was once a member of the Godwin-Holcroft circle, and her novel has therefore been read as a representation and critique of Wollstonecraft's "free love" relationship with Godwin. But the novel is also, as one contemporary pointed out, as much "a satire on our prejudices in favour of marriage" as on those who theorized against it. And like Brooke's novel *Lady Julia Mandeville* it puts the evidence of its own exemplarity in question to the point of becoming double-voiced.

Like Sidney Bidulph, Adeline Mowbray governs her life by her mother's ideals and example, "imitating her in those pursuits and studies on which were founded Mrs. Mowbray's pretensions to superior talents" and desiring in her turn to be "a pattern of imitation to others . . . for the benefit of society." But where her mother only writes books to inspire admiration and imitation, Adeline makes the theories she has imbibed from books the rule of her practice. Adeline thus becomes what every reader of conduct books and exemplary novels is supposed to be: a living application and exemplification of what she has read.

Convinced from her reading of Glenmurray's work of "the superior purity and happiness of a union cemented by no ties but those of love and honour" over any union established by "an idle ceremony . . . muttered over me at the altar," Adeline resolves to live with Glenmurray on the basis of the principles in his book. Rather than marry Glenmurray according to the prescriptions of the Marriage Act, therefore, she is determined that they shall be joined together in the old way, by faith and troth, and thus "act independent of society, and serve it by our example even against its will."

The novel makes it clear that, at the turn of the nineteenth century, fifty years after the Marriage Act, this is no longer a practical option. The Matriarchs' construction of female virtue had prevailed, and regarding her as a "fallen woman" for living with Glenmurray without the proper ceremonial forms, the respectably married women in the novel will neither receive Adeline nor give her countenance. Unlike Carolyn or Lady Bidulph, Mrs. Beauclerc tells Adeline not only that she cannot help her but also that she can no longer afford even to be seen with her: "My rank in life is not high enough to enable me to countenance you with any chance of leading others to follow my example; I should not be able to serve you, but should infallibly lose myself."

Living with Glenmurray in the old way, without the "Ceremony and Circumstance" required by the act, now makes Adeline a complete social outcast. It leads to her being taken for a kept woman and a whore; it exposes her to insult and injury from other men; it leaves her without support from Glenmurray's estate or from his relations upon his death; and during his lifetime, it makes her an object of shame and embarrassment to Glenmurray himself. Even Glenmurray finally urges her to abandon the irresponsible principles he taught in his book and to marry him in due form. The exemplarity here is heavily marked. Adeline's example of faith and troth is said by the more Christian women in the novel to be ineffectual, because it sets itself up against the "Ceremonies and Circumstances" that, fifty years after the Marriage Act, are already being naturalized as "the custom of ages." Adeline is, they say, "the victim of a romantic, absurd, and false conception of virtue" and her example is beneficial to society only as "a warning to all young people" of the terrible price to be paid for having the self-conceit to live one's life as a rare example of uncommon principles.

Opie undercuts the evidence of this exemplarity by undercutting the Matriarchs' ideological opposition between "virtuous" and "fallen" women. Transplanting the conduct expected of respectable wives into the unrespectable place of the fallen woman, which Adeline occupies, Opie repeatedly illustrates Adeline's "wifely" devotion to Glenmurray and Christian charity to others. She also uses a series of authoritative men, who observe her conduct with Glenmurray, to present Adeline as the epitome of sexual and domestic virtue. Mr. Maynard, for instance, says, "She shone so brightly in the graceful awefulness of virtue that I gazed with delight and somewhat of apprehension lest this fair perfection should suddenly take flight to her native skies." Dr. Norberry observes that Adeline is "possessed of every quality of head and heart," that "her love comes in aid of her integrity," and that he cannot help admiring her. And Glenmurray's relation, Berendale, finds her in possession of "every gift of heart and mind and person which could make a woman amiable . . . not only an adept at every useful feminine pursuit, but modest in her demeanour and gentle in her manners."

Adeline is in all respects — but the omission of an "idle ceremony," which marks her as "vicious" among the ladies — the perfect exemplar of wifely, domestic, and Christian virtue. There is more than one suggestion in the novel that Adeline is ostracized by other women — who have nothing to recommend them but the Matriarchal observance of that "idle ceremony," which they mistake for virtue — because they are jealous of her many excellences. Mr. Maynard's sisters, for instance, are happy to discover that she is a "kept woman," because they declare that they "hate prodigies" and feel themselves "unworthy to associate with them"; and Dr. Norberry's wife declines to give Adeline even common charity, because, being "a woman of narrow capacity and no talents or accomplishments she had, like all women of the sort, a great aversion to those of her sex who united to feminine graces and gentleness, the charms of a cultivated understanding, and pretensions to accomplishments or literature."

There is also more than one suggestion that by virtue of her constancy and fidelity to Glenmurray, Adeline occupies a position that not only differentiates her from both mistresses and wives but also puts both mistresses and wives into a single category, one which is opposite to hers. As Adeline tells Mary Warner, though conventionally categorized as his mistress, she is as "virtuous" as if she were Glenmurray's legal wife, because "mistresses or kept ladies in general are women of bad character and would live with any man; but I never loved, nor ever shall love, any man but Mr. Glenmurray. I look upon myself as a wife in the sight of God; nor will I quit him till death shall separate us."

The difference between Adeline and a mistress is that there is only one man for her. This is also her difference from a wife, for the marriages to which Adeline's union with Glenmurray is compared indicate that fidelity such as theirs is as rare in the married state as it is among libertines and whores. The wives of Glenmurray's cousins, who look down on Adeline and refuse to associate with her, are anything but faithful. One is having an affair with her husband's intimate friend, the other is coquetting with many men (but sleeping with them one at a time). Unlike Adeline, however, both are received in "respectable society." Adeline's mother, Mrs. Mowbray, is married to an Irishman who "did not consider his union with the mother as a necessary check to his attempts on the daughter" and "looked upon her as his certain prey." It is to flee his advances that Adeline first offers to live with Glenmurray as his wife in the sight of God. And when, at Glenmurray's dying request, Adeline marries Berendale according to all the proper ceremonial forms, she finds not only that he is far less good to her than Glenmurray was without them but also that going through the ceremony neither guarantees his fidelity nor safeguards her position as a wife.

While the marriage register may have prevented Berendale from deserting Adeline and remarrying in England, it does not prevent him from going to Jamaica and marrying a rich widow there. And once he has done so, Adeline can no more prove the legality of her marriage and the legitimacy of her daughter to the satisfaction of the lawyers — given Berendale's denial of the marriage, the possibility of tampering with the marriage register, and the death of the two witnesses — than a woman could prove herself a wife before the Marriage Act was passed. Adeline therefore finds herself in the same bigamous situation that women found themselves in before the act. Hearing that Berendale's new wife has also given birth to a child, Adeline determines to take no further legal steps against him, even to obtain the maintenance for herself and her daughter that she desperately needs, but leaves him instead to the reproaches of his conscience.

The law is of no more use to Adeline than it is to her mother, who has likewise been abandoned by her husband. The Marriage Act could punish women for not marrying in due form, but it could not make marriages more stable, eliminate bigamy, or prevent wives from being abandoned to destitution. The novel's response to Mary Warner's question — Why not marry in form if one plans to be faithful to one man anyway? — is therefore that it makes little real difference to a woman's maintenance and security whether she marries in due form or not.

The only argument for the forms of marriage required by the act that Adeline can finally propose, therefore, is based on the uncommonness of her own example. Her argument for the legalizing forms of marriage is not, she emphasizes, the result of her own experience but of "a more serious, unimpationed and unprejudiced view of the subject than I had before." It is precisely because she has learned that married couples are rarely as happy as she was in her pure, but outlawed, union with Glenmurray that she realizes that her example is "dangerous" and impractical for others to follow. It is precisely because she realizes that constancy such as hers and Glenmurray's is so rare and unusual that she argues that the legal forms of marriage are needed to impose a constancy "of which few are capable" unless they are "forced" to it. But constancy has to be imposed on people who prefer "licentiousness" and "change" — not for the benefit of women or to make *them* happy or secure — but for the benefit of children. Alluding to a letter that Wollstonecraft wrote Amelia Opie, in which she intimated that she would not have become "femme Godwin" had she not "been a mother,"[60] Adeline Mowbray states that the argument which has finally swayed her in favor of marriage, despite the misery she has experienced in that state, "is founded on a consideration of the interest of children." "Connexions capable of being dissolved at will" are, she says, echoing the Marriage Act's pious hope, more likely to induce parents to neglect the welfare and education of their children.

Opie uses Adeline's and her mother's marriages to show that there was

little evidence that the act had succeeded in enforcing "constancy," in preventing connections from being dissolved at will, or in contributing to the
safety and support of daughters. The Marriage Act's designs to make marriage more stable and publicly useful appear no less "ideal," "theoretical,"
and "impractical" than Glenmurray's ideas about marriages founded on
faith and troth; and these Adeline, like society itself, has been obliged to
give up.

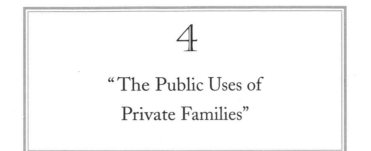

4

"The Public Uses of
Private Families"

To put matters on a fair and equitable footing between the sexes
... necessarily involves many public and political, as well as private and domestic concerns. And in its progress, new points of
view must open. — MARY HAYS

THE PRIME ISSUE for public policy in the Marriage Act, as we have
seen, was to ensure that husbands and fathers supported their families, educated their children, and discharged their procreative and domestic responsibilities for the public good. Enlightenment family ideology in
the latter half of the eighteenth century accompanied and forwarded these
goals. Public men told private men that England's prosperity depended on
men's "rational love" and "judicious education" of their children; that the
industry and good order of the polity depended on each gentleman's
government of his family and dependents; and that by his domestic economy and beneficent care of his family, friends, and immediate community,
each private gentleman promoted the order, wealth, and well-being of the
nation.

Male ideologues feared that they were writing to a moment when "domestic pleasures . . . appear[ed] to a great part of mankind, insipid, unmanly, and capable of satisfying none but the weak, the spiritless, the inex-
perienced, and the effeminate."[1] For too many men, "Paradise Hall" still
consisted of being born into, marrying into, or buying one's way into the
careless, leisured, aristocratic, and "dissipated" lifestyle of the rich and fa-
mous.[2] Male ideologues therefore tried to naturalize men's paternal affections and to magnify their dignity and public importance in order to persuade men to take them on. Public men told private men that paternal
supervision of children's health and education was "by no means unmanly"
and that "the nursery" had "often alleviated the fatigues of the bar and sen-

ate house."[3] They said that the nursing and management of children had been "too long fatally left to the management of women, who cannot be supposed to have proper knowledge to fit them for such a task" and that "fathers should take more interest in their children's upbringing."[4]

Male ideologues also said that it was "natural" for a man to feel the warmest affection for his children and kin: "After himself, the persons in his own family, those who usually live in the same house with him, his parents, his children, his brothers and sisters, are naturally the objects of his warmest affection."[5] Public men told private men that, though a man's care for his family and supervision of his children stemmed from "private affections," which "tend towards the private good, this does not hinder them from being public affections too, or destroy the good influence of them upon society, and their tendency towards the public good."[6] Private gentlemen could make invaluable contributions to the public good through "virtuous" private affections, which "naturally" led them to the care of their children and dependents, to the conscientious discharge of their domestic and parental offices, and to fixing a plan of education for their children which would raise them to become productive and "useful Commonwealthsmen."[7]

Enlightenment feminists were thus taking a leaf out of men's book when they told ladies, as Hannah More put it, that "it is the profession of ladies to be wives, mothers and mistresses of families," and when they urged *ladies* to discharge these domestic and parental offices for the public good. Far from asking ladies to confine themselves to some marginal institution identified with women and with women's "proper role," they were inviting private ladies to undertake the tasks that Enlightenment ideologues were urging on private gentlemen. And they were extending Adam Smith's dictum, that every man is a burden to society who does not contribute to the public good, to women too: "*both* sexes, in order to render themselves beneficial members of society, are equally required to comply with these terms."[8]

Dr. Johnson pointed out, long before Raymond Williams did, that "as any opinion grows popular, it will innovate speech in the same proportion as it alters practice."[9] In the eighteenth century, the opinion which "innovated speech" by equating "domestic" exclusively with the home and the home with women and which placed the family in a "private" sphere outside of politics and public life, was not popular yet. It is easy to misread eighteenth-century texts by overlooking the fact that key words — *domestic, private, public, family, society* — occupied different signifying spaces then than they do now. As we will see, the eighteenth-century significations of these words were not only different; they also opened onto a network of presuppositions about what Paley called "the public uses of private families" which are foreign to liberalism's later "bipolar view of social life" — its "tendency to split itself into distinct parts: what is private and what is public."[10] These presuppositions made the family more central to social and political thought than it later became. They also made the government of families, tenants, and dependents and the education of children the public work of private men. It is in this context that both eighteenth-century feminisms' diverse constructions and their promotion of the "domestic woman" will be reevaluated and read.

The Domestic, the Private, and the Public

In the eighteenth century, the word *domestic* was still applied to men as well as to women, arguably to men more properly than to women. Johnson's own examples in the revised 1799 edition of his *Dictionary* were Addison's maxim that "the faithful, prudent husband is an honest, tractable and *domestick* animal" and a sentence from Richardson's *Clarissa:* "the practical knowledge of the *domestick* duties is the principal glory of a woman." The word *domestic* was applied not only to people living in the same household but to members of different households who shared the same chief or family head. For instance, in 1747, Hutcheson wrote: "After the proper parental power expires, there often succeeds that of the head of the family, which is of such extent as the *domesticks* make it by their own consent, express or tacit, by voluntarily continuing it or entering into a family, where they knew such a degree of power was assumed."[11] By extension, the term *domestic* was applied to men within the same country or nation who shared the same monarch or governor. Johnson's example is a quote from King Charles: "Next to the sin of those who began that rebellion, there must needs be, who hindered the speedy suppressing of it, by *domestick* dissentions." But Hume was also still employing the word in this sense when he spoke of the "*domestic* government of the state, where the public good, which is or ought to be the [government's] object, depends on a multitude of causes" and of the ways "*domestic* manufacturers emulate the foreign."[12] In these examples, the word *domestic* is being used in reference to what we would today call the public sphere.

This confusion of public and private in the same word may be attributable to the fact that *domestic* originally designated ministers, courtiers, chaplains, and other servants in a king's or prince's household. It therefore goes back to a time when the king and his household *were* the government. But there are also traces of this usage in Hutcheson's phrase: "should one allege that a potent head of a family, with his numerous *domesticks,* might have conquered, and thus compelled his neighbours around to submit to him as their prince."[13]

Eighteenth-century usage of the words *private* and *public* was also significantly different from ours. In one of its senses, *private* meant "withdrawn from public life" or "deprived of office" — we still use the word in this way when we speak of private members of Parliament or of privates in the army. In this sense, however, one could be a "private man" in what is now considered the public sphere. One could also be a "private man" in any space occupied by persons of quality or rank. Adam Smith uses the term *private man* in this way, by contrast with "the man of rank and distinction," in the 1790 edition of his *Theory of Moral Sentiments:* "The most perfect modesty and plainness joined to as much negligence as is consistent with the respect due to the company, ought to be the chief characteristic of the behaviour of a private man."[14]

Used in this sense, *private* also had connotations of "privateness" — "the state of a man in the same rank with the rest of the community"[15] — which directly conflicted with eighteenth-century connotations of *domestic.* The word *domestic* had come into English from the French[16] where it designated "all those persons subordinate to someone, who constitute his household . . . [and] owe him submission, respect and fidelity."[17] The connotations of *domestic* were feudal and hierarchical, those of *private* were not.

A second meaning of *private* was "secret," "not open," as distinct from *public,* in the sense of "open," "offered to general notice," "generally known," or "published to the world." As Johnson indicates, Granville used the words in this sense when he wrote: "In private grieve, but with a careless scorn, / In public seem to triumph, not to mourn." In this sense, one could be public in what we now consider the private sphere — in one's household, before one's servants, amongst one's friends — as well as private in public. Maria Edgeworth uses the words in this sense when she classes *Castle Rackrent* with "secret memoirs and private anecdotes," arguing that "we cannot judge either of the feelings or of the characters of men with perfect accuracy from their actions or appearance in public." But this is also why the story she tells is the story of the family's private life only insofar as it has already become public — open, generally known — to her narrator, a family retainer who "pour[s] forth anecdotes and retail[s] conversation with all the minute prolixity of a gossip in a country town."[18]

A third meaning of *private* was "particular" as distinct from "public" in the sense of "general" or "common," and thus "pertaining to a particular person or group" as distinct from "public" in the sense of "pertaining to the community, the state, or the nation at large." But in the earlier part of the century, at least, this was not yet the primary or obvious meaning — as John Dennis tells us in 1724, when he struggles to understand what Mandeville could possibly have meant by his subtitle to *Fable of the Bees,* "Private Vice, Public Benefit." Dennis's attempt to work out "what the author means by Private Vices" is quite wonderful, and deserves to be quoted in full:

> by which Words, he does not mean Vices or Sins which are committed secretly, though that perhaps is the natural Signification of the Words; because such a Meaning would exclude almost every sort of Luxury: Nor can he mean by Private Vices, the Vices of Private Persons; because by such a meaning he must affirm, That the Vices of publick Persons, such as Legislators, Ministers of State, Magistrates and public Officers are not Public Benefits, and such an Assertion might imply that they are publick Mischiefs; but to affirm or imply either must be either very far from his Intention, or must make him contradict himself. By Private Vices then, however ambiguously he has expressed himself, he can mean nothing but the Vices of particular Persons, of every individual Member of the Civil Community, whether they are public or private Persons.[19]

Dennis clearly feels that this is a tour de force. The phrase "Public Benefit" does not present him with the same difficulty: "the word Benefit can certainly need no explaining," he says, and "by the word Publick, he who speaks of a Free People . . . can mean nothing but the whole collective Body of that Free People."[20]

Enlightenment ideology recognized a distinction between private and public in all these senses, but it did not assume a binary opposition. Though very diverse in other ways, Shaftesbury, Mandeville, Sidney, Dennis, Hutcheson, Hume, Beattie, Butler, Godwin, Burke, Steuart, and Adam Smith all thought that the nature, happiness, and prosperity of the Public (i.e., of the whole collective body of the people) was a function of the nature, happiness, and prosperity of the private (i.e., particular) persons composing it. They thought the happiness and advantage of each particular or private person was analogical to, and continuous with, that of the public, the community, state, or nation at large:

> Man is made to promote the good of society equally with his own good . . . These ends do indeed perfectly coincide, and to aim at public and private good are so far from being inconsistent, that they mutually promote each other.[21]

> The same course of life which contributes to the general prosperity, procures also to the agents the most stable and most worthy felicity . . . The general happiness is the result of the happiness of individuals.[22]

> By acting according to the dictates of our moral faculties we necessarily pursue the most effectual means for promoting the happiness of mankind.[23]

> Matrimonial Union promotes the happiness of the individual by means of the most friendly society . . . It must therefore promote the public weal; both because the public is made up of individuals; and also because by this institution the race of men is continued from age to age.[24]

> National Religion is the only Fountain both of general publick and private virtue . . . Charity, that makes the happiness of Particulars, tends to the Felicity of the whole Community.[25]

> It is the combination of every private interest which forms the public good.[26]

Enlightenment feminists shared these views. Matriarchs and Egalitarians both believed "political and private happiness are invariably connected"[27] and saw the virtue, happiness, and well-being of the public as an outgrowth of the virtue, happiness, and well-being of the private or particular persons composing it. "Public virtue is only an aggregate of the private," said Mary Wollstonecraft, for "public affections, as well as public virtues, must ever grow out of the private character."[28] Hannah More agreed: "Private Virtue is Public Benefit."[29] Because the public good was an aggregate of the private good, and because the public was whatever it was by virtue of the persons composing it, Enlightenment thinking also assumed that the morals, ideas, and conduct of private (i.e., particular) persons was a matter of legitimate public (i.e., common or general and open or published) concern.[30]

This Enlightenment identification of the private and the public good was strengthened by the assumption that man was, by nature, a social being.[31] When nineteenth-century sociology, marxism, or their postmodern derivatives say that man is a social being, they mean that he is a socialized being, the particular product or effect of a particular education and culture. This idea was already present in the eighteenth century, since it followed from Locke's doctrine that children are born *tabula rasa,* that they become whatever they become as a result of education and culture.[32] But when Enlightenment thinkers called man a social being, they meant that "man, who can subsist only in society, was fitted by nature to that situation for which he was made."[33] Even when they recognized that human failings could disturb as well as promote the well-being of society, or argued that society was evil and corrupt, they assumed that Newton's Nature — that nature which demonstrates Divine Providence and through whose laws God rules the world — or God in the Scriptures, or both, had equipped man with such faculties, needs, desires, reason, and affections as drew him to the society of others and made it necessary for him to live amongst them:

> God having made Man such a Creature that, in his own Judgement it was not good for him to be alone, put him under strong Obligations of Necessity, Convenience and Inclination to drive him into Society, as well as fitted him with Understanding and Language to continue to enjoy it.[34]

> Men are creatures fitted by Nature for Civil Polity.[35]

> We are so formed by nature that no man in solitude without the aid of others and an intercourse of mutual Offices, can preserve himself in safety or even in life, not to speak of any pleasure or happiness.[36]

No man, strictly speaking is independent. The Author of our being has connected us by mutual wants to each other; and has given noone the power of
saying I will be happy in spite of my fellows.[37]

This idea that God and/or Nature fitted man for society by ensuring that
each requires the assistance of others to provide for his wants expressed itself in political economy as a doctrine of dependence. It also underlay Enlightenment conceptualizations of "family society."

"Family Society" and Men's Domestic Government

During the latter half of the eighteenth century, Enlightenment ideologues represented the family both as a natural phenomenon and as "an
adventitious state, founded upon some human deed or institution."[38] Enlightenment ideologues saw no contradiction here, and the same writers
speak of it both ways. Even Rousseau: "The most ancient of all societies,
and the most natural society, is that of the family . . . The family is therefore the first model of political societies."[39] For whether they viewed the
"adventitious" institution — with its marriage laws and conventional organization — as evidence of man's rational understanding of natural principles (Hutcheson), as "the result of human passions cooperating with human reason" (Beattie), as a supplement for the shortcomings of individuals
who failed to live up to their natural obligations (Hume), as degenerate in
[its] current social form (Rousseau), or as a culturally variable response to
different local, climactic, and natural conditions (Montesquieu, Hume),
Enlightenment thinkers argued that there was continuity, harmony, or interrelation between nature and society. As Blackstone put it, marriage is
"founded in nature, but modified by civil society; the one directing man to
continue and multiply the species, the other prescribing the manner in
which that natural impulse must be confined and regulated."[40]

This articulation of nature and civil society made it possible for Enlightenment ideologues to represent the private family as playing crucial
public roles, which were consistent with public policy's promotion of the
"public uses of the marital institution" through the Marriage Act. Significantly, the "public uses" of private families in Enlightenment family ideology bore on the "natural" dimensions of the family as much as on the "adventitious state." The political uses of the marital institution were thus
naturalized, and its natural uses politicized.

As a natural phenomenon, the private family was said to promote the public good by ensuring the perpetuation of human society through the procreation and support of children. No surprise there! Nature, so the argument went, had ordained that the male and female of all species come together, not only to procreate, but also to care for each other and, conjointly, for their young:

> Nature has implanted in the two sexes a strong mutual affection, which has a wonderful power, and has in view a friendly society for life.[41]

> Nature has implanted in all living creatures an affection between the sexes, which, even in the fiercest and most rapacious animals, is not merely confined to the satisfaction of bodily appetite, but begets a friendship and mutual sympathy, which runs through the whole of their lives.[42]

Even among savages, man's "natural" liking for and growing attachment to those who depended on him ensured that he would wish to care for his infant and its mother. Nature was providential and wise in thus designing man's affections, because human infants were "of all animals the most helpless" and because "mothers are insufficient alone for the necessary and laborious work" of nourishing, protecting, and educating their young. The family was "the most natural society," for it embodied all those naturally and divinely ordained affections and mutual needs that "naturally" drove men and women to live together in a "friendly" society" for the protection of their young.[43]

As an adventitious institution that was the result of men's deeds, the family was considered "the first society" in four different ways, which again straddle our modern public-private divide.

The family was the first society to have been established historically, and thus the origin of society and of government. Even Hume — who thought the state of nature "a philosophical fiction"[44] and ridiculed the idea that societies had been established by consent rather than by conquest, usurpation, and force — assumed that the family had been the first historical society. Apart perhaps from his emphasis on the emergence of civil law from domestic government, Hume's description of how polities evolved from the family is perfectly commonplace:

> Suppose the conjunction of the sexes to be established in nature, a family immediately arises; and particular rules being found requisite for its subsis-

tence, these are immediately embraced; though without comprehending the rest of mankind within their prescriptions. Suppose that several families unite together into one society, which is totally disjoined from all others, the rules which preserve peace and order enlarge themselves to the utmost extent of that society.[45]

Society had come into being as a development and enlargement of the family.

The family also remained the first society in the present, inasmuch as the family (not the "unencumbered" individual of nineteenth-century liberalism) was represented as the kingdom's basic component unit. In Enlightenment family ideology, private (i.e., particular) families were not treated as separate from society or as marginal to the state's "real" concerns. They were described as the components and building blocks of the nation. As Bolingbroke put it, "the first societies, and those which compose all others, are family societies. These are natural, and the better they are regulated, the more surely will political societies, whose component parts they are, be put and maintained under good regulations."[46] Or as Gally said: "Private Families ought to be, and have always been, considered as the constituent Parts of large Communities. And from thence it follows, that whatever Power temporal Princes have to make Laws for the Good Order and Peace of Communities, they must have the same for the making of Laws for the Good Order and Peace of Private Families."[47]

As the constituent parts or component elements of the nation, private families had important political uses. William Paley — whose compendium of later eighteenth-century commonplaces became an established textbook for students throughout the first half of the nineteenth century — conveniently lists them. Private families, he said, do not merely ensure "the comfort of individuals"; they create the wealth and prosperity of the nation through "the encouragement of industry" and "the production of the greatest number of healthy children."[48] Private families also promote "the better government of society, by distributing the community into separate families, and appointing over each the authority of a master of a family, which has more actual influence than all the civil authority put together" and "the same end in the additional security the state receives for the good behaviour of its citizens from the solicitude they feel for the welfare of their children, and from being confined to permanent habitation."[49]

The government of private families was linked both to public prosperity and to public order, for the propertied private family was the kingdom's basic economic and administrative unit.[50] The private man who, as master of his family, confined himself to a permanent habitation and used his authority and influence there to govern his children, servants, tenants, and dependents was therefore said to promote the public good. As Hutcheson argued, "there are very few who have either abilities or opportunities of doing anything which can immediately and directly affect the interests of all; and yet everyone almost can contribute something to the advantage of his kinsmen, his friends and his neighbours, and by so doing plainly promotes the public good."[51] Princes would pass laws for the good order of private families, and masters of families would govern them for the good of all. Or, in Hume's more cynical version of this argument, "each man, being a sovereign in his own family, has the same interest with regard to it as the prince with regard to the state; and has not like the prince any opposite motives of ambition and vainglory which may lead him to depopulate his little sovereignty." In his little domestic sovereignty, each private man could be a prince; and as a better, wiser, and more beneficent ruler of his own family kingdom than some princes were of the state, he could join with his peers in "privateness" to build the new society as an association of little sovereigns, each benevolently governing his own children, domestics, tenants, and dependents for the public good.

The family was represented as the first *society* because all the fundamental elements of society were still enshrined in the family. That was why, in the eighteenth century, one spoke of "conjugal society," of "family society" or of "domestick society" rather than, as we do today, of marriage, "the" family, and "the" home.

The family was a society inasmuch as a primary meaning of *society* was still "a union of many persons in one general interest."[52] The general interest of the assorted persons united in a family was understood to be economic. As Jane Rendall points out, the family was still in all classes primarily "an economic institution, for the mutual support, even survival, of all members of the family."[53] And, as Bridget Hill and Davidoff and Hall have shown, the family household — composed of master, mistress, unmarried children or kin, servants, and fieldworkers or apprentices — remained the primary locus of production throughout the eighteenth century.[54] Whether agricultural or commercial, family society among the propertied classes was often a complex and extended economic unit.

It was also as a complex, economically based, interdependent association of persons under the direction of a domestic governor that family society continued to seem analogous to the state. This is why James Steuart and Adam Smith conceived of their new science of political economy as a public version of the oeconomics (from *oikos*, household) of private families. In the introduction to his *Inquiry into the Principles of Political Economy*, Steuart explains that he had invented political economy by analogy with the economy of private families:

> Oeconomy in general is the art of providing for all the wants of a family with prudence and frugality . . . The object of it in a private family is to provide for the nourishment, the other wants, and the employment of every individual . . . What oeconomy is in a family, political oeconomy is in a state; with these essential differences, however, that in a state there are no servants, all are children: that a family may be formed when and how a man pleases, and he may there establish what plan of oeconomy he thinks fit; but states are found formed, and the oeconomy of these depends on upon a thousand circumstances.[55]

Political economy was an analogical translation, or transposition, onto the public arena and nation at large of the planning and organization of the "Master of a Family" in providing for the wants of his family and the employment of its members. Steuart notes differences as well as similarities, because the relation between the economy of a private family and the economy of a nation is analogical; there are different constraints and a different level of complexity, for instance. But even some of these differences return us to the model of the paternalistic family: "in a state there are no servants, all are children." As Adam Smith later did, Steuart "often recur[s] to private oeconomics for clearing up [his] ideas concerning the political."[56] After all, as Hume said, "each man being a sovereign in his own family, has the same interest with regard to it, as the prince with regard to the State."[57] Or, as Hester Chapone pointed out, "it is with a family, as with a Commonwealth, the more numerous and luxurious it becomes, the more difficult it is to govern it properly."[58]

From this point of view, the private family (e)state continued to seem most emblematic of the state. On the land, the complexity, size, and difficulty of governing the family society increased in the latter half of the eighteenth century, as the "engrossment" of small farms extended family estates and turned more and more freeholders into tenants and dependents of large landlords, whose "sovereignty" extended to everyone on their domain. John Throsby observed in 1791 of a Leicestershire landlord who owned 1100 acres: "If he chuse to govern, he may give laws to all that breathe in this place, [for] not only all the land owns him for its lord, but every dwelling also; the patronage of the Church and the living are all his own."[59] Though generally identified now with Tory glorifications of England's medieval or "Gothic" past, images in women's novels of the frighteningly tyrannical or benevolently paternalistic domestic government of private families in ancient castles or on family estates might also be read as allusions to the contemporary effects of engrossment and to a contemporary empowerment of great landlords analogous to that of the great barons of the medieval or gothic past.

The family was a society not only in the sense that it was an often-complex, governed association of persons bound by economic interest but also in the sense that it was a structured space of social interactions in which certain rules of behavior applied and the assorted members had diverse roles, duties, and obligations relative to one another. From this point of view, the family was also represented as "the first society" to which children were exposed and, thus, as their primary locus of training, education, and sociality: "Men are necessarily born into a family society and are trained up by their parents to some rule of Conduct and behaviour."[60] "Man, born in a family, is compelled to maintain society from necessity, from natural inclination and from habit. The same creature, in his farther progress, is engaged to establish political society in order to administer justice."[61]

Although there was considerable public debate about the relative advantages of educating children in schools or at home in the second half of the eighteenth century, there was as yet no compulsory public schooling, certainly for the propertied ranks. The sort of education that children received, if they received any useful education at all, depended largely on their family. The perceived importance of children's care and education steadily increased in the course of the century, for economic reasons that were examined in the previous chapter. At the same time, the belief that children are born *tabula rasa* and that their characters and conduct are the effect of the examples they are given and of the principles and habits instilled in them substantially increased the impact attributed to education. Supporters of the idea that education was one of the prime public functions of the family argued that the family's ability to act as a school for society was enhanced by the fact that it was not only an adventitious but also a natural institution. Like Adam Smith, they said, "domestic education is the instrument of nature; public education the contrivance of man."[62] Or, like Beattie, they insisted, "Domestic discipline is found to be as friendly to virtue, and is certainly more agreeable to nature" than boarding schools and nowhere but in family society "is the child likely to meet with so much tenderness, and so zealous a concern for his temporal and eternal welfare, as in the house of those who gave him birth."[63]

As a society, where certain rules applied and where members had certain duties relative each to each, the family was also described as the place where, along with children, servants, dependents, and domestics were taught, by precept and example, those principles, relative duties, and rules of conduct on which the well-being, some said "the very existence," of the larger society depended. Here the recurrent assumption that the public (the body of the nation as a whole) was whatever it was as a result of the character and conduct of private (particular) persons kicked in. The sentiments expressed in Tillotson's "Sermon on Family Religion" were often repeated, for instance, by John Dennis in *Vice and Luxury Publick Mischiefs* (1724):

> Families are the first Seminaries of Religion . . . The Neglect of due Preparation of our Children and Servants at Home can hardly ever be corrected afterwards . . . If they continue void of the Fear of God, which there hath been no care taken to plant in them, they will almost necessarily be bad in all Relations: undutiful Children, slothful and unfaithful Servants, scandalous members of the Church, unprofitable to the Commonwealth, disobedient to Governors, both Ecclesiastical and Civil; in word, Burthens of the Earth, and so many Plagues of Human Society.

These were not the only values that "Human Society" was expected to acquire from the family. Patriotism, love of country and devotion to the public good were also to be imbibed from the family, along with those habits of decency and good conduct on which civilized life was thought to depend:

We begin our public affections in our families. No cold relation is a zealous citizen . . . The love of the whole is not extinguished by this subordinate partiality. Perhaps it is a sort of elemental training to those higher and larger regards, by which alone men come to be affected, as with their own concerns, in the prosperity of a kingdom.[64]

There is scarce any man, who by discipline, education and example, may not be so impressed with a regard to general rules, as to act on almost every occasion with tolerable decency, and through the whole of his life to avoid any considerable blame. Upon a tolerable observance of these duties depends the very existence of human society which would crumble into nothing if mankind were not generally impressed with a reverence for those important rules of conduct.[65]

Conceived as the place where children, servants, dependents and domestics were to be taught, by precept and example, those principles and general rules of conduct on which the virtue of society depended, family society played a central, and indeed a foundational, pedagogical public role.

Both as a complex and often extended economic unit serving one general interest and as a space of sociality and education where certain habits, principles, and rules of conduct were practised, imparted, and imposed, family society was a permanent testimony to men's dependence on the society of others for all their needs and wants, as well as to the importance of avoiding "confusion in families" by determining, a priori, where the superiority and authority lay. The word *governor* linked these two facets of "the little society of the family," since it was used in the eighteenth century for men performing either the domestic governing or the domestic educative tasks.

These public uses of the private family constituted a patriarchal ideal and bore for the most part on propertied families (whether aristocratic, genteel, or of the middling sort) rather than on the poor. It was an ideal with considerable cultural currency and which Enlightenment feminists held up for critique or ridicule in their novels, as did some of their male contemporaries.[66] There is little evidence that, except in fictions — whether philosophical, political, or literary — propertied families really functioned like this.

In their novels and tracts, Matriarchs generally agreed with Wollstonecraft's description of the sad condition of family society at the end of the eighteenth century.[67] In the English propertied classes, she said, "the sordid calculations of blind self-love" directed to perpetuating and increasing the family estate supplied the place of any wider benevolence and precluded all possibility of what Lawrence Stone has called "affective individualism."[68] Parents promoted matches that would force their children to "do violence to a natural impulse and run into legal prostitution to increase wealth or shun poverty." In the propertied ranks, husbands and wives made coquetry and adultery "the grand business of genteel life," and "children are neglected for lovers" by mothers and fathers alike.[69] In the propertyless ranks, gaming laws, press gangs, and enclosures, which increased the wealth and security of family estates, caused "the distress of industrious mothers whose helpmates have been torn from them, and the hungry cry of helpless babes."[70] England was composed of dysfunctional families at all ranks, she claimed. The only difference between Wollstonecraft's analysis of the situation and that of the Matriarchs lay in the attribution of cause: Wollstonecraft attributed the evils plaguing family society to the corrupting effect of "the perpetuation of property in our families";[71] Matriarchs attributed them to the lack of good Christian principle and to imitation in all ranks of the "dissipation" of aristocratic life.[72]

Although they critiqued and discredited the patriarchal ideal of benevolent domestic sovereigns governing and educating their wives, children, servants, and domestics for the public good, Enlightenment feminists in the latter half of the eighteenth century shared with proponents of this ideal most of the assumptions outlined above. They shared patriarchal ideologues' ideas about the public uses of private families and about the importance of the domestic governor's governing role. This is certainly one reason why the family was such a central issue for them, too, but it was not the only reason they urged ladies to take over "the proper government of our families" and to occupy as "lawful possessors" a "domestic territory" that men, prejudice, custom, church doctrine, Enlightenment family ideology, and public policy had gifted to men.[73]

Ladies' Domestic Government and Women's Work

As the story was told until recently, women were left behind in the household at the beginning of the Industrial Revolution in the eighteenth century, when men followed the means and locus of production out of the household and into a workplace. This, in turn, was said to have led ipso facto to women's confinement to domesticity, to the separation of women in private life from civil society, which was conceived as men's public domain, and to the doctrine of "separate spheres." More recent historical studies have shown, however, that the Industrial Revolution and the separation of the workplace from the household both occurred rather later than earlier calculated — in the beginning and middle of the nineteenth century, respectively — and that the agricultural household and commercial "house" remained the primary economic units throughout the eighteenth century.[74] This makes better sense of the importance given to men's domestic and paternal government by Enlightenment family ideology, but it raises the question of why Enlightenment feminists would have urged ladies to take over "the proper government of our families" from men and called on ladies to make the domestic sphere "a sphere of properly female action" *before* the separation of workplace from household and of private from public life. One clue lies in the kinds of women these feminists were primarily addressing.

One significant group that Enlightenment feminists were speaking to when they called on women to work at being wives, mothers, and mistresses of families were ladies without means. Enlightenment feminists sought to reopen marriage as an economic refuge and as a method of economic and social advancement for women not unlike themselves — daughters of the gentry with small portions; daughters of clergymen, military officers, once prosperous merchants, professional men, younger sons, and gentlemen of small means; daughters abandoned or disinherited upon the death of one parent and the remarriage of the other and left to fend for themselves — who, as we saw, were finding it harder and harder to support themselves by their work in the marketplace.[75] Educated to a genteel style of life and left without adequate means of support, such "indigent gentlewomen" could no longer afford to remain single. Yet, dowerless, impoverished, or with only small fortunes, these ladies were not competitive in the marriage mart either. As Clara Reeve complained, "a great number" were being "condemned to a life of perpetual celibacy" because:

> there are but few men, comparatively, that will take for a wife an amiable maiden without fortune suitable to his own. Every young man is taught to look out where he can marry to advantage; wealth is supposed to include every thing . . . Thus the ugly, the deformed, the foolish, the distempered,

are preferred with fortunes; while the lovely, the amiable, the accomplished, who are in every way qualified to be wives and mothers, are past by, neglected, despised and forgotten.[76]

By marrying only to raise *their* fortunes, men with some fortune (or their families) were, in effect, preventing women without fortune from doing the same. Among the daughters of peers alone, as Susan Staves has shown, a quarter were doomed to spinsterhood at the end of the eighteenth century because they "were too underfunded to compete on the marriage market, either because their portions were too small to attract suitable husbands, or because the assets that were supposed by the settlement to be made available for their portions were not available when needed."[77]

In the latter half of the eighteenth century, it was ladies without fortune or earning power — not men, as in the nineteenth century — who needed a domestic haven or asylum from what they described as a cruel, competitive, and money-driven world where indigent gentlewomen who could not find work faced want, abandonment, prostitution, and death. The plight of such ladies is movingly portrayed in Egalitarian tracts, as well as in Egalitarian novels from Charlotte Smith's *Emmeline* and *The Old Manor House* to Mary Hays's *Memoirs of Emma Courtney* and *The Victim of Prejudice*. Lovely, amiable, and admirably qualified to be wives and mothers by their education, principles, and virtues, the impoverished and orphaned heroines of such novels are thwarted at every turn by fiscal prejudice and by the manifold cruelties of a heartless world. Rejected by their lovers' family despite all their education, principles, and virtues, or abandoned by their lovers for a wealthier and more worldly match, they are also unable to find any way of living on their earnings independently of some sort of family. These suffering heroines therefore exist bleakly as outcasts from society, as skivvies in someone's attic or as transitory guests in other women's homes; or, despite their best efforts to evade it, they follow the alternative route of destitution, prostitution, and death. They are only ever saved from such dreadful fates by an ideal lover who loves them enough to marry them (often in secret) against all the social and economic odds. Egalitarians often presented women in a "deserted and friendless condition" as "poor unfortunate victims" whose "feeble powers of resistance" made them of all God's creatures "least able to defend themselves,"[78] for they hoped to ameliorate the lot of unfortunate women by appealing to society's conscience.

Matriarchs developed a more cynical strategy. Reasoning that the marital route to financial security and social advancement would remain blocked as long as women had nothing to bring to a marriage in lieu of the money they lacked, Matriarchs took a leaf out of political economy's book. As political economy insisted that labor had replaced gold as "the real measure of value," Matriarchal tracts and novels insisted that the work a wife could do in her diverse domestic roles supplanted fortune as the real measure of a woman's value. Translating back into the domestic arena political economy's dictum that "the state of a nation's wealth is not to be estimated from the state of its coffers . . . but from the number, frugality, industry and skill of its people,"[79] Matriarchs turned frugality, industry, virtue, and professional skill as mothers, wives, and mistresses of the family into the dowry of the dowerless. They promulgated the desirability to "a man of sense and fortune" of acquiring an amiable, useful, and capable wife who could act as a companion and "helpmeet" to him.

This is why the proto-Alger story of "poor but capable girl makes good in the marriage mart" recurs, in one form or another, in the plots of Matriarchal novels from Lennox's *Sophia* to Edgeworth's *Belinda* and Austen's *Pride and Prejudice* and *Mansfield Park*. Such novels describe a trajectory in which the capable heroine's skill and good sense in the domestic and familial arena (as well as her superiority in these regards to more wealthy and flighty female characters) enable her to overcome any obstacle created by her lack of fortune, lack of proper family background, and need to get a husband. Her virtues in the domestic sphere enable her to become a valued member of genteel society and to marry well, and having earned herself a conjugal haven, she can disappear from history to preside over her retreat.[80]

The other group whom Enlightenment feminists were addressing when they called on women to take over government of their families from their husbands and to work at being wives, mothers, and mistresses of the family were married women of means. When Enlightenment feminists spoke of an exodus of men from the household even at the turn of the nineteenth century, it was not of an exodus of shopkeepers, manufacturers, or tradesmen that they spoke. The men they described as having occupations that took them away from home were professional men (doctors, lawyers, and such), military men, men in public office, and above all, members of the gentry, aristocracy, and moneyed ranks whose gallantries

— or preoccupation with horses, dogs, drinking, and gambling — led them to neglect their families and spend their time elsewhere. Enlightenment feminists were addressing the idle, well-to-do, pleasure-seeking wives of such men when they called on ladies to withdraw from their pursuit of pleasure, their flirtations, and their dissipations, in order to work in their households at being mothers, wives, and mistresses of the family. When they addressed the wives of merchants, shopkeepers, manufacturers, and such, they gave quite different advice: they told the wives of such men to be sure to learn bookkeeping and whatever skills they needed to make themselves their husband's indispensable partners at work and to run the business alone in the event of their husband's demise.

Both feminisms sought to "restore the female character to its dignity and independence" by urging reasonably well-to-do wives in the middling and upper ranks to undertake those domestic offices which were said to promote the public good. They wanted married ladies to demonstrate through their domestic work that "women are not so despicable as Men would have them believe themselves" and that women could "by their abilities and virtues exact respect."[81] Especially in reference to women, we today hear these words — *dignity* and *respectability* — with the negative and rather piddling connotations that they eventually obtained by association with the conduct that Victorians recommended as their merely outward marks: a certain stateliness or formality, a certain propriety of appearance and behavior. But when Enlightenment feminists spoke of dignifying women, they meant enabling women to acquire "true worth and excellence"; and when they spoke of making women respectable, they meant "worthy of respect."[82]

To Enlightenment feminists, "dignity" and "respect-ability" were still male, rather than female, attributes: "Men exclude us from that power and dignity which we have a right to share with them" and "deny us the equality of esteem which is our due."[83] Dignity and respectability were attributes that men possessed by virtue of their reason or their rank or, in the upwardly mobile middling ranks, as a result of their demonstrated abilities and virtues: "Abilities and virtues are absolutely necessary to raise men from the middle ranks to notice, and the natural consequence is notorious; the middle rank contains most virtue and abilities . . . but the whole female sex are in the same condition as the rich."[84] If women wanted to share men's dignity, feminists reasoned, they too must develop "abilities and virtues" which would "raise" them in their own eyes and in the eyes of men.

To dignify their sex and make it worthy of respect, therefore, Matriarchs and Egalitarians espoused for ladies in the upper and middling ranks the Protestant, "middle class" work ethic of advancing oneself by one's virtues and abilities. They taught ladies that by reconceiving their diverse *roles as women* as *professional work* — work requiring reason, ability, education, effort, persistence, virtues, and specialized knowledges — ladies could demonstrate their solid ability and worth against those who argued that wives were helpless and useless creatures, capable perhaps of performing household duties as their husbands' "upper servants" but incapable of all the more important and publicly valued offices of domestic government.

The division of labor that preoccupied both Enlightenment feminisms, and constituted an area of debate among women and of dispute between women and men, lay not between the household and the workplace or between the public and the private spheres, *but within the domestic arena itself.* Men made a distinction in the household between "domestic Offices" (such as domestic government and the government and education of children), which were designed to be the province of the master of the family, and "household duties," which could be left to fond mothers and foolish wives to carry out under the direction of their husbands. Domestic offices were placed on a par with civil offices, and like civil offices, they were said to be beyond women's abilities and outside their jurisdiction: "There are many household duties for which nature has not qualified the man; and many Offices, both domestick and civil, whereof women are not capable. In a word, the two sexes are natural associates, feminine weakness being compensated by masculine strength."[85]

Women were said to be dependent on men for the performance of those domestic offices they were said to be incapable of performing for themselves and their children, and the assistance that men were required to render women and children by their domestic offices in turn constituted an argument for the legitimacy of men's "uncontroll'd indisputable power and superiority" over women: "To do good in any kind, by Money, Councel and Assistance, by Favour or Authority, does naturally give Men an uncontroll'd indisputable Power and Superiority; the Benefactor will always be uppermost in Praise and Honour and Esteem of all that see and know, as well as of such that feel his Goodness."[86] "Uncontroll'd indisputable Power and Superiority" over women, children, and dependents was the reward Enlightenment ideologues proposed to private men for performing their domestic offices for the public good.

The corrolary to this was that conduct books for women written by men urged women to eschew all exercise of power over men, however subtle and indirect, and to do all they could to ensure that men remained "uppermost in Praise and Honour and Esteem." William Duff, for instance, pointed out in 1783 — while conciliating ladies by agreeing that they might indeed be rational beings and companions to their husbands — that "there are many of our sex, who though sound Whigs in their political principles, retain a little tincture of Jacobinism in their principles of domestic government; and how much soever they detest those exploded doctrines of passive obedience and non-resistance in the government of the State, they are not for excluding them altogether in the government of their households."[87] Though distancing himself from these harsher measures, Duff himself insisted that wives demonstrate that meekness, obedience, and "subordination of the gentler sex to their male companions, which results from their different constitutions both mental and corporeal"; and he argued, on the basis of this difference in constitution, that while a wife might be usefully employed "in the management of her family concerns," she must "beware of claiming or exercising a *governing* power."[88]

Gisbourne makes the same point: "Whatever may be the influence which the amiable virtues of a wife may obtain over her husband, let not the consciousness of it ever lead her to seek opportunities of displaying it nor cherish a wish to intrude into those departments which belong not to her jurisdiction."[89] Women were instructed to leave to their husbands undisputed charge of all those "departments" of domestic life which were dignified with the title of "domestic Offices" and compared to civil offices in the state. Conduct books for women written by men urged women to adopt behavior emphasizing their complete dependence on the superior judgment and abilities of men; they even instructed women to conceal their abilities and attainments in order to make themselves appear even more helpless, meek, and dependent than they were.

Enlightenment feminists saw this division of labor within the family between domestic offices and household duties as perpetuating women's supposedly "natural" inferiority and subordination to the government of men, and as detrimental to their domestic happiness as well as to their "respect-ability." Matriarchs and Egalitarians both thought that it was by the "tyranny" and "vices" of their domestic governors that most women were primarily oppressed: "The calamities of an unhappy marriage are so much greater than can befal a single person, that the unmarried woman may find abundant argument to be contented with her condition, when pointed out to her by Providence." "A greater share of care, perplexity, pain and sorrow belong to the matron than to the spinster."[90] Difficult and frustrating as it might have been in the latter half of the eighteenth century to be "women of superior cast [who] have not a road open by which they can pursue more extensive plans of usefulness and independence," it was infinitely worse for a woman to be "the upper servant of her husband," and "the sport of the vices and infirmities of her Tyrant."[91]

It was this division of labor within the family between domestic offices and household duties, and between domestic government and domestic employments, that Enlightenment feminists were tackling when they advised ladies to take over "the proper government of our families" and proposed an *as yet ideal and idealized division of labor* between private woman and public man as a way of improving the domestic and social lot of ladies in the middle and upper ranks. The division of labor which both feminisms proposed and promoted was later naturalized as the doctrine of "separate spheres." Conventional and constraining as this might later have become, at the end of the eighteenth century, it represented what Kathryn Sutherland calls "a revolutionary appropriation of the family unit" by women.[92] And the debate among women was still about how it might be brought about.

Matriarchs saw the removal of professional men and idle gentlemen from the household — and any reluctance on their part to undertake the role of "nursing Fathers" which the Enlightenment's politicized family ideology and fictional typologies were urging on men — as an opportunity for ladies to step in and take over that domestic territory themselves. Matriarchs therefore preached unilateral female action: ladies must, they insisted, work at being faithful wives, capable mothers, and conscientious mistresses of the family, *regardless* of whether their spouses were faithful husbands and conscientious fathers and governors or not. As far as the Matriarchs were concerned, the fact that men thought it necessary to exert their efforts abroad was even something to be encouraged; the family as workplace was not a place to be shared. It was a place to be appropriated by ladies as "a special sphere of female action."[93] And while, like Hester Chapone, recognizing that "the due regulation of a family" is "seldom the wife's province, and that many men do not choose even to acquaint her with the real state of their affairs," Matriarchs continued to urge ladies to take charge of the domestic economy and of the family's "general plan of domestic government."[94]

Men's analogy between the performance of domestic and civil offices was central to the Matriarchal argument here: for instance, when Hannah More urged ladies to take over government of the family by working with the "same spirit of perseverance in the home, which the father thinks it necessary to be exerting abroad in his public duty or professional engagement."[95] It was also evident when she constructed women's work in the family as a profession on a par with men's professions in civil society: "Most men are commonly destined to some profession, and their minds are consequently turned each to its respective object . . . The profession of ladies, to which the bent of *their* instruction should be turned, is that of daughters, wives, mothers, and mistresses of families."[96] Matriarchs assured ladies that they would not merely be performing "household duties" — there would be servants for the merely menial tasks. For ladies, the profession of mother, wife, and mistress of a family would be a branch of government, for ladies would be performing those domestic offices, which consisted of governing children, servants, and the domestic economy to their good:

> Economy, such as a woman of fortune is called to practice, is not merely the petty detail of small daily expenses, the shabby curtailing and stinted parsimony of a little mind operating upon little concerns; but it is exercise of sound judgement exerted in the comprehensive outline of order, of arrangement, of distribution, of regulation, by which alone well-governed societies, great and small, subsist. She who has the best regulated mind will, other things being equal, have the best regulated family.[97]

The profession of ladies as mothers and mistresses of families would be equal in dignity to the professions of men, not only because ladies would govern those "departments" of domestic life which Enlightenment ideology constructed as significant enough to assign to men, but also because, like men's professions in civil society, the profession of ladies required superior intellectual abilities, superior personal qualities, and specialized knowledge.

Matriarchs also provided ladies with a specific and carefully worked out program of action: their conduct books and novels instructed ladies in the profession they were proposing to them and taught ladies how to behave and what they needed to know to be the sort of mothers, wives, and mistresses of families the Matriarchs envisioned.

Matriarchs rewrote the role of mother of a family as its governess or teacher.[98] They made her responsible, not only for her children's physical well-being and moral and religious education, but also for "instruct[ing] her family in every branch of useful or ornamental knowledge."[99] The mother-as-governess was no sweet, meek, and pliant creature: "A mother whose displeasure is not feared is never really loved," said Jane West. "She becomes a nonentity and nothing can be so detrimental to domestic good government as maternal insignificance."[100]

There was little danger of maternal insignificance, however, for mother-governesses who understood their powers. If children were "a source of wealth" to the nation, and if those children were born *tabula rasa* as Locke had argued, then education alone made them whatever they became. "By opposite tendencies of education," wrote Maria Edgeworth, "opposite characters from the same original disposition are produced."[101] By choosing the tendency of her children's education and by taking charge of their instruction herself, a mother-governess could make of them whatever she would.

Matriarchs had long argued that mothers were better suited than men to the education of children. When Locke had made fathers and male governors and tutors responsible for the new "rational" and enlightened method of educating children — by getting them to internalize principles and develop virtuous habits — writers like Lady Damaris Masham argued against his *Thoughts on Education,* saying that it was more "natural" for women to perform these educative offices:

Since the Affairs either of Men's Callings, or of their private Estates, or the Service of their Country . . . allow them not the leisure to look daily after the Education of their Children; and that otherwise also they are naturally less capable than Women of that Complaisance and Tenderness which the right Instruction and Direction of that Age requires . . . this so necessary a work of forming betimes the Minds of Children so as to dispose them to be hereafter Wise and Vertuous Men and Women, cannot but be performed by Mothers only.[102]

Bathsua Makin had used biblical precedent to make the same point: "None have so great an advantage of making most deep impression on their Children as Mothers. What a prudent and virtuous Mother commends by Precept and Example sticks long; witness Lemuel and his Proverbs, many of which he suckt with his Mother's Milk."

A century later, therefore, when public policy and Enlightenment ideologues were outlining the public benefits of education and debating the relative virtues of educating children at home or in schools, Matriarchs had only to iterate and modernize their predecessors' arguments. To be fully effective, Matriarchs argued, education had to be carefully adapted to the particular disposition, situation, and destination (professional or other) of each individual pupil; and mothers, who knew their children better than anyone else and cared for each child, and who had fewer children to educate than a teacher in a school, were better equipped than either schools or tutors to adapt their teaching to the needs and abilities of each child — even if they had less formal knowledge and education than a father or tutor.

But it was on the acknowledged public benefit of domestic education that these latter-day Matriarchs really set their sights. In refurbishing their predecessors' arguments, they were careful to point out that as educator-in-chief of her family, a mother-governess acquired real power, or as Hannah More put it, "acknowledged power: a power wide in its extent, indefinite in its effects and inestimable in its importance."[103] Through the power she exercised in her own little kingdom to fashion the character, principles, and habits of the rising generation like a demi-god, a mother-governess determined the manners, habits, values, and beliefs of England itself: "On YOU depend in no small degree the principles of the whole rising generation . . . To YOU is made over the awful important trust of infusing the first principles of piety into the tender minds of those who may one day be called to instruct not families merely, but senates. Your private exertions may at this moment be contributing to the future happiness, your domestic neglect to the future ruin, of your country."[104]

It was this wider power over society which Matriarchs urged mothers to recognize, to seize, and to exercise by taking charge of their children's education. As Clara Reeve said: "Nothing is of equal consequence to the health of a state as the education of Youth . . . Education is the source from which Manners proceed . . . There is no kind of schooling equal to that Instruction which children receive at home under a virtuous and well-informed mother, who gives up her time and abilities to care for them."[105]

Toni Bowers has shown that "Augustan representations of maternity" were "most often representations of failed authority and abdicated responsibility."[106] And it is against such representations of maternal failure, rather than against our contemporary cultural construction of maternal nurturing and education as "natural" to women, that Matriarchal representations of the respectable mother-governess should be read. Matriarchs were countering cultural images of maternal failure, as well as philosophical, political, and fictional images of nursing fathers using their authority and "natural tenderness" to successfully guide their children's education. In this discursive context, the exemplum of the mother-governess can be said to have been dignifying and empowering to women. One might add, however, that Matriarchs themselves were often spinsters, who had spent at least some of their lives, before turning to writing, as teachers of other women's children; and from this point of view, the projection onto mothers of their own "professional" roles as teachers and governesses might be said to mark the self-dignifying limits of their imagination.

Like male ideologues who argued that every private gentleman contributed to the public good by governing his domestics, tenants, and immediate community and by giving charity to his needy neighbours, Matriarchs insisted that the effectiveness of the mother-governess as educator and contributor to the public good extended far beyond her children — to her servants, to tenants and villagers on the family estate, to the poor, and to all those other family societies with which she came into contact: "In our relative situation, as mothers and mistresses of families, we possess so much influence, that if we were uniformly to exert it in the manner which the times require, we might produce a most happy change in the morals of the people . . . Such a change would conduce more to extricate us from our present difficulties than the wisdom of our counsellors or the valour of our fleets and armies."[107] Matriarchs taught that as mistress-governess of her household, a matron who consistently rewarded merit and combated immorality could reeducate slatterly or dissipated servants and make them industrious, frugal, honest, and modest. They told ladies that by working among the lower orders, especially on the family estate, the mistress of an affluent or high-ranking family could reeducate the lower orders to industry and virtue, perform essential public works, and cement the different classes each to each.

Matriarchs wanted ladies, through their work, to make societies great and small not only more Christian (and therefore more virtuous) and more industrious and frugal (and thus more prosperous) but also more closely cemented. They shared the assumption of male ideologues that societies both domestic and national were "glued together" by mutual dependencies: "The very frame and being of societies, whether great or small, public or private, is joined and glued together by dependence. Those attachments which arise from and are compacted by a sense of mutual wants, mutual affection, mutual benefit and mutual obligation, are the cement which secures the union of the family as well as the state."[108] If Matriarchs set their faces so firmly against profligacy and dissipation, therefore, it was not only for good Christian reasons. It was also because they thought that profligacy and dissipation in fashionable society and in the ranks that imitated it destroyed those cementing attachments and mutual dependencies in the family and in the state on which the stability of Britain's hierarchical order depended.

This is also why Matriarchs argued, in the wake of the French Revolution, that as long as the upper ranks continued to devote themselves to their fashionable pleasures, absenting themselves from their estates and ignoring the "obligations" of their rank towards "those whom Providence, in the distribution of human lots, have placed under their immediate protection," popular disaffection would grow. The large caste of servants, the peasantry, and the manufacturing ranks were already, they said, developing "the too general prejudice" that "lords and ladies are but poor creatures, were it not that they have got the upper hand in this world," and complaining that these creatures who led useless or infamous lives and cared for no one but themselves should not be "*permitted* to possess wealth."[109] Profligacy, luxury, and dissipation in the upper ranks thus fostered a dangerously "democratical spirit" in the lower ranks of society which, after the unfortunate example of the French Revolution, threatened to unglue the social hierarchy and unseat Britain's aristocratic and monarchical government yet again.

Matriarchs taught that it would be the "glory" of ladies to reform society by discouraging profligacy and dissipation, by mitigating through their public works the evils afflicting the deserving poor, and by "befriending" their inferiors in the proper spirit of "affability and condescension" in order to inspire them with such affection, loyalty, and admiration as would save hierarchical society from itself. They told private ladies in the middling and upper ranks that they had a duty to "conciliate and attach the lower orders" by showing "a kind remembrance of their wants, an affectionate concern for their welfare, and a desire to promote their real interests."[110] And, as we will see in the next chapter, in their novels, they exemplified the superiority of the mistress of a family's performance of these public functions over the master's.

Philanthropy as the Matriarchs conceived it was therefore not a marginal or apolitical pastime; it was a "beneficent" act of government to be undertaken by wealthy ladies, well-to-do ladies, and genteel ladies with small competencies for the public good. Beth Fowkes Tobin has argued that Matriarchs like Hannah More were among those who "championed the emergent middle class's right to superintend the poor" by new "capitalist" and Foucauldian methods of regulation and surveillance and that this was part of a "battle" by the middle class against the hegemony of the landed classes with their old face-to-face "paternal system of charity."[111] But what is most striking about the Matriarchs' position in these terms is that their construction of the mother and mistress of a family borrowed *both* from the regulating middle-class manager *and* from the beneficent patriarch. Matriarchs joined the "paternal relation of duty and dependence" and the face-to-face charity of the old landed paternalism to the regulatory practices of the new professional middle-class male economic managers, in order at once to displace the old patriarchal government of family, villagers, and tenants and to preserve it in women's more competent hands.[112] Matriarchs thus worked to cement in the impoverished ranks of society a hierarchical subordination of men and women which they were also subverting and inverting for classes of women more like themselves.[113]

To "dignify" ladies by enabling them to demonstrate that they could contribute to the public good by their government of others, Matriarchs constructed well-to-do ladies as the "domestic governors" and "philanthropic" educators and reformers of their children, servants, and social or economic inferiors. By appropriating for private ladies the domestic and charitable offices that Enlightenment ideologues had assigned to private gentlemen, the Matriarchal imaginary carved out for ladies a position in family society superior to that of "upper servants" to their husbands and improved their domestic lot. As Mitzi Myers has said, as far as they were concerned, "virtue and usefulness justif[ied] assertion, activity, responsibility; ultimately doing good even confer[red] power."[114] But, as Elizabeth Langland has shown, this also introduced a class division into the household.[115] Displaced, the difference between household duties and domestic offices that once marked a hierarchical difference between women and men became a hierarchical mark of distinction among women of different ranks in the same domestic economy.[116] If dignifying themselves by appropriating the governing and regulatory domestic offices to themselves has laid Matriarchs open to modern charges that they acted as agents of discipline and punishment for the hegemonic ideology,[117] it laid them open in the eighteenth century to Egalitarian condemnation of their will to power and to Egalitarian caricature as petty domestic tyrants and mean-spirited tormentors of their children, domestics, and dependents.

Disconcertingly perhaps, the Egalitarians agreed with the Matriarchs both about the substance and about the importance of married ladies' maternal and domestic roles. As Anne Mellor says, even Wollstonecraft "advocated 'family politics' as a political program that would radically transform the public sphere."[118] Egalitarians agreed with Matriarchs that the circumstances of fashionable life undermined family society and the public good and that "attention to children and family ought to be the prominent feature in the character and employment of every woman who has children and families to attend to."[119] If anything, the Egalitarians extended the maternal role. A mother, they said, must not only be firm and educated enough to instruct her children, form their moral character, "inspire a love of home and of domestic pleasures," and prepare future citizens for their roles in society at large. She must also nurse and raise her own children herself — "a wife in the present state of things who neither suckles nor educates her own children scarcely deserves the name of wife, and has no right to that of citizen," said Mary Wollstonecraft.[120] A wife and mother must also have enough knowledge of anatomy and medicine not only to look after her own health but also to be a "rational nurse" and diagnostician for all the members of her household.[121]

There are, however, important differences between the Egalitarians and the Matriarchs about ladies maternal and domestic roles, which become most evident when they seem to agree most closely. In the passage that follows, for instance, Wollstonecraft is accepting — not only in principle, but also as some sort of ideal — a division of labor between men and women which makes work in and on family society a sphere of properly female action. Like the Matriarchs, she is presenting men's work in civil society and women's work in family society as equally demanding jobs of equal value to society:

> Society will at some time or other be so constituted that while he was employed in any of the departments of civil life, his wife, also an active citizen, should be equally intent to manage her family, educate her children and assist her needy neighbours.[122]

But Wollstonecraft differs from the Matriarchs on two crucial points.

First, in Wollstonecraft's imaginary, the lady managing her family, educating her children and assisting her needy neighbor is no one's "mistress" — not the mistress of her family, not the mistress of her servants or subordinates in the social order, and (Wollstonecraft is very firm about this) not a mistress to her husband. Nor has she taken command of what is still officially her husband's department of domestic life by default, stealth, or guile. The lady managing her family, educating her children, and assisting her neighbors, in Wollstonecraft's imaginary, is an independent, patriotic, fully active voting citizen, just like her husband, who inhabits a rationally constituted society in which a particular division of labor prevails and in which women are doing one of society's equally necessary and valued jobs. Thus, where the Matriarchs sought to persuade ladies individually to take over the government of their families and to supply their husbands' place, Wollstonecraft displaces responsibility for this change in domestic government from individual women to society and from the family to the state. She expects "society" to be "so organized" as to "compel" men and women to "freely" perform their respective duties in this division of labor between women in the family and men in civil life: "Society is not properly organized which does not compel men and women to discharge their respective duties by making it the only way to acquire the countenance from their fellow creatures which every human being wishes in some way to attain."[123]

The pressure here is not only social but also political, for Wollstonecraft expects the state to be governed in such a way as to make it in each person's rational interest to perform her or his respective duties in the family or in the state. Wollstonecraft's ideal society is therefore not at all the anarchical and immoral space that her eighteenth-century and early-nineteenth-century detractors pretended it was: "A truly benevolent legislator always endeavours to make it in the interest of each individual to be virtuous; and thus private virtue becoming the cement of public happiness, an orderly whole is consolidated by the tendency of all parts towards a common centre."[124] There is that word *cement* again, but this time it indicates that for her, as for Godwin, the cement of societies, domestic or political, is not a hierarchical relation of dependence — as Matriarchs and patriarchal Enlightenment ideologues supposed — but the independent performance of duties and of virtuous actions by citizens who share a common social and political goal.

The difference between what Matriarchs meant by dependence and what Wollstonecraft meant by "independence" therefore has less to do with *what* is done than with *how* it is to be done, for doing one's duty relative to one's family and to society is what Wollstonecraft means by "independence": "The being who discharges the duties of its station is independent."[125] The difference is only that people who are independent are *free* to do their duty as reason and interest dictate for the common good, as opposed to being bound to dependence and obedience to a superior's commands. For Wollstonecraft, if this condition is met, a woman can be as independent and worthy of respect as a mother and wife in a division of labor that gives her the domestic offices and her husband the civic offices to perform, as her husband can be when performing his civic offices in the same independent way:

> The maternal solicitude of a reasonable affectionate woman is very interesting, and the chastened dignity with which a mother returns the caresses that she and her child receive from a father who has been fulfilling the serious duties of his station, is not only a respectable, but a beautiful sight . . . I have viewed with pleasure a woman nursing her children, and discharging the duties of her station . . . I have thought that a couple of this description, equally necessary and independent of each other, because each fulfilled the respective duties of their station, possessed of all that life could give.[126]

For Wollstonecraft, as for Locke, Hutcheson, Ferguson, and Jane West, freedom is not a matter of doing whatever one pleases but of "the security that others shall not do as they please to you." And Wollstonecraft's concept of independence turns out to be synonymous with self-government — the right to govern oneself as the laws of reason, right, and duty require without the intermediary of any person. Wollstonecraft merely extends the scope of women's self-government from matters bearing on their own individual minds, consciences, and life choices to all those "duties" to others in the family which constitute government of the domestic sphere.

Wollstonecraft's second crucial difference from the Matriarchs' position is that she projects that division of labor which makes domestic government women's work onto some indeterminate time in the future: "Society will at some time or other be so constituted . . ." Egalitarian feminists did not envision the division of labor between public man and private woman as a goal attainable in their present as the Matriarchs did, because for them everything in society was so interconnected and interdependent that nothing in society could change until everything was changed. Egalitarians argued that ladies could not be expected to become faithful wives, devoted mothers, and conscientious mistresses of their families until men became faithful husbands, devoted fathers, and conscientious masters of their families: "Faithless husbands will make faithless wives," said Wollstonecraft; and "till men become attentive to the duty of a father, it is vain to expect women to spend that time in the nursery which they now choose to spend at their glass."[127] "While a man is squandering his fortune at the gaming house or on the turf . . . can he reasonably expect that his wife will dedicate her time to domestic drudgeries at home?" asked Mary Hays. Wives would change their behavior when husbands changed theirs, and husbands would change their behavior when wives changed theirs. As Catherine Macauley said, "till both are reformed, there is no expecting excellence of either."[128] To change the status quo, "both sexes must act from the same principle."[129]

At the same time, since men and women could not help "being educated to a great degree by the opinions and manners of the society they lived in," it was evident to the Egalitarians at the end of the eighteenth century that "till society be differently constituted, much cannot be expected from education."[130] Men's and women's principles and conduct would be altered only when they could be educated and acculturated differently, and they could be educated and acculturated differently only when society was constituted differently. Freedom would be nothing but a convenient British political fiction as long as the old feudal-hierarchical institutions remained in place, and women could not expect to act as independent governors of their families as long as hierarchy, obedience, and proper subordination remained the organizing principles of government and of societies great and small. For the Egalitarians, therefore, nothing could really change for women in their domestic situations until everything was changed: there would have to be a revolution to scrap society and start again.

While the Matriarchs proposed that women gradually change their families, society, and their lot within both by reeducation and by acting unilaterally to take over the domestic offices that public ideology still assigned to men, the Egalitarians argued that "much could not be expected from education" and that without reconstituting society from the ground up, there was no real practicable way forward. While the Matriarchs told ladies to positively encourage their husbands to pursue their interests away from home and to take full advantage of men's reluctance to devote themselves to their domestic offices, in order to take over "the proper government of our families" from men, the Egalitarians vindicated women's rights and wrote appeals to the men of Great Britain. And while the Matriarchs plotted out exactly what each lady could do, at once, by herself, to better her own domestic and social lot, the Egalitarians made it clear that even the changes they proposed in the patriarchal family depended on women's securing the acquiescence and willing cooperation of men.

If ladies distanced themselves from Wollstonecraft and the Egalitarians at the turn of the nineteenth century, therefore, it was not only, or not so much, because Matriarchs — in what was certainly not their finest hour — managed to identify Egalitarians with sexual immorality and with the destabilizing excesses of the French Revolution. It was also, and perhaps primarily, because the Egalitarians offered them no way forward. They gave ladies no immediately practicable program of action and no relief from their position as upper servants of their husbands.

As we saw in Chapters 1 and 2, both in the political and feminist debates of the eighteenth century and in the novel's fictional representations of exemplary families, whatever sketch of the family one represented as "natural" or as "virtuous" remained a crucial emblem for one's concept of the polity as a whole. As Francis Hutcheson put it, although "parental power" could no longer be considered "the foundation of the civil," it remained "a natural sketch and emblem of it."[131] Women novelists could therefore deploy fictional images of propertied families imbricated with their localities as what Burke called so many "little images of the great country" to represent and debate "the public uses of private families" which have been discussed here. More particularly, in their rewritings of Rousseau, they used their images of the family and their emplotments of domestic life to exemplify and compare — or to question and critique — the effectiveness of competing forms of patriarchal and matriarchal domestic government. They also used their exempla of the family and their emplotments of domestic life to raise issues bearing on the "public Good" as much as on women's lives.

5

Governing Utopias and
the Feminist Rousseau

Government, in its very principle, deduces its primary origin from family rule . . . States and nations are but families upon a larger scale. — THOMAS DUTTON, 1802

CITING MME. DE GENLIS, Clara Reeve pointed out that Rousseau's great achievement had been to popularize Locke.[1] And indeed, when *Julie, ou la Nouvelle Héloïse* and *Emile, ou Traité de l'Education* were first translated into English by William Kendrick in the early 1760s, Rousseau was — quite rightly — read by the enlightened male establishment in England as a proponent and imitative translator of their own, Lockean, family romance. While Voltaire in France called *Héloïse* "a silly book," the *Critical Review* in England said that it provided "the most enchanting description of conjugal life and pastoral happiness ever written," and the *London Chronicle* gave its readers eight excerpts describing "the domestic economy" at Clarens.[2] And while *Emile* was being burned by the common hangman in Paris as dangerously innovative stuff, the *Critical Review* praised the book for "throwing new light on subjects which have been thought exhausted," and the *London Magazine* published nineteen excerpts of Book 5 to illustrate the compatibilities necessary for a successful marriage and the proper education for prospective wives.[3]

By the end of the century, however, Rousseau was being excoriated by Burke, or lionized by the canonical male Romantics, as an egalitarian and (deliciously) dangerous revolutionary; and Hannah More was blaming the fact that many eighteenth-century English novels had become "dangerously democratical" on translations of foreign authors, and more particularly of Rousseau: "Incredible pains have been taken to obtain translations of every book which was supposed likely to be of use in corrupting the heart and misleading the understanding . . . [Novels] are at once employed to defuse destructive politics, deplorable profligacy and impudent infidelity. Rousseau was the first popular dispenser of this complicated drug."[4] In a gesture that was repeated by historians on both sides of the Channel for almost three hundred years, this conveniently made egalitarianism a foreign import and Rousseau the originator and bearer into England of revolutionary, democratic, and republican ideas. Rousseau's versions of Locke thus came to figure as originals, and Rousseau, the patriarchal translator and elaborator of the Enlighteners' patriarchal family romance, came to figure as a dangerously democratic leveler of hierarchies and persons.

This curious transformation of Rousseau in England from establishment patriarch in the 1760s to revolutionary leveler in the 1790s undoubtedly owes more than we remember to the impact at the end of the eighteenth century of "dangerously democratical" women novelists like Inchbald, Smith, Radcliffe, Fenwick, Williams, Wollstonecraft, and Hays, who rewrote Rousseau as an egalitarian and whose positions came to be mistaken for his.[5] The impact of these women's work has been papered over by repetitions of the story about Rousseau's quarrel with Hume and British men of letters during his visit to England and of the story about the French Revolutionary Assembly's tribute to him, which was constructed by British conservatives during the revolutionary decade. In the 1790s, demonizing Jean-Jacques — the vulgar little foreigner that no one had liked — helped to shore up Britain's aristocratic and hierarchical society against the reimportation of her own republican revolution and the recurrence of civil war; and for Matriarchs, it conveniently erased the impact of their Egalitarian rivals, while tarring the latter with Julie's profligacy and the Savoyard Vicar's heretical brush.

Even in the 1790s, however, this conservative British story about Rousseau as a dangerous leveler had only the slenderest basis in fact. *The Social Contract,* arguably Rousseau's only egalitarian text, had virtually no readership in England during the latter half of the eighteenth century, as Edward Duffy, among others, has pointed out.[6] During the decades when Rousseau was being transformed from a proponent of benevolent patriarchal family values into a dangerous revolutionary, England's knowledge of Rousseau consisted of his most conventionally patriarchal writings: the *First and Second Discourses, Héloïse,* and *Emile.* And, in attacking Rousseau as a dangerous leveler of traditional feudal hierarchies in his *Letter to a*

Member of the National Assembly in 1791, even Burke could still find nothing to say against the "domestic economy" of Clarens or the patriarchal education of Emile and Sophie. Burke bases his entire case for Rousseau's
revolutionary "egalitarianism" on Saint-Preux's desire to marry Julie while
a domestic in her father's house — an event in fact foiled in Rousseau's
novel by L'Etange's reassertion of paternal authority and by the transfer of
property in the estate at Clarens and of property in Julie between l'Etange,
the old-style patriarch, and Wolmar, his rational and "benevolently" patriarchal heir. As Nicola Watson has shown, it was also this first half of *Héloïse* that created the framework for those Matriarchal readings and novelistic rewritings of Rousseau at the turn of the nineteenth century, in
which, like Burke, the authors sought to identify "the plot of revolution"
with "the plot of female seduction" and with anarchic private sensibility, in
order to suppress both.[7]

We can hear Hannah More and the conservative backlash at the turn of
the nineteenth century with another ear, however, if we recall that in the
1760s and 1770s Matriarchs like Frances Brooke, Sarah Scott, and Lady
Mary Hamilton had been among the first to rewrite Rousseau,[8] and that
during the revolutionary decade, when leveling rewritings of Rousseau began to proliferate, Egalitarians were critiquing Rousseau for not being radical enough. For women writers at each of these different junctures, Rousseau's usefulness lay not only in the popularity and familiarity of his plots[9]
but also in the fact that he had conveniently narrativized Locke's politico-
historical argument about the natural origin of society and government in
the patriarchal family, while fleshing out for the imagination at Clarens
the British male establishment's mid-century idyll of paternalistic good
order and benevolent domestic government. Transposing British prejudices about woman's inferiority into his natural utopias, Rousseau had
also presented her domestic subjection in the patriarchal family, total
dependence on men for her needs and wants, and willing submission to
men's injustice and cruelty as "the natural woman's" naturally designated
lot. Denying women reason, learning, and an education comparable to
Emile's, Rousseau argued that nature's assignation of childbearing to
women made marriage their only destination, pleasing and serving men
their only goal, household duties their only suitable occupation, and restraint of their own wishes, passions, and desires their most distinctive and
admirable virtue. Wollstonecraft used her critique of Rousseau in *Vindica-*

tion of the Rights of Woman to underline the affinities between Rousseau's expectations of women and those of influential and much reprinted British male conduct book writers like Gregory, Fordyce, and Lord Chesterfield.[10] It was precisely the affinity between the benevolent patriarchal ideals of England's enlightened male establishment and Rousseau's utopian fictions which made the latter such a convenient butt for British Egalitarians and Matriarchs. By foregrounding the reference of their own novels to Rousseau's French narratives, Matriarchs in the 1760s and 1770s and Egalitarians in the revolutionary decade could mask their attacks on English patriarchal prescriptions for the family, the polity, and women's conduct; and by rewriting Rousseau's novels otherwise, they could disseminate their own views of the family, the polity, and women's social and familial situations in their place.

We can hear Hannah More's observations about importing "dangerously democratical" translations with another ear too, if we recall that throughout the long eighteenth century there had been considerable two-way traffic between England and France both in interlinear translations and in imitations of novels and philosophical tracts.[11] Translations on both sides of the Channel ranged from the more or less exact to the more or less allusive. Interlinear translators thought nothing of omitting whole portions of imported texts, of changing endings, or of adding entire sections of their own. "Imitations" and paraphrases of foreign novels were still considered a species of translation, and writers used "the freedom of the translator" to "embellish and perfect" foreign works by rewriting them and adapting them to the different tastes and different social and political circumstances of their target audience. Alongside interlinear translations of foreign novels like *Héloïse* and *Emile,* therefore, there was also a host of "popularizations" and more or less allusive imitations. The more allusive imitations of *Julie, ou la Nouvelle Héloïse,* like Frances Brooke's *Lady Julia Mandeville* (1763), Helen Maria Williams's *Julia* (1790), and Charlotte Smith's *Montalbert* (1795) and *Desmond* (1792), adapted or transposed the characters and altered the story line. The less allusive imitations, like Scott's *Millenium Hall* (1762) and Lady Mary Hamilton's *Munster Village* (1778), appropriated Clarens, Rousseau's image of a model pastoral domestic economy in retreat from society, and perfected it according to their lights; or, like Mary Hays's *The Victim of Prejudice* (1799) and Eliza Fenwick's *Secresy* (1795), they joined elements borrowed from *Emile* (1762) to elements borrowed from *Héloïse* (1761). Since excerpts from *Héloïse* were also presented in the English periodicals in such a way as to set up an opposition between pastoral natural happiness and society that was "even starker than might be discerned in the novel itself,"[12] Matriarchal novels like Frances Brooke's *The Excursion* (1777) or Jane West's *A Gossip's Story* (1797) and Egalitarian novels like Radcliffe's *Romance of the Forest,* Inchbald's *Nature and Art,* or Charlotte Smith's *Marchmont* (1796), which contrast utopian natural scenes of domestic happiness with scenes of fashionable depravity and social injustice, can also be said to have been written "after the manner of Rousseau." As a result, "the logic of Rousseau's plot came to inform much of the discourse stimulated by the Revolution in England, to the point where even the most passing allusion to its heroine, Julie, might operate as a convenient shorthand," as Nicola Watson has pointed out.[13]

An effect of multiple translations, transpositions, imitations, citations, critiques, and rewritings, "Rousseau" thus became a *topos* where women's differences from each other and from their male counterparts could be inscribed, explored, and debated and where Enlightenment feminists themselves could "shed new light on subjects which had been thought exhausted." Exploring some facets of this "feminist Rousseau" will bring out their differences, their critiques of each other, and their respective designs to ameliorate the domestic, social, and political status quo.

Rousseau and Utopian Matriarchal Fictions

In considering the prehistory of the "domestic novel," let us recall that Locke's politico-historical argument in *Two Treatises on Government* in fact offered *two* origins and foundations for society: the social contract and the family. Rousseau, working on his imitative translations from Pierre Coste's already incomplete interlinear translation,[14] had therefore only to fracture Locke's politico-historical narrative into two alternate versions of itself by splitting it at its fault lines. While stressing the opposition between natural equality and social inequality that Locke had papered over, Rousseau highlighted the disparity between Locke's two accounts of the origin and foundation of society by treating them as separate stories in separate texts. Rousseau "embellished and perfected" each — the compactual origin in *The Social Contract,* and the familial origin in *Héloïse* and *Emile.* Thus, in the parlance of his fellow eighteenth-century French translators, Rousseau "extracted from the English [Locke] a French

[Locke] agreeable to" his target nation so that his text could be "read with interest without thinking about whether it is an original or a copy";[15] and he did so by using "the freedom of the translator" to "break the shell" of Locke's *Treatises* "into many pieces"[16] and by adapting each to the different political circumstances of his French audience.[17]

Using the Bible and other ancient writings, as we saw, Locke had placed the patriarchal family at the beginning of recorded history and at the beginning of his text because he was arguing, after a long civil war and as a prelude and foundation to the Revolutionary Settlement, that society could be reconstructed and legitimized in the present by returning to its pattern and origin in the benevolent patriarchal family. Headed by a "nursing father, tender and careful of the public weal" in the person of King William, "our great Preserver," this benevolent patriarchal family was to be the Glorious Revolution's alternative and corrective to absolutist Stuart fathers and to the tyrannical family of Filmerian patriarchs.

"Discontented with [the] present state" of France, Rousseau too wanted "to be able to go backward in time" to "the age at which [he] could desire that the species had stopped."[18] Like Locke, Rousseau wanted to return to the benevolent patriarchal family, which, as "the most ancient of all societies, and the only natural society," also constituted for him "the first model of political societies."[19] But writing in the midst of the *ancien régime* in France, Rousseau could only create a credible opening in his present for Locke's corrective to absolutism by placing the benevolent patriarchal family in the midst of nature, on its rural estate, as an isolated utopia in retreat from the luxury and corruption of society and from France's feudal-absolutist regime. Like Crusoe's island,[20] Clarens and the menage in *Emile* are isolated utopian retreats dominated by Lockean nursing fathers who educate servants, children, and women, as well as any other adult male within their reach, and who rationally and "benevolently" govern these, their "natural" subordinates and subjects, "to their Good." Clarens and the households in *Emile* thus iterate Locke's gesture by offering themselves as a rational alternative and virtuous corrective to the luxury and corruption prevailing in Paris and to France's feudal-absolutist regime. As Julie points out when she says that Wolmar's household represents "on a smaller scale, the order established for the government of society," Rousseau's novel assumes the family-state analogy.[21]

For British readers and reviewers in the 1760s, Clarens and the households in *Emile* also tapped into what Virginia Kenny has called the conservative British "country house ethos" which, between 1688 and 1750, used "the concept of country-house life and the role of the landlord at the apex of a manageable little power structure" in the "microcosmic society of the estate" as a "vivid metaphor" for political control of the "larger society of the state." This conservative poetic and political idyll, which was iterated by Addison and Steele in *The Spectator* and *The Tatler* at the beginning of the eighteenth century and at mid century by Bolingbroke, Lyttelton, Chesterfield, Pope, and Thomson (most of whom either had works translated into French or were themselves exiled in France), contrasted the "redemptive" rural retreat that the benevolent landlord created for his family and dependents by right government of his estate with urban luxury and depravity. Based on an idealization of the past, and most particularly of "the legendary age of Gothic government," it also represented the country estate, much as Rousseau represented Clarens, as a society characterized by public and private virtue, frugality, order and degree among dependents and visitors, and good stewardship by "the standards of the natural economy."[22]

When they reimported this country house idyll in the 1760s and 1770s, British Matriarchal novelists like Sarah Scott or Mary Hamilton refashioned and extended Rousseau's image of the benevolent patriarch's country retreat as a rational alternative and virtuous corrective for society's domestic and political ills.[23] Grafting Locke's and Rousseau's patriarchal ideal of beneficent domestic government onto Astell's ideal of a Protestant retreat for ladies,[24] and crossing both with the longstanding conservative British literary and political tradition of pastoral country house panegyrics, Sarah Scott in *Millenium Hall* offered a powerful Matriarchal image of a virtuous hierarchical "family"[25] on its rural estate which is governed by ladies for what *they* perceive to be the public good. Mary Hamilton highlights this moment of substitution of matriarchal for patriarchal government in *Munster Village* by having her idealized mistress of a family, Lady Frances, refuse to marry the man to whom she has been engaged for sixteen years as long as her nephew, Lord Munster, is a minor, so that she can have sole charge of her nephew's fortune and estate at Munster Village and can act without interference as an educating mother-governess to him and to his sister. Scott and Hamilton also ensured that their capable and virtuous Shunamite heroines got all the intradiegetic admiration and deference from men, properly positioned at their feet, which was the Shunamite's due.

Like Wolmar in the admiring descriptions of Clarens that Saint-Preux composes for Lord B——'s edification, Lady Frances and the governing ladies at Millenium Hall are constructed as exemplary governors for the imitation of men. Scott achieves this in *Millenium Hall,* much as Rousseau did: by having a male narrator, Sir George Ellison, report and publish to another man his abject admiration for the "uncommon society" he finds at the hall. Hamilton achieves the same effect by concluding her novel with a masque in which the great men of Greece (Demosthenes, Aristotle, Plato, and others), of Italy (the Medicis, Raphael, Ariosto, Tasso, and others), and of England (Locke, Sir William Petty, Dryden, and Waller) do "homage" to Lady Frances's "superlative merit" by "expatiating on the advantages she had procured to society" and on the ways "she had obliged the whole nation, as every one individual might receive improvement or pleasure by her means."[26] But where Wolmar's patriarchal artifice at Clarens collapses at Julie's death, Lady Frances and the ladies at Millenium Hall are assured of enduring political progeny: Lord Munster will imitate Lady Frances "like the *halo* of the *rainbow,* exhibits *the same* though *fainter colours*";[27] and Ellison, who resolves to pattern his domestic government after the example of Millenium Hall, goes on to do so — with some help from the ladies — in the novel's sequel, *The History of Sir George Ellison* (1766).

Although analogical, Locke's and Rousseau's imaginary of benevolent domestic government and Scott's or Hamilton's Matriarchal imaginaries were not the same. Scott underlines the differences between them in *Sir George Ellison* by banishing the political ideal operative at Clarens to a slave plantation in the West Indies and by presenting it as the most benevolent form of government a kindly gentleman like Ellison could imagine prior to his first encounter with the ladies at Millenium Hall.[28] For Matriarchs like Frances Brooke and Sarah Scott, Clarens was only the old tyrannical patriarchy in more benevolent and cynically manipulative disguise.[29] Saint-Preux makes the connection clear in his admiring explanation of Wolmar's government of Clarens: "How are we to keep servants and mercenaries under proper regulations, otherwise than by force and restraint? The art of a master consists in disguising this restraint under the vail of pleasure and of interest, that what they are obliged to do, may seem the result of their own inclination."[30] As Mira Morgenstern put it, "Wolmar uses the metaphor of the family to perpetuate an atmosphere conducive to the internalization of Wolmar's own interests by every member of the estate," and though he employs love and benevolence "instead of command and brute force, as the principle of running not only his family, but also his servants," love and benevolence are in fact a "cover for authoritarian domination" that is "all the more effective for being camouflaged."[31] One might add that in "duping" those he educates and governs by creating a controlled environment where internalizing certain principles seems to be to their rational advantage as well as his, Wolmar was only imitating the conduct Locke recommended to children's governors in *Thoughts on Education*.[32] In masking his demands for unfailing habitual obedience to his authority as benevolence and concern, Wolmar was only inscribing in his domestic utopia the mechanism of dependence which British Enlighteners considered the "glue" of society.

James Steuart, for instance, reasoned that if people come into society and remain in society because they require the offices of others to supply their wants, "dependence is the only bond of society" and that therefore "the best way of binding a free society together is by multiplying reciprocal obligations and creating a general dependence between all its members."[33] Adam Smith went a step further by arguing that men had from the first "voluntarily" subordinated themselves to the authority of local chiefs, feudal barons, or landowners because they depended on these men for their food, shelter, or protection, and that men would continue to "voluntarily" subordinate themselves to their superiors in civil polity as long as they continued to draw benefits from their subordination.[34] It was therefore the dependence of inferiors on superiors which cemented society. "Virtue" — understood as the duty of performing "good offices" for one's inferiors and as the duty of obedience to one's superiors — was crucial to the preservation of the hierarchical social order. In principle, as Blake was later to put it with bitter irony, "if all do their duty, none need fear harm."[35]

Ellison's "benevolence" in the West Indies consists in governing his slaves by just such prescriptions. Like Wolmar, who treats Julie, Saint-Preux, and his "family" of servants as obedient children to be educated, directed, provided for, and watched over (he describes himself as "a living eye"[36]), Ellison provides food, shelter, protection, direction, work, and schoolmasters for his slaves on the plantation, telling them: "As long as you do your duty, I shall look upon you as free servants, or rather like my children, for whose well-being I am anxious and watchful." Like Wolmar, who designs Clarens as an orderly society in which everyone is "united in his service" and dependent upon him in all things, Ellison forms a plan "to render our slaves obedient without violating the laws of justice and humanity." As Wolmar ensures obedience to his will by "subduing" the passions of his wife, Saint-Preux, and his servants, by regulating their pleasures, and by ensuring that they live an orderly life, Ellison corrects the "faults" of his slaves, imposes a regular and orderly routine, and "promotes innocent amusements" among them. As Wolmar dismisses any domestic who is not wholly obedient and devoted to the order he demands, Ellison sells any slave who breaks his laws. And as Wolmar's servants serve him "willingly" and well because they understand that greater benefits accrue to them in his household than in any other man's, so Ellison's slaves serve him "willingly" and well because they understand that they are better off with him as their master than any other man. Like Wolmar, Ellison therefore enjoys the affection of his slaves, even while he benefits economically from his benevolence, since his profits increase beyond everyone else's as a result his slaves' better physical health and grateful devotion to his interests.[37]

Scott emphasizes that Ellison "exerts a power merely political" and that he has "no natural right to enslave" anyone. She also links Locke's and Rousseau's "benevolent" paternalism and the British Enlightenment's doctrine of dependence to domestic slavery. In doing so, she suggests that, far from being a suitable form of government for a "free people," this was a mode of government which subordinated the people to authoritarian masters while relegating women and servants to domestic enslavement. By linking slavery on the plantations to domestic life in conjugal societies and by marking similarities between men's cruel treatment of the wives and daughters, whom they considered their property, and their cruel treatment of their slaves, Scott also prepares the ground for Ellison's exposure to the superior government of Millenium Hall, which its Matriarchal governors have designed as a refuge for all "the persons those ladies had removed from a state of mortifying dependence."[38]

Millenium Hall and *Munster Village* underline the differences between matriarchal and patriarchal conceptions of domestic government by inserting a series of personal histories of ladies attached to the hall or to the village. These personal histories illustrate the evils produced by women's "mortifying dependence" on others in patriarchal family societies outside the village or the hall.[39] They tell of lustful guardians masquerading as nursing fathers, of forced marriages to vicious or physically repulsive men, of domestic misery under cruel and tyrannical husbands, of love matches stymied by inequalities of wealth, and of humiliation and abandonment at the hands of husbands who publicly set up mistresses or wasted their fortunes gambling. And they describe all the horrors of embarking on marriage when, like Mrs. Lee in *Munster Village,* a lady:

> cannot help shuddering at a contract which nothing can dissolve but death. To me, it is terrible to reflect that it is a strangely unequal conflict, in which the man only ventures the loss of a few temporary pleasures, the woman the loss of liberty; and almost the privilege of opinion. From the moment she is married, she becomes the subject of an arbitrary lord; even her children, the mutual pledges of their affection, are absolutely in his power, and the law countenances him in the use of it — and a woman finds no redress for the indelicate abuses of an uncivil, a passionate, an avaricious, an inconstant, or even a drunken husband — from matrimonial decisions there is no appeal.[40]

Echoing Astell, Scott and Hamilton portray women's subjection to their husbands in patriarchal family society as "the perfect condition of slavery."

By contrast with these evils of patriarchal domestic government, the "family" at Millenium Hall provides "an assured asylum against every evil" and shows what else it might mean to govern others "to their Good." While occupying themselves with all the "dignified and rational pursuits of life" and harmoniously surrounding themselves with foster "daughters" whom they educate to be like themselves, the ladies who govern Millenium Hall gather in and assist other subaltern victims of Enlightened British society. They provide the poor, the old, and the physically challenged or deformed with a roof over their heads and the means of earning their own living with dignity. They pay lower-class mothers on their estate to stay at home and nurse their children, and they set up schools for their sons and daughters. They ensure that impecunious young women are taught all the useful arts and accomplishments that will make them marriageable, and they provide a house where indigent gentlewomen can live and work in security. And while they eschew marriage for themselves and devote their lives to others, they indicate what Hannah More and Jane

West will later preach:[41] that some such acts of assistance and beneficence to others are also within the power of every married lady, regardless of her fortune or rank.[42]

Besides helping the indigent, giving poor young couples a house and the means of earning their subsistence, and allowing artificers to live in Munster Village rent-free for two years while they build up their trade, Lady Frances uses her nephew's fortune to improve agriculture and to perform "works of national magnificence." In Munster Village, Lady Frances builds a hospital for incurables, a compendious public library (both of which she says England lacks), and a university where all the liberal arts and sciences are taught and practiced and where young men are helped to choose the profession to which they are best suited. Lady Frances also provides an education for her niece comparable to that which she provides for her nephew, as well as university education and maintenance for twenty ladies, many of whom then "married very well in the neighbourhood."

The principle of mutual dependency underlies both Matriarchal utopias — if that is the word for collections of projects later undertaken by philanthropic ladies, and later still by the welfare state. The ladies replace the patriarchal idea that society is cemented by dependence based on self-interest, however veiled, with the idea that society is cemented by "the circulation of kindness." "Can there be anything more evidently our duty," Lady Frances asks, "than that we should return the kindness we receive; and that, if many are employed in promoting our interest, we should be as intent on advancing theirs?" The ladies' government of Millenium Hall assumes that, as "there is no creature in the universe that is not linked into some society," so human "society is a state of mutual confidence, reciprocal services and correspondent affections." And Lady Frances's government of Munster Village embodies the principle that "society is manifestly maintained by a circulation of kindness; we are all of us, in some way or other, wanting assistance, and in like manner qualified to give it. None are in a state of independency on their fellow creatures. The most slenderly endowed are not a mere burthen on the community; even they can contribute their share to the common good."[43] Therefore, rather than exploit the poor and grow rich on their labor, as Wolmar and Ellison do (and as the novel says "the Squires" do), the ladies at Millenium Hall implement the principle of the mutual exchange of kindly good offices on an entirely different level:

Now there is neighbour Susan and neighbour Rachel; Susan is lame so she spins cloaths for Rachel; and Rachel cleans Susan's house and does such things for her as she cannot do for herself. The ladies settled all these matters at first, and told us, that as they, to please God assisted us, we must in order to please him, serve others; and that to make us happy, they would put us in a way, poor as we are, to do good to many.[44]

Where Wolmar and Ellison demand that their subject-slaves depend on them alone and think it in their own self-interest to serve faithfully in return for food, shelter, and protection, the ladies at Millenium Hall create networks of mutual dependence in which each supplies others' lacks and each serves others while being served. Where Wolmar and Ellison seek to control their subject-slaves by using a concealed art to harness human nature to their will, the ladies at Millenium Hall provide the members of their society with the means of subsistence and the means to be of assistance to others and they "advise," "encourage," visit, and educate; but having done so, they leave those they have helped to govern themselves by the principles of virtue and industry they have been taught. Since the ladies continue to monitor the poor and demand a disciplined life, one could read their methods of government as a manifestation of Foucault's panoptikon. I am reading them here, however, through the positions outlined in Chapter 1, which distinguish between law and license, and between subordination to another's will and "free" self-government by principles of virtue and law.

From this point of view, the difference between these patriarchal and matriarchal conceptions of government is marked by their different representations of their "assured asylums" as Gardens of Eden. Rousseau represents Elysium, Julie's "delightful asylum," as an extension of Wolmar's political principles. It is a walled garden, to which Wolmar has the key. Within it, a "superintendent's" concealed art has redirected nature according to human will, and once-free creatures, like birds, are drawn and kept there by the superintendent's steady provision of food and shelter.[45] Scott, by contrast, represents her delightful asylum for animals as a wood, which owes nothing to art, where animals are protected as much as possible from "natural evil" and left their entire liberty. And she represents her walled garden as a space that cannot be entered by anyone, even the ladies, without the inhabitants' permission. Within it, the physically deformed can build a harmonious community for themselves, safe from "the tyranny of those wretches who seem to think that being being two or three feet taller gives them a right to make them a property, and expose their unhappy forms to the contemptuous curiosity of the unthinking multitude."

Wolmar's benevolence is confined to the circle of his family and dependents at Clarens, and thus to the people subject to him from whose obedience and good will he can also profit. The matriarchs, on the other hand, use the profits of the estate at Millenium Hall to increase the number of people they can help.[46] They also offer the example of a more far-reaching philanthropy, the effects of which extend beyond any single estate or family circle, from which they do not directly profit; and it is this philanthropic possibility — the possibility of an excess of giving without consideration of any return but the pleasure of doing good — that Ellison takes away from his visit to Millenium Hall and practices in areas where ladies could not credibly intervene. In the latter part of *Sir George Ellison,* after his return to England, Ellison becomes a justice of the peace whose benevolence extends beyond his family and servants to neighboring families and their children, to the village poor, to those subject to the parish priest and local government, to those undeservedly imprisoned for debt in his own and in neighboring counties, and ultimately to the enfranchisement of his West Indian slaves. But whether his philanthropy is extended to his neighbors, the village poor, imprisoned debtors, or slaves, Ellison's endeavor is not only to free them from the oppression of the moment but to give them the means to earn a dignified living, free of any "mortifying dependence," and he acts without expecting any return. From this point of view, his conduct to Miss Alin is typical. Setting aside with difficulty his own passion for her, he frees her from an avaricious father and enables her to marry and support her children with another man by providing her with the dowry and the funds she needs.

As Ellison points out, he is "no leveller." He "raises noone to the same affluence [he] enjoy[s]" and is "far from destroying the subordination" that, his cousin Sir William argues, is "necessary for the stability and preservation of society." Ellison never asks why there is so much cruelty, suffering, and injustice requiring his philanthropic interventions nor suggests that some wider change in society or in the law might be required to right the wrongs he finds all around him. His views are limited, like those of the Matriarchs themselves, to the idea that "by changing the household, we influence history,"[47] which Kathryn Sutherland imputes to Hannah More. Like those of the Matriarchs, too, Ellison's views are bounded by his own duty and by the means Providence has given him of doing good: "I consider every thing I possess, my fortune, my talents, and my time, as given me in trust to be expended in the service of the Giver. I am but a steward . . . The best manner in which I can serve my master, is in benefitting his creatures." And finally, Ellison's views are bounded by the Enlighteners' assumption that "self-love and social are the same" and by the associated political assumption that all society could become as utopian as Millenium Hall or as happy as Ellison's household and immediate environment if other men followed the Matriarchs' precepts and were converted to virtue, benevolence, and philanthropy by their Christian example.

Until then, however, and in absence of any extant female retreat like Millenium Hall, the Matriarchs' best advice to their meeker daughters was to avoid domestic slavery, both of the viciously tyrannical and of the viciously fashionable sort, by retreating to domestic sanctuaries with the Ellisons of this world. Frances Brooke's *The Excursion* and Jane West's *A Gossip's Story*, for instance, demonstrate the wisdom of young ladies' remaining in "assured asylums" (however dull) and the folly of their venturing on risky excursions. They do so by contrasting natural scenes of domestic happiness with scenes of fashionable profligacy "after the manner of Rousseau," while tapping into the traditional Matriarchal story of two sisters, one of whom has lamentable coquettish tendencies.[48]

The Excursion and *A Gossip's Story* seem to begin where *Sir George Ellison* leaves off. At the end of Scott's novel, Providence has rewarded Ellison's benevolence by giving him the widowed Miss Alin to wife and blessing him with two daughters whom he tenderly educates. This enables him to exemplify the advantages of virtuous, benevolent, and philanthropical family government, by showing that "it is impossible to imagine a scene of more perfect felicity on earth, than this family represented." Louisa and Maria Villers in *The Excursion* are in the position of Ellison's daughters. They are brought up in "the little paradise of Belfont" by Colonel Dormer, their uncle and guardian, "an enthusiastic admirer of truth, nature and genuine beauty." Here, they too experience nothing but benevolence, virtue, and philanthropy. Likewise, when *A Gossip's Story* opens, Louisa and Marianne are living happily in domestic retirement with their father, Mr. Dudley, a man "possessed in an eminent degree of the virtues of the head and the heart." In *The Excursion*, Louisa, the sensible daughter, chooses to remain with her father, content with "the heart-felt pleasures of retirement and the tranquil joys of a rural life," while Maria, who is "quick, impatient," and "ambitious," makes the dangerous excursion to London to pursue her dream of happiness — a "ducal coronet on her coach" — and is almost ruined by the fashionably vicious and charming Lord Melvile. The Louisa in *A Gossip's Story* likewise chooses to remain with her benevolent father. She even goes with him to the relative poverty of a small Lancashire estate where she will find "a sanctuary safe from every misfortune," rather than marry the wealthy but vicious Sir William. Her flighty sister, Marianne, by contrast, refuses the suitor who is her father's double and chooses to wed the fashionable Mr. Clermont, who matches "her own romantick idea of a lover" instead; and as a result of her folly, she finds herself an abandoned and miserable wife.

In these novels, social evil seems to be identified with worldly ambition, romantic illusions about men and love, gossip, detraction, and the fashionable life; and sense and virtue, as demonstrated by both Louisas, consist of retirement in an assured domestic asylum and of such caution in the choice of a spouse as can be predicated on judicious restraint of emotion and desire. The underlying social abuses and injustices to women are therefore couched (as they will be couched in Austen and in the so-called "realist novel") as matters of manners and morals, and the novels seem to share the limitations of Ellison's views by making social happiness a matter of individual character and choice and by assuming that "if all do their duty, none need fear harm." In fact, however, these novels indicate the more shocking politics they also conceal, by constructing the sisters' choices among suitors as choices between different principles of domestic government.

Stern, haughty Sir William, in *A Gossip's Story*, has all the makings of an old-style domestic tyrant. Recently returned from the East, where he could treat people like slaves, Sir William thinks his money can also purchase him a wife. "Too long accustomed to a servile adulation," he finds the idea of making a dowerless woman like Louisa his humble dependent "flattering to his pride." Having forgotten that "freeborn Britons are seldom inclined to admit the claims of wealth and arrogance, if men possess no superior title to respect and esteem," he never troubles to be "amiable" or "gracious" to his inferiors. Mr. Dudley, Louisa's father, recognizes that only a wife with an extremely "accommodating temper" will be able support Sir William's "asperity" and "ungracious method of bestowing favours" with the requisite patience and cheerfulness. The marriage to Louisa is called off when his self-serving cruelty to helpless dependents is revealed by the discovery that Sir William has abandoned his mistress and child without provision, after promising her marriage and living with her for some years.

Mr. Clermont in *A Gossip's Story*, and Lord Melvile in *The Excursion*, on the other hand, are fashionable gentlemen who treat women as commodities in a different way. For them, women are objects of pleasure — to be acquired by courtship, consumed sexually, and thrown away. Lord Melvile therefore thinks nothing of compromising Maria while trying to set her up as his mistress in place of a mistress of whom his worldly father has helped rid him; likewise, when his marriage to her becomes irksome to him, Clermont thinks nothing of abandoning the distraught Marianne to solitude in the country while he pursues his pleasures elsewhere.

The men both Louisas marry, and Maria's eventual spouse, on the other hand, are made from Ellison's mould. Louisa in *A Gossip's Story* marries Mr. Pelham (the suitor foolishly rejected by her sister), who is a man of proven virtue, "generous friendship," and "manly tenderness" to women.[49] Like Ellison, he also "measure(s) his conduct to the unfortunate by that divine benevolence, which regards the keen susceptibility of misery." Louisa in *The Excursion* marries a genteel, well-educated country squire with the same utopian "country" values that her father exercises at Belmont. And once saved from ruin in town by the philanthropy of Mr. Hammond, a friend and substitute for her nursing father, Maria finds her own Belmont with Colonel Herbert, a man frank, benevolent, "open, brave, generous, sincere, well-bred," who "esteems" women. Like Frances Brooke's husband once again, Colonel Herbert is a soldier who depends on his own abilities to support himself, rather than being one of the fashionable elite.

Marianne and Maria, the foolish sisters, are misled in their choices of Clermont and Melvile — and all but destroyed — by excesses of passion and romantic sensibility, like that of Saint-Preux for Julie. Their romantic sensibility prevents them from avoiding domestic slavery by reading their lovers aright, and their excesses of passion prevent them from directing their desire towards the suitor who will neither prove a tyrant once he is a husband nor treat them as a disposable object of consumption. Each novel therefore rewrites Saint-Preux's inconquerable passion for Julie, even after she becomes Wolmar's wife at her father's behest, to show that romantic feelings and imaginary projections can and must be overcome before a woman can make the proper choice. Overcoming "the dangerous excess of the passions" and "the violence of love, grief, despair and jealousy" — as Ellison does while Miss Allin is married to the man her father has chosen, as Maria does in *The Excursion* when Lord Melvile marries the woman his father has chosen for him, and as Louisa does in *A Gossip's Story* while the man she loves is her sister's prospective husband — is presented by these Matriarchal novels as the key to obtaining a husband who will not make his wife a slave to his domestic tyranny and as the condition for utopian domestic bliss. In this respect, as April London says, Matriarchal novels taught women to "accept self-denial as normative."[50] But in rewriting Rousseau in this way, these Matriarchal novels also repeated him: for overcoming "the dangerous excess of the passions" is also Wolmar's "cure" for Julie and Saint-Preux's vain attempt to escape subjection to the filiations of property and rank by creating a space for "natural" virtue and emotion outside the patriarchal hierarchy.

Rousseau and Fictional Egalitarian Critiques

"Dangerously democratical" women novelists in England during the 1790s also "cited" Locke's and Rousseau's utopian image of the benevolent patriarchal family governed by a nursing father in its rural retreat. They used it, as Rousseau and the Matriarchs had used it, to critique the dissipations, luxury, and corruption of fashionable society; but they also used it as Rousseau and the Matriarchs had not used it: to challenge the privileges of rank and the tyrannical disregard of the wealthy for the impoverished lower orders. In Helen Maria Williams's *Julia*, Radcliffe's *Romance of the Forest*, Mrs. Inchbald's *Nature and Art*, and Charlotte's Smith's *Marchmont*, for instance, the happy beneficent families with nursing fathers (the Cliffords, the families of the lake, the Henry Norwynnes, and the Marchmonts, respectively) are presented as alternatives and correctives to rich, ambitious, fashionable, and worldly families (the Seymours, the feudal families of the forest, the William Norwynnes, and the Dacres), who exploit their subordinates, abuse the poor at their pleasure, and take ruthless advantage of innocent and defenseless women.[51]

Iterating Rousseau in England a century after Locke, by presenting the beneficent patriarchal family with its nursing father as a society that could be established only in retreat from the larger society and in opposition to its values, could itself be construed as a comment on what Price called the "incompleteness" of the Glorious Revolution and on its failure to do its job. But "dangerously democratical" women novelists went further, by turning this device against itself.

Not content with using the benevolent patriarchal family to critique the society of the time, *Nature and Art, The Victim of Prejudice, Romance of the Forest*, and *Marchmont* also demonstrate the impotence of nursing fathers, and thus of their families, before the depredations of society's wealthy, vicious, violent, and powerful men. In Radcliffe's novel, the humble, beneficent, and virtuous Le Lucs (pointedly located in Switzerland, Rousseau's birthplace) only escape the destruction and death at the hands of the powerful and tyrannical Marquis to which Adeline's father has already succumbed, by the introduction of a *deus ex machina* at the end of the story. Mr. Raymond, Mary's tutor and nursing father in *The Victim of Prejudice*, tells her upon her first exposure to society what her life will demonstrate: that he has no means of protecting her from society's corrupt norms or from men who are richer and socially more powerful than he. In Mrs. Inchbald's novel, *Nature and Art*, Rebecca, Hannah, and the benevolent Henry Norwynne repeatedly fall victim to a system of British law and justice which is administered by rich, self-interested, and dishonest judges like Henry's worldly brother, William. And *Marchmont's* benevolent hero is unjustly dispossessed of his inheritance and prevented from helping his impoverished mother and sister by the machinations of more rapacious and worldly men who derive their abusive power from the unholy alliance of money, political influence, and the law.

These novels thus demonstrate, against the Matriarchs, the practical impossibility of finding refuge even in a benevolent patriarchal family with an Ellison-type father or husband from a society in which, despite the Glorious Revolution, inferiors have no recourse against superiors and arbitrary power and corruption prevail. Disputing Locke and Rousseau and the British Enlighteners, they also argue that in a regime governed by violence, greed, and injustice, nursing fathers — those hybrids of "masculine" reason and "feminine" nurturance — are ejected from their commanding place as "Lords of Creation" to partake of the helplessness and disabilities traditionally associated with women.[52] By demonstrating the incapacity of nursing fathers to occupy this commanding place, these novels also indicate, in opposition to the Matriarchs, the inadequacy of supposing that society can be cured of its evils by increasing the number of men who, like Ellison, model their conduct on female virtue, beneficence, and philanthropy. Matriarchal philanthropy and changes in the conduct and tasks of the propertied household are not, *by themselves,* sufficient to correct social ills and alter the course of history, they suggest.

Williams, Smith, and Hays take another radical step by rewriting Julie's story in *Héloïse* in such a way as to demonstrate the inadequacy of the Enlighteners' image of the kingdom as a hierarchy of orderly family societies, rationally and benevolently governed by little domestic sovereigns.

In *Julia,* Helen Maria Williams unmasks the property, power, and privilege underlying the domestic economy at Clarens by making Frederick, her Saint-Preux character, the one to contract the marriage that separates him from Julia, and by showing Mr. Clifford, the novel's nursing father, acting just as L'Etange did with Julie, by making his daughter Charlotte's marriage to Frederick possible through a transfer of property between men. Like Frances Brooke in *Lady Julia Mandeville* thirty years earlier, she indicates that from this point of view there is little difference for women between old-style and new-style patriarchs. But Williams also deconstructs the idyll at Clarens more radically than Brooke did, by rewriting it through the perspective provided by Pope's poetic rendition in "Eloisa to Abelard" of the letters that the original Eloisa wrote to Abelard from her cloister:

> Yet here for ever must I stay;
> Sad proof how well a lover can obey!
> Death, only death, can break the lasting chain;
> And here ev'n then, shall my cold dust remain,
> Here all its frailties, all its flames resign,
> And wait till 'tis no sin to mix with thine.
> Ah wretch! believ'd the spouse of God in vain,
> Confess'd within the slave of love and man . . .
> Unequal task! a passion to resign,
> For hearts so touch'd, so pierc'd, so lost as mine.[53]

Translated into French and known to Rousseau, Pope's version of the story reappears as the retroactive ambiguity created by Julie's confession, in her last posthumous letter, that her passion for Saint-Preux has survived her marriage to Wolmar: "Long have I indulged the salutary·delusion, that my passion was extinguished; the delusion is now vanished, when it can no longer be useful. You imagined me cured of my love . . . In vain, alas! I endeavoured to stifle that passion which inspired me with life; it was impossible; it was interwoven with my heart-strings."[54] Rousseau also gives Wolmar all the rational and sexual coldness of Pope's Abelard:

> For thee the fates, severely kind, ordain
> A cool suspense from pleasure and from pain;
> Thy life a long, dead calm of fix'd repose;
> No pulse that riots, and no blood that glows.

While changing the character functions around, Williams uses this palimpsest of Pope's "Eloisa and Abelard" in Rousseau's novel to unmask Wolmar's folly in supposing that, as a nursing father, he can cure Julie and Saint-Preux of their passions through reason and good order and construct his family at Clarens as a utopia by governing others "to their Good." Williams also uses this palimpsest of Eloisa's situation and feelings to stigmatize Julie and Wolmar's "salutary delusion" of married happiness at Clarens as a most unsalutary form of hypocrisy.

In Williams's novel, Mr. Clifford does everything a nursing father should: he arranges a marriage for his daughter, Charlotte, to Frederick, a man she profoundly loves; he takes in his orphaned and impoverished niece, Julia (who like Claire in *Héloïse* is also Charlotte's closest friend); he treats Julia like a daughter; and he cares for the poor on his estate. Mr. Clifford asks only that everyone should be happy and content in the well-ordered little family he so benevolently governs. But Mr. Clifford's family is disrupted by what neither reason, benevolence, nor good order can control. As the narrator repeatedly points out, a passion may be controlled or suppressed only before it has acquired "strength" and "force," that is, before it has become a passion at all.

At the prompting of his worldly brother, Frederick agrees to marry Charlotte for any number of good, rational reasons, despite his growing passion for Julia. But notwithstanding Julia's "cool suspense of pleasure and of pain" and "severely kind" conduct towards him, he finds that his passion for her simply cannot be overcome; and although he fulfils his marital duties to Charlotte to the letter (as Julie does with Wolmar), Frederick's passion for Julia prevents him (like Saint-Preux) from using his great talents to do anything useful in the world. Against the Matriarchs' Rousseauesque argument that overcoming "the dangerous excesses of passion" is the key to utopian domestic bliss, therefore, Williams shows that while Frederick can control his passions sufficiently to do the expected thing by marrying Charlotte — a person who by reason and circumstance ought to be able to make him happy — the violence he does to his own feelings every day of their marriage makes his conjugal life a scene of torment and pretence and their domestic happiness a lie.

Torn between his duty to Charlotte and his passion for Julia, and half-maddened with pain, Frederick finally contracts a fever on the brain which kills him. His dying words echo and alter those of the letter bearing Julie's dying wishes. Dispensing with Wolmar and Julie's delusion that honorably obeying the forms and duties of marriage can be "salutary" or "useful" to anyone, he insists: "It is fit that I should die, who have only lived to embitter the lives of those to whom my soul is most devoted." And as Julie commends Saint-Preux and Claire to each other and asks them to care for her children and for the aging Wolmar, Frederick commends Charlotte to Julia, who together will bring up Frederick's child and care for the aging Mr. Clifford. The only intact remnant of the extended patriarchal family benevolently governed by Mr. Clifford, therefore, is the close friendship between two women, which has withstood all the buffetings of passion and bitter trials of fortune. And the only commitment that proves capable of surviving the sort of suitable, dutiful, and dis-passionate marriage that Rousseau and the Matriarchs recommended is the strong affection and commitment to a female intimate and companion which Rousseau and the Matriarchs both insisted a woman ought to give up on her wedding day.[55]

In *Montalbert* and *The Victim of Prejudice,* Charlotte Smith and Mary Hays also punctured the patriarchs' and Matriarchs' tidy image of the kingdom as a collection of families, by drawing attention to the presence, even in the ranks of the wealthy and titled, of whole groups of outcast women who were being ignored.[56]

In *Montalbert,* Charlotte Smith rewrote *Héloïse* through the perspective provided by another palimpsest in Rousseau's novel — Eloisa's child by Abelard, who was abandoned to the care of others when Eloisa was directed by Abelard to imprison herself in the nunnery and become the bride of God. This abandoned child appears in *Héloïse* only fleetingly, as Julie's still-born child by Saint-Preux — a child conveniently aborted, like their union, by the violence of Julie's father when their relationship becomes known. Smith revived the child Rousseau buried, as a daughter (Eloisa bore Abelard a son), to exemplify what it meant for a woman to be an outcast from the filiations of property and rank on which Rousseau's patriarchal family utopia at Clarens depends. And she used that forgotten daughter, Rosalie, to rewrite Julie's story as a story about the marginality of the growing number of orphaned, illegitimate, and dispossessed women in England at the end of the eighteenth century: women born to families in the propertied ranks who would not acknowledge them, to fathers who had disinherited them, and to a gentility that they could no longer sustain.

Julie's story is embedded in *Montalbert* as the story of Rosalie's mother, Mrs. Vyvian, née Montalbert. Ormsby, her lover and Rosalie's father, was, like Saint-Preux, young and passionate and full of sensibility, but poor. Like Saint-Preux, he came to stay at the Montalberts' country house and was "carelessly" allowed to spend all his time with Miss Montalbert, because it "never occurred" to her father (who like L'Etange was a despot and a snob) that a poor dependent would dare raise his eyes to his daughter. Like Julie's "friends" in Rousseau's novel,[57] Miss Montalbert's friends all conspired to "save her reputation" when she found herself "likely to become a mother." Like L'Etange and Lord B——, her father and Ormsby's brother made Ormsby renounce her, sent him overseas, and "forced" her into a "detested marriage" with the well-to-do Mr. Vyvian, by whom she (like Julie with Wolmar) subsequently had other children. And like Claire, her friend Mrs. Lessington saved her reputation by helping Miss Montalbert to conceal her "fatal secret" — but this time by taking her daughter at birth and bringing her up in her own family. Like Julie and Eloisa, Mrs. Vyvian has since done her duty as a wife without being able to renounce what has been the great love of her life: "though my hand was not at my own disposal, never has it acknowledged any sovereign but him to whom my first vows were given. Yet I very sincerely tried, when under the cruel necessity of giving myself to Mr. Vyvian, to fulfil the duties that were imposed upon me."[58]

However, this novel condemns the conduct of everyone involved. As Rosalie points out, "her mother had been betrayed by some or all of those whom she considered her best friends." *Montalbert* demonstrates, against Rousseau and the Matriarchs, that, instead of leading to blissful domestic utopias, such "contrivances, which cunning and caution have invented for the security of property" in the ranks of the wealthy led only to "unfeeling" domestic arrangements that produced estrangement and dysfunctional families into the second and third generations.

Without any "natural feeling" or affinity to bind Mrs. Vyvian to her husband or Rosalie to the Lessingtons, each is condemned to live, without illusions or delusions, as a "solitary and isolated being in the midst of her family." Mrs. Vyvian is imprisoned in a loveless marriage with a cold, domineering, and sometimes violent man, who, like Wolmar, knows that she has loved another; and, living as an outcast in her family, her only support in her domestic misery is "the consolation of having sacrificed [herself] to duty," the affection of one of her children by Vyvian, and the consciousness that she is "expiating" through the bitterness and duration of her sufferings "the errors of her early life."

Mrs. Vyvian's daughter Rosalie is doubly dispossessed. Dispossessed first in the Lessington parsonage of the maternal "tenderness" and paternal "fondness and protection" she would have enjoyed if her natural parents' early "indiscretion" had been effaced by a "happy union" between them, Rosalie is dispossessed again, in the parson's household, from any proper place in the filiation of property and rank. As Rosalie says, comparing her prospects of marrying Mrs. Vivyan's nephew, Montalbert, in her current situation with what they would have been had her natural parents been allowed to marry: "I should not then have been despicable in the eyes of Montalbert's relations — I might have been received by *his* mother with pride and pleasure from the hands of my own; but now I am an outcast, and have no right to claim the protection of any human being." Neither a Vyvian nor an Ormsby, neither a Lessington nor a Montalbert, lacking any proper name and any proper place in the symbolic order, Rosalie has no family to claim and no right to a family. Casually sacrificed at birth to the "contrivances which cunning and caution have invented" for the transmission of property in daughters and estates between men of substance, Rosalie is in every domestic and social sense an outcast and a "cypher."

Rosalie's life therefore iterates Julie's and her mother's as an even newer Eloisa — a woman precariously perched on the margins of gentility who has to make her way in the world without family or fortune.[59] Like her predecessors, Rosalie has in her turn to make the fatal choice between wedding the secret lover, Montalbert, with whom she has assignations in the woods, and acceding to the pressure of "friends" who try to force her into a distasteful but economically advantageous marriage. The "contrivances of cunning and caution" remain, but the economic reasoning has shifted in keeping with this newer Eloisa's social marginality. In urging Rosalie to marry what she describes as "a little, dirty, drunken curate," the Lessingtons tell her she must: "consider, you have no fortune . . . it is your business to endeavour to procure an establishment instead of affecting these fine romantick airs . . . Mr. Hughson is a young man of fortune; he is, in his family, in his situation and prospects, in every way unexceptionable." And Montalbert urges Rosalie to agree to a clandestine marriage before a Catholic priest to stave off the disinheritance he fears from a marriage displeasing to his family and to protect his place in the filiation of property and rank.

Rosalie's marital options challenge the comparatively rosy choices of domestic government that were imagined for women in Matriarchal typologies: there are no fashionable gallants, no wealthy and aristocratic domestic tyrants, and no well-to-do benevolent country gentlemen here. Rosalie can trade the vestiges of her gentility for a legal but miserable marriage to a vulgar and drunken curate, or she can follow her heart, confirm her marginality, and reinscribe her illegitimacy by agreeing to a clandestine and unlegitimized marriage to Montalbert.

Rosalie chooses the clandestine marriage to Montalbert, updating Julie, who, as William Kendrick points out in a translator's note, marries Saint-Preux by exchanging vows in private in a manner that was by then precluded in England by the Marriage Act. Unlike both Julie and her mother, however, Rosalie flees to distant parts with Montalbert when she, too, finds herself "likely to become a mother." Yet, though she has seemingly chosen a path contrary to theirs, she, too, is, in her turn, "buried yet living." The difference in her case lies only in the form this burial takes. Rosalie is buried by events and motifs that make her a continual outcast: she is imprisoned in a conventlike fortress, while Montalbert mistakenly thinks she has died in an earthquake; still separated from Montalbert but back in England, she is treated as absent while present by the repeated refusal of the "unfeeling" to notice, remember, or pity her; and then, when Montalbert mistakenly assumes that she has betrayed him with another, he uses his authority as a husband to deprive her of her child and of everything that for her represents living. As she says: "*I* have no father! Do not mock me! . . . I had a husband — indeed I had a child, but both are gone, and now I am a wretched outcast." Even the novel's happy ending — produced by the now wealthy Ormsby's unexpected return and by the help suddenly forthcoming from Charles Vyvian and William Lessington — only underscores the importance, even for a married woman, of having family to protect her, fortune to recommend her, and men of substance in the social and symbolic order to bring her husband to heel. The influence of these men eventually constitutes Montalbert, Rosalie, and their child as a viable family unit for the first time.

As Mrs. Vyvian and her daughter demonstrate in *Montalbert,* a woman was "buried yet living" whether she was in an unfeeling family cobbled together for economic motives or an outcast from family and fortune. Rosalie's life with Montalbert and their son at the end of the novel intimates that living "unburied" depended on the slim chance that a woman could realize precisely those social and emotional aspirations which the Lessingtons, Rousseau, and the Matriarchs characterized as "romantick." As one of the characters says: "If we were to give up every sentiment as ridiculous that your writers or your dramatists attempt to render so, there would not be left, in the human heart, one virtue to reconcile us to the misery of existence."

Hays, in turn, joins elements of *Emile* to elements of *Héloïse* to address other difficulties faced by ladies of the middle and upper ranks without family or fortune in an England where rising numbers of orphaned, illegitimate, and spinster women were forced to exist outside the boundaries of any family unit while being precluded from finding remunerative work. Mary Hays's heroine in *The Victim of Prejudice* is an orphan, she is illegitimate, and she has no fortune. The novel opens on a citation and feminist alteration of Rousseau's pedagogical utopia: William and Mary are brought up in the bosom of nature to be perfect companions and ideal spouses, like Emile and Sophie; but unlike Sophie, Mary has in Mr. Raymond a tutor and nursing father who educates her to principle and rational independence, rather than to flattery and female subordination. Mary, like Julie, loses the great love and companion of her youth to social prejudice when William's father insists that William marry elsewhere for rank and fortune. But Mary's single exposure to sexuality has an outcome more realistic in England at the end of the eighteenth century than Julie's. Though raped through no fault of her own by a nobleman who thinks her fair game, Mary's "loss of innocence" and loss of "character" herald her fall

outside family into destitution and perpetual victimization at the hands of
a society that equates female virtue with chastity and social acceptability
with a family estate. Lacking Julie's or Mrs. Vyvian's noble father and large
fortune, Mary has no way back, no means of redeeming her past by becoming a "virtuous" wife, mother, and mistress of a family. And, in accordance with the Enlighteners' assumption that women were, or ought to be,
subsumed in the patriarchal family and "covered" by men, society provides
Mary with no way of earning an honest living either. An outcast and without the means of sustaining life, Mary (like her mother, who was seduced
rather than raped) has nothing to do but to die.

Mary's death can be read as a critique of society's cruelty to illegitimate,
impoverished, orphaned, and fallen women. As Eleonor Ty says, her life is
"a catalogue of possible 'wrongs' or acts of social injustice perpetrated on
the eighteenth-century . . . female."[60] But Mary's death can also be read as
a comment on the Matriarchs' blithe assumption that, by making their virtue their dowry, young women without fortunes would be able to obtain
some purchase in the marriage mart and find a "safe asylum" for themselves with the right man. If anything, Mary's staunch virtue proves her
undoing: it makes her refuse both the "legal prostitution" her ravisher
eventually offers and the "protection" that William would give her were
she willing to become the mistress of a married man; and her philanthropy
to the Nevilles deprives her even of the little nest egg that Mr. Raymond
has been able to leave her. Despite her virtue, despite her almost super-
human persistence in trying to earn an honest living, and despite the "philanthropy" of those good people who occasionally try to help her, there is
no "assured asylum from all evil" anywhere for Mary. Even more radically,
therefore, Hays's novel must be read as an indictment of the political assumption, which patriarchs and Matriarchs shared, that the family was society's most original and fundamental social, economic, and political unit
and that the strengthening, well-governing, and philanthropy of the
family would act as society's cure-all. Mary represents all that this political
assumption excluded and ignored. For women like Mary, who were forced
by society to exist outside of any family and who sought to live honorably
as particular, independent, and "unrelative" persons, there was as yet no
doctrine of "individualism," no political, ideological, social, or economic
provision, and no hope.

Hays's use of imagery from the Garden of Eden to characterize Mary's youthful life with William and Mr. Raymond in the bosom of nature, and of imagery of the Fall to characterize Society's interruption of their idyll, repeats Rousseau's opposition between nature and society, to indicate, against both Rousseau and the Matriarchs, the impermanence and permeability of society's pastoral "outside." For Hays, it is not an Emile or an Ellison who will change the world; it is the world which will change them. As Mr. Raymond tells Mary:

> The guileless, generous, ardent, youth, brought up in rural shades, on his entrance into society, will, by irresistible contagion and insensible gradations, become *a man of the world* . . . In the opinion of those who class with the higher ranks of society, poverty, obscure birth, and the want of splendid connections, are the only circumstances by which he can be degraded. The beauty, virtue, talents of my child, in the eye of philosophy, are an invaluable dowry; but philosophers are not yet legislators of mankind. William is destined for the theatre of the world; he will imbibe the contagion of a distempered civilization.[61]

Indeed, Mr. Raymond himself is "forced into contradictions that belie [his] precepts" by the opinion of the world. Despite his many kindnesses to Mary, he faithfully carries out his "trust" to those who "class with the higher ranks of society," by helping them to enforce their sentence of exclusion on her. In this context, it is significant that, in Hays's rewrite of Eve's plucking of the apple, it is Man who drives Woman to commit the prohibited act for love of him; in *The Victim of Prejudice*, it is from Raymond's weakness and William's worldliness, as much as from Sir Peter Osborne's violence, that Mary's destruction stems.

Hays's imagery of Eden and the Fall also invokes Locke's politico-historical argument about Adam's original benevolently patriarchal family, the fall into tyrannical political patriarchies, and the second coming of that original "natural" Adamic family through King William's government of England as a nursing father. Reminding us that Locke's politico-historical argument was an adaptation for a secular and politicized world of the Christian story of the Fall and Redemption, Hays's imagery in *The Victim of Prejudice* underscores the fact that, for Mary, the promised political and social redemption has not come to pass. In this context, the names Hays gives her characters — William and Mary — are significant. Together with William's abandonment of Mary and Mary's unredeemed fall, this suggests that for women all hopes that the Revolutionary Settlement would be the "great Preserver" of "their just and natural rights" have proved false, and Locke's and Rousseau's claims for "nursing fathers, tender and carefull of the public weal" have proved an empty fiction. The reality, as Hays says, has "mock[ed] the toil of the visionary projector."

In these Egalitarian novels of the 1790s, there was, on the whole, no privileged oppression by class or gender. The Egalitarians' "dangerously democratical" Rousseau did not privilege the sufferings of women or those of the lower classes, as nineteenth-century marxism and certain forms of twentieth-century liberalism would later do. Their views are more accurately represented by Laclau and Mouffe's postmarxist concept of "alliance politics."[62] Egalitarian novels showed that there was, equally, oppression of women in the middle and upper ranks (like Mary, Rosalie, Mrs. Vyvian, Adeline, Rebecca, and Gwendolyn), nursing fathers of all ranks (Le Luc is a pastor, Marchmont a peer, Raymond a country gentleman, and Henry Norwynne of country shopkeeper stock), women in the lower orders (like Hannah in *Nature and Art* and Phoebe or the day laborer's wife in *Marchmont*), and families in the lower orders (like that of the London printer's journeyman in *Desmond*, the village poor in *Nature and Art*, or the servants at Eastwoodleigh in *Marchmont*). All suffered equally from their governors' unfeeling perversions of justice and self-interested abuses of power and place, as well as from their subordination to their (domestic, political, social, or economic) "superiors" in Britain's hierarchical society, though their sufferings are shown to take different forms.

The Egalitarians' "dangerously democratical" rewrites of Rousseau also model ways in which the oppressed groups in different ranks of society can make common cause, by allying across class and gender lines to help each other against their oppressors, through what Foucault would call "local resistances." Though an outcast and victim herself, Mary, in *The Victim of Prejudice*, manages to help a curate's family set themselves up afresh when her ravisher, Sir Peter Osborne, deprives them of the living, cottage, and little farm on which their subsistence depends; and Mr. Raymond's old domestic, James, gives Mary shelter and support after her vain attempts to earn her living honestly have brought her to a debtor's prison. In Radcliffe's *Romance of the Forest*, Peter, a servant long unpaid, helps the upper-class La Motte and his family survive while they are hiding from merciless pursuers; the pastor, Le Luc, and his family give shelter and protection to Adeline, the penniless and outcast daughter of an aristocrat; and, though themselves endangered and pursued, both La Motte and his servant help Adeline escape the Marquis's abuses of power, as Adeline will later help M. Le Luc and his soldier son. In *Nature and Art*, the dean's nephew, Henry, and the curate's daughter, Rebecca, save a baby born to Hannah, the daughter of a poor cottager, and keep it alive until she can claim it. And in *Marchmont*, Wansford — a servant at Easterleigh, who has himself "suffered from the lower retainers of the law" and knows enough of their "cunning and cruelty" to "abhor" them — hides the noble but impoverished Marchmont from retainers of the law who are serving "the malignant tyranny of two rich men," until Marchmont can flee to France. Using the language of "virtue" and "philanthropy" as patriarchs and Matriarchs did, Egalitarian novels thus showed oppressed men and women of different ranks making common cause against British society's diverse legalized and publicly countenanced forms of oppression.

By representing virtue, philanthropy, and mutual aid as the affirmation and response of disenfranchised women and men in all ranks of British society to the cruelties and injustices of a social order dominated by principles of self-interest and by greedy, ambitious, and exploitative persons, these Egalitarian rewritings of Rousseau also gave the lie to idealized Matriarchal and patriarchal representations of virtue and philanthropy as a property of the genteel and well-to-do which invariably proceeded from the top down. In so doing, they also exposed the cynicism of an ideology that taught superiors to do their duty by graciously relieving the distresses of the "deserving" amongst their social and economic inferiors, in order that the latter might do their duty by "voluntarily" submitting to their governors in return for benefits received. As Henry in *Nature and Art* says to Lord Bendham of his Christmas "gift" to the poor on his estate: "I thought it was prudent in you to give a little; lest the poor, driven to despair, should take all." Or, as the narrator observes of William's "Christian" ministry, with its "rigid attention to the morals of people in poverty, and total neglect of their bodily wants": "to be very poor and very honest, very oppressed yet very thankful, is a degree of sainted excellence not to be attained without the aid of zealous men to frighten into virtue."

In *Marchmont*, Charlotte Smith also deconstructed the oppositions —

between country and town, high and low, well-governed families and fashionable society, law and license, (English) liberty and (French) tyranny — on which Rousseauesque patriarchal and Matriarchal images of family government as a model and cure-all for the state relied. *Marchmont* is a more effective rewrite of Rousseau from this point of view than is *Desmond,* despite the latter's overt political debates.[63] It also intimates perhaps the most radical "final solution" of all for outcast British women and men of all ranks, the solution towards which Smith's last novel, *The Young Philosopher,* also tends. It is with *Marchmont* that I will therefore conclude.

Althea in *Marchmont* is another Rosalie. An outcast and a "cypher" like Rosalie, Althea is disinherited in her infancy and displaced from her natural family by her father's remarriage and newfound political and economic ambitions. Like Rosalie, Althea refuses the match forced upon her by Sir Audley with a brutal and corrupt lawyer, Mohun, in favor of an improvident love-match with Armyn Marchmont, the young and impoverished scion of a noble, Tory family. They meet and fall in love at Eastwoodleigh, a Gothic country mansion where Althea is "buried yet living," sent there by her father when she refuses to "sell" herself to Mohun, and where Marchmont has gone to hide, an outlaw from Sir Audley's legal henchmen, who are trying to put him in a debtor's prison.

Eastwoodleigh now belongs to Sir Audley, who lives in London and considers "money and power the two things which every man of sense makes it the business of his life to obtain." Unlike Clarens and Matriarchal domestic retreats, therefore, Eastwoodleigh represents no escape for Althea or Marchmont either from Sir Audley's abusive patriarchal government or from the corruption of fashionable society in town. Smith shows that "in a country celebrated for its equal laws," the long arm of magistrates and lawyers extends Sir Audley's self-serving abuses of property and power even into the most rural areas and that "those who have imagined that at a great distance from London, there reigns Arcadian simplicity, and that envy, detraction and malice only inhabit great cities, have been strangely misled by romantic description."[64] There are malicious detractors and corrupt lawyers at Eastwoodleigh as well as in London, and if there is any Arcadian simplicity there, it is the simplicity of abject poverty and of honest souls who are no match for Sir Audley and his lawyers, and know no means of redress.

Smith uses her portrait of the country estate at Eastwoodleigh to demythologize Clarens and its Matriarchal surrogates as models and cure-alls for society at large. Neither a refuge from the evils of society nor a utopian domestic sovereignty established through the transmission of property between men, Eastwoodleigh is a model of domestic, social, and economic dispossession. Once home to the Marchmonts, who were in bygone days the friends and protectors of kings, it is now the property of Sir Audley and Lady Dacre, who have progressively wrested it from the Marchmonts by using dishonest lawyers and shady legal tricks. Deprived of his property and heritage and an outlaw in the land, Marchmont now uses Eastwoodleigh as his hide-away from Vampyre (one of Sir Audley's legal henchmen), while he considers fleeing to France. As Marchmont points out, therefore, despite the vaunted British "liberty," his situation in England is not so very different from the situation of aristocrats like himself during the Reign of Terror in France: "Whether I am to pass my life in the Fleet or the Abbaye, whether I am to exist under the tyranny of Robespierre or a victim to the chicanery of Vampyre, seems to me a matter so immaterial, that it ought not to induce me to cross the water to embrace the one or escape the other." The English and French nobility have both been ruined, exiled, and dispossessed of their estates. Both have been turned into social outcasts: "an exile from society, and compelled either to live as a wretched vagabond or submit to see my whole life wasted within the walls of a prison."

The difference, if there is a difference, is that in England — as Althea's banishment and dispossession also show — money is displacing birth as the measure of social status. As Althea and Lucy, Marchmont's equally impoverished sister, agree, their "ancestors will *now* do nothing for" them, for "not a citizen, not even a wealthy tradesman, will take either of us to ennoble his house; for in this country, it is very certain money is respected most . . . What then are we to do?" Likewise, because it is money rather than birth which is valued, "Marchmont's poverty, however incurred, seemed in the opinion of gentlemen [like Sir Audley and Mohun] to be a crime which should throw him at a distance from all human society."

Clarens — Rousseau's utopian well-born and well-governing family living independently, in retreat from society, on its country estate — was, therefore, already old-fashioned. The old landed aristocracy was being "thrown at a distance" from its land and its privileges in England as well as in France, where Marchmont finds himself treated as a social outcast too.

"Society" was now the province of ruthless, rising, ambitious, moneyed men like Sir Audley who, with the connivance of the law, were exploiting the countryside and tearing apart the "family" on its country estate.

At Eastwoodleigh, the law gives Sir Audley the license to exploit, dispossess, and "throw at a distance" all the other traditional inhabitants of the estate as well. The effects of what Smith calls the "iron ploughshare of oppression in the form of law" are not only inscribed on the landscape, in the derelict mansion that signals the Marchmonts' depropriation and in the deforestation of the land of its ancient woods by "the unfeeling rapacity of their creditors." The effects of the law's oppression are also inscribed on the lives of villagers and tenants who have been depropriated just like the Marchmonts. The Wansfords, for instance, have been thrown off their farm and Mary Moseley deprived of her living as an upper servant at the great house. Vampyre — the corrupt local attorney who has helped Lady Dacre's father make Marchmont's father destitute and is now helping Sir Audley put Armyn Marchmont in a debtor's prison — has likewise "undone many poor people" who "have died in jail, and whose children have been turned out to beggary or gone to the parish." Once these people become dependent on the charity of the parish, the parish officers complete their dispossession with "unfeeling tyranny" by implementing the poor law in such way as to give the abandoned, half-naked, half-starved family of a day laborer "a parish allowance that did not afford them even bread" or by menacing Mary Moseley with loss of her cottage and transfer to the workhouse.

By showing that "the very means provided by men in society for their mutual protection" have been "converted into those of oppression, plunder and ruin," Smith's representation of the country estate at Eastwoodleigh gives the lie to "visionary projectors" like Locke, Hutcheson, and Ferguson who claimed: "Laws are so far from excluding liberty that they are it's natural and surest defence . . . a people is denominated free when their important interests are well secured against any rapacious or capricious wills of those in power."[65] To show that the law was being capriciously manipulated by dishonest lawyers to serve men of property and power and that no one's important interests were secure was to go for the jugular of Britain's political system.[66] For, on the one hand, Britain's social hierarchy was predicated on governors' and magistrates' faithful performance of their trust, and on the other, Britain's social contract had promised the law's protection of the people's rights to life, liberty, and property.

Sir Audley has no interest in fulfilling any Trust — whether to his daughter, to his social subordinates, or to the aristocracy. He "adheres to the existing powers in the administration" and pays attention only to those of his inferiors who can "be made useful to him in the existing circumstances." Meanwhile, "buried yet living" at Easterwoodleigh, Marchmont and Althea are deprived, with the connivance of the law, both of their liberty and of their property, while many of the villagers and tenants are losing their lives to starvation besides. With consummate irony, Smith showed that, in "a country celebrated for its equal laws," the law was proving a great leveler of high and low despite itself, by ensuring that unfortunate people at all ranks could be impoverished and dispossessed.

The Dacres' ambition for property and power tears the traditional Clarens-like "family" at Eastwoodleigh, with its master, mistress, children, servants, and tenants, apart; and it has an analogous effect on every particular family associated with the estate. In this novel, property — posited by the Matriarchs as well as by Rousseau in *Héloïse* as the precondition for founding families that would be stable economic, social, and political units — in fact "throws" family members "at a distance" from family society. As Althea is "exiled" and "thrown at a distance" by Sir Audley and Lady Dacre to preserve their family property intact, so the Marchmonts are kept at a distance by Lady Chichester, who wants nothing to do with her poor relations. At Eastwoodleigh, where Marchmont has, as he says of his mother and sisters, been "driven from my family, not allowed even to afford them the protection they want," Marchmont is exiled and driven from Althea too. He becomes "a poor wanderer . . . without a home and without friends," seeking his fortune abroad. Other dispossessed families from the Eastwoodleigh estate are also driven from their homes and families, "thrown at a distance" to seek their fortunes elsewhere. Phoebe Prior, whose mother was a servant at Eastwoodleigh, is driven by the failure of her husband's shop to make a dangerous trip to the West Indies. The day laborer, whose wife and children were now living at Eastwoodleigh "on a parish allowance that did not afford them even bread," has "gone for a soldier in mere despair, to avoid the sight of his family's misery." As Althea observes: "If scenes like these are to be found in the cabin of the industrious labourer, who can wonder any more that any man should quit his paternal cottage? — Or how can it be strange that our peasantry fly to America?"

"Dangerously democratical" feminist rewrites of Rousseau therefore challenged the governing, legally defined, benevolently patriarchal domestic economy conceived by the British Enlighteners as a safeguard for the wealth of the nation and fleshed out by Rousseau. They also challenged the dispassionately virtuous, dutiful, philanthropic, and reasonably well-to-do family society that was represented as an asylum for women and children by the Matriarchs. They did so by showing that each was secured and framed by its manifold exclusions. As in the representation of a vase which from a different optical perspective yields two facial profiles, these Egalitarian novels brought to the fore what patriarchal and Matriarchal constructions of the proper and propertied family rendered invisible: the profiles of outcast daughters and subjected mothers, of disempowered nursing fathers and dispossessed families, and of divided kin and exiled breadwinners. Like anatomists, "dangerously democratical" novelists dissected the dispassionate and well-calculated couplings recommended to the propertied and would-be propertied ranks by the Matriarchs and by Rousseau, to display the brutalities, the repression of natural affections, the domestic estrangement, the violence, the torments, and the pretence concealed by their respectable facade. The Egalitarians valorized that which was dismissed as eccentric or romantic by the governing image of the kingdom as a hierarchy of orderly and economically viable family societies, rationally and benevolently governed by domestic sovereigns "to their Good." They told women to trust the bonds of natural affection, both in marital choices and in intimate friendships between women. They indicated the virtue, among the excluded and oppressed, of mutual aid and of democratic alliances across class and gender lines. They underlined the importance of education to rational independence and the dignity of work for women, and indeed for men, who were forced to live without family, friends, or fortune as "isolated and unrelative beings." And they indicated the revolutionary possibility that the impoverished, outcast, and dispossessed might seek their subsistence from "a new heaven and a new earth," as exiles from their native land.

CONCLUSION

The Domestic
Revolution

Power is the law of man; make it yours
— MARIA EDGEWORTH

The world's a masquerade! The masquers, you, you, you.
— OLIVER GOLDSMITH
for Charlotte Lennox

IN THE eighteenth century, as we have seen, the public functions of private families were at the forefront of theoretical, prescriptive, and fictional debates about the family. Enlightenment feminists shared with their male counterparts the conviction that in a well-ordered state, each private family ought to play a foundational governing, economic, and educative role in its own particular locality. But Matriarchs and Egalitarians had different visions of the proper structure of societies great and small and correspondingly different conceptions of the family and of women's proper place relative to men.

Egalitarians imagined a family based on consensual relations, where husbands and wives performed their duties independently, had equal "softness" and equal "sense," and were, in principle, equally capable of nurturing and educating their children and of assisting their needy neighbors. Matriarchs imagined a family in which hierarchy and due subordination prevailed, and men kneeled admiringly at the foot of the pedestal from which angelically superior, capable, and virtuous wives governed, while seeming to obey. Constructing themselves as moralists and social reformers, Matriarchs and Egalitarians translated the different domestic revolutions they proposed, their different critiques of patriarchal domestic government, and their different analyses of the social and political status quo into different fictional exemplars and emplotments of women's domestic lives. While offering their readers new patterns of imitation and desire, Matriarchal and

Egalitarian writers therefore injected into every conduct book and novel what Jane West called "prejudice and party" and made domestic fictions the place where the war of domestic systems was fought out.

In urging both well-to-do leisured ladies and women without means to become "domestic women" and to make government of the family their province, Enlightenment feminists were enjoining women to make themselves responsible for an institution that was still being represented — by men to men — as crucial to the health, wealth, morality, order, and well-being of the nation. The public importance attributed to the family and to men's domestic government in Enlightenment ideology, the priority given to the care and education of children in political economy and public policy, the severe loss of jobs in the marketplace for ladies of small means in the middling and upper ranks, and the "cruel" strictures of the Marriage Act — all these contributed to making Enlightenment feminists tackle the division of labor in the family between men's "domestic offices" and women's "household duties" in an attempt to "enlarge" themselves and improve their domestic lot. While promoting an as yet ideal and idealized division of labor between women and men which appropriated the patriarch's domestic offices for ladies in the middling and upper ranks and left the civil offices and civil professions to men, Matriarchs and Egalitarians both stressed the virtue and the practical necessity for ladies to refashion themselves as "domestic women" whose "profession" it would be to govern the family, educate their children, and assist the needy for the public good. Matriarchs exemplified in their novels the superior woman's talents and abilities in the domestic arena and her success in getting a good husband. Egalitarians critiqued the social order for victimizing "amiable" women without family or fortune by preventing them from obtaining any such respectable domestic place, and highlighted the legal, social, and political oppressions that tore virtuous and benevolent families apart. But both feminisms sought to "dignify" women, to raise them from the position of "upper servants" to their husbands, and to provide them with a safe marital "asylum," by making men's "domestic offices" women's work.

For Enlightenment feminists throughout the long eighteenth century, changes in the government, character, conduct, education, and relative position of women in the domestic hierarchy were logically related both to changes in the character, conduct, and government of the family and to changes in the character, conduct, and government of the polity. Like their male counterparts, both kinds of feminists argued that the private or particular good and the public or general good were connected and mutually reflecting poles, inasmuch as the public was whatever it was by virtue of the values and conduct of the particular families composing it.

This mirroring of the particular and the general, of the private and the public, of the family and the state, made exemplification possible. It enabled Matriarchal and Egalitarian writers to represent whichever revolution in the family and in female manners they proposed at once as the conduct of a particular woman in a particular family and as conduct bearing on the larger public issues of the time.

Although they both acknowledged the interrelation of the particular and the general in these ways, Matriarchs and Egalitarians ultimately gave the public and private poles different weights as levers for social change. Unlike the Matriarchs, the Egalitarians ultimately lacked faith in the ability of individual women in particular families to effect domestic and social change without a corresponding change in the structure and values of society as a whole; and, while Matriarchs continued to offer ladies empowering images of themselves as domestic Shunamites and to show each lady how she might act at once, in her own domestic situation, to dignify herself and improve her own domestic lot, Egalitarians increasingly offered the public images of domestic and social victimization and represented the domestic revolution as inseparable from a social and political revolution in the state.

One reason for this difference in their gender politics was the difference in Matriarchal and Egalitarian views of education and of how much might be expected from education in the way of unilateral personal, domestic, and social change. Another and perhaps profounder reason for the difference in their gender politics, as we will see below, had to do with the different analyses of power and competition in the hierarchical patriarchal family and kingdom on which Matriarchal and Egalitarian gender politics were based.

Analyses of power and competition underlay both the domestic strategies that Matriarchs recommended to ladies for managing their husbands and taking over government of the family from men, and Egalitarian critiques of these strategies. Linked as it was to the issues of hierarchy and equality explored throughout this book, this Enlightenment feminist debate about power and gender politics reveals lacunae in some of the Enlightenment's classical political and economic texts, while shedding light on "the great forgetting" of Enlightenment feminist debates.

Competition and Domestic Power

Matriarchs realized that, to strengthen their own position in the household and those attachments and dependencies they thought cemented domestic society, it was not going to be enough in the long run to encourage men to leave the domestic offices to ladies while they pursued their occupations abroad. Ladies would have to wean their husbands away from their dissipations and vices and "domesticate" them. Men's taste for dissipated, fashionable entertainments, they reasoned, "undomesticated" men and unglued family society, for profligate and dissipated men did not have to depend on their wives for pleasures, comforts, and benefits they could get elsewhere, and men did not trouble to give pleasure or confer benefits where they did not seek to receive them. An undomesticated man who did not depend on family society for his wants and comforts was a man whom his wife could not "attach:" he moved outside her sphere of action and beyond the reach of her good government. Matriarchal advice to wives was therefore to try to "attach" and domesticate their wayward husbands, much as one would try to attach and domesticate a wild and rather dangerous bird, by tempting him back to fireside comforts with unfailing kindness, patience, and good sense: "A man should come to his own fireside as a weary bird does to his nest, not as a captive in a prison." Never reproach him, said the Matriarchs; never show anger or ill-humor or resentment, never let him see the bars of his cage.[1]

At the same time, Matriarchs were giving ladies empowering images of themselves as latter-day Shunamites holding sway over men from the superior heights of dignity, piety, sense, and virtue. Here is Hannah More at the end of the eighteenth century, speaking of medieval courtly love and of the desirability of restoring the eminence — and "despotic sway" — it had once given ladies:

> *religion* and *chastity,* operating on the romantic spirit of those times establish[ed] the despotic sway of women; and though, in this altered scene of things, she no longer looks down on her adoring votaries from the pedestal to which an absurd idolatry lifted her; yet let her remember that it is the same religion and the same chastity which once raised her to such an elevation, that must still furnish the noble energies of her character; must still attract the admiration, still retain the respect, of the other sex.[2]

Here again, men are present on the scene only to honor and obey women, positioned center stage, who are infinitely above them; and the implication is that, despite the altered state of things, ladies can reestablish the same "despotic sway" over men that they once enjoyed under courtly love, by means of the same chastity and the same religion.

The strategic question for Matriarchs was how to reconcile the two — how women could "attach" and "domesticate" men and subordinate them to women's good government while restoring women in the household to their proper towering eminence center stage. The Matriarchs' short answer was: unobtrusively and without alerting men. Women must shun all "ostensible" superiority and use their "intrinsic" superiority to govern while seeming to obey. But this apparently simple solution, which hid the Shunamite in a masquerade and made her seem almost indistinguishable from "the proper lady," rested on complex and now forgotten Enlightenment feminist analyses of the uses and abuses of different kinds of power and of the effect of competition on societies great and small, which consciously elaborated and explored the unthought in male ideologues' representations of power and competition.

From mid century on, Egalitarians and Matriarchs both described the reality of family society not merely as a Foucauldian space where all interpersonal relations were relations of power but also as a space — unthinkable in Foucault's theory — where official and unofficial technes of power compete for mastery and where the *unofficial* ones almost invariably prevail.[3] Egalitarian Jane Collier, for instance, divided her satirical tome, *An Essay on the Art of Ingeniously Tormenting*, into two parts which correspond to these two kinds of power: "The first Part is addressed to those who may be said to have an exterior power from visible authority, such as is invested by law or custom, in masters over their servants, parents over their children, husbands over their wives, and many others. The second Part will be addressed to whose who have an interior power, arising from the affection of the person on whom they are to work, as is the case of the wife, the friend, etc."[4] In the first part of her essay, Collier demythologized conduct books, which presented purely idealized portraits of the relative duties of husbands and wives, parents and children, and masters and servants and which claimed that the good of society depended on the preservation of traditional forms of exterior power, which subordinated inferiors to the authority of their social and domestic "superiors." By humorously chronicling the multiple extant abuses of exterior power in each of these relative situations, Collier indicated that exterior power was still governed by arbitrary will and that, far from benefiting society, "visible authority such as is vested by law and custom" was too often used only to "torment" those subject to it. Women appear in this first part too, for being a good Egalitarian, Collier showed that ladies who had a measure of exterior power — over servants, companions, and poor female dependents living in their households, for instance — were quite as capable of using it to oppress and torment their subordinates as were men.[5]

But it is in the essay's second part, devoted to the abuses of interior power, that women really come into their own. Collier made it clear that, in practice, interior power was far more effective in the domestic arena than exterior power: "This interior power, if properly used for the Torment of those whose affections you have gained, will be found strong enough greatly to overbalance any exterior power."[6] While men assumed that power could be contained in and controlled by the purely formal and legal structures they invented — legislative, executive, and judiciary in the state; moral, religious, and paternalist in the family and locality — women knew that what actually came to pass also depended on the play of power interior to interpersonal relations and on the exercise of forms of power over others for which there is no law.

Collier showed how ladies could play on their husbands' nerves and affections to torment them and how, by thus tormenting them, they could bring a husband to heel. One technique was to be as contrary about trivial things as possible: "Be out of humour when your husband brings company home; be angry if he goes abroad without you; and troublesome if he takes you with him."[7] Should her husband try to insist that his wife receive and welcome his friends when he brings them home, a wife is advised that she can follow this up by pleading her affection for him as a reason *not* to oblige him:

> Own your self a weak, silly, fond woman, apt, you may confess, to take prejudices, nay aversions, to those who would endeavour to share with you the least portion of your husband's affections. Then, bursting into tears, you may add that nothing but the most hard-hearted wretch in the world could be angry at his poor wife, for hating anyone for love of him; but you *did* and *would* hate and detest them all as long as you lived. On this your husband

will be forced to sue for reconcilement; which you must by no means grant, till you have brought him to acknowledge that the highest mark of affection you can show towards him, is to hate and abhor all he esteems and loves.[8]

By constantly turning the tables on him in this way, a wife could bring her husband around to accepting anything she did, however contrary to his wishes or commands. She could also accustom him to doing whatever *she* wanted in order to secure his own peace.

Interior power thus reversed the relations of power between husbands and wives prescribed by exterior power, for the husband was made to placate and obey the wife rather than she him. As Collier said, "the husband may bluster and rave, and talk of his authority and power, as much as he pleases;" a wife who knows how to use her interior power to torment him and get her way will treat all such storms with "a perfect disregard" and with "a proper degree of contempt."[9]

Mary Hays observed that one could not really blame women for resorting to this sort of "mean subterfuge, whining and flattery, feigned submission and all the dirty little attendants which compose the endless train of low cunning," because "the weak have no other arms against the strong" and "necessity owns no law but her own."[10] By contrast, in "Essay on the Noble Science of Self-Justification," her equally satirical rewrite of Collier's *Essay,* Matriarch Maria Edgeworth indicated that, far from being a sign of weakness, such conduct was a successful form of gender politics which embodied the principle: "Power is the law of Man, make it yours."

Edgeworth indicated that women's stratagems and low cunning were successful bids to "obtain power by all means," rather than signs of women's helplessness or weakness; and she showed just how effectively a wife could use the weaknesses men attributed to her as a woman to "maintain unrivalled dominion at home and abroad" and to make her husband "rue the day when first he made her promise to *obey.*"

The fundamental law of this "noble science," which Edgeworth called "peculiar to the female sex," is for the adept always to acknowledge her husband's authority and superior powers of reason, judgment, and wit, while playing relentlessly on her own supposed *lack* of these attributes to block his every move. In a dispute, for instance, a wife would justify her own position against her husband's by going over the same ground again and again and again, making sure that she wandered as far as possible from the point and that she supported the volubility and dull prolixity of her monologue with every resource of the voice — such as the plaintive, the petulant, the peevish, and the monotonous. This would rout her opponent and teach him to give way to her rather than submit to more of the same. Should her husband try to make his position and his commands clear to her by painstakingly retracing every link in the chain of his reasoning, she would wait until he was sure he had fixed her with his very *best* argument — and allow her eye to wander, discover that a candle wanted snuffing, or recall that she had some household matter to attend to. And having harassed and stymied him at every turn, she would "grow calm as he grows angry, and wonder at his rage."[11]

Edgeworth makes it clear that such methods easily permitted a wife to "enforce implicit obedience to her authority" — for what husband would persist in trying to dictate to such a wife, or if he did, be able to prevail? But Edgeworth also indicated that for her, as for Hayes, the problem with such methods was that they were grounded in female imbecility, and yet were — despite or because of this — more effective with men than all "the arts of women of sense, wit and feeling."[12] As Jane West said bitterly: "Men are ever most easily vanquished by the *meanest* antagonists. An artful woman is a despicable creature . . . Yet I hardly know a proficient in deception who did not govern all her male connections, and moreover persuade them that she was the most amiable creature."[13]

Like West, Collier and Edgeworth were not saying that ladies had no power over their husbands; they were using satire and ridicule to make the feminist point that ladies were using the wrong *kinds* of power to the wrong kinds of end. This is a point that Enlightenment feminists repeatedly made in their tracts and conduct books too:

> Aware of the impossibility of vanquishing by violence, many women have attempted to raise their empire out of their imbecility; and thus originated a numerous group of exquisite creatures, who founded their empire on being really *good for nothing*, either as friends, companions, helpmates or handmaids.[14]

> It happens that many a helpless, fretful and dawdling wife acquires a more powerful ascendancy, than the most discrete and amiable woman; and that the most absolute female tyranny is established by these sickly capricious humours.[15]

[Women] cunningly obtain power by playing on the weakness of men; they may well glory in their illicit sway, for, like Turkish bashaws, they have more real power than their masters.[16]

Egalitarians and Matriarchs both acknowledged that ladies could easily build their empire over men upon men's imbecility and their own. They recognized that ladies could "easily vanquish" men by low cunning, by their supposed weaknesses, by exploiting their sexuality or by "playing off those contemptible infantile airs that undermine esteem even while they excite desire." But they said that doing so was degrading to women. It encouraged men to regard women with condescension and contempt, and it reinforced stereotypes about women's uselessness, childishness, and lack of reason. For Matriarchs, the conduct of imbecile-exquisites was a betrayal of women's "superiority of sense and virtue" over men, and it let the side down badly. For Egalitarians, the problem with the conduct of imbecile-exquisites was that it kept ladies in the subject positions of tyrant and slave: female slaves to male tyrants, with the slaves turning tyrant as their tyrants became enslaved.

In this context, the Egalitarians' and the Matriarchs' opposite portraits of women as powerless victims or powerful Shunamites both took on supplementary significance as unmasking and consciousness-raising devices. The image of women as powerless victims became an attempt to make women understand their real powerlessness and victimization in patriarchal society. What Diane Hoeveler has called "victim feminism" became an attempt to show women that powerlessness and victimization underlay — and were concealed by — their very *success* in using their supposed imbecility, their sexuality, their feigned submission, and all the other marks of their inferior station to bolster their own power.[17] If women had the same exterior power as men and the same independence to pursue their goals, they would not have to play off their silly airs or exploit their beauty, their sexuality, and their interior power over men to their own ends. By the same token, the image of the powerful Shunamite became an attempt to show women that there were other effective, honorable, and nondegrading kinds of power at their disposal, despite their subordinate station in patriarchal society. It became an attempt to get women to envision dignified and respectable alternatives to building their empire over men on their exquisiteness and imbecility. Victim and Shunamite thus became different ways of

eschewing the "illegitimate sway" women obtained by using highly effective, but degrading forms of interior and unofficial power over men.

The Shunamite, however, also represented a shift in the grounds of female power over men from feminine sorts of incapacity to capacities that
were clearly within the masculine domain. Unlike the imbecile-exquisite
who exploits her sexual difference and her "amiable defects" to gain her ascendancy over men, the Shunamite builds *her* ascendancy on her intrinsic
superiority to men in sense, ability, and virtue. Competition was central to
Matriarchal analyses of power, because the Matriarchs understood that
this shift in the grounds of women's power would put women in direct
competition with men on their own ground: "Knowledge and understanding are distinctions of which the lords of creation are highly tenacious; and
they are most unwilling to allow that more than a few particles of these
precious metals can possibly be amalgamated with the sophisticated rib."[18]

Matriarchs had long said that men kept women ignorant, subordinate,
and childlike because they feared competition from women:

> Had we the same literature, he would find our brains as fruitful as our
> bodies . . . [Men keep women from learning] lest our pregnant wits should
> rival the towring Conceits of our insulting Lords and Masters.[19]

> [Men knew] the Abilities of Mind of our Sex and feared that we, who in
> the Infancy of the World were their Equals and Partners in Dominion,
> might in the process of time by Subtlety and Stratagem, become their
> Superiors.[20]

> > They're wise to keep us Slaves, for well they know,
> > If we were Lette, we soon should make them so . . .
> > They fear we should excell their sluggish Parts
> > Should we attempt the Sciences and Arts,
> > Pretend they were designed for them alone,
> > So keep us Fools, to raise their own Renown.[21]

Given the chance to compete, declared these early feminists, women
would not only rival but excel men in precisely those areas where men
claimed superiority. Men kept women subordinate and submissive by all
the legal and customary forms of exterior power they could command, not
because they were secure in their own superior abilities, but, on the contrary, precisely because they were not. Men in the middling ranks were

particularly prone to fearing competition from women, because, unlike the
nobility and gentry who derived their social superiority from their birth
and estates, all their claims to notice and precedence, and indeed all their
power to "rise in the world," depended on demonstrating the superiority of
their "abilities and virtues."

As Matriarchs recognized, this placed women in a double-bind whenever they sought to demonstrate *their* superior abilities and virtues, especially in supposedly masculine preserves like learning or domestic government. For, on the one hand, women's inferiority was so generally assumed
that women had to prove themselves markedly superior to men before
men could be brought to acknowledge that women were even their equals.
But on the other hand, the fact that men's superiority to women was a
baseless conceit meant that any demonstration of the Shunamite's superior
sense and ability would arouse men's fear of competition from women and
provoke men's resistance to women's rule: "His pride revolts against the
power to which his reason tells him he ought to submit. What then can a
woman gain from reason?"[22] "The native pride of human nature renders us
very hostile to the claims of superiority . . . It is sure to have its pretensions
contested."[23] The idea that men and women should both submit to the
same principles of reason or religion rather than to one another was not
going to work if it awakened men's fear of competition from women.[24]

This first double-bind was complicated by another. On the one hand,
Matriarchs recognized that to "dignify" themselves and to institute that
division of labor in which they would take over the "proper government" of
their families from men, ladies would have to compete with men on their
own patriarchal terrain. On the other hand, their analyses showed that
competition was fundamentally incompatible with the preservation of the
social and political hierarchy, with the attachments and mutual dependencies that were supposed to cement members of society each to each, with
the tenets of Christian morality, and with people's personal happiness.
Here their analyses of the social effects of competition differ markedly
from those of political economists like James Steuart and Adam Smith,
with whom they otherwise agreed.

James Steuart had argued that division of labor was the best means of
promoting a general dependency among members of a society. By setting
different people to work in different aspects of agriculture, manufacture,
and commerce, the division of labor connected people through their mu-

tual wants and ensured that each group depended on other groups to supply its needs. Division of labor therefore ensured that members of society were cemented together by the exchange of "good Offices." Adam Smith went a step further by arguing that efficiency and productivity were increased in the workplace, not only through the greater speed and dexterity of each workman under the division of labor, but also through the fact that by dividing and *combining* their labor, all could produce more than each could produce alone. By analogy to the workplace, the division of labor in society at large permitted different men to develop different skills, talents, professions, and expertise; and once *combined* by commerce, which "render[ed] that difference useful," this enriched the common stock: "Among men, the most dissimilar geniuses are of use to one another; the different produce of their respective talents, by the general disposition to truck, barter and exchange, being brought as it were into a common stock, where every man may purchase whatever part of the produce of another man's talents he has occasion for."[25] Barter, purchase, and exchange were thus signifiers and vehicles of those mutual good offices that glue the members of society each to each. Such commerce should therefore "naturally" serve as "a bond of union and friendship" among individuals and among nations.

Like Hume, Adam Smith acknowledged that *in practice* "commerce which ought naturally to be, among nations as among individuals, a bond of union and friendship, has become the most fertile source of animosity."[26] Steuart and Smith also acknowledged that *in practice* "the spirit of monopoly" was preventing commercial exchange between individuals and between nations from cementing people and countries each to each and from working for the public good. But, unlike Enlightenment feminists, they were unable to think of these phenomena as discordant and divisive symptoms or side effects of competition itself. Convinced that "it is the combination of every private interest which forms the public good" and that "what is prudence in the conduct of every private family can scarce be folly in that of a great kingdom,"[27] they attributed the animosity and jealousy they saw around them to mistaken perceptions — to people's failure to understand the all-round benefits of competition. They were convinced that commercial exchange "naturally ought to be" a bond of union and friendship, that rivalry and "emulation" naturally ought to produce excellence and spur every man to better himself, and that "the uniform, constant and uninterrupted effort of every man to better himself" ought naturally to be "the principle from which public and national, as well as private, opulence is originally derived."[28]

Matriarchs, too, wanted to promote a division of labor between the domestic and civil economy in order to "better" themselves, but they argued that competition was incompatible with the mutual dependencies, mutual benefits, and attachments which cemented hierarchical societies and on which their peace and harmony depended. They argued from their observation of "the conduct of every private family" that wherever there was rivalry and competition, there was also envy, selfishness, contention, divisiveness, vanity, hatred, and greed. "We call the society of children *society in miniature*," Maria Edgeworth said, and we discover by observation that children's sympathy and concern for each other, their sense of shared purpose, and their readiness to assist one another, disappear as soon as their abilities, passions, and appetites are placed in "direct competition" with those of other children:

> Two hungry young children with their eager eyes fixed on one and the same bason of bread and milk, do not sympathize with each other, though they have the same sensations; each perceives that if the other eats the bread and milk, he cannot eat . . . We may observe that the more quickly children reason, the sooner they discover how far their interests are in any way incompatible with the interests of their companions. The better a boy is at calculating, the sooner he will perceive that if he shares a bason of bread and milk with a dozen friends, he will have very little left.

When children are placed in direct competition with each other for relative superiority and inferiority, she continues, this sort of rational self-interest, with its accompanying unconcern for the well-being of others, rapidly deteriorates into envy and hatred: "If experience convinces them that they must lose in proportion as their companions gain, either in fame or in favour, they will necessarily dislike them as rivals; their hatred will be as vehement as their love of praise and affection is ardent."[29]

Edgeworth points out that in the same sort of competitive situations, "men of superior knowledge and abilities" behave in the same way as these children: "all their social and all their public affections lose their natural warmth and vigour, whilst their selfish passions are cherished and strengthened, being kept in constant play by rivalship." The Matriarchs argued that in any society, great or small, where it is found competition, rather than cementing people each to each, keeps people contending with one another for relative superiority and inferiority, promoting divisiveness and undermining "the sense of mutual dependence" from which, according to Enlightenment ideologues, "the first principles of social intercourse are deduced."[30]

Also, unlike the analyses of Enlightenment ideologues who argued that the competition of private persons resulted in the public good, Matriarchal analyses showed that these mechanisms of competition were incompatible with the preservation of the social and political hierarchy. Competition — understood as each man's attempt to "better" himself — made it impossible to preserve "the line that separates the several orders of men," because it meant that each rank of society was seeking to rival and displace the one above it in fortune, appearance, and lifestyle. In a commercial state like England, where wealth and success were increasingly "overbalancing" birth in the determination of power and rank, such competition enabled each rank of society to "encroach on the position and privileges" of the rank or ranks above it. This destabilized the "right and true subordination" that should characterize a "well-regulated state" by enabling members of each rank to supply and usurp their superiors' proper place. Moreover, if private virtue was necessary to the public good, as Enlightenment ideologues and Enlightenment feminists both argued, competition must be seen as absolutely antithetical to it, for competition that held wealth and advancement in the hierarchy as its principal goals produced and promoted "keen, designing, selfish, ambitious men, who study mankind in order to turn them to their own account."[31] In the aggregate, men anxious to advance only their own interests, ambitions, wealth, and importance produced a society in which "rank [is] flattered, fame coveted, power sought, beauty idolized, money considered as the only thing needful . . . profit held up as the reward for virtue, and worldly estimation as the just and highest prize of laudable ambition."[32] And this did not, Matriarchs insisted, make for a good, much less a pious and Christian, society.

The Matriarchs pointed out that competition did not make for private happiness either. There is no happiness, they said, in possessing an envious temper and a malevolent disposition or in being driven by ambition or avarice to discontent with one's rank or lot. There is no happiness in advancements that turn on securing the admiration and applause of others or in rivalries and power struggles that provoke others to all the jealousy, hatred, detraction, and revenge of which they are capable. If men in a commercial state contend with each other to "rise in the world," they are to be pitied; but "they are not models of imitation," for "they sacrifice happiness to some strong passion or interest."[33]

Matriarchal analyses of competition therefore backed the woman of superior sense and virtue into a corner where she must and must not compete. She must compete with men on their own terrain, because, like men, she must "dignify" herself and "rise in the world" through her superior abilities and virtues and because she must ground her power, her ascendancy, and her domestic government on her superiority to men in sense, ability, and virtue. But at the same time, she must not compete with men on their own terrain, because she must not suborn "the right and true subordination" characterizing "well-ordered" families and states, because she must not undermine the attachments and mutual dependencies that cement societies great and small, and because she must not sacrifice her true happiness even to her strong passion for and interest in female supremacy. Above all, the woman of superior sense and virtue must not compete with men on their own terrain because to do so would defeat her purpose by arousing male resistance to her rule.

The Matriarchs resolved this dilemma by concealing the Shunamite beneath a masquerade. The masquerade allowed the woman of superior virtue, abilities and sense to *compete by not competing* and to gain her ascendancy over men by not seeming to. Through this masquerade, which disguised the Shunamite as the sort of proper lady described by male conduct book writers like Gregory, Fordyce, and Gisbourne, the superior woman carefully concealed her superiority in order to avert all the dangers of competition.

Matriarchs understood that "the native pride of human nature renders us very hostile to the claims of superiority ... It is sure to have its pretensions contested. The same may be observed of every natural or acquired eminence, unless the envied distinction is so enveloped in modesty and complaisance as to diminish all the invidious effects of superiority."[34] The masquerading Shunamite must therefore, they taught, ensure that her outward conduct consisted of a tissue of signals that she was not in direct competition with men. In conversation, her superior knowledge and learning "must rarely assume so dense a body as to be discernible to vulgar eyes." The masquerading Shunamite must never talk about herself, never contradict a man, never presume to offer advice; she must listen to everyone, especially to men, in "attentive silence" — though she might, on rare occasions, convey "silent intimations of dissent." If by mischance she attracted notice or admiration, she must be careful not to respond with "just remarks and acute observations," for she must quite aggressively avoid any situation (including displays of musical, artistic, or literary skill) in which her superior abilities might attract admiration, celebrity, or applause. She must envelop even her expert professional government of family society in conduct that constantly signaled her proper "feminine" subordination to men and her recognition of women's proper place. The Shunamite masquerader must *never* under any circumstances remind men, or even allow them to suspect, that she *could* rival their performance in any domain. For the law of her being was to shroud the interior power she derived from her abilities, designs, and true superiority over men behind the seven veils of female propriety: silence, modesty, deference, unwillingness to attract notice, complaisance, dutifulness, and obedience to God.

The masquerading Shunamite thus exploited what Terry Castle calls "the logic of symbolic inversion" that informed the masquerades so prevalent in eighteenth-century social life and required everyone to "wear a Habit which speaks him the Reverse of what he is." The Shunamite wore the veils of female propriety as she wore the domino to these masquerades — as "a sign of negativity, of the erasure or voiding of all form" which completely covered and concealed the real, capable female form beneath.[35] By this conduct, Matriarchs assured ladies, the Shunamite would obtain all the ascendancy she desired and all the admiration she deserved: "If she resolve so to husband her faculties as to confine intelligence to *acquiescence*, and discernment to *compliment* she will infallibly rise in the scale of wonders to something that is supernatural." "By ingeniously aiming at performing her own duty, she will acquire that eminence for which ostentation wearies itself in vain."[36]

The Shunamite who masked her superior sense and ability under the seven veils of female modesty would be elevated through her apparent subjection by activating the biblical principle that "whoever exalteth himself shall be abased, and he that humbleth himself shall be exalted." By displaying the modesty, humility, diffidence, and deference "proper" to her female station, the woman of superior sense, ability, and virtue would attain her rightful eminence. By exalting the lords of creation, she would ensure that they submitted to her rule. And by leaving husbands all "the name and th'addition to a king" in the domestic hierarchy while capably performing his domestic offices as "vice-regents," the masquerading Shunamite would neutralize all the dangers of direct competition and of "ostensible rivalship," "attach" her husband, and overbalance all masculine resistance to her plan of domestic good government.

It was therefore by competing without competing that the Matriarchs competed with men for supremacy and ascendancy in the family. And it was by competing without competing that they won. By engaging men on their own ground but in such a way as to neutralize the dangers of direct competition, the Matriarchal wife, mother, and mistress of a family would once again rise in the world to ascend the pedestal at center stage that Matriarchs had always reserved for the supernaturally angelic and capable Shunamite. It is an ironic tribute to the success of this strategy that, even when emptied of all substance, the veils of female propriety which the Matriarchs recommended as a mask became the very mark of female superiority and the visible signal that there was an "angel in the house."

The masquerading Shunamite also used her noncompetitiveness to gain a competitive edge in the market for wives:

> The more a woman's understanding is improved, the more obviously she will discern that there can be no happiness in any society where there is a perpetual struggle for power; and the more her judgement is rectified, the more accurate views will she take of the station she was born to fill, and the more readily will she accommodate herself to it; while the most vulgar and ill-informed women are ever most inclined to be tyrants, and those always struggle most vehemently for power who, at the greatest distance from deserving it, would not fail to make the worst use of it.[37]

Matriarchs marketed the masquerading Shunamite's superiority as a wife over imbecile-exquisites and vulgar coquettes who used and abused their interior power to subject men to their "despotic sway," by demonstrating in novels and conduct books that she made the better wife precisely because she understood, as imbecile-exquisites did not, that (overt) competition with men for power and ascendancy in the family did not make for domestic happiness. Unlike the female exquisite who built her empire over men on her infantility and imbecility, the Shunamite masquerading as a proper lady would never be so foolish, so vulgar, or so ill-informed as to struggle with her husband for power. For she had "accurate" views (as we saw!) of the station she was born to fill and knew just how to accommodate herself — and her husband — to her proper place.

Adopting what Diane Hoeveler calls "the masquerade of femininity" thus allowed the Shunamite to "submit to the dominant economy of desire in an attempt to remain on the [marriage] market in spite of everything." It allowed her to exploit all the eroticism that, as Ruth Yeazell has shown, men attached to the signs of female ignorance and modesty, however fictional they might be; and this enabled her to compete without competing with the imbecile-exquisite, who was her principal rival for the attentions and the affections of propertied and well-born men.[38] Matriarchs were thus able, not entirely without truth, to emplot their fictions to show that the masquerading Shunamite *manifestly* was the complaisant, subordinate, "feminine," noncompetitive and nonthreatening wife that the imbecile-exquisite only promised to be, and that she was ultimately to be preferred as a wife by "men of sense and fortune."

As the Egalitarians observed with considerable distaste, however, this also meant that masquerading Shunamites differed from imbecile-exquisites less than Matriarchs liked to suppose. The Matriarchs had shifted the source of female power from the body to the mind and from infantile female incapacity to superior female ability, but they had not changed its stratagems. Like imbecile-exquisites, Egalitarians said, masquerading Shunamites obtained their ascendancy over men by dissimulation, by "deluding" men with "mock ensigns" of their power, and by practising that "winning softness" which "governs by obeying." Like imbecile-exquisites, too, masquerading Shunamites were seeking to "overbalance" men's "exterior power" by means of their own, less visible and more "interior" forms of power, in order to elevate themselves from inferiority and subordination into men's ascendant place. Like the imbecile-exquisites they despised, therefore, the Matriarchs were proceeding on the principle, "Power is the law of man; make it yours." They were building the Shunamite's empire on "a little knowledge of human weakness, justly termed cunning, softness of temper, *outward* obedience, and a scrupulous attention to a puerile kind of propriety" — instead of on the demand that men "respect in us the majesty of a rationality on which he so justly values himself."[39]

Egalitarians critiqued the Matriarchs, not only for the way they urged women to build their empire over men, but also for treating empire over others as the supreme good. From the Egalitarians' point of view, the problem was that Matriarchs and imbecile-exquisites were both going after the wrong thing: "It is not empire, but equality that they should be contending for."[40] Egalitarians argued that power over others was an evil, not a good. Matriarchal arguments that women should use their empire over others to "noble ends" overlooked the fact that power over others is almost invariably abused by women as well as men, and that it inevitably corrupts those who exercise it. Men could not be trusted with sovereign power in family society because "power is an engine too dangerous, and of too ready execution in domestic life, to be trusted in the hands of men — subject as all human beings more or less are to error, to passion and caprice."[41] For the same reason, women could not be trusted with sovereign power in domestic society either: "Women lose all dignity of mind in acquiring power, and act as men are observed to act when they have been exalted by the same means."[42] Women become (like) tyrannical men when they purloin men's power and rotate into their governing place. As Lacan might say, all those who occupy the place of the phallus come to be spoken by it. When women sank men to exalt themselves and exercise power from the patriarch's commanding place, they were only casting down patriarchal power to replace it with the equally nefarious and oppressive power of Matriarchs. As Wollstonecraft put it, "one power should not be thrown down to exalt another — for all power inebriates weak men."[43]

Consistent with their vision of independence, the Egalitarians insisted that they "did not wish women to have power over men, but over themselves."[44] They no more wanted women to rule over men than they wanted men to rule over women or over other men. Where Matriarchal analyses of power centered on competition, because they were interested in competing for domestic power and for ascendancy over men, Egalitarian analyses of power centered on hierarchy, because they wanted to eliminate competition for power and place relative to others altogether. And where Matriarchal analyses of power showed the destructive effects of direct competition on hierarchical societies, which were cemented by mutual dependencies, Egalitarian analyses of power showed the "pernicious" effects of structuring societies as hierarchies, which encouraged dependency and competition for relative position in the first place.

Wollstonecraft agrees that in hierarchies, superiors and inferiors are mutually dependent, but not in the benevolent way that Matriarchs and male Enlightenment ideologues argued cemented societies for the public good. Superior power, she said, creates and "multiplies dependents," because the number of dependents and the extent of their dependency is a measure of the superior's power. At the same time, it puts those dependents in a situation where their major concern must be to please and placate their superiors, and this precludes the exercise of sense and virtue both in women and in men.

Wollstonecraft adduced the professions — the army, the navy, and the clergy — as evidence of the way men are "necessarily made foolish or vicious by the very [hierarchical] constitution of their professions." Among the clergy, for instance, "the curate . . . must obsequiously respect the opinion of his rector or patron, if he means to rise in his profession." He is made foolish by being required to demonstrate "blind submission" to his superiors rather than to think for himself and act independently according to the dictates of his own reason and conscience. By the same token, in the army, blind submission to superiors turns every corps into "a chain of despots who, submitting and tyrannizing without exercising their reason, become dead weights of vice and folly on the community."[45]

Wollstonecraft argued, by analogy with men's professions in civil society, that preserving hierarchies of superiority and dependence in domestic society, as the Matriarchs wanted to do, was bound to have the same negative effects on the profession of ladies as wives, mothers, and mistresses of families:

> If women be educated for dependence, that is to act according to the will of another fallible being and submit, right or wrong, to power, where are we to stop? Are they to be considered as *vice-regents* allowed to reign over a small domain and answerable for their conduct to a higher tribunal liable to error? It will not be difficult to prove that such delegates will act like men subjected by fear, and make their children and servants endure their tyrannical oppression.[46]

Wollstonecraft argued that ladies would not be able to govern the family, much less act like Shunamites from principles of sense and virtue, in the structural position of "vice-regent" that Matriarchs were preparing for them by professionalizing women's domestic offices and advising women to conceal their real government of the family by leaving their husbands the "name and all th'additions to a king." In the position of vice-regent, the professional wife and mistress of the family was, like the curate and the soldier, still subordinate to the power of another whom she must please and placate. Like the dependent curate and soldier, the dependent wife would be afraid not to follow her husband's orders; like them, she would therefore submit to those above and tyrannize those below without exercising her reason, to preserve or advance her own interests.

The other even more pernicious effect of hierarchies, Wollstonecraft argued, was that in practice men did not rise in them by ability and merit but by interest and pandering servility: "A man of rank or fortune, sure of rising by interest, has nothing to do but to pursue some extravagant freak; while the needy *gentleman* who is to rise, as the phrase turns, by his merit, becomes a servile parasite or a vile pander." In hierarchies, she insisted, "respectability is not attached to the relative duties of life, but to the station." Hierarchies are corrupt and corrupting because they deflect attention and rewards from the ability with which tasks are performed to a person's standing in the hierarchy, and thus turn all competition into competition to obtain or retain station and place. A minister of state's "chief merit" consists of "the art of keeping himself in place," because that is what makes him "respect-able"; "it is not necessary that a minister should feel like a man when a bold push might shake his seat." By the same token, the ranks who were seeking to "encroach on the place and privilege of the rank or ranks above them," as the Matriarchs said, were seeking wealth, because wealth, not merit and virtue, was the means of obtaining the station to which respectability was attached. "One class presses on another; for all are aiming to procure respect on account of their property; and property once gained, will procure the respect due only to talents and virtue. Men neglect the duties incumbent on man, yet are treated like demi-gods."[47] Hierarchy was therefore the cause of competition and the origin of all the moral and social ills that the Matriarchs argued competition entailed.

Egalitarians insisted that all uses of power which suborned men and women's independence were to be eschewed. Consequently, the only power over men that Egalitarians would permit themselves to use was the persuasive power of language. They believed in "human nature" as some of the more optimistic Enlightenment ideologues had portrayed it: man was a rational being, and pity and benevolence were innate and "natural" to him. They therefore focused their efforts on deploying well-thought-out rhetorical strategies to mobilize what Mary Hays called "the only true grounds of power[, which] are reason and affection for humanity."[48]

The Egalitarians assumed that, as rational beings, men could be persuaded by rational arguments that their views about women were false and their practices nefarious: "it is neither absurd nor chimerical," insisted Mary Hays, "to suppose that men may by degrees and by calm representation, be brought to consider the subject as they ought, and are bound in justice and honour to do."[49] All the evils of women's situation, said Mary Ann Radcliffe, "proceed from one of the three following causes: viz, a want of reflection from its being a precedent of long standing; a wilful blindness, through avaricious views; or a downright want of understanding."[50] The Egalitarians therefore used rational arguments to persuade men to rethink all those longstanding, unfounded doctrines, customs, and prejudices that deprived women of their dignity and rights. They argued passionately against the prejudices that kept women ignorant, against the customs that kept them dependent, against the laws that kept them helpless, against the doctrines that assumed their inferiority, against the tyrannies that oppressed them, and against all the practices responsible for lives spent in apparently unmitigated suffering. They explained and explained and explained again all those points on which men continued to show a curious want of understanding. And they determined that what men could not be brought to understand they must be made to feel.

Egalitarians reasoned that, as inately compassionate and benevolent as well as rational beings, men were also susceptible to persuasion through their hearts and consciences: "Justice — Pity — Gratitude — and other virtues are inherent in the human mind . . . Consequently, no thinking or rational being can deviate from them without violating the laws of his nature, and thus wounding his conscience."[51] If men's wilful blindness and avaricious views could not be discredited by rational arguments, this law of human nature meant that they could be circumvented by heart-rending portraits of the terrible effects on women of the injustices committed against them. The Egalitarians painted moving portraits of the abuses women faced inside and outside family society: at the hands of husbands who displayed all manner of cruelties from willfulness and neglect to alcoholism and physical brutality, at the hands of family and kin who offered women insult and injury instead of protection, and at the hands of friends, employers, and seducers who duped, raped, or degraded women when they were already sunk by illness, poverty, and despair. Using what Diane Hoeveler has called "staged female weakness" to make their case, the Egalitarians duplicated and exploited patriarchal associations of femininity with helplessness, weakness, dependence, and incapacity by presenting women as helpless victims of intolerable cruelty, unreason, and injustice, who had been completely "reduced to a state of submission and dependence" and "rendered mutely the humble companions of men, the tools of their interest or the sport of their authority."[52]

The Matriarchal story of superior female ability and virtue was designedly a success story, even when disguised by the proprieties required by the Shunamite's strategic masquerade. "You too can succeed in marrying well and occupying your proper eminence centre-stage if you imitate this heroine and use her strategies to govern your man," the Matriarchal narrative seemed to say. Whatever its simultaneous status as a reflection of reality, the story of female suffering and victimization was a strategic story too. The victim story was designed to serve Egalitarian goals. The Egalitarians' emotive language and moving descriptions of women as "poor, unfortunate victims" were powerful rhetorical instruments, aimed at the heart and designed to wound — or awaken — society's conscience. As their hopes that England would complete her Glorious Revolution faded in the last decade of the eighteenth century, Egalitarians increasingly devoted their efforts and their fictions to awakening society's conscience by exemplifying the victimizations caused by the failures of the Glorious Revolution to actualize its utopian, paternalistic dream.

Separate Spheres and the "Great Forgetting"

Exemplified in eighteenth-century novels, conduct books, essays, and tracts and imitated during the nineteenth century both in England and in America (where Matriarchs like More and Edgeworth were published and read), it was the Matriarchal imaginary of the family and of the virtuous "domestic woman" governing her household, educating her children, and assisting the needy for the public good which initially prevailed. The Matriarchs' strategy for elevating ladies in the domestic hierarchy onto the pedestal reserved for the capable and angelically virtuous Shunamite eventually changed the relative duties ascribed to husbands and wives, fathers and mothers, and masters and mistresses of families. And, although no doubt aided and abetted in the nineteenth century by the Industrial Rev-

olution and the separation of workplace from home, it was eighteenth-
century Matriarchs' fictional exemplars of virtuous Christian ladies unilaterally making government of the family "a sphere of properly female action" which eventually became naturalized in the doctrine of "separate
spheres."

We might therefore construe the domestic revolution as the successful
effect of Enlightenment feminist work. We might conclude that, as a program designed to elevate women from their inferiority and to free them
from subordination "in all things," the division of labor between women
and men imagined by Enlightenment feminists actually improved the situation of certain classes of women for a hundred years or more. But we
cannot simply stop there, for "feminization," marginalization, and dis-
empowerment of the family, and of the eighteenth-century women's novels that had debated and transformed it, almost immediately accompanied
implementation of this particular domestic revolution as its shadow. The
Matriarchs' very success therefore raises ongoing questions about the
mixed and problematical consequences of even the most successful feminist revolution at a different historical moment and in different social and
cultural circumstances.

From this point of view, it is interesting to note that it was only in the
middle of the nineteenth century — when the family had been recentered
on ladies' domestic government and on women's work — that political
ideology and public policy installed the individual "unencumbered subject" as society's fundamental component unit, downplayed the public
benefit of private domestic offices, and represented the family as increasingly separate from the real economic and political business of society. It
was in the latter half of the nineteenth century — only after Matriarchs
had taught private ladies to eschew their dissipations and to make themselves responsible for the education of their children — that the schooling
of children was moved, by law and public policy, out of the family and into
the public domain. The Public Education Act was passed in England in
1870, and universal compulsory schooling became law in 1880.[53] It was after ladies without means in the middle and upper ranks had reconceived
private families as more or less peaceful asylums for themselves from a
cruel and money-driven world, by centering them on ladies' good offices,
that the family began to be construed as *men's* haven in a heartless world.
And only after eighteenth-century women novelists had transformed

women's reading matter, built up a faithful readership, and turned the novel into a forum for social, political, and feminist debate did the "domestic novel" become a privileged *male* genre of nineteenth-century middle-class writing. This is also when canonical histories of the novel began to iterate James Beattie's narrative aphasia by claiming that the only four, reasonably popular, male eighteenth-century novelists Beattie could think of were responsible for the transformation of the old romance into the domestic novel,[54] with the consequence that important eighteenth-century women writers, like Frances Brooke, Sarah Scott, Eliza Haywood, Charlotte Lennox, Frances Sheridan, Elizabeth Inchbald, Charlotte Smith, Mary Hays, Jane West, Maria Edgeworth, and Eliza Fenwick, were written out of history.

The domestic revolution modeled in women's eighteenth-century conduct books and novels and debated by Enlightenment Matriarchs and Egalitarians was thus effaced by what Clifford Siskin has called the "Great Forgetting."[55] The naturalization of separate spheres and of the domestic arena as woman's proper domain was predicated, in other words, on a number of significant erasures. But, rather than arguing that these erasures were produced solely by what Astell called men's habit of writing histories to "recount each other's Great Exploits" or by patriarchal *resentment*, we ought to consider where at least some of history's subsequent erasures stemmed from the Matriarchal strategies of masquerade and concealment discussed above, as well as from Matriarchal silencing and discrediting of their Egalitarian rivals.

The first erasure for which Matriarchs themselves can be held wholly or partly responsible was erasure of the family as a feminist issue and of the domestic as a "territory" which women had ever disputed with men. As we saw, the Matriarchs' bid for domestic power required the superior lady to avoid direct competition and "ostensible rivalship" with men. It required masking the Shunamite's superior abilities and virtues under the proper lady's veils of modesty, silence, deference, and unwillingness to attract notice. Matriarchal strategy for taking over domestic government from men advised ladies to govern while seeming to obey. It taught them to surreptitiously use their superior internal power and any opportunities afforded by their husbands' pursuit of their pleasures or obligations abroad to take over "the plan of domestic economy" while preserving the appearances of the patriarchal family by presenting themselves as their husbands' "vice-

regents." No part of this Matriarchal strategy was served by alerting or reminding men that the "domestic woman" was, or had ever been, anything
but a properly complaisant, noncompetitive, and obedient wife. No part of
this Matriarchal strategy was served, either, by reminding men that it was
men who had once been called upon by Enlightenment ideology to stay at
home to raise and educate their own children, to find their pleasures in the
nursery, to volunteer their time and assistance to their needy neighbors,
and to take charge — tenderly, benevolently, and responsibly — of the domestic economy and of the welfare and employment of everyone in it.
Thus, if the nineteenth-century doctrine of separate spheres sealed the
victory of the domestic woman in the domestic sphere, it also tied her
hands and made the Great Forgetting of women's role in the domestic revolution the condition and result of her success.

A second erasure for which Matriarchs can be held at least partly responsible was that of the complex role played by law in the domestic revolution. The domestic revolution owed much of its impulse, as we saw, to
the Enlightenment conviction that "the government of laws not men"
promised "enlargement," and to feminist uses of reason, education, and the
law of God to translate this promise of enlargement into self-government
for ladies and into transformations of the domestic domain, which offered
greater scope for female action. But the domestic revolution also owed
much of its urgency in the latter half of the eighteenth century to the detrimental economic and social effects on women of restrictive laws — like
the 1753 Marriage Act and laws proclaiming all children bastards whose
parents had not been legally married before their birth[56] — which penal-
ized women's sexual activity outside registered forms of marriage in order
to control the proper "multiplication of the population" and to subordinate
the reproduction of children to the production of wealth. Together with
the steady decrease in jobs for women in the economy at large and
women's decreasing ability to support themselves, the penalties inscribed
by such laws made it increasingly urgent that women in the middling and
upper ranks "get husbands" and confine themselves, their sexuality, their
talents, and their abilities to whatever domestic society had to offer.

Judged purely by their material results, of course, eighteenth-century
laws bearing on marriage and reproduction were a triumph for political
economy and for public "police" — in the triple eighteenth-century sense
of policy, civil administration, and enforcement of public order. The popu-

lation's growth rate accelerated steadily in the latter half of the eighteenth century, according to Rickman's first census in 1801; and Britain's population almost doubled between 1791 and 1831, when it went from 7.74 million to 13.28 million in a generation and a half.[57] Together with laws that voided traditional canonical practices of retroactive legitimation for illegitimate children *per subsequens matrimonium*, the Marriage Act — by voiding the "troth" of all unions not preceded by the ceremonies it prescribed — helped to drive down the age of marriage and increase the demand for "marriage and a maintenance" as a condition for "commerce" between the sexes. But such legislative acts also helped drive up the frequency of those related phenomena, prenuptial pregnancies (pregnant brides) and "illegitimate" births, as Egalitarian rewritings of Rousseau remind us,[58] while driving a permanent wedge between legality and morality.

The Matriarchs identified private morality with public legality, and they magnified the distance between the "virtuous" woman, who "conquered" before yielding a man possession of her person, and the "fallen" woman, who yielded upon the promise of marriage in the mistaken belief that she would conquer. They enhanced this distinction, initially at least, to bring home to women the message that trusting to men's promises in the old way under the new marriage law would only turn more and more of the population into bastards and whores and reduce women and children to poverty by depriving them of any right to a man's economic "maintenance." Identifying morality with legality and advising women to conquer before yielding constituted a more immediately practical defense for women against the strictures of the law than anything proposed by the Egalitarians. It also conformed to the longstanding Matriarchal practice of arguing that women could govern themselves better than men could govern them, by showing that women knew better than men how to adhere to moral, religious, and positive law.

But this strategy, in turn, erased all question about the law. It eliminated all questioning of that disjunction between morality and legality which the government admitted it had created, as well as uncomfortable questions about those "corrupt" implementations of law which were dramatized and condemned by Egalitarians. As a result, the Matriarchs' self-righteous cult of the "virtue" prescribed by civil law and their moral condemnation of "fallen" women also sank into the Great Forgetting the radical effects, on their own and less fortunate women's lives, of laws that had all but created

the "unmarried mother" and the "fatherless child" by no longer acknowledging and upholding the "troth" of the union that had produced them.

A third erasure for which Matriarchs can be held responsible was the
partial erasure of the analogical mirroring between the private and public,
the particular and the general, which made fictional exemplification possible. Although Matriarchs represented the private domestic woman as
playing a governing public, philanthropic role, they were consistently blind
to what the particular objects of her benevolence — the poor tenant, the
imprisoned creditor, the outcast daughter, the crippled soldier, the dispossessed farmer, the illegitimate child — exemplified in public and social
terms. By the same token, although Matriarchal revisionings of the patriarchal family exemplified the possibility of inverting or disabling hierarchies between men and women, which placed the Shunamite in a position
of subordination and dependence which to her was intolerable, Matriarchs
were often blinded, by their own will to power, to the analogies between
the politics they espoused in their own private, subordinate, and dependent domestic situations and those of men and women in ranks subordinate
to and dependent on their own.

We might also say that there was a complementary partial erasure of
the mirroring between private and public (this time in the sense of "published to the world") in the Matriarchs' consistent strategy of making
themselves appear more conventional than they were. Matriarchs were often double-faced and double-voiced: in their careful selection of one feminist goal at a time, in the way they used morality as a mask in their fictions, and in their advice to would-be Shunamites to masquerade as
proper ladies. And we might argue that whenever the mask she presented
to the world was mistaken for the true object of imitation, the Matriarchs'
powerful feminist model of the admirably capable Shunamite was erased.

The final erasure for which we can hold Matriarchs responsible was the
discrediting and repression of their Egalitarian rivals. We might say that
this silencing was a function of all the other erasures, since (as we saw), despite their own shortcomings, Egalitarian fictions foregrounded the blindness profiled by the Matriarchs' insight and dismantled Matriarchal models of the family and of the domestic woman by pointing to the
complacency, the coldness, the cunning, and the will to power that lay at
their core. Of course, the Egalitarians' imaginary of the family and their
dream of equality and reciprocity between women and men at home and

abroad lived on as a "subjugated knowledge," to reemerge in different guises at different times.

What was plunged into the Great Forgetting, therefore, were the terms of the Enlightenment debate between women and of the war of systems in their novels, and with it the cogency and topicality of the Matriarchs' and Egalitarians' respective positions, the centrality of their concerns to Enlightenment thinking, and the common issues women faced. This has obscured the extent to which our discussions about the family and about women's proper place are still framed by the motifs that recurred in their work. These were motifs of power and domestic government, of hierarchy and equality in family societies, and of women's work and women's worth. They were motifs of "virtue," economics, and female sexuality, and of children as a source of wealth or want. They were motifs of subjection, victimization, and exclusion, of education and law, and of the power of fictions to mold us for good or ill. For those of us who are still willing to look to the past for examples, there may be a moral here about the impossibility of any permanent victory by one feminism or another, once the links of filiation and dialogue are lost.

NOTES

1. Judith Phillips Stanton, "Statistical Profile of Women Writing in English from 1660 to 1800," in *Eighteenth-Century Women and the Arts,* ed. Frederick M. Keener and Susan Lorsch (New York: Greenwood, 1988): 250–51. Dale Spender's landmark work rediscovered a hundred women novelists; Stanton identified over one thousand women writers and was still uncovering more as the book went to press. See Dale Spender, *Mothers of the Novel: One Hundred Good Women Writers before Jane Austen* (London: Pandora, 1986). See also Jane Spencer, *The Rise of the Woman Novelist: From Aphra Behn to Jane Austen* (Oxford: Blackwell, 1986); and Clifford Siskin, *The Work of Writing: Literature and Social Change in Britain, 1700–1830* (Baltimore: Johns Hopkins Univ. Press, 1998).

2. Cheryl Turner, *Living by the Pen: Women Writers in the Eighteenth Century* (London: Routledge, 1992), 57, 59. See also Margaret J. Ezell, *Writing Women's Literary History* (Baltimore: Johns Hopkins Univ. Press, 1993); and, for the power of writing during the long eighteenth century, Nancy Armstrong and Leonard Tennenhouse, *The Imaginary Puritan: Literature, Intellectual Labor, and the Origins of Personal Life* (Berkeley: Univ. of California Press, 1992); and Siskin, *Work of Writing*.

3. *Public woman* meant prostitute in the eighteenth century and indeed, until the middle of the century, it was a common *topos* in prefaces to play on the seductiveness of the woman writer and of the body of her text as they offered themselves to readers. As we will see, one of the things that Enlightenment feminists changed during the long eighteenth century — along with the image of women as by nature passionate, licentious, and disorderly — was this image of the woman writer as a public woman who was prostituting herself. Enlightenment feminists from mid century on gave women and women writers — both — a new respectability by identifying them with principle, morality, and service to the public good. For

the change in images of women's nature between the end of the seventeenth and the end of the eighteenth century, see Felicity Nussbaum, *The Brink of All We Hate* (Lexington: Univ. Press of Kentucky, 1984).

The term *patriarchy* has been used by political theorists as a label for a particular political philosophy and by historians for social and domestic situations in which men control women and children (or at least keep telling women and children that they must submit to being controlled by men). I use this term with Margaret Ezell's and Anthony Fletcher's caveats in mind that patriarchy covers a variety of older and newer patriarchal situations in the sixteenth and seventeenth centuries too, and that it needs to be considered a flexible term. See Margaret Ezell, *The Patriarch's Wife* (Chapel Hill: Univ. of North Carolina, 1987); and Anthony Fletcher, *Gender, Sex, and Subordination in England, 1500–1800* (New Haven: Yale Univ. Press, 1995).

4. Quoted words are by "Sophia," who wrote two feminist pamphlets in 1751, one Egalitarian ("Woman Not Inferior to Man") and the other Matriarchal ("Woman's Superior Excellence over Man"). No one quite knows who she was or whether she was a "she" at all, but the pamphlets capture what were by then already quite longstanding feminist positions. Extracts from the essays can be found in Moira Ferguson, ed., *First Feminists: British Women Writers, 1578–1799* (Bloomington: Indiana Univ. Press, 1985), 270, 277.

5. Ibid., 283.

6. Janet Todd, *The Sign of Angellica: Women, Writing and Fiction, 1660–1800* (New York: Columbia Univ. Press, 1989), 9.

7. Ibid., 2.

8. Eleanor Ty, *Unsex'd Revolutionaries: Five Women Novelists of the 1790s* (Toronto: Univ. of Toronto Press, 1993), 4.

9. Anne Mellor, *Romanticism and Gender* (New York: Routledge, 1993), 83–84.

10. Mitzi Myers, "Hannah More's "Tracts for the Times": Social Fiction and Female Ideology," in *Fetter'd or Free? British Women Novelists, 1670–1815,* ed. Mary Anne Schofield and Cecilia Macheski (Athens: Ohio Univ. Press, 1986), 277–78; and Patricia Myer Spacks, *Desire and Truth: Functions of Plot in Eighteenth-Century English Novels* (Chicago: Univ. of Chicago Press, 1990), 6.

11. Ezell, *Patriarch's Wife,* 54. Ezell is speaking of the seventeenth century, but as we will see, the situation of the family and of the patriarch within it was still being debated and recast in the eighteenth century.

12. Jacques Derrida, "Les Langues et les Institutions de la Philosophie," *Texte* 4 (1985): 4; see also "Des Tours de Babel," in Jacques Derrida, *Psyche: Invention de l'Autre* (Paris: Seuil, 1987); and Eve Tavor Bannet, "The Scene of Translation: After Jakobson, Benjamin, De Man, and Derrida," *New Literary History* 24, no. 3 (1993): 577–95.

13. Jacques Derrida, *The Ear of the Other: Otobiography, Transference, Translation* (New York: Schoken, 1982), 122.

14. Elizabeth Grosz, "Sexual Difference and the Problem of Essentialism," in *The Essential Difference,* ed. Naomi Schor and Elizabeth Weed (Bloomington: Indiana Univ. Press, 1994), 95. *Emersion* seems to mean "immersion in and emergence from."

15. Elizabeth Kowalski-Wallace, *Their Fathers' Daughters: Hannah More, Maria Edgeworth, and Patriarchal Complicity* (Oxford: Oxford Univ. Press, 1991), 110.

16. Anne Phillips, *Democracy and Difference* (University Park: Pennsylvania State Univ. Press, 1993), 95.

17. Alice Browne, *The Eighteenth-Century Feminist Mind* (Detroit: Wayne State Univ. Press, 1987), 19.

18. Janet Barker, Preface to *Exilius; or the Banish'd Woman* (1715; reprint, New York: Garland, 1973).

19. Clara Reeve, *The Progress of Romance* (1785; reprint, New York: Facsimile Editions, 1974), 2:41.

20. Ezell, *Patriarch's Wife,* 65; Mellor, *Romanticism and Gender,* 8. Gallagher makes the same point. The difference between the seventeenth and eighteenth centuries appears to lie only in the form the *topos* took. In the seventeenth century, according to Ezell, it was proper to deny an economic motive for publication; in the eighteenth, according to Gallagher, it was proper to claim that one was publishing from economic necessity. As Gallagher puts it: "Grub Street had become pathetic . . . it harbored a new breed of worthy starvelings." See Catherine Gallagher, *Nobody's Story: The Vanishing Acts of Women Writers in the Marketplace, 1670–1820* (Berkeley: Univ. of California Press, 1994), 155.

21. I have found such scholarship extremely helpful, especially the work of Katherine Sobba Green, Anne Mellor, Kate Ellis, Claudia Johnson, and Ann Williams, which contrasts men and women's uses of the "same" Gothic, Sentimental, or Romantic genres, and the work of Lennard Davis and Michael McKeon, which un-

derlines the undecidability of the line between fact and fiction in eighteenth-century narratives.

22. James Thompson, *Models of Value: Eighteenth-Century Political Economy and the Novel* (Durham: Duke Univ. Press, 1996), 7, 12.

23. Turner, *Living by the Pen,* 17.

24. Ralph A. Houlbrooke, *The English Family, 1450–1700* (New York: Longman, 1984), 5; Peter Laslett and Richard Wall, eds., *Household and Family in Past Time* (Cambridge: Cambridge Univ. Press, 1972), 64.

25. J. C. D. Clark, *English Society, 1688–1832: Ideology, Social Structure, and Political Practice during the Ancien Régime* (Cambridge: Cambridge Univ. Press, 1985), 6.

26. John Cannon, *Aristocratic Century: The Peerage in Eighteenth-Century England* (Cambridge: Cambridge Univ. Press, 1984), 170.

27. Clark, *English Society,* 67. See also James J. Sack, *From Jacobite to Conservative: Reaction and Orthodoxy in Britain, 1760–1832* (Cambridge: Cambridge Univ. Press, 1993); and Dustin Griffin, *Literary Patronage in England, 1650–1800* (Cambridge: Cambridge Univ. Press, 1996). Although she takes a more plural view of Britain, Linda Colley generally agrees with this neo-Tory representation. She also denies that economic growth was a modernizing agent, arguing that landed men continued to dominate all the high offices of the land to the end of the Victorian period and that "the elite believed rightly that commercial energy, imperial dominion, a taste for liberty, and stable rule by an exclusive elite could be painlessly combined." Linda Colley, *Britons: Forging the Nation, 1707–1837* (New Haven: Yale Univ. Press, 1992), 61.

28. Robert B. Shoemaker, *Gender in English Society, 1650–1850* (London: Longman, 1998), 11–12.

29. Harold Perkin, *The Origins of Modern English Society, 1780–1880* (London: Routledge, 1969), 24.

30. Naomi Schor and Elizabeth Weed, eds., *The Essential Difference* (Bloomington: Indiana Univ. Press, 1994), xiv.

31. Linda J. Nicholson, *Gender and History: The Limits of Social Theory in the Age of the Family* (New York: Columbia Univ. Press, 1986), 17.

32. Zillah Eisenstein, *The Radical Future of Liberal Feminism* (New York: Longman, 1981): 89. Some of the other classical texts here are: Melissa Butler, "Early Liberal Roots of Feminism: John Locke and the Attack on Patriarchy," *American*

Political Science Review 72 (1978): 135–50; Mary Lyndon Shanley, "Marriage Contract and Social Contract in Seventeenth-Century English Political Thought," *American Political Science Review* 32 (1979): 79–91; Teresa Brennan and Carole Pateman, "Mere Auxiliaries of the Commonwealth: Women and the Origins of Liberalism," *Political Studies* 27 (June 1979): 183–200; Jean Bethke Elshtain, *Private Woman and Public Man: Women in Social and Political Thought* (Princeton: Princeton Univ. Press, 1982); Carol Pateman, "Feminist Critiques of the Public/Private Dichotomy," in *Public and Private in Social Life,* ed. S. I. Benn and G. F. Ganz (New York: St. Martin's, 1983); Genevieve Lloyd, *The Man of Reason: Male and Female in Western Philosophy* (London: Methuen, 1984); Jean Grimshaw, *Philosophy and Feminist Thinking* (Minnesota: Univ. of Minnesota Press, 1986); Nicholson, *Gender and History;* and Ellen Kennedy and Susan Mendus, eds., *Women in Western Philosophy: Kant to Nietzsche* (New York: St. Martin's, 1987).

33. Rosalind Coward, *Our Treacherous Hearts* (London: Faber & Faber, 1992), 5.

34. Judith Evans, *Feminist Theory Today: An Introduction to Second-Wave Feminism* (London: Sage, 1995).

35. See for instance: Deborah L. Rhode, *Theoretical Perspectives on Sexual Difference* (New Haven: Yale Univ. Press, 1990); Mariane Hirsch and Evelyn Fox Keller, *Conflicts in Feminism* (New York: Routledge, 1990); Pamela Abbott and Claire Wallace, *The Family and the New Right* (London: Pluto, 1992); Schor and Weed, *Essential Difference;* and Moira Gatens, *Feminism and Philosophy* (Bloomington: Indiana Univ. Press, 1991).

36. Carol Lee Bacchi, *Same Difference: Feminism and Sexual Difference* (Sydney: Allen & Unwin, 1990); Constance H. Buchanan, *Choosing to Lead: Women and the Crisis in American Values* (Boston: Beacon, 1996); Betty Friedan, *Beyond Gender* (Washington, D.C.: Woodrow Wilson Center Press, 1997).

Chapter 1 / The Question of Domestic Government

1. Martyn P. Thompson, *Ideas of Contract in English Political Thought in the Age of John Locke* (New York: Garland, 1987).

2. This was also the argument against Locke made by Second Wave liberal feminist theorists. For the key texts, see above, Introduction, n. 32.

3. John Locke, *Two Treatises upon Government,* edited and introduced by Peter Laslett (Cambridge: Cambridge Univ. Press, 1967), 2: #82. References are to treatise and paragraph number.

4. Mary Astell, *Some Reflections upon Marriage* (1694; reprint, New York: Source Book Press, 1970).

5. Locke, *Two Treatises,* 2: #86.

6. Astell, *Some Reflections,* 107.

7. This was not a marginal issue. Susan Staves observes of the court cases she read that justices generally "resisted scrutinizing very closely" what went on in families; "each husband and father was in important ways to be the judge of what went on in his own family, and public justices disliked interfering with this jurisdiction." Susan Staves, *Married Women's Separate Property in England, 1660–1833* (Cambridge: Harvard Univ. Press, 1990), 228. As Shoemaker points out, "in this hierarchical society, violence was an accepted method of disciplining social inferiors who misbehaved, whether they were servants or wives." Robert B. Shoemaker, *Gender in English Society, 1650–1850* (London: Longman, 1998), 104. By the nature of her subject, Staves focuses on the propertied ranks, for whom Astell largely spoke. Matters might have been a little different among villagers, since neighbors would intervene in situations of marital violence. See Susan Dwyer Amussen, *An Ordered Society: Gender and Class in Early Modern England* (Oxford: Blackwell, 1988); and John Gillis, *For Better or Worse: British Marriages 1600 to the Present* (Oxford: Oxford Univ. Press, 1985).

8. Astell, *Some Reflections,* 107 (Astell's emphasis).

9. Ibid. England could be said to have "elected" her sovereigns (i.e., freely chosen them and consented to be ruled by them) in the Revolutionary Settlement, which brought William and Mary and their heirs to the throne of England in place of the Stuart monarchs. The stipulations about the monarch's constitutional powers in the Act of Settlement could likewise be compared to the stipulations about the husband's freedom to dispose of property coming to him with his wife's marriage settlements.

10. Nancy Armstrong and Leonard Tennenhouse, *The Imaginary Puritan: Literature, Intellectual Labor, and the Origin of Personal Life* (Berkeley: Univ. of California Press, 1992), 173.

11. Daniella Gobetti, *Private and Public: Individuals, Households, and Body Politic in Locke and Hutcheson* (New York: Routledge, 1992). For the prevalence and uses of the family-state analogy in seventeenth-century England, see Amussen, *An Ordered Society.* Roderick Phillips shows that Locke continued to argue in the terms established by the Civil War debate when "protagonists both on the royalist and parliamentary sides attempted to justify their respective causes by appeals to im-

ages of marriage and the family. Both sides agreed that the relation between a king and his subjects was analogous to the contractual relation between husband and wife. The question was whether in the case of a tyrannical husband (the king at the political level), the wife (the kingdom) was permitted to rebel and finally divorce." See Roderick Phillips, *Putting Asunder: A History of Divorce in Western Society* (Cambridge: Cambridge Univ. Press, 1988), 166.

12. Peter Laslett, Introduction to John Locke, *The Two Treatises on Government* (Cambridge: Cambridge Univ. Press, 1967), 112. The work of Laslett and Schochet (see n. 13) was the basis for Second Wave liberal feminist arguments that there is no family-state analogy in the *Treatises* and that the modern divide between the public and private spheres and between "private woman" and "public man" began with Locke. I am using Laslett and Schochet's arguments to show that this is not the case even in their terms.

13. Gordon J. Schochet, *Patriarchalism in Political Thought* (Oxford: Blackwell, 1975), 263, 265.

14. Locke, *Two Treatises*, 2: #78, #14.

15. It was to keep the analogy on this point that Locke had to allow divorce after the "Endes" of conjugal society had been served. See n. 11. Locke's eighteenth-century followers did not follow him here.

16. Laslett, Introduction, 112.

17. Locke, *Two Treatises*, 2: #63.

18. Ibid., 2: #65.

19. John Dennis, *Vice and Luxury Publick Mischiefs; or Remarks on a Book Intituled the Fable of the Bees or Private Vices Public Benefits* (London: 1724), 8.

20. Francis Hutcheson, *Collected Works* (Hildesheim, Germany: Georg Olms Facsimile Edition, 1969), 4:279, 282.

21. Ibid., 282.

22. For the hierarchical character of civil and political society, see especially Amussen, *An Ordered Society;* Harold Perkin, *The Origins of Modern English Society, 1780–1880* (London: Routledge, 1969); and J. C. D. Clark, *English Society, 1688–1832: Ideology, Social Structure, and Political Practice during the Ancien Régime* (Cambridge: Cambridge Univ. Press, 1985). Paul Langford has countered with the argument that the hegemony belonged to property rather than to aristocracy as such, and he has foregrounded the presence of countermovements. Paul Langford,

Public Life and the Propertied Englishman, 1689–1798 (Oxford: Clarendon, 1991). For the hierarchical character of domestic society, see Anthony Fletcher, *Gender, Sex, and Subordination in England, 1500–1800* (New Haven: Yale Univ. Press, 1995). Fletcher argues against Lawrence Stone that even "the very essence of the companionate marriage was the subordination of women . . . during the eighteenth century, patriarchal relations between men and women were reinforced by a potent secular ideology of subordination" (395). Carol Pateman and Susan Staves make the same point, arguing respectively that contract theory "justified" both civil and domestic subordination and that "contract theory was used in the eighteenth century to legitimize the husband's power over his wife." In Carol Pateman, *The Sexual Contract* (Stanford, Calif.: Stanford Univ. Press, 1988) 33; and Staves, *Married Women's Separate Property*, 167. Suzanne Trill explores how, in addition, "Christianity provided the ideological basis for a patriarchal system of social order that defined femininity negatively and justified female subjection and subordination." See her essay, "Religion and the Construction of Femininity," in *Women and Literature in Britain, 1500–1700*, ed. Helen Wilcox (Cambridge: Cambridge Univ. Press, 1996), 31–32.

23. Lawrence Stone, *The Road to Divorce: England 1530–1987* (Oxford: Oxford Univ. Press, 1992), 13.

24. Quoted in Shoemaker, *Gender in English Society*, 103; Philip Dormer Stanhope, Lord Chesterfield, *Letters to His Son* (London, 1775, 2nd ed.), 2:330.

25. Locke, *Two Treatises*, 2: #58, #61, #58, #60.

26. Ibid., 1: #67.

27. Judith Drake, *An Essay in Defence of the Female Sex* (1696; reprint, New York: Source Book Press, 1970), 33.

28. Ibid., 28.

29. Quoted in Hilda Smith, *Reason's Disciples: Seventeenth-Century English Feminists* (Urbana: Univ. of Illinois Press, 1982), 106.

30. Mary Hays, *Appeal to the Men of Great Britain in Behalf of Women* (1798; reprint, New York: Garland, 1974), 97.

31. Ibid., 159.

32. Ibid.

33. Eliza Haywood, *The Female Spectator*, 4 vols. (London, 1775), 3:79.

34. Lady Chudleigh, "The Ladies' Defence; or the Bride Woman's Counsellor Answer'd" (1700), in *First Feminists: British Women Writers, 1578–1799,* ed. Moira Ferguson (Bloomington: Indiana Univ. Press, 1985), 221. The character speaking is Sir John.

35. Masham, Lady Damaris, *Occasional Thoughts in Reference to a Vertuous or Christian Life* (London, 1705), 55.

36. Lady Chudleigh, "Ladies' Defence," 231. The character speaking is Sir William.

37. Mary Wollstonecraft, *Vindication of the Rights of Woman with Strictures on Moral and Political Subjects* (New York: Whitston, 1982), 64.

38. See Sylvia Harcstark Myers, *The Blue-Stocking Circle: Women, Friendship, and the Life of the Mind in Eighteenth-Century England* (Oxford: Clarendon, 1980).

39. Wollstonecraft, *Rights of Woman,* 350.

40. Locke, *Two Treatises,* 2: #63.

41. This became a commonplace, which was repeated by men and by women throughout the eighteenth century.

42. Locke, *Two Treatises,* 2: #59.

43. One could argue that this kind of personal power, and its abuse, continue alongside and as the underside of the impersonal technes of power that Foucault describes. This other sort of power is ignored by him, however. From this point of view, his theory buys into Enlightenment assumptions about the automatism of laws and government which were modeled on Newtonian readings of God's government of the world as a great machine obeying ineluctable laws. See Eve Tavor Bannet, "Analogy as Translation: Wittgenstein, Derrida, and the Law of Language," *New Literary History* 28, no. 4 (1997): 655–72. As we will see in the concluding chapter, women recognized and deployed both "official" and "unofficial" kinds of power.

44. Locke, *Two Treatises,* 2: #57.

45. Hutcheson, *Works,* 6:282.

46. Adam Ferguson, *Institutes of Moral Philosophy,* new enlarged edition (Basil: James Decker, 1800), 218.

47. For women's view of the polity's failure to live up to its promises, see Chapter 5.

48. Astell, *Some Reflections,* 107, 108.

49. Jane West, *Letters to a Young Lady in which the Duties and Characters of Women are Considered,* 3 vols. (2nd ed. of 1806; reprint, New York: Garland, 1974), 2:447.

50. Clara Reeve, *Plans of Education, with Remarks on the Systems of other Writers* (1792; reprint, New York: Garland, 1976), 37.

51. Locke says that "the greatest part of mankind govern themselves chiefly, if not solely by this law of fashion; and so they do that which keeps them in reputation with their company, little regard the laws of God and the Magistrate." *Essay Concerning Human Understanding,* (London, Everyman, 1947), 2:28, #12.

52. See the next section, which shows how they deployed the law of God to their own advantage.

53. Astell, *Some Reflections,* 34.

54. Hannah More, *Works,* vol. 8, *Strictures on the Modern System of Female Education* (London: 1818), 34.

55. J. G. A. Pocock, *Virtue, Commerce, and History* (Cambridge: Cambridge Univ. Press, 1987).

56. Dennis, *Vice and Luxury Publick Mischiefs,* 8.

57. Montesquieu, *De L'Esprit des Lois,* 6 vols. (Paris, 1834), 1:42.

58. From this point of view, Locke's *Treatises* resembled the Twenty-Nine Articles of the Church of England, which sought to build a broad base of agreement between opposing religious camps.

59. See Andrew Sharp, ed., *Political Ideas of the English Civil Wars, 1641–1649* (London: Longman, 1983); and Richard Ashcraft, *Revolutionary Politics and Locke's "Two Treatises of Government"* (Princeton: Princeton Univ. Press, 1986).

60. As Rousseau understood, there were in effect two origins for society in Locke: the social contract and the family. See Chapter 5.

61. Locke, *Two Treatises,* 2: #10.

62. Ferguson, *Institutes,* 218.

63. Pocock, *Virtue, Commerce, and History,* 224.

64. Joseph Nicolas has shown that "the English Civil War became a frame of reference throughout the Romantic period for contemporary political events on the Continent," with explicit parallels being drawn, for instance, between Cromwell and the revolutionary tyrants in France. See Joseph Nicolas, "Revolutions Com-

pared: The English Civil War as Political Touchstone in Romantic Literature," in *Revolution and English Romanticism: Politics and Rhetoric,* ed. Keith Hanley and Raman Selden (New York: St. Martin's, 1990). For adaptations of English thought by the French, see Lynn Hunt, *The Family Romance of the French Revolution* (Berkeley: Univ. of California Press, 1992). For English responses to the French Revolution, see Ronald Paulson, *Representations of Revolution, 1789–1820* (New Haven: Yale Univ. Press, 1983). For the continuity in radical thought in England between 1688 and the French Revolution, see Caroline Robbins, *The Eighteenth-Century Commonwealthsman* (Cambridge: Harvard Univ. Press, 1959); J. G. A. Pocock, *The Ancient Constitution and the Feudal Law* (Cambridge: Cambridge Univ. Press, 1987); and Bridget Hill, *The Republican Virago: The Life and Times of Catherine Macauley* (Oxford: Clarendon, 1992).

65. Stephen Prickett, *England and the French Revolution* (London: Macmillan, 1989), 31.

66. In Marilyn Butler, ed., *Burke, Paine, Godwin and the Revolutionary Conspiracy* (Cambridge: Cambridge Univ. Press, 1984), 29. For the relation between Price's position on electoral representation, that of Locke and that of the Levellers before him, see Ashcraft, *Revolutionary Politics.*

67. Hill, *Republican Virago.* There is also a good discussion here of how the Whigs at mid century rediscovered Locke and the political pamphlets of the Civil War.

68. Edmund Burke, *Reflections on the Revolution in France,* in *The Writings and Speeches of Edmund Burke,* vol. 8, ed. Paul Langford (Oxford: Clarendon, 1989), 63, 66. As Marilyn Butler points out, Burke was giving the Revolution "one possible revolutionary plot" and there were others. See her essay, "Revolving in Deep Time: The French Revolution as Narrative," in *Revolution and English Romanticism: Politics and Rhetoric,* ed. Keith Hanley and Raman Selden (New York: St. Martin's, 1990), 1–22.

69. Burke, *Reflections,* 147.

70. Ibid., 143.

71. Ibid., 110.

72. Quoted in Hill, *Republican Virago,* 75.

73. Written in 1738 and published only in 1749, Bolingbroke's *Letters on the Spirit of Patriotism and on the Idea of a Patriot King* (Oxford: Clarendon, 1982) used "the ordinance of God" to argue for "the just authority of kings and the due obedience of subjects" (53). It also castigated any attempt to overthrow a king.

74. For analyses of Wollstonecraft's response to Burke, see Paulson, *Representations of Revolution;* Eleonor Ty, *Unsexed Revolutionaries: Five Women Novelists of the 1790s* (Toronto: Univ. of Toronto Press, 1993); Tom Furniss, "Gender in Revolution" in *Revolution in Writing: British Literary Responses to the French Revolution,* ed. Kevin Everest (Buckingham, England: Open Univ. Press, 1991); and Claudia Johnson, *Equivocal Beings: Politics, Gender, and Sentimentality in the 1790s: Wollstonecraft, Radcliffe, Burney and Austen* (Chicago: Univ. of Chicago Press, 1995).

75. Pocock, *Virtue, Commerce, and History,* 102.

76. Sophia, "Woman Not Inferior to Man," 270, 277.

77. See Hunt, *Family Romance;* and Olwen H. Hufton, *Women and the Limits of Citizenship in the French Revolution* (Toronto: Univ. of Toronto Press, 1992).

78. Barbara Taylor, *Eve and the New Jerusalem: Socialism and Feminism in the Nineteenth Century* (New York: Pantheon, 1983), 21.

79. Sophia, "Woman's Superior Excellence over Man," 283.

80. Astell, *Some Reflections,* 117–18.

81. For a strong argument against this reading, see Katherine Sutherland, "Hannah More's Counter-Revolutionary Feminism" in *Revolution in Writing: British Literary Responses to the French Revolution,* ed. Kevin Everest (Buckingham, England: Open Univ. Press).

82. See Christopher Durston, *The Family in the English Revolution* (Oxford: Blackwell, 1989); and Shoemaker, *Gender in English Society.*

83. Margaret Fell Fox quoted in Ferguson, *First Feminists,* 115.

84. Quoted in Durston, *Family in the English Revolution,* 13.

85. Quoted in Hilda Smith, *Reason's Disciples,* 55.

86. Elaine Hobby describes two periods of women's writing in the seventeenth century and demonstrates how women "transformed proscriptions into a kind of permission," for instance, when they said that they were commanded by God to write and that their writing was therefore proof of their obedience and modesty. See Elaine Hobby, *Virtue of Necessity: English Women's Writing, 1646–1688* (London: Virago, 1988), 7. Also Hilary Hinds, *God's Englishwomen: Seventeenth-Century Radical Sectarian Writing and Feminist Criticism* (Manchester: Manchester Univ. Press, 1996).

87. Astell, *Some Reflections*, 122, 100; Masham, *Occasional Thoughts*, 27. See also Ruth Perry, *The Celebrated Mary Astell: An Early English Feminist* (Chicago: Univ. of Chicago Press, 1986); and Joan Kinnaird, "Astell and the Conservative Contribution to English Feminism," *Journal of British Studies* 19, no. 1 (1979): 53–75.

88. Bathsua Makin, *An Essay to Revive the Antient Education of Gentlewomen in Religion, Manners, Arts and Tongues* (London, 1673): 3.

89. Ferguson, *First Feminists*, 233.

90. Astell, quoted in Perry, *The Celebrated Mary Astell*, 56.

91. Lady Chudleigh, Introduction to "Ladies' Defence," 214.

92. Ibid., 236.

93. William Seymour, *Marriage Asserted: In Answer to a Book Entitled Conjugium Conjurgium* (1674; reprint, New York: Garland, 1976), 17.

94. Astell, *Some Reflections*, 100.

95. This is a point also made by Poullain de la Barre: "I think it is no less unworthy to imagine (as the vulgar commonly do) that women are naturally servants of man; than to pretend that they who have received talents and particular endowments from God, are servants and slaves of those for whose good they employ them." François Poullain de la Barre, *The Woman as Good as the Man; or the Equality of Both Sexes,* trans. A. L. (1677; reprint, Detroit: Wayne State Univ. Press, 1988). Some critics have claimed that Astell was influenced by Barre because they sometimes used similar arguments; she could have found the same arguments elsewhere.

96. "Letter on Religion I," in Elizabeth Carter, *Memoirs of the Life of Mrs. Carter,* 3 vols. (London, 1816), 1:374.

97. West, *Letters to a Young Lady,* 2:292; 3:71.

98. Carter, *Memoirs,* 374.

99. William Gouge, *Domesticall Duties* (1622), quoted in Smith, *Reason's Disciples,* 51. Attempts were made by some clerics and conduct book writers in the eighteenth century to soften this a little by pointing out that husbands had a reciprocal duty to be reasonable and kind to their wives.

100. Wollstonecraft, *Rights of Woman,* 86, 58; Catherine Macauley, *Letters on Education* (1790; reprint, New York: Garland, 1974), 100.

101. Wollstonecraft, *Rights of Woman*, 40.

102. Macauley, *Letters*, 201.

103. Mary Hays, *Letters and Essays, Moral and Miscellaneous* (1793; reprint, New York: Garland, 1974), 122.

104. Wollstonecraft, *Rights of Woman*, 376; West, *Letters to a Young Lady*, 2: 365.

105. Hays, *Appeal*, 169.

106. Ibid., 260.

107. See Adrienne Rich, *Of Woman Born: Motherhood as Experience and Institution* (New York: Norton, 1976); and Carol Gilligan, *In a Different Voice: Psychological Theory and Women's Development* (Cambridge: Harvard Univ. Press, 1982).

108. For discussion of these types, see Paul K. Korskin, *Typologies in England, 1650–1820* (Princeton: Princeton Univ. Press, 1982); and John K. Sheriff, *The Good-Natured Man: the Evolution of a Moral Ideal, 1660–1800* (Birmingham: Univ. of Alabama Press, 1982). See also Gary Kelly's argument about the "feminization" of men in this period. Curiously, his marxist argument reproduces the position of the most patriarchal (as opposed to paternalistic) of eighteenth-century male commentators.

109. The ideological underpinnings of this figure in the latter half of the eighteenth century will be explored in Chapter 4.

110. See Caroline Gonda, *Reading Daughters' Fictions, 1709–1834* (Cambridge: Cambridge Univ. Press, 1996). Gonda explores shifts in the representation of paternal authority in women's novels from tyrannical rule (in *Clarissa* and *Sir Charles Grandison*) to moral and pedagogical care.

111. West, *Letters to a Young Lady*, 2:365; 3:239.

112. *King Lear*, act I, sc. 1.

113. West, *Letters to a Young Lady*, 3:140.

114. For survey of male conduct books on women's proper position in relation to men, see Ellen Messer-Davidow, "For Softness She" in *Eighteenth-Century Women and the Arts*, ed., Frederick M. Keener and Susan Lorsch (New York: Greenwood, 1988). See also n. 22 above.

115. William Fleetwood, *The Relative Duties of Parents and Children, Husbands and Wives, Masters and Servants* (1705; reprint, London: Scholartis Press, 1928), 60, 165, 175.

116. Thomas Gisbourne, *An Inquiry into the Duties of the Female Sex* (1797; reprint, New York: Garland, 1984), 231.

117. William Paley, *Paley's Moral Philosophy*, with annotations by Richard Whateley (London, 1859), 226.

118. West, *Letters to a Young Lady*, 2:321. "Bashaws" or "Pashahs" was supposed to invoke "Oriental" tyranny. Many histories of the world and accounts of manners in different climes at this time described British women as freer and more fortunate than women in the Orient, who were portrayed as confined to harems by tyrannial pashas. These accounts used men's civility, gallantry, and "politeness" to ladies as an index of Britain's superiority to the Orient and more advanced and cultivated mores. West is saying, "Don't flatter yourselves, gentlemen; we're not in a better situation at all."

Chapter 2 / Domestic Fictions and the Pedagogy of Example

1. Roland Barthes, *Sollers Ecrivain* (Paris: Seuil, 1979), 20, 39.

2. Clara Reeve, *The Progress of Romance* (1785; New York: Facsimile Editions, 1974), 1:97.

3. Hugh Blair, *Lectures on Rhetoric and Belles Lettres* (1763; reprint, London, 1812), 304.

4. Catherine Macauley, *Letters on Education* (1790; reprint, New York: Garland, 1974), 330.

5. Ibid., 334, 332. Eighteenth-century reactions to the spread of printing and literacy and to the proliferation of popular fiction it brought with it emphasize the presence of an important new influence. Blair points out that novels "might be employed to very useful purpose" (*Lectures,* 304). The Edgeworths observed that "formerly it was wisely said, 'Tell me what company a man keeps and I will tell you what he is;' but since literature has spread a new influence over the world, we must add, 'Tell me what company a man has kept and what books he has read, and I will tell you what he is.'" Maria Edgworth and Richard Lovell Edgeworth, *Practical Education* (1798; reprint, New York: Garland, 1974), 385. And Macauley says that "to confine literary occupation entirely to novels . . . cannot fail to have a powerful influence over the manners of society" (*Letters on Education*, 148). It is a commonplace in text after text — indeed, one which is illustrated in the novels themselves — that the characters and expectations of young people are formed by the novels they read. As Clifford Siskin has said, "to classify the innumerable warnings

against young girls reading novels as simply a manifestation of Augustan conservatism is to miss the historical point — the particular attitude to change was secondary to a primary issue: writing's capacity to produce that change." Clifford Siskin, *The Work of Writing: Literature and Social Change in Britain, 1700–1830* (Baltimore: Johns Hopkins Univ. Press, 1998), 3.

6. Jane Barker, preface to *Exilius; or the Banish'd Woman* (1715; reprint, New York: Garland, 1973).

7. Anna Laetitia Barbauld, *The British Novelists with an Essay and Prefaces Biographical and Critical,* 50 vols. (London, 1810), 1:50.

8. Ibid., 1:59.

9. Jane West, *Letters to a Young Lady in which the Duties and Characters of Women are Considered,* 3 vols. (1806 [2nd ed.]; reprint, New York: Garland, 1974), 2:455, 461; Hannah More, *Works,* (London, 1818), 7:33.

10. Reeve, *Progress of Romance,* 85.

11. West, *Letters to a Young Lady,* 2:309, 312.

12. See also Eve Tavor, *Scepticism, Society, and the Eighteenth-Century Novel* (London: Macmillan, 1987; New York: St. Martin's, 1987), 150ff.

13. Reeve, *Progress of Romance,* 85.

14. More, *Works,* 7:287.

15. For boundary crossing, see Lennard J. Davis, *Factual Fictions: The Origin of the English Novel* (New York: Columbia Univ. Press, 1983); and Michael McKeon, *The Origins of the English Novel, 1600–1740* (Baltimore: Johns Hopkins Univ. Press, 1987).

16. Blair, *Lectures,* 160.

17. Mary Delariviere Manley, Preface to *The Secret History of Queen Zarah, and the Zarazians* (London, 1705).

18. Eliza Haywood, *The Female Spectator* (London, 1775), 5, 6. This was probably written early in 1744.

19. Edgeworth and Edgeworth, *Practical Education,* 351. See also Henry Home, Lord Kames, *Elements of Criticism* (1763; reprint, New York: 1855), 70.

20. More, *Works,* 7:210.

21. *Familiar* was still the adjective of the noun *family,* and *familiarity* meant "proper to the head of a family," "proper to a person of the family," and hence "the behaviour due among members of a family or household" (*Oxford English Dictionary*).

22. Sarah Fielding, *Remarks on "Clarissa"* (1749; reprint, Los Angeles: William Clark Memorial Library, no. 231, 1985), 7. Compare this with Samuel Johnson's more familiar statement in *The Rambler,* no. 4 (1751) that "when an adventurer is levelled with the rest of the world, and acts in such scenes of the universal drama as may be the lot of any other man; young spectators fix their eyes upon him with closer attention, and hope by observing his behaviour and success to regulate their own practices, when they shall be engaged in like part. For this reason these familiar histories may perhaps be made of greater use than the solemnities of professed morality, and convey the knowledge of vice and virtue with more efficacy than axioms and definitions." Sarah Fielding does not speak of individual adventurers journeying through the universal drama of the world.

23. Mary Wollstonecraft, *A Vindication of the Rights of Woman, With Strictures on Moral and Political Subjects,* (1792; reprint, New York: Whitston, 1982), 229.

24. Henry St. John Bolingbroke, *Works,* vol. 2, *Letters on the Study and Use of History,* 186; Blair, *Lectures,* 17–18, 305.

25. Barbauld, *British Novelists,* 1:48, 49.

26. Timothy Hampton, *Writing from History: The Rhetoric of Exemplarity in Renaissance Literature* (Ithaca: Cornell Univ. Press, 1990), 4.

27. Johnson, *Rambler* 4.

28. Reeve, *Progress of Romance,* 102. Compare with Montaigne's: "Fabulous testimonies, provided they are possible, serve like true ones. Whether they happened or no, in Paris or in Rome, to John or Peter, they exemplify at all events some human capacity." Quoted in John D. Lyons, *Exemplum: The Rhetoric of Example in Early Modern France and Italy* (Princeton: Princeton Univ. Press, 1989), 142.

29. Kames, *Elements of Criticism,* 70.

30. Sir William Jones, "On the Imitative Arts," in *Eighteenth-Century Critical Essays,* ed., Scott Elledge (Ithaca: Cornell Univ. Press, 1961), 88.

31. John Locke, *Some Thoughts Concerning Education* (Oxford: Clarendon, 1989), 1: #67.

32. Haywood, *Female Spectator,* 1:151.

33. More, *Works*, 8:57.

34. West, *Letters to a Young Lady*, 3:347.

35. Gary Kelly, *Revolutionary Feminism: The Life and Career of Mary Wollstonecraft* (New York: St. Martin's, 1992), chap. 1.

36. Johnson, *Rambler* 4; Robert Dodsley, *An Essay on Fable* (1764; reprint, Los Angeles: Augustan Reprint Society, no. 112, 1965), lxi.

37. Kames, *Elements of Criticism*, 51.

38. Elizabeth Cooper, Preface to *The Muses' Library* (London, 1737); Macauley, *Letters on Education*, 283.

39. Macauley, *Letters on Education*, 115; More, *Works*, 7:53; Reeve, *Progress of Romance*, 126.

40. As Janet Todd says, "sentimental literature is exemplary of emotion." See Janet Todd, *Sensibility: An Introduction* (London: Methuen, 1986), 4. For the intended effect on readers, see Todd, op. cit., and Ann Williams, *Art of Darkness: A Poetics of Gothic* (Chicago: Chicago Univ. Press, 1995).

41. Johnson, *Rambler* 121; Mrs. Barbauld uses this phrase also.

42. Sarah Fielding, Preface to *The History of Countess Dellwyn* (London, 1759).

43. Lyons, *Exemplum*, 19. John Oldmixon made the same point about induction in the eighteenth century: "History is designed to instruct Mankind by Example, to shew what Men were by what they did, and from particular Instances to form general Lessons in all the various Stations of Life." John Oldmixon, *An Essay on Criticism* (1728; reprint, Augustan Reprint Society, no. 107–8, 1964), 18.

44. "Knowledge is nothing but the perception of the connection and agreement or disagreement and repugnancy of ideas." John Locke, *Essay Concerning Human Understanding*, IV, 1:2.

45. Dodsley, *Essay on Fable*, lix–lx, lxi.

46. Stephen Greenblatt, *Renaissance Self-Fashioning from More to Shakespeare* (Chicago: Univ. of Chicago Press, 1980).

47. In Ioan Williams, *Novel and Romance, 1700–1800: A Documentary Record* (New York: Barnes & Noble, 1970), 147.

48. More, *Works*, 7:57, 34–35.

49. West, *Letters to a Young Lady,* 2:323, 325.

50. Spacks reads the "messages and countermessages" in eighteenth-century women's novels as emerging from the plot; Gonda points out that "the power of the example" may also be working against the grain of the moral. In Patricia Myer Spacks, *Desire and Truth: Functions of Plot in Eighteenth-Century English Novels* (Chicago: Univ. of Chicago Press, 1990); and Caroline Gonda, *Reading Daughters' Fictions, 1709–1834* (Cambridge: Cambridge Univ. Press, 1996).

51. See Lorraine McMullen, *An Odd Attempt in a Woman: The Literary Life of Frances Brooke* (Vancouver: Univ. of British Columbia Press, 1983).

52. Frances Brooke, *Lady Julia Mandeville* (1764; reprint, London: Scholartis Press, 1930), 47.

53. David Hume, *Essays Literary, Moral and Political* (London: Ward, Locke & Tyler, n.d.), 413.

54. Quoted in McMullen, *An Odd Attempt,* 64–65.

55. Ibid., 63. See also Janet Todd's reading of this novel in *The Sign of Angellica: Women, Writing, and Fiction, 1660–1800* (New York: Columbia Univ. Press, 1989).

56. The issue here is not merely one of patriarchal power; it has to do with eighteenth-century uses of law to preserve estates under family names. As Paul Langford has pointed out, the turnover of landed property in the eighteenth century was blatant and troubling to contemporaries: of the 100 largest estates in Buckinghamshire, for instance, 37 changed hands between 1700 and 1750, and 17 more between 1750 and 1780. To keep estates in the family, fathers used a variety of legal devices, from wills and entails to jointures and marriage settlements, including — when the last heir was a daughter — making marriage to her conditional on her husband's taking her family's name. This is also the issue on which Cecilia's marriage to Mortimer Delvile initially founders in Burney's *Cecilia,* where Delvile Senior refuses to let Mortimer take her name and Cecilia loses her fortune on marrying him as a result. See Paul Langford, *Public Life and the Propertied Englishman, 1689–1798* (Oxford: Clarendon, 1991), 35ff.; and Susan Staves, *Married Women's Separate Property in England, 1660–1833* (Cambridge: Harvard Univ. Press, 1990).

57. Kowalski-Wallace has argued that there was no fundamental difference between new-style benevolent and old-style authoritarian or "tyrannical" patriarchy. See Elizabeth Kowalski-Wallace, *Their Fathers' Daughters: Hannah More, Maria Edgeworth, and Patriarchal Complicity* (Oxford: Oxford Univ. Press, 1991). But her argument that Matriarchs like Edgeworth and More were "Daddy's girls" assumes

that eighteenth-century feminists did not understand this. Brooke's novel shows that they did understand that the iron fist had only been covered by a velvet glove, and so do many of the other feminist rewrites of Rousseau later in the century, which will be considered in Chapter 5. See also Mitzi Myers defense of Edgeworth against Kowalski-Wallace's charges, "Daddy's Girl as Motherless Child: Maria Edgeworth and Maternal Romance," in *Living by the Pen,* ed., Dale Spender (New York: Teacher's College Press, 1992).

58. Barbauld, *British Novelists,* 27:1. The *Monthly Review* had written, "we doubt not, but the exemplary fate of the rash and infatuated Mandeville, will preach more powerfullly against the horrid practice of duelling, than all the dispassionate reasoning in the world; not excepting, perhaps, even the masterly arguments contained in Rousseau's *Eloisa.*" (29 August 1763). Jonathan Clark suggests that "duelling is the best index to and proof of the survival and power of the aristocratic ideal as a code separate from and ultimately superior to the injunctions of law and religion" and that, from the 1770s to its demise after 1832, attacks on duelling were attacks on the aristocratic code of honor. If this is the case, Mrs. Barbauld may also be hinting that Brooke's novel was subversive of the aristocratic political ideals cited at Belmont. See J. C. D. Clark, *English Society 1688–1832: Ideology, Social Structure, and Political Practice during the Ancien Régime* (Cambridge: Cambridge Univ. Press, 1985), 108ff.

59. Mary Hays, Preface to *Memoirs of Emma Courtney* (1796; reprint, London: Pandora, 1987).

60. Barbauld, *British Novelists,* 1:51. Mrs. Barbauld is echoing Fanny Burney's Preface to *Evalina.*

61. See Katherine Anne Ackley, "Violence against Women in the Novels of Early British Women Writers" in *Living by the Pen,* ed. Dale Spender (New York: Teachers' College Press, 1992).

62. Betty Rizzo shows that (real) women like Elizabeth Montagu (Matriarch leader of the Bluestocking circle) and Lady Elizabeth Chudleigh "outpatriarched the patriarchs" and "dictated the terms" of their dependents' lives to their dependents. See Betty Rizzo, *Companions without Vows: Relations among Eighteenth-Century British Women* (Athens: Univ. of Georgia Press, 1994), 111. Mme. Duval has also been read as a reference to (and punishment of) Fanny Burney's aunt, who lived with the Burneys and tried to force Fanny to accept a proposal of marriage from a man who had come to tea and decided he liked the look of her; Fanny was saved from this awful fate by her father's intervention.

63. For the importance of a "blessed competence" to eighteenth-century women like Evalina, see Edward Copeland, *Women Writing about Money: Women's Fiction in England, 1790–1820* (Cambridge: Cambridge Univ. Press, 1995). Copeland defines a "competence" as "that amount of money that it takes to live 'genteelly,'" and says that "the competence scale, universally understood, settles even the most outrageous plots into a translatable, recognizable social persepctive" (10).

Julia Epstein and Catherine Gallagher have explored questions connected to Evalina's lack of any proper family name; they say that Evalina, like Burney herself, whose father was a music teacher and servant to the genteel, was a "nobody" in social terms, seeking a name. Epstein argues that the novel shows that for eighteenth-century women self-determination derived "first and foremost from social legitimation" and that Evalina is somewhat two-faced and manipulative in this respect, showing both an innocent and a knowing (and thus critical, ironic, and rebellious) face in her letters, and using her innocence to control Villars and Orville in order to make an ultimately conventional place for herself in the patriarchy. Other critics have shared these views, often reading Evalina as an extension of Burney herself. See Julia Epstein, *The Iron Pen: Frances Burney and the Politics of Women's Writing* (Madison: Univ. of Wisconsin Press, 1989); Catherine Gallagher, *Nobody's Story: The Vanishing Acts of Women Writers in the Marketplace, 1670–1820* (Berkeley: Univ. of California Press, 1994); Judy Simons, "The Tactics of Subversion," in *Living by the Pen*, ed. Dale Spender (New York: Teachers' College Press, 1992); Kristina Straub, *Divided Fictions: Fanny Burney and Feminine Strategy* (Lexington: Univ. Press of Kentucky, 1987); Joanne Cutting-Gray, *Woman as "Nobody": The Novels of Fanny Burney* (Gainsville: Univ. Press of Florida, 1992).

As we will see in Chapter 5, however, the question of "name" as a problem of family affiliation and of the situation of middle- and upper-class women who lacked both family and finances becomes an increasingly important issue in Egalitarian feminist novels as the century progresses, for sociohistorical reasons that transcend Burney's personal psychology and biography. I am arguing here that *Evalina* exemplifies the Egalitarian ideals for family relations described in the previous chapter and that one has to distinguish among eighteenth-century ideologies and visions of the family to determine what is conventional and what is subversive in a particular discursive context.

64. Terry Castle, *Masquerade and Civilization: The Carnivalesque in Eighteenth-Century English Culture and Fiction* (Stanford: Stanford Univ. Press, 1986), 279, 283. Castle reads this as the end of the novel (which it is not), in order to argue that Cecilia's carnivalesque career represents Burney's wish fulfilment and that, having

punished herself and her character for having such unrealistic wishes, she forces herself and her character back into conventional feminine subordination. Katharine Rogers likewise argues that *Cecilia* "demonstrates that even a woman who apparently has every resource of independence" cannot retain them. See Katharine M. Rogers, *Frances Burney: The World of Female Difficulties* (New York: Harvester Wheatsheaf, 1990). but see also nn. 56 and 70 to this chapter. One could argue that loss of fortune upon marrying against patriarchal wishes is being shown to be the consequence of acquiring money, as both Cecilia and Mortimer do, by inheritance rather than by work (as Burney does). As Charlotte Smith understands in *Emmeline,* money or "a financial independence" is the precondition for freedom of choice and independence of conduct in Burney's early novels. See also Gonda, *Reading Daughters' Fictions,* chap. 3.

65. *Emmeline* has also been read as a rewrite of Goethe's *Werther* and of Rousseau and as a Gothic novel. See Syndy McMillen Conger, "The Sorrows of Young Charlotte: Werther's English Sisters, 1785–1805," *Goethe Yearbook* 3 (1986): 21–56; and Diane Long Hoeveler, *Gothic Feminism: The Professionalization of Gender from Charlotte Smith to the Brontes* (University Park: Pennsylvania State Univ. Press, 1995).

66. As Katharine Rogers says, "Taught to value herself primarily as a sexual being, Miss Milner can conceive no way to gratify her ego except by exerting power over men." Katharine Rogers, "Elizabeth Inchbald: Not Such a Simple Story," in *Living by the Pen,* ed. Dale Spender (New York: Teachers' College Press, 1992), 83. However, in this respect, Miss Milner may be said to represent the patriarchy's model for the proper lady; see Spacks, *Desire and Truth,* 100. One might even suggest that Inchbald is subverting the conventional patriarchal pattern of proper female development from the young and beautiful woman, who reigns over men before marriage, to the compliant and subservient wife.

67. This insistence that the roles of lover and mentor or guardian be separated is an important move in the lover-mentor theme in eighteenth-century novels, first discussed by Dale Spender, since it may be seen as a precondition for egalitarian reciprocity between husband and wife. For the lover-mentor theme, see also Jane Spencer, *The Rise of the Woman Novelist: from Aphra Behn to Jane Austen* (Oxford: Blackwell, 1986); and Spacks, *Desire and Truth.* In important and troubling respects, the lover-mentor theme intersects with the incest theme in eighteenth-century womens's novels. See particularly Eleanor Ty, *Unsex'd Revolutionaries: Five Women Novelists of the 1790s* (Toronto: Univ. of Toronto Press, 1993), chap. 5.

68. Mrs. Stafford was read at the time as speaking for Charlotte Smith, whose marital experience was similar. She likewise left her husband and supported her eight children through her writing.

69. John Stuart Mill, *The Subjection of Women* (London: Virago, 1983), 1.

70. Since many readings of Burney's novels are biographical and they stand accused of social and patriarchal conformism, it may be worth pointing out that Burney herself eschewed any conventional place in the social hierarchy: she hated her time at court and married a French emigré, D'Arblay, whom she had to support through her writing. One might read this egalitarian extension of reciprocity between husband and wife to the family finances as the foundation for the possibility of supporting a husband who could not provide for her.

71. Janet Todd has pointed out that Jacobin novels try to incorporate "both gentleness and humanity" and "firmness of nerve" in a "dualistic balanced ideal" of men's and women's characters. Pat Elliot has likewise pointed out that Charlotte Smith "often blurred gender distinctions." See Todd, *Sensibility*, 189; and Pat Elliott, "Charlotte Smith's Feminism," in *Living by the Pen*, ed. Dale Spender (New York: Teachers' College Press, 1992), 94. This has proved a problem for critics like Gary Kelly, who speaks of the "feminization" of eighteenth-century culture, and Claudia Johnson, who argues against these "equivocal beings," saying that when men became feminized, women had to become hyperfeminine. One might point out that, in different ways, both are allying themselves with eighteenth-century critiques of "nursing fathers" and of Egalitarian feminists. These critiques of "effeminate men" and "female Amazons" likewise assumed that it was problematic or wrong for men and women to have the same "human nature." See Gary Kelly, *Women, Writing and Revolution* (Oxford: Clarendon, 1993); and Claudia Johnson, *Equivocal Beings: Politics, Gender, and Sentimentality in the 1790s: Wollstonecraft, Radcliffe, Burney, Austen* (Chicago: Univ. of Chicago Press, 1995).

72. Mrs. Selwyn is preferred to Evalina by many modern critics. She is often read as a feminist or female Amazon and as an expression of Burney's real desires. See, for instance, Katherine Sobba Green, *The Courtship Novel, 1740–1820* (Lexington: Univ. Press of Kentucky, 1991); and Spencer, *Rise of the Woman Novelist*.

73. For the Shunamite, see Chapter 1, "The Issue of Relative Place."

74. For a less idealized view of the situation of female companions in other women's households, see Rizzo, *Companions without Vows;* Janet Collier's chapter on the subject in *An Essay on the Art of Ingeniously Tormenting* (London, 1753); and the "little histories" in Sarah Scott's *Millenium Hall* (1762; Ontario: Broadview,

1994). One might also read these scenes as what Spencer calls "a dramatized conduct book" for downtrodden female companions.

75. For links between Lennox, West, and Austen, see Patricia Myer Spacks, "Sisters," in *Fetter'd or Free? British Women Novelists, 1670–1815,* ed. Mary Anne Schofield and Cecilia Macheski (Athens: Ohio Univ. Press, 1986); and Marilyn Butler, *Jane Austen and the War of Ideas* (Oxford: Clarendon, 1975). For a study of Lennox's career, see Gallagher, *Nobody's Story,* chap. 4.

76. Much of the important work on Maria Edgeworth and *Belinda* has been done by Marilyn Butler — which is just as well, since she is one of the few critics who likes *Belinda.* In *Jane Austen and the War of Ideas,* Butler reads *Belinda* as an equivocal novel, because she assumes that Edgeworth was a Jacobin like her father and Thomas Day. In *Maria Edgeworth: A Literary Biography* (Oxford: Clarendon, 1972), Butler compares *Belinda* favorably to *Cecilia* and reads it as an exemplary novel. Beth Kowalski-Wallace critiques *Belinda*'s "domestic ideology." For the issues here and Marilyn Butler's response, see n. 57 above. See also Elizabeth Harden, *Maria Edgeworth* (Boston: Twayne, 1984); and Gallagher, *Nobody's Story.*

77. Nancy Armstrong argues that "the domestic woman executes her role in the household by regulating her own desire . . . Self regulation alone gave a woman authority over a field of domestic objects and personnel where her supervision constituted a form of value in its own right." I don't disagree with her there; I do think, however, that Armstrong overlooks the role this self-government initially played in eighteenth- and early-nineteenth-century Matriarchal feminism and in the complexities of feminist thinking about virtue and self-regulation. For Matriarchs, self-restraining virtue was at once a tactic for inverting power relationships in the household and a means of demonstrating women's respect-ability, and Matriarchal images of capable women supervising the household were designed both to supply the place of fortune in the marriage mart and to show that women could take on (i.e., usurp) the important domestic roles that patriarchal ideology assigned to men (see Chapter 4). Because her work is primarily focused on the nineteenth century, Armstrong does not see the feminist underpinnings of the domestic woman; she reads her only as an agent of hegemonic patriarchal ideology. This the domestic woman may, indeed, have become in the later nineteenth century, once the doctrine of separate spheres and the public-private, family-state divide were in place. But, as Mitzi Myers has pointed out, "paradigms universalized from Victorian fiction cannot fully account for women's writing generated from and contingent on a different situation." See Nancy Armstrong, *Desire and Domestic Fiction: A Political History of the Novel* (Oxford: Oxford Univ. Press, 1987); and

Myers, "Daddy's Girl," 138. For other critics of Armstrong's thesis, see the introduction to this book.

78. In *The Courtship Novel,* Katherine Sobba Green argues that the Percivals represent Maria Edgeworth's ideal of marriage. But their marriage is reciprocal and egalitarian, with husband and wife nurturing and educating their children; Belinda's is not. Her marriage gives Belinda the ascendancy over and supervision of others, and there are several scenes in the novel which show her to be superior to and more capable than her prospective groom in dealing with domestic matters (the scene with his servant for instance). For Edgeworth's disagreement with Egalitarian principles, see also Marilyn Butler, "Edgeworth's Stern Father: Escaping Thomas Day, 1795–1801," in *Tradition in Transition: Women Writers, Marginal Texts and the Eighteenth-Century Canon* (Oxford: Clarendon, 1996).

79. See Wollstonecraft's comparison of Matriarchs and imbecile coquettes in Chapter 6.

80. Sarah Fielding, Preface to *The Lives of Cleopatra and Octavia* (1757; reprint, London: Scholartis Press, 1928), xxxix.

81. West, *Letters to a Young Lady,* 3:139–40.

82. Wollstonecraft, *Rights of Woman,* 94.

83. See especially Haywood, *Female Spectator,* book 4, which is almost a rough draft of *Betsy Thoughtless.*

84. Ibid., 1:106.

85. Ibid., 1:243.

86. Ibid., 1:208.

87. The reformed coquette theme goes back to the 1690s; today, following Spacks and Kelly, she is often identified exclusively with the aristocratic lady. See Todd, *Sign of Angellica;* Spacks, *Desire and Truth;* Spencer, *Rise of the Woman Novelist;* Kelly, *Women, Writing, and Revolution.* See also n. 66.

88. Haywood, *Female Spectator,* 1:276, 2:94, 4:304.

89. Ibid., 1:71.

90. Ibid., 2:97.

Chapter 3 / Sexual Revolution and the Hardwicke Marriage Act

1. There have been two generations of historians of the eighteenth-century family during the past thirty years. The first either took the government at its word or ignored the act; the second quite often begins its story in the last decades of the eighteenth century, therefore after the act had taken effect; it also shades into gender studies. For the first generation, see esp. Peter Laslett, *Household and Family in Past Time* (Cambridge: Cambridge Univ. Press, 1972); Jean Louis Flandrin, *Families in Former Times* (Cambridge: Cambridge Univ. Press, 1976); Lawrence Stone, *The Family, Sex, and Marriage in England, 1500–1800* (New York: Harper & Row, 1976); and Randolph Trumbach, *The Rise of the Egalitarian Family* (New York: Academic Press, 1978). Important works of the second generation include Leonore Davidoff and Catherine Hall, *Family Fortunes: Men and Women of the English Middle Class, 1780–1950* (Chicago: Univ. of Chicago Press, 1987); John Gillis, *For Better or Worse: British Marriages, 1600 to the Present* (Oxford: Oxford Univ. Press, 1985); Jeffrey Weeks, *Sex, Politics, and Society* (London: Longman, 1989); Amanda Vickery, "Golden Age to Separate Spheres: A Review of the Categories and Chronology of English Women's History," *Historical Journal* 36 (1993): 383–414; Anthony Fletcher, *Gender, Sex, and Subordination in England, 1500–1800* (New Haven: Yale Univ. Press, 1995); and Robert B. Shoemaker, *Gender in English Society, 1650–1850* (London: Longman, 1998).

2. *Letter to the Public containing the Substance of what Hath been offered in late Debates upon the Subject of the Act of Parliament for the better preventing of Clandestine Marriages* (London, 1753), 55; Henry Gally, *Some Considerations upon Clandestine Marriages* (London 1729), 34.

3. Henry Stebbing, *An Inquiry into the Force and Operation of the annulling Clauses of a late Act for the better Preventing of Clandestine Marriages* (London, 1753), 5.

4. See George Elliott Howard, *A History of Matrimonial Institutions,* 3 vols. (Chicago: Univ. of Chicago Press, 1904); and R. B. Outhwaite, ed., *Marriage and Society: Studies in the Social History of Marriage* (New York: St. Martin's, 1981).

5. See Thomas Salmon, *A Critical Essay Concerning Marriage* (London, 1724); and Stebbing, *Inquiry.*

6. Sir William Blackstone, *Commentaries on the Laws of England,* reprinted from the British copy of 1765 (Philadelphia, 1771).

7. *Gentleman's Magazine* 23 (October 1753): 453.

8. There is a good account of the multitude and variety of local marriage rites in Gillis, *For Better or Worse.*

9. Parliamentary Debate on the Clandestine Marriage Bill. In Cobbett's *Parliamentary History of Great Britain* (London: Hansard), 15:76.

10. Ibid., 58, 59.

11. F. Douglas, *Reflections on Celibacy and Marriage* (London: 1771), 32.

12. It is worth remembering that child labor was not merely a product of nineteenth-century factories. In this period, children were put to work in home industries, agriculture, and mining (for instance) even as young as four or five.

13. Adam Smith, *The Wealth of Nations* (Oxford: Clarendon, 1979), 65.

14. Adam Ferguson, *Institutes of Moral Philosophy*, new enlarged edition (Basil: James Decker, 1800), 209.

15. James Steuart, *An Inquiry into the Principles of Political Economy* (1767, 1780; Edinburgh: Oliver & Boyd, 1966), 78. The term *political economy* was apparently coined by Steuart in this text, and as far as I can tell, his distinction between productive and unproductive propagation of the species actually preceded that between productive and unproductive labor.

16. Cobbett's *Parliamentary History*, 15:63.

17. William Paley, *Paley's Moral Philosophy*, with annotations by Richard Whateley (London: Parker & Sons, 1859). This is a particularly interesting edition of Paley because it tells us that Paley, who wrote at the end of the eighteenth century and summarized thinking about the "Public Uses of the Marriage Institution" embodied in and surrounding the Marriage Act, was still being used as an authoritative university textbook in 1859. According to Whateley, Paley had "laid the foundation of the Moral Principles of many hundreds — probably thousands — of Youths while under a course of training designed to qualify them of being the Moral Instructors of Millions."

18. Pinchbeck and Hewitt point out that "the training of children in some kind of work or craft so that they might learn habits of industry and have the ability to support themselves when they were grown up was a distinctive feature of sixteenth century social policy" too. The difference, they argue, is that then the goal was to promote social stability, whereas in the eighteenth century, the goal was to promote economic growth and wealth. See Ivy Pinchbeck and Margaret Hewitt, *Children in English Society*, 2 vols. (London: Routledge, 1969), 2:223, 309.

19. For one signficant exception, see Leah Leneman and Rosalind Mitchison, "Clandestine Marriage in the Scottish Cities, 1660–1780," *Journal of Social History* 24 (1993): 845–61. The Marriage Act did not apply to Scotland, and Leneman and Mitchison's study of the somewhat chaotic situation there agrees very well with what eighteenth-century Britons were saying about the state of the marriage institution before and immediately after passage of the Marriage Act.

20. Eliza Haywood, *The Female Spectator* (London, 1775), 3:138–39.

21. Cobbett's *Parliamentary History*, 15:7, 3.

22. Gally, *Clandestine Marriages*. This was apparently written some twenty years before the bill but became a central point of reference in the debates surrounding the bill. See Howard, *Matrimonial Institutions*, vol. 1.

23. Haywood, *Female Spectator*, vols. 1 and 2; and Maria Delariviere Manley, "The Wife's Resentment," in *The Meridian Anthology of Early Women Writers: British Literary Women from Aphra Behn to Maria Edgeworth, 1660–1800*, ed. Katharine M. Rogers and William McCarthy (New York: St. Martin's, 1964).

24. Martin Ingram, "The Reform of Popular Culture," in *Popular Culture in Seventeenth-Century England*, ed. Bary Reay (New York: St. Martin's, 1985).

25. Cobbett's *Parliamentary History*, 8.

26. Daniel Defoe, *Conjugal Lewdness or Matrimonial Whoredom: A Treatise Concerning the Use and Abuse of the Marriage Bed* (1717), 366–67.

27. Haywood, *Female Spectator*, 1:24.

28. Abductions in eighteenth-century novels have been treated as a purely literary *topos* borrowed from Richardson's *Clarissa;* in fact, they might be described as the eighteenth-century equivalent of date rape: they always involve the woman's being borne off against her will in a carriage by a man she knows and being ravished or seduced. Such abductions are reported in contemporary diaries, though they seem to have occasioned most comment when there was something extraordinary about them, for instance, when the abducted young lady was rescued by the Prince of Wales. The abduction scenes in *Evalina, Emmeline,* and *Self-Control,* for instance, can be read as different exempla of how to escape ravishment; it is to be noted that none of the characters in these women's novels is passive, like *Clarissa,* and all discomfit or turn the tables on their would-be ravishers.

29. Cobbett's *Parliamentary History*, 51. See also Roger Lee Brown, "The Rise and

Fall of Fleet Marriages," in *Marriage and Society,* ed. R. B. Outhwaite (New York: St. Martin's, 1996), 117–36.

30. *Letter to the Public,* 18.

31. *Paley's Moral Philosophy,* 216. See also *Letter to the Public,* 20.

32. It is interesting that just before passage of the Marriage Bill, the House had defeated a bill requiring each man in the country to be listed in a public register. The members of the House argued that this was an intolerable infringement of Englishmen's freedom and that the register would be used for purposes of forced taxation.

33. Blackstone, *Commentaries,* 1:455.

34. *Letter to the Public,* 18.

35. *Paley's Moral Philosophy,* 204.

36. *Letter to the Public,* 19.

37. Francis Hutcheson, *Collected Works,* (Hildesheim: Georg Olms, 1969), 6:154.

38. Douglas, *Celibacy and Marriage,* 23.

39. Compare Hutcheson, *Works,* 6:154; and Blackstone, *Commentaries,* 1:447.

40. Thomas Malthus, *First Essay on Population* (London, 1798), 200–201.

41. For a social science view of the connection between the steep rise in illegitimate births at the end of the eighteenth century and the Marriage Act of 1753, see Jona Schellekens, "Courtship, the Clandestine Marriage Act, and Illegitimate Fertility in England," *Journal of Interdisciplinary History* 25 (1995): 433–44; and Belinda Meteyard, "Illegitimacy and Marriage in Eighteenth-Century England," *Journal of Interdisciplinary History* 10 (1980): 479–89. For an excellent account of the sexual demographics of the period, see Michael Anderson, "The Social Implications of Demographic Change," in *The Cambridge Social History of Britain, 1750–1950,* ed. F. M. L. Thompson (Cambridge: Cambridge Univ. Press, 1990).

42. Their observations have been confirmed and demonstrated by modern feminist work like that of Alice Browne, Ivy Pinchbeck, and Louise Tilly. See also, more recently, Edward Copeland, *Women Writing about Money: Women's Fiction in England, 1790–1820* (Cambridge: Cambridge Univ. Press, 1995).

43. Clara Reeve, *Plan of Education* (1792; reprint, New York: Garland, 1974), 138.

44. Cobbett's *Parliamentary History*, 26.

45. *Gentleman's Magazine*, 23:452, 24:145.

46. Cobbett's *Parliamentary History*, 14.

47. Neo-Tory historians like Clark and liberal historians like Langford disagree on whether the dividing line in society fell between gentlemen and plebeians or between the propertied and the unpropertied. From the point of view of Enlightenment feminists, the answer seems to have been that, to stay on the right side of the line, a woman required both money and gentility. See J. C. D. Clark, *English Society, 1688–1832: Ideology, Social Structure, and Political Practice during the Ancien Régime* (Cambridge: Cambridge Univ. Press, 1985); and Paul Langford, *Public Life and the Propertied Englishman, 1689–1798* (Oxford: Clarendon, 1991). For Enlightenment feminists on this subject, see Chapters 4 and 5 of this volume.

48. See Gillis, *For Better or Worse.*

49. The Egalitarians were also speaking from their own experience here. Cheryl Turner discusses the "function [of authorship] as a source of income for the impecunious, literate woman" and suggests that by the second half of the eighteenth century, writing might have been perceived as a way for a woman to earn money without losing respectability. Her study of the social backgrounds of more than sixty eighteenth-century women writers shows that most wrote for money because they had been disinherited by their fathers or married to younger sons, professional men, or wastrels, who could not support them adequately. See Cheryl Turner, *Living by the Pen: Women Writers in the Eighteenth Century* (London: Routledge, 1992), 65.

50. Jane West, *Letters to a Young Lady in which the Duties and Characters of Women are Considered,* 3 vols (2nd ed. of 1806; reprint, New York: Garland, 1974), 2:335–36.

51. Some of the men had said the same of marriages designed to unite fortunes or estates. See, for instance, William Ramsay, *Conjugium Conjurgium* (1673; reprint, New York: Garland, 1976); and Defoe, *Conjugal Lewdness.*

52. There may have been real cause for concern about public indifference to the new act. As *The Gentleman's Magazine* sarcastically reported: "By letters from diverse parts, we have advice that the reading of the Marriage Act in churches has produced a wonderful effect on the minds of the fair sex . . . On Sunday 4th, when a minister of Kingston-in-Surrey began (after prayers were over) to read the Marriage Act, almost all of the congregation went out of the church." *The Gentleman's Magazine* 23:538.

53. For the role of promises in producing illegitimate births in France, see Cissie Fairchild, "Female Sexual Attitudes and the Rise of Illegitimacy," in *Journal of Interdisciplinary History* 8, no. 4 (spring 1978): 627–67. For changes in pornography and sex manuals addressed to men which encouraged sexual practices that would make women more likely to conceive, see Shoemaker, *Gender in English Society,* chap. 3.

54. Carolyn Woodward, "Sarah Fielding's Self-Destructive Utopia," in *Living by the Pen: Early British Women Writers,* ed. Dale Spender (New York: Teacher's College Press, 1992); and Spacks, *Desire and Truth: Function of Plot in Eighteenth-Century English Novels* (Chicago: Univ. of Chicago Press, 1990), 136.

55. Frances Sheridan, *Memoirs of Miss Sidney Bidulph* (1761; reprint, Oxford: Oxford Univ. Press, 1995), 46–47, 294.

56. Julia Wright suggests that *Secresy* is a rewrite of *Liaisons Dangereuses* and a "mosaic of the gothic, the romantic, the libertinist, and the didactic." See Julia M. Wright, "'I am ill-fitted': Conflicts of Genre in Eliza Fenwick's *Secresy*," in *Romanticism, History, and the Possibilities of Genre: Reforming Literature, 1789–1837,* ed. Tilottama Rajan and Julia M. Wright (Cambridge: Cambridge Univ. Press, 1998), 149, 154.

57. Eliza Fenwick, *Secresy; or Ruin on the Rock* (1795; reprint, Ontario: Broadview, 1994), 250.

58. Ibid., 339.

59. Ibid., 345.

60. See Cecilila Lucy Brightwell, *Memorials of the Life of Amelia Opie* (London, 1854), 61.

Chapter 4 / "The Public Uses of Private Families"

1. Vicissimus Knox, *Essays, Moral, and Literary,* 2 vols. (1792; reprint, New York: Garland, 1974), 2:69.

2. Anthony Fletcher likewise points out that "social aspiration was a driving force in Hanoverian England, unifying the middle ranks in an obsessive engagement in seeking entry into the ranks of the gentry, by aping their style of life, manners, and morals." Anthony Fletcher, *Gender, Sex, and Subordination in England, 1500–1800* (New Haven: Yale Univ. Press, 1995), 325. See also Introduction, n. 27.

3. Knox, *Essays,* 2:69. Knox had clearly never spent a lot of time with small children himself!

4. Quoted in Alice Browne, *The Eighteenth-Century Feminist Mind* (Detroit: Wayne State Univ. Press, 1987), 19.

5. Adam Smith, *The Theory of Moral Sentiments,* ed. Raphael Macfie (Oxford: Clarendon, 1979), 219. Notice the absence of wives in this catalogue of objects of man's natural affections.

6. Joseph Butler, *Fifteen Sermons preached at the Rolls Chapel* (1774; reprint, London: Bell, 1949), 37.

7. Sterne's *Tristram Shandy* might be read as a satire on such ideas.

8. Priscilla Wakefield, *Reflections on the Present Condition of the Female Sex* (1798; reprint, New York: Garland, 1974), 2.

9. Johnson's *Dictionary* (London, 1799 rev. ed.), 3.

10. S. I. Benn and G. F. Ganz, *Public and Private in Social Life* (New York: St. Martin's, 1983), 25.

11. Francis Hutcheson, *Collected Works* (Hildesheim, Germany: Georg Olms Facsimile, 1969), 4:271.

12. David Hume, *Essays Literary, Moral. and Political* (London: Ward, Locke & Tyler, n.d.), 150, 156.

13. Hutcheson, *Works,* 4:282.

14. Adam Smith, *Moral Sentiments,* 55.

15. Johnson's *Dictionary.*

16. See the *Oxford English Dictionary.*

17. See *domestique* in *Encyclopédie ou Dictionnaire Raisonne des Sciences, des Arts et des Métiers,* ed. Diderot and D'Alembert (Paris, 1751).

18. Maria Edgeworth, *Castle Rackrent* (1800 ed.; reprint, Oxford: Oxford Univ. Press, 1991).

19. John Dennis, *Vice and Luxury Publick Mischiefs or Remarks on a Book Intituled The Fable of the Bees or Private Vices Public Benefits* (London: 1724), 2–3.

20. Ibid., 3–4.

21. Butler, *Fifteen Sermons,* 29, 33.

22. Hutcheson, *Works,* 4:37, 120.

23. Adam Smith, *Moral Sentiments,* 166.

24. James Beattie, *Collected Works,* ed. F. O. Wolf (Stuttgart: Friedriech Frommen Verlag, 1970), 3:580.

25. Dennis, *Vice and Luxury,* 78, 122.

26. James Steuart, *An Inquiry into the Principles of Political Economy* (Edinburgh: Oliver & Boyd, 1966), 145. There is no antithesis between public and private even in Mandeville's *Fable of the Bees* (1714). He too assumed that public prosperity was the outcome of the actions of all members of the nation. His shocking paradox only turned on the binary opposition between virtue and vice — on the idea that the selfishness, avarice, pride, ambition, and hyprocrisy of private or particular persons could somehow turn into their opposite — the wealth, prosperity, and benefit of the collective body.

27. Mary Radcliffe, *The Female Advocate; or an Attempt to Recover the Rights of Women from Male Usurpation* (1788; reprint, New York: Garland, 1974), 421.

28. Mary Wollstonecraft, *A Vindication of the Rights of Woman with Strictures on Moral and Political Subjects* (New York: Whitston, 1982), 406.

29. Hannah More, *Works* (London, 1818), 8:32.

30. This also underpins the argument that "Example is a duty we owe all the world." See Chapter 2.

31. Indeed, for the purpose of this argument, the words *public* and *social* could be used as synonyms: "The nature of man, considered in his public or social capacity, leads him to right behaviour in society." Butler, *Fifteen Sermons,* 45.

32. For the links established during this period between education, culture, cultivation, and legislation, see Zygmunt Baumann, *Legislators and Interpreters* (Cambridge: Polity Press, 1987).

33. Adam Smith, *Moral Sentiments,* 85.

34. John Locke, *Two Treatises on Government,* ed. Peter Laslett (Cambridge: Cambridge Univ. Press, 1967): 2: #77.

35. Hutcheson, *Works,* 4:279.

36. Ibid., 4:82.

37. John Aiken, *Letters from a Father to a Son* (1792–93; reprint, New York: Garland, 1971), 318.

38. Hutcheson, *Works,* 4:255.

39. Jean-Jacques Rousseau, *Du Contrat Social* (Paris: Editions Sociales, 1955), 55, 56.

40. Sir William Blackstone, *Commentaries on the Laws of England in Four Books* (1765; reprint, Philadelphia, 1771), 1:422. This position can also be read as a response to those in the debates surrounding the Marriage Act who argued that the government was not entitled to pass laws regulating marriage, because "Marriage has a natural Existence of its own, antecedent to and abstracted from all the laws of Civil Society" and that "no Man by entering into Society, can or ought to be presumed to have yielded up into the Hands of Society, his natural right to contract Marriage, as shall seem to him most expedient." The government position was that the public good took precedence over private freedoms, because society was "founded on the power to limit" private freedoms for the public good, and that it was the government's duty to foster "the public uses of the marital institution." This latter position is inscribed in Blackstone's *Commentaries.* See also Henry Stebbing, *A Dissertation on the Power of States to Deny Civil Protection to the Marriages of Minors made without the Consent of their Parents or Guardians* (London, 1754), 1; and Henry Gally, *Some Considerations Upon Clandestine Marriages* (London, 1729), 6, 122, 130). See also the debate in the House, in Cobbett's *Parliamentary History of England.*

41. Hutcheson, *Works,* 4:70.

42. Hume, *Essays,* 77.

43. Beattie, *Works,* 3:576.

44. Hume, *Essays,* 419.

45. Ibid., 421.

46. Henry St. John Bolingbroke, *Works* (Philadelphia: Carey & Hart, 1841), 4:228.

47. Gally, *Clandestine Marriages,* 5.

48. He is virtually citing the Marriage Act here; see Chapter 3.

49. *Paley's Moral Philosophy with Annotations by Richard Whateley* (London: Parker & Son, 1859), 203–4.

50. Henry Fielding is credited with founding the London police force in the latter

part of the century. It was still incumbent on the masters of prominent families, especially in the country, to keep public order and act as justices of the peace.

51. Hutcheson, *Works*, 4:81.

52. Johnson's *Dictionary*. This is a meaning the word retains today only when we speak of the Society of Friends or Society for the Prevention of Cruelty to Animals.

53. Jane Rendall, *The Origins of Modern Feminism, 1780–1860* (Chicago: Lyceum, 1985), 5.

54. The Industrial Revolution and the separation of workplace from the household has been put back to the early or middle nineteenth century by a number of historians of different schools and persuasions. See, for example, Bridget Hill, *Women, Work, and Sexual Politics in Eighteenth Century England* (Oxford: Blackwell, 1989); Leonore Davidoff and Catherine Hall, *Family Fortunes: Men and Women of the English Middle Class, 1780–1850* (Chicago: Chicago Univ. Press, 1987); J. C. D. Clark, *English Society, 1688–1832: Ideology, Social Structure, and Political Practice during the Ancien Régime* (Cambridge: Cambridge Univ. Press, 1985). See also "Some Questions of History and Time" in the Introduction to this book.

55. Steuart, *Political Economy*, 15, 16.

56. Ibid., 68.

57. Hume, *Essays*, 228.

58. Hester Chapone, *Letters on the Improvement of the Mind*, 2 vols. (London, 1774, 4th ed.), 2:71.

59. Quoted in Beth Fowkes Tobin, *Superintending the Poor: Charitable Ladies and Paternal Landlords in British Fiction, 1770–1860* (New Haven: Yale Univ. Press, 1993), 26. J. C. D. Clark argues that rural society became more hierarchical as the eighteenth century progressed and that the essential components of patriarchy were strengthened. See *English Society*, 68.

60. Hume, *Essays*, 420.

61. Ibid., 25–26.

62. Adam Smith, *Moral Sentiments*, 163.

63. Beattie, *Works*, 4:280.

64. Edmund Burke, *The Writings and Speeches of Edmund Burke*, ed. Paul Langford, vol. 8, *Reflections on the Revolution in France* (Oxford: Clarendon, 1989), 244.

65. Adam Smith, *Moral Sentiments*, 163.

66. For example, Fielding's *Tom Jones* and Goldsmith's *Vicar of Wakefield.* For Enlightenment feminist critiques, see Chapter 5.

67. Wollstonecraft was responding to Burke's glowing portrait of happy English families under Britain's "antient constitution." For Wollstonecraft's argument with Burke, see Chapter 1, n. 74.

68. *Affective individualism* was a term promulgated in Lawrence Stone, *The Family, Sex and Marriage in England, 1500–1800* (New York: Harper & Row, 1977).

69. Mary Wollstonecraft, *Vindication of the Rights of Man,* ed. Sylvana Tomaselli (Cambridge: Cambridge Univ. Press, 1995), 21.

70. Ibid., 14.

71. Ibid., 19.

72. This attribution of blame is picked up by liberal and marxist historians when they characterize the emphasis on virtue and the regulation of the family as an attack by the middle class on the aristocracy. However, many of the Matriarchs themselves belonged to the landed gentry; they also repeatedly complained that dissipation was characteristic of all the propertied ranks (including their own).

73. Hannah More, *Works,* 8: 26.

74. See n. 54.

75. For the social backgrounds of women writers and for the economic difficulties they faced at the end of the century, see esp. Cheryl Turner, *Living by the Pen: Women Writers in the Eighteenth Century* (London: Routledge, 1992); and Edward Copeland, *Women Writing about Money: Women's Fiction in England, 1790–1820* (Cambridge: Cambridge Univ. Press, 1995).

76. Clara Reeve, *Plans of Education, with Remarks on the Systems of other Writers* (1792; reprint, New York: Garland, 1974), 121–22.

77. Susan Staves, *Married Women's Separate Property in England, 1660–1833* (Cambridge: Harvard Univ. Press, 1990), 217. For the predicament of women in unpropertied ranks also, see Bridget Hill, *Women, Work, and Sexual Politics,* chap. 12; Alice Clark, *Working Life of Women in the Seventeenth Century* (London: Routledge, 1919); and Louise Tilly and Joan Scott, *Women, Work, and Family* (New York: Methuen, 1978).

78. Mary Ann Radcliffe, *The Female Advocate,* 407, 409.

79. Adam Ferguson, *Institutes of Moral Philosophy*, new enlarged edition (Basil, 1800), 209.

80. Since the Renaissance, there had been a version of the Horatio Alger story centered on younger sons. See Michael McKeon, *The Origins of the English Novel, 1600–1740* (Baltimore: Johns Hopkins Univ. Press, 1987), 219ff.

81. Mary Hays, *Letters and Essays Moral and Miscellaneous* (1793; reprint: New York: Garland, 1974), 19; Sophia in *First Feminists: British Women Writers, 1578–1799*, ed. Moira Ferguson (Bloomington: Indiana Univ. Press, 1985), 270; Wollstonecraft, *Rights of Woman*, 37.

82. Fleetwood, for instance, says, "The foundation of respect is some supposed excellence or worth, and in this case some kind of superiority." William Fleetwood, *The Relative Duties of Parents and Children, Husbands and Wives, Masters and Servants* (1705; reprint, New York: Garland, 1985), 12.

83. Wollstonecraft, *Rights of Woman*, 125.

84. Ibid., 130.

85. Beattie, *Works*, 3:583. See also Shoemaker, *Gender in English Society*, 115ff.

86. Fleetwood, *Relative Duties*, 255. Fleetwood is echoing Hobbes, who said that "there can be no greater argument to a man of his own power" than assistance to his wife, children, and kin. Hobbes called such assistance "charity."

87. William Duff, *Letters on the Intellectual and Moral Character of Women* (London, 1807 ed.), 134, 274.

88. Ibid., 273, 41, 134.

89. Thomas Gisbourne, *An Enquiry into the Duties of the Female Sex* (1797; reprint, New York: Garland, 1974), 251.

90. Chapone, *Improvement of the Mind*, 2:200; Jane West, *Letters to a Young Lady in which the Duties and Characters of Women are Considered* (2nd ed. of 1806; reprint, New York: Garland, 1974), 3:88.

91. Mary Hays, *Appeal to the Men of Great Britain* (1798; reprint, New York: Garland, 1974), 58, 134.

92. Kathryn Sutherland, "Hannah More's Counter-Revolutionary Feminism," in *Revolution in Writing: British Literary Responses to the French Revolution*, ed. Kevin Everest (Buckingham, England: Open Univ. Press, 1991), 35.

93. Wakefield, *Present Condition of the Female Sex,* 8.

94. Chapone, *Improvement of the Mind,* 2:56, 74.

95. More, *Works,* 8:38.

96. Ibid.

97. Ibid., 7:154.

98. For the mother-teacher and extension of this role into the authorial persona, see also Mitzi Myers, "Daddy's Girl as Motherless Child: Maria Edgeworth and Maternal Romance," and Jane Spencer, "Of use to her daughter: Maternal Authority and Early Women Novelists," both in *Living by the Pen: Early British Women Writers,* ed. Dale Spender (New York: Teachers' College Press, 1992); and Mitzi Myers, "Hannah More's 'Tracts for the Times,'" in *Fetter'd or Free? British Women Novelists, 1670–1815* (Athens: Ohio Univ. Press, 1986).

99. West, *Letters to a Young Lady,* 3:269.

100. Ibid., 239.

101. Maria Edgeworth and Richard Lovell Edgeworth, *Practical Education* (1798; reprint, New York: Garland, 1974), 305–6. Maria published this with her father but insisted she wrote most of it.

102. Lady Damaris Masham, *Occasional Thoughts in reference to a Vertuous or Christian Life* (London, 1705), 186–87. Compare this to Locke, *Thoughts on Education,* #70.

103. More, *Works,* 7:62.

104. Ibid.

105. Reeve, *Plan of Education,* 29, 112.

106. Toni Bowers, *The Politics of Motherhood: British Writing and Culture, 1680–1760* (Cambridge: Cambridge Univ. Press, 1996), 16.

107. West, *Letters to a Young Lady,* 2:484.

108. More, *Works,* 7:187.

109. West, *Letters to a Young Lady,* 2:345; 3:291.

110. Ibid., 3:301.

111. Tobin, *Superintending the Poor,* 2, 6.

112. See Michael Hurst, *Maria Edgeworth and the Public Scene: Intellect, Fine Feeling, and Landlordism in the Age of Reform* (Coral Gables, Florida: Univ. of Miami Press, 1969). Hurst argues that for Edgeworth, "the ideal instrument for revolutionizing Irish conditions was an enlightened governing class, by which she meant the aristocracy and gentry made aware of their duties and willing to mitigate the full rigor of their technical rights." (30) Like More, Edgeworth belonged to the landed gentry, and was intimately involved with estate management on the family estate at Edgeworthtown. West was married to a clergyman and lived in the country. The eighteenth-century clergy were much more closely associated with the gentry and aristocracy, on whom they were dependent for their livings, than with the middle class, and have indeed been described as "pseudo gentry" as a result. Compare Paul Langford's description of public philanthropy as the local government of associations of middle-class men in *The Propertied Englishman*, 207ff. One sees why Matriarchs needed to preserve the patriarchal face of philanthropy to distinguish themselves from the philanthropy of local government by men in the middling ranks.

113. By arguing that even women of very small means could perform these philanthropic functions if they practised sufficient economy, and by representing destitute gentlewomen as subordinate to their more wealthy benefactresses, Matriarchs crossed and blurred the lines now drawn between the middle and upper classes, a distinction that in any case seems to have been borrowed from much later analyses of the French Revolution. Harold Perkin argued that the old society was "a finely graded hierarchy of great subtlety and discrimination, in which men were acutely aware of their exact relation to those immediately above and below them and that "the one horizontal cleavage of great import" was "between the gentleman and the common people." J. C. D. Clark and John Cannon agree with him there; and this seems to be true to women's texts. However, eighteenth-century women writers who wrote for money knew all about the dangers of losing caste and slipping down the social hierarchy; they therefore saw the relation between these gradations as more fluid than Perkin, Clark, and Cannon say it was, and more closely connected to wealth. This is why, for Matriarchs and Egalitarians alike, the operative distinction was between the wealthy or propertied and the poor, and why the disjunction between wealth and birth on the marriage mart became a focal issue in their work. See Harold Perkin, *The Origins of Modern English Society, 1780–1880* (London: Routledge, 1969), 24; John Cannon, *Aristocratic Century: The Peerage in Eighteenth Century England* (Cambridge: Cambridge Univ. Press, 1984); Clark, *English Society;* and for women writers' attitudes to poverty and wealth, Edward Copeland, *Women Writing About Money: Women's Fiction in England, 1790 –1820* (Cambridge: Cambridge Univ. Press, 1995). See also Chapter 5 of this volume.

114. Myers, "Hannah More's 'Tracts for the Times,'" 268.

115. Compare Elizabeth Langland's analysis of nineteenth-century households in *Nobody's Angels: Middle Class Women and Domestic Ideology in Victorian Culture* (Ithaca: Cornell Univ. Press, 1995) with Bridget Hill's analysis of eighteenth-century households in *Women, Work, and Sexual Politics.*

116. One might also argue that this distinction between household duties and domestic offices collapsed when ladies could no longer afford servants and had to perform the household duties themselves again, and that *housewife* became the name for this collapse. As the more publicly important domestic offices came to be taken over by public instititutions (education, welfare, etc.), the domestic woman found herself back in the role of "upper servant."

117. See also Chapter 2, n. 77.

118. Anne Mellor, *Romanticism and Gender* (New York: Routledge, 1993), 84.

119. Hays, *Appeal,* 169.

120. Wollstonecraft, *Rights of Woman,* 310. Wollstonecraft repeats this point several times in the course of the tract. See also her *Thoughts on the Education of Daughters.*

121. Donzelot has argued that "it was this promotion of woman as mother, educator, and medical auxiliary which was to serve as a point of support for the main feminist currents in the nineteenth century." See Jacques Donzelot, *The Policing of Families* (New York: Pantheon, 1979), 21.

122. Wollstonecraft, *Rights of Woman,* 309.

123. Ibid., 300.

124. Ibid., 306.

125. Ibid., 307.

126. Ibid., 302, 303.

127. Ibid., 25.

128. Catherine Macauley, *Letters on Education* (1790; reprint, New York: Garland, 1974), 216.

129. Wollstonecraft, *Rights of Woman,* 367.

130. Ibid., 25.

131. Hutcheson, *Works,* 4: 284.

Chapter 5 / Governing Utopias and the Feminist Rousseau

1. Clara Reeve, *Plans of Education with Remarks on the Systems of Other Writers* (1792; reprint, New York: Garland, 1974), 43.

2. Henri Roddier, *Jean-Jacques Rousseau en Angleterre au Dix-huitième Siècle* (Paris: Boivin, 1950), 86.

3. Edward Duffy, *Rousseau in England: The Context of Shelley's Critique of the Enlightenment* (Berkeley: Univ. of California Press, 1979), 16.

4. Hannah More, *Works* (London, 1818), 7:33, 44.

5. Rousseau was also imitated, popularized, and rewritten by male authors in Britain, for instance in Henry Brooke's *The Fool of Quality,* Thomas Day's *Sandford and Merton,* and Oliver Goldsmith's *The Vicar of Wakefield.* Some of these imitations by male authors probably influenced the Egalitarian representations of disempowered nursing fathers discussed below. Alice Browne relates Rousseau to Henry Mackenzie's *Julia de Roubigné* and to two male novelists in the Godwin circle. There is a fuller list of imitations in Roddier, but he makes it sound as if all ideas in England had originated in France. See Alice Browne, *The Eighteenth-Century Feminist Mind* (Detroit: Wayne State Univ. Press, 1987); and Roddier, *Jean-Jacques Rousseau.*

6. Duffy, *Rousseau in England,* 16.

7. Nicola Watson, *Revolution and the Form of the British Novel, 1790–1825* (Oxford: Clarendon, 1994), 4. For the argument about excessive female sensibility, revolutionary energy, and their suppression by conservatives at the turn of the century, see also Ronald Paulson, *Representations of Revolution, 1789–1820* (New Haven: Yale Univ. Press, 1983).

8. For Frances Brooke's *Lady Julia Mandeville,* see Chapter 2.

9. There were multiple editions of *Héloïse* and of *Emile* both in French and in English translation between their first publication in 1761 and 1762 respectively and the last decade of the eighteenth century. See Joseph Texte, *Jean-Jacques Rousseau and the Cosmopolitan Spirit in Literature* (New York: Stechert, 1899); and Roddier, *Jean-Jacques Rousseau.* For translation theories and practices, see Lawrence Venuti, *The Translator's Invisibility: A History of Translation* (New York: Routledge, 1995); and Flora Ross Amos, *Early Theories of Translation* (New York: Columbia Univ. Press, 1920).

10. See the chapter called "Animadversions on some of the writers who have rendered women objects of pity, bordering on contempt," in Wollstonecraft's *Rights of Woman*, chap. 5. For the parallels between Rousseau and Gregory and other writers of English conduct books, see Ruth Bernard Yeazell, *Fictions of Modesty: Women and Courtship in the English Novel* (Chicago: Univ. of Chicago Press, 1991).

11. For the traffic in translations from England to France, see Harold Wade Streeter, *The English Novel in French Translation* (New York: Institute of French Studies, 1936); for traffic in the other direction, Roddier, *Jean-Jacques Rousseau;* and Texte, *Cosmopolitan Spirit in Literature.*

12. Duffy, *Rousseau in England,* 13.

13. Watson, *Revolution,* 4.

14. Rousseau could not read English.

15. Pierre Le Tourneur, the French translator of Shakespeare and Young. Quoted in Streeter, *French Translation,* 26.

16. W. L. Gent, Preface to his translation of Virgil's *Eclogues.* Quoted in Flora Ross Amos, *Early Theories,* 146.

17. *Héloïse* was also, of course, a rewrite of the story of the original Abelard and Eloisa. For a brilliant analysis of their original letters, see Peggy Kamuf, *Fictions of Feminine Desire* (Lincoln: Univ. of Nebraska Press, 1982), chap. 1. For a comparison of Rousseau's *Héloïse* with Richardson's *Clarissa,* see Janet Todd, *Women's Friendship in Literature* (New York: Columbia Univ. Press, 1980).

18. Jean-Jacques Rousseau, *First and Second Discourses,* ed. Roger D. Masters (New York: St. Martin's, 1964), 104.

19. Jean-Jacques Rousseau, *Du Contrat Social* (Paris: Editions Sociales, 1955), 55, 56.

20. *Robinson Crusoe* is the only novel Emile is allowed to read.

21. *Julia; or the New Eloisa. A Series of Original Letters Collected an Published by J. J. Rousseau,* trans. William Kendrick, 3 vols. (Edinburgh, 1794), 3:83. For Clarens as exemplary of the state, see William Ray, *Story and History: Narrative Authority and Social Identity in the Eighteenth-Century French and English Novel* (Oxford: Blackwell, 1990). For Rousseau's portrait of Wolmar as the good father in relation to treatments of the family-state analogy in France (which followed a somewhat different trajectory than it did in England during these years), see Lynn Hunt, *The Family Romance of the French Revolution* (California: Univ. of California Press, 1992). For the family-state analogy in England, see Chapter 1 of this volume.

22. Virginia C. Kenney, *The Country-House Ethos in English Literature, 1688–1750* (Sussex: Harvester, 1984), 5, 6, chap. 3.

23. *Millenium Hall* was published in 1762. Rousseau's *Héloïse* (1761) was already being read in England in 1761 when Richardson said he did not like it and Gray called it "absurd and improbable." See Texte, *Cosmopolitan Spirit in Literature,* 231. Although we cannot prove that she read *Héloïse* at this point, because she had all her letters burned, Sarah Scott was herself a translator of novels from the French and could certainly have read the novel as early as this.

24. See Bridget Hill, "A Refuge from Man: The Idea of a Protestant Nunnery," *Past and Present* 117 (1987): 107–30; Joan K. Kinnaird, "Astell and the Conservative Contribution to English Feminism," *Journal of British Studies* 19, no. 1 (1979): 53–75; and Barbara Schnorrenberg, "A Paradise like Eve's: Three Eighteenth-Century British Utopias," *Women's Studies* 9, no. 3 (1982): 263–73.

25. Sarah Scott, *Millenium Hall* (1762; reprint, Ontario: Broadview, 1994), 62, 64. In the eighteenth century, *family* referred to a man and his dependents or domestics (wife, children, servants, tenants, kin).

26. Lady Mary Hamilton, *Munster Village* (1778; reprint, London: Pandora, 1987), 130, 133.

27. Ibid., 139.

28. *Sir George Ellison* was published four years after *Millenium Hall* but frames it in story time: Ellison visits Millenium Hall for the first time half-way through *Sir George Ellison; Millenium Hall* represents his account of that visit; *Sir George Ellison* goes on to recount Ellison's life and relations with the ladies of the hall after that first visit.

29. Moira Ferguson reads Sarah Scott as favoring the conservative, "pro-ameliorative" position on slavery taken by people like Powell who sought to combine philanthropy and profit, and she describes Ellison's plantation in the West Indies as "reenact[ing] *Millenium Hall* in a Carribean context." See Moira Ferguson, *Subject to Others: British Women Writers and Colonial Slavery, 1670–1834* (London: Routledge, 1992), 101, 304 n. 32.

Scott was not a leveler, but as I will be arguing here, Ellison's West Indian estate and Millenium Hall represent different concepts of government and of philanthropy. It should be noted, too, that Ellison does free his West Indian slaves once he has learned the superior principles of the ladies at Millenium Hall.

30. Rousseau, *Julia; or the New Eloisa,* trans. Kendrick, 2:338.

31. Mira Morgenstern, *Rousseau and the Politics of Ambiguity: Self, Culture, and Society* (University Park: Pennsylvania State Univ. Press, 1996), 207–8.

32. Beth Kowalski-Wallace likewise argues that "Locke's milder sort of government amounts to a psychological manipulation of the child's affections" and that the governance of parents is designed to "act in the service of established ideology." We differ, in that it seems to me that eighteenth-century Matriarchs repeatedly demonstrated, at least from mid century on, that they were well aware of this. See Elizabeth Kowalski-Wallace, *Their Fathers' Daughters: Hannah More, Maria Edgeworth, and Patriarchal Complicity* (Oxford: Oxford Univ. Press, 1991), 19.

33. James Steuart, *An Inquiry into the Principles of Political Economy* (Edinburgh: Oliver & Boyd, 1966), 107, 89.

34. Adam Smith, *An Inquiry into the Nature and Causes of the Wealth of Nations* (New York: Modern Library, 1937).

35. This is the last line of William Blake's "The Chimney Sweeper" (1789).

36. Rousseau, *Julia; or the New Eloisa,* trans. Kendrick, 2:329; 3:35.

37. See n. 32.

38. Sarah Scott, *The History of Sir George Ellison* (1766; reprint, Lexington: Univ. Press of Kentucky, 1996), 101. For an alternative view, see Anne Mellor, "'Am I not a Woman and a Sister?' Slavery, Romanticism, and Gender," in *Romanticism, Race, and Imperial Culture, 1780–1834,* ed., Alan Richardson and Sonia Hofkosh (Bloomington: Indiana Univ. Press, 1996); and Felicity Nussbaum, *Torrid Zones: Maternity, Sexuality, and Empire in Eighteenth-Century English Narratives* (Baltimore: Johns Hopkins Univ. Press, 1995).

39. Caroline Gonda indicates the extent of this "mortifying dependence" for daughters by pointing out that Blackstone (unlike Locke) stressed that English law did "not hold the tie of nature to be dissolved by any misbehaviour of the parent" and that "most of Scott's work suggests that daughters acting on inward resistance are doomed to failure in the patriarchal family, whether the patriarchy is 'old' or 'new.'" *Millenium Hall,* she says, represents "an alternative to this world of human sacrifices." See Caroline Gonda, *Reading Daughters' Fictions, 1709–1834* (Cambridge: Cambridge Univ. Press, 1996), 110.

40. Hamilton, *Munster Village,* 150. See also Chapter 1 of this volume.

41. For West's and More's social program, see Mitzi Myers, "Hannah More's 'Tracts for the Times,'" in *Fetter'd or Free? British Women Novelists, 1670–1815,* ed.

Mary Anne Schofield and Cecilia Macheski (Athens: Ohio Univ. Press, 1986); and April London, "Jane West and the Politics of Reading," in *Tradition in Transition: Women Writers, Marginal Texts, and the Eighteenth-Century Canon*, ed. Alvaro Ribeiro and James G. Basker (Oxford: Clarendon, 1996). See also Chapter 4 of this volume. It sounds to me as if West and More had read *Millenium Hall*, since their tracts often repeat the ladies' programmatic speeches in Scott's novel word for word.

42. One possible real life genealogy here is suggested by Gary Kelly, who makes Sarah Scott a member of the Bluestocking circle presided over by her sister, Elizabeth Montagu, and argues that her novel is representative of the Bluestocking reforms of "gentry capitalism." See Gary Kelly, Introduction to *Millenium Hall* (Ontario: Broadview, 1994). Like Sylvia Myers, Kelly places Hannah More among second generation Bluestockings. Betsy Rizzo, however, positions Sarah Scott as something of an outsider to her sister's circle and describes Scott's (failed) attempts to establish a female utopia along the lines of Millenium Hall with Lady Babs, whose companion she was. See Sylvia Harcstark Myers, *The Bluestocking Circle: Women, Friendship, and the Life of the Mind in Eighteenth-Century England* (Oxford: Clarendon, 1990); and Betsy Rizzo, *Companions without Vows: Relations among Eighteenth-Century British Women* (Athens: Univ. of Georgia Press, 1994).

43. Hamilton, *Munster Village*, 121. This could be described as a literal application of the Enlighteners' ideas about the individual as a social being — see Chapter 4.

44. Scott, *Millenium Hall*, 66.

45. For the garden as an image of Wolmar's polity, see Ray, *Story and History*, chap. 12.

46. The contrast is explicity drawn in *Millenium Hall*, pp. 221–22 and 158.

47. Kathryn Sutherland, "Hannah More's Counter-Revolutionary Feminism," in *Revolution in Writing: British Literary Responses to the French Revolution* (Buckingham, England: Open Univ. Press, 1991), 45.

48. For West's *Gossip's Story* as a story about two sisters, one exemplary, the other at fault, see Patricia Myer Spacks, "Sisters," *Fetter'd or Free: British Women Novelists, 1670–1815*, ed. *Mary Ann* Schofield and Cecilia Macheski (Athens: Ohio Univ. Press, 1986).

49. Eleonor Ty argues that West "speaks from the position of the Father." See *Unsexed Revolutionaries: Five Women Novelists of the 1790s* (Toronto: Univ. of Toronto Press, 1993). For a counterargument, see April London, "Jane West and the Politics

of Feminism," in *Tradition in Transition: Women Writers, Marginal Texts, and the Eighteenth-Century Canon,* ed. Alvaro Ribeiro and James G. Basker (Oxford: Clarendon, 1996); and Katherine Sobba Green, *The Courtship Novel, 1740–1820* (Lexington: Univ. Press of Kentucky, 1991).

This is another example of the migration of ideas between feminist camps explored in Chapter 1. Matriarchs were appropriating and adapting part of the Egalitarian position on wedded happiness here, but as we will see in the next section, Egalitarians responded by denying that there was a safe haven to be found in this way and by fictionally demonstrating the inability of virtuous and benevolent men to prevail against society's corrupt, patriarchal, and hierarchial order any better than women.

50. London, "Jane West," 62.

51. For the use of Gothic novels to critique tyrannical and/or worldly family structures, see Kate Ferguson Ellis, *The Contested Castle: Gothic Novels and the Subversion of Domestic Ideology* (Urbana: Univ. of Illinois Press, 1989); Ann Williams, *The Art of Darkness: A Poetics of Gothic* (Chicago: Univ. of Chicago Press, 1995); Mark Madoff, "The Useful Myth of Gothic Ancestry," *Studies in Eighteenth-Century Culture* 8 (1979): 337–50; and Harriet Guest, "The Wanton Muse: Politics and Gender in Gothic Theory after 1760," in *Beyond Romanticism: New Approaches to Texts and Contexts, 1780–1832,* ed. Stephen Copley and John Whale (London: Routledge, 1992).

52. This is a point made by several critics. Caroline Gonda says that "the good fathers in Gothic and other novels are the weak figures, incapable of protecting or providing for their daughters" and that daughters feared the father's weakness; Caroline Woodward speaks of "the crippling effect" of men's "feminine virtues"; and Spacks points out that "sentimental novels declare the inadequacy of plots of power" and "appear to develop no adequate alternative." Marianne Yurchuk and George Haggerty argue, by contrast, that Radcliffe equalizes her heroes and heroines by giving all of them both feminine and masculine traits. See Gonda, *Reading Daughters' Fictions,* xvi; Catherine Woodward, "Sarah Fielding's Self-Destructive Utopia: The *Adventures of David Simple,*" in *Living by the Pen,* ed. Dale Spender (New York: Teacher's College Press, 1992); Patricia Myer Spacks, *Desire and Truth: Functions of Plot in Eighteenth-Century English Novels* (Chicago: Univ. of Chicago Press, 1990); and Deborah D. Rogers, ed., *The Critical Response to Ann Radcliffe* (Westport, Conn.: Greenwood, 1994).

53. Alexander Pope, "Eloisa to Abelard," in *The Poems of Alexander Pope,* ed. John Butt (1717; London: Methuen, 1963), 11.

54. Rousseau, *Julia; or the New Eloisa,* trans. Kendrick, 3:84.

55. Unlike Eleanor Ty, who reads *Julia* as "present[ing] a communal arrangement motivated by caring, connectedness, and sensibility, which according to Chodorow and Gilligan's theories would be associated with the maternal," I think this novel is less about female community than about friendship — a term used in the eighteenth century to describe ideal marital relations as well as close companionship between women, like that between Julia and Charlotte. In this novel, friendship is also shown to be the basis of Frederick's love for Julia; it is lacking in his relationship with Charlotte. See Eleanor Ty, *Unsexed Revolutionaries;* and Anne Mellor, *Romanticism and Gender* (New York: Routledge, 1993).

56. For the large number of women remaining unmarried and for the perilous economic and social situation of genteel writing ladies, see Chapter 4, nn. 75, 77.

57. In the eighteenth century, the term *friend* meant family or kin, as well as what it means now.

58. Charlotte Smith, *Montalbert* (1795; reprint, New York: Scholars Facsimiles, 1989), 2:10.

59. This was the situation of many women writers too.

60. Ty, *Unsexed Revolutionaries,* 60.

61. Mary Hays, *The Victim of Prejudice* (1799; reprint, Ontario: Broadview, 1994), 52. This could also be read as a comment on the Matriarchal idea of turning women's virtue and work into the dowry of the dowerless. See Chapter 4.

62. Ernesto Laclau and Chantal Mouffe, *Hegemony and Socialist Strategy: Towards a Radical Democratic Politics* (London: Verso, 1985).

63. Charlotte Smith in *Desmond* also rewrites *Héloïse* to sanction adulterous love between the Julie and Saint-Preux characters and to draw explicit parallels between public and domestic politics. There are many excellent discussions of this novel already. See, for instance, Watson, *Revolution,* 37ff; Diana Bowstead, "Charlotte Smith's *Desmond:* The Epistolary Novel as Ideological Argument," in *Fetter'd or Free? British Women Novelists, 1670–1815,* ed. Mary Anne Schofield and Cecilia Macheski; Pat Elliott, "Charlotte Smith's Feminism," in *Living by the Pen,* ed. Dale Spender (New York: Teacher's College Press, 1992); and Ty, *Unsexed Revolutionaries,* chap. 8.

64. Millenium Hall is described as a "female Arcadia."

65. Hutcheson, *Works,* 6:282. See also Chapter 1 of this volume.

66. Carroll Fry points out that attacks on lawyers "had become dangerous by 1796," after the sedition trials of John Thelwell, Thomas Holcroft, Horne Tooke, and nine others in 1794 and Parliament's "Two Acts" extending treason to forbid discussion of the constitution and of public grievances. See Carroll L. Fry, *Charlotte Smith* (New York: Twayne, 1996), 207.

CONCLUSION

The Domestic Revolution

1. Jane West, *Letters to a Young Lady in which the Duties and Characters of Women are Considered*, 3 vols. (2nd ed. of 1806; reprint, New York: Garland, 1974), 3:221–22. West is also turning the tables on the men, who had long used this image of caged birds to describe wives' proper reaction to their loss of freedom in the marriage state. Here is Philogamus: "As soon as the Parson has pronounced the fatal words, he [the husband] puts on the Lord and Master, and in a short time lets her [his new wife] see that she must obey; the Bird is lured into the Cage where it may beat itself against the Sides until it is forced to live in Thrall or beat its brains out." Here is Fleetwood: "To be meek and quiet under injuries and hard usage, that is not otherwise to be avoided or removed is acting with Reason . . . The wild Birds beat themselves almost to Pieces in the same Cage where tame ones sit and sing; and yet the Prison is the same." See Philogamus, *The Present State of Matrimony* (1739; reprint, New York: Garland, 1975), 54; and William Fleetwood, *The Relative Duties of Parents and Children, Husbands and Wives, Masters and Servants* (1705; reprint, New York: Garland, 1985).

2. Hannah More, *Works* (London, 1818), 7:20.

3. Patricia Spacks has also argued that women's plots were plots of power. See Patricia Myer Spacks, *Desire and Truth: Functions of Plot in Eighteenth-Century English Novels* (Chicago: Chicago Univ. Press, 1990).

4. Jane Collier, *An Essay on the Art of Ingeniously Tormenting* (London: A. Miller, 1753), 19.

5. For relations between women and their dependent female companions, see Betty Rizzo, *Companions without Vows: Relations among Eighteenth-Century British Women* (Athens: Univ. of Georgia Press, 1994); for contemporary accounts of the life of a governess in another woman's household, see Edward Copeland, *Women Writing about Money: Women's Fiction in England, 1790–1820* (Cambridge: Cambridge Univ. Press, 1995).

6. Collier, *Ingeniously Tormenting*, 104.

7. Ibid., 126.

8. Ibid., 117.

9. Ibid., 109.

10. Mary Hays, *Appeal to the Men of Great Britain* (1798; reprint, New York: Garland, 1974), 91.

11. Mrs. Bennett in Jane Austen's *Pride and Prejudice* is described as having driven her husband into his library and out of domestic government by means such as this.

12. Maria Edgeworth, "Essay on the Art of Self-Justification," in *The Meridian Anthology of Early Women Writers,* ed. Katharine M. Rogers and William McCarthy (New York: St. Martin's, 1964), 360.

13. West, *Letters to a Young Lady,* 3:139–40.

14. Ibid., 2:402.

15. More, *Works,* 8:141.

16. Mary Wollstonecraft, *A Vindication of the Rights of Woman with Strictures on Moral and Political Subjects,* ed. Ulrich H. Hardt (New York: Whitston, 1982), 94.

17. Diane Lang Hoeveler, *Gothic Feminism: The Professionalization of Gender from Charlotte Smith to the Brontës* (University Park: Pennsylvania State Univ. Press, 1995), 7.

18. West, *Letters to a Young Lady,* 3:4.

19. Hannah Woolley, quoted in Hilda Smith, *Reason's Disciples: Seventeenth-Century English Feminists* (Champaign-Urbana: Univ. of Illinois Press, 1982), 107.

20. Judith Drake, *An Essay in Defence of the Female Sex* (1696; reprint, New York: Source Book Press, 1970), 34.

21. Sara Egerton in *First Feminists: British Women Writers, 1578–1799,* ed. Moira Ferguson (Bloomington: Indiana Univ. Press, 1985), 169. See also Chapter 1.

22. Maria Edgeworth, *Letters for Literary Ladies* (1795; reprint, New York: Garland, 1974), 9. Edgeworth's speaker represents a lady who builds her power on sexuality and "feminine" defects.

23. West, *Letters to a Young Woman,* 3:28.

24. See Chapter 1.

25. Adam Smith, *An Inquiry into the Nature and Causes of the Wealth of Nations* (New York: Modern Library, 1937), 16.

26. Ibid., 460.

27. James Steuart, *An Inquiry into the Principles of Politial Economy* (Edinburgh: Oliver & Boyd, 1966), 145; Adam Smith, *Wealth of Nations,* 426.

28. Adam Smith, *Wealth of Nations,* 326.

29. Maria Edgeworth and Richard Lovell Edgeworth, *Practical Education* (1798; reprint, New York: Garland, 1974), 274–75.

30. Ibid., 278, 292. See also Chapter 2 above.

31. Clara Reeve, *Plans of Education with Remarks on the Systems of other Writers* (1792; reprint, New York: Garland, 1974), letter ix.

32. More, *Works,* 7:137–38.

33. Edgeworth, *Practical Education,* 279.

34. West, *Letters to a Young Lady,* 3:28.

35. Terry Castle, *Masquerade and Civilization: The Carnivalesque in Eighteenth-Century Culture and Fiction* (Stanford: Stanford Univ. Press, 1986), 5, 77–78. For the actual practices at masquerade parties, see her first chapter. See also Mary Anne Schofield, *Masking and Unmasking the Female Mind: Disguising Romances in Feminine Fiction, 1713–1799* (Newark: Univ. of Delaware Press, 1990).

36. West, *Letters to a Young Lady,* 3:28, 22.

37. More, *Works,* 8:17.

38. Ruth Bernard Yeazell, *Fictions of Modesty: Women and Courtship in the English Novel* (Chicago: Univ. of Chicago Press, 1991), 7; and Hoeveler, *Gothic Feminism,* 48. Yeazell also shows how the modest lady's plot accommodates "aggressive energies and desires which her modesty might superficially appear to deny" (ix).

39. Mary Hays, *Letters and Essays, Moral and Miscellaneous* (1793; reprint, New York: Garland, 1974), 24; Wollstonecraft, *Rights of Woman,* 55.

40. Wollstonecraft, *Rights of Woman,* 223.

41. Hays, *Appeal to the Men,* 264.

42. Wollstonecraft, *Rights of Woman,* 223.

43. Ibid., 105.

44. Ibid., 48.

45. Ibid., 51–52, 51, 5.

46. Ibid., 110–11.

47. Ibid., 140, 298.

48. Hays, *Letters and Essays,* 23.

49. Hays, *Appeal to the Men,* 129.

50. Mary Ann Radcliffe, *The Female Advocate: or an Attempt to Recover the Rights of Women from Male Usurpation* (1788; reprint, New York: Garland, 1974), 430.

51. Hays, *Appeal to the Men,* 129.

52. Hoeveler, *Gothic Feminism,* 7; Radcliffe, *Female Advocate,,* 407, 404; Hays, *Appeal to the Men,* 138, 160.

53. See, for instance, S. J. Curtis and M. E. Boultwood, *An Introductory History of English Education since 1800* (London: Univ. Tutorial Press, 1960).

54. James Beattie, *Works,* vol. 3, *Dissertations Moral and Critical* (1783), ed. F. O. Wolf (Stuttgart: Friedrich Frommen Verlag, 1970), "On Fable and Romance."

55. Clifford Siskin, *The Work of Writing: Literature and Social Change in Britain, 1700–1830* (Baltimore: Johns Hopkins Univ. Press, 1990).

56. See Sir William Blackstone, *Commentaries on the Laws of England in Four Books* (1765; reprint, Philadelphia, 1771), 1:454ff.; and Sir Frederick Pollock and Maitland Pollock, *A History of English Law* (Cambridge: Cambridge Univ. Press, 1898).

57. See E. A. Wrigley, *People, Cities, and Wealth: The Transformation of Traditional Society* (Cambridge: Blackwell, 1987); and R. I. Rotberg and Theodore K. Rabb, eds., *Marriage and Fertility* (Princeton: Princeton Univ. Press, 1980).

58. For the connection between the steep rise in illegitimate births at the end of the eighteenth century and the Marriage Act of 1753, see Chapter 3, n. 41.

WORKS CITED

Primary Texts

Aiken, John. *Letters from a Father to a Son.* 1792–93. Reprint, New York: Garland, 1971.

Astell, Mary. *Some Reflections Upon Marriage.* 1694. Reprint, New York: Source Book Press, 1970.

Barbauld, Laetitia. *The British Novelists with an Essay and Prefaces Biographical and Critical.* 50 vols. London, 1810.

Barker, Jane. *Exilius; or the Banish'd Woman.* 1715. Reprint, New York: Garland, 1973.

Barre, François Poullain de la. *The Woman as Good as the Man; or the Equality of Both Sexes.* Trans. A.L. 1677. Reprint, Detroit: Wayne State Univ. Press, 1988.

Beattie, James. *Works.* Ed. F. O. Wolf. Stuttgart: Friedriech Frommen Verlag, 1970.

Blackstone, Sir William. *Commentaries on the Laws of England.* 4 vols. 1765. Reprint, Philadelphia: Robert Bell, 1771.

Blair, Hugh. *Lectures on Rhetoric and Belles Lettres.* 1763. 12th ed., London, 1812.

Bolingbroke, Henry St. John. *Letters on the Spirit of Patriotism and on the Idea of a Patriot King.* 1749. Reprint, Oxford: Clarendon, 1982.

———. *Works.* Philadelphia: Carey & Hart, 1841.

Booth, George, Earl of Warrington. *Considerations upon the Institution of Marriage.* 1739. Reprint, New York: Garland, 1985.

Brightwell, Cecilia Lucy. *Memorials of the Life of Mrs. Opie.* London, 1854.

Brooke, Frances. *The Excursion.* 1777. Reprint, Lexington: Univ. Press of Kentucky, 1996.

———. *Lady Julia Mandeville.* 1764. Reprint: London: Scholartis Press, 1930.

Brunton, Mary. *Self-Control.* 1810. Reprint, London: Pandora, 1986.

Burke, Edmund. *The Writings and Speeches of Edmund Burke.* Vol. 8. *Reflections on the Revolution in France* and *Letter to a Member of the General Assembly.* Ed. Paul Langford. Oxford: Clarendon, 1989.

Burney, Fanny. *Cecilia; or the Memoirs of an Heiress.* 1782. Reprint, Oxford: Oxford Univ. Press, 1988.

———. *Evalina.* 1778. Reprint, Oxford: Oxford Univ. Press, 1968.

Butler, Joseph. *Fifteen Sermons preached at the Rolls Chapel.* 1774. Reprint, London: Bell, 1949.

Carter, Elizabeth. *Memoirs of the Life of Mrs. Carter.* 3 Vols. London: Rivington, 1816.

Chapone, Hester. *Letters on the Improvement of the Mind.* 4th ed. London, 1774.

Clarke, John. *An Essay Upon Study.* 1731. Reprint, Yorkshire: Scolar Press, 1971.

Cobbett's *Parliamentary History of England.* Vol. 15. London: Hansard, 1813.

Collier, Jane. *An Essay on the Art of Ingeniously Tormenting.* London, 1753.

Collier, Mary. *Felicia to Charlotte.* 1749. Reprint, New York: Garland, 1974.

Considerations on the Causes of the Present Stagnation of Matrimony. 1772. Reprint, New York: Garland, 1984.

Cooper, Elizabeth. Preface to *The Muses' Library.* London, 1737.

Defoe, Daniel. *Conjugal Lewdness or Matrimonial Whoredom. A Treatise Concerning the Use and Abuse of the Marriage Bed.* 1727. Reprint, Gainesville, Fla.: Scolars Press, 1967.

Dennis, John. *Vice and Luxury Publick Mischiefs; or Remarks on a Book Intituled The Fable of the Bees or Privat Vices Publick Benefits.* London, 1724.

Dodsley, Robert. *An Essay on Fable.* 1764. Reprint, Los Angeles: Augustan Reprint Society, no. 112, 1965.

Douglas, F. *Reflections on Celibacy and Marriage.* 1771. Reprint, New York: Garland, 1984.

Drake, Judith. *An Essay in Defence of the Female Sex.* 1696. Reprint, New York: Source Book Press, 1970.

Duff, William. *Letters on the Intellectual and Moral Character of Women.* 1807 ed. Reprint, New York: Garland, 1974.

Edgeworth, Maria. *Belinda.* 1801. Reprint, Oxford: Oxford Univ. Press, 1996.

———. *Castle Rackrent.* 1800. Reprint, Oxford: Oxford Univ. Press, 1991.

———. *Letters for Literary Ladies.* 1795. Reprint, New York: Garland, 1974.

Edgeworth, Maria, and Richard Lovell Edgeworth. *Practical Education.* 1798. Reprint, New York: Garland, 1974.

Elledge, Scott. *Eighteenth-Century Critical Essays.* Ithaca: Cornell Univ. Press, 1961.

Encyclopédie ou Dictionnaire Raisonné des Sciences, des Arts, et des Métiers par une société de gens de lettres. 6 vols. Ed. Diderot and D'Alembert. Paris, 1751.

Fenelon, François de Salignac de la Mothe. *Education des Filles.* 1687. Paris: Lagny, 1937.

Fenwick, Eliza. *Secresy; or Ruin on the Rock.* 1795. Reprint, Ontario: Broadview, 1994.

Ferguson, Adam. *Institutes of Moral Philosophy.* New enlarged ed. Basil: James Decker, 1800.

Ferguson, Moira, ed. *First Feminists: British Women Writers, 1578–1799.* Bloomington: Indiana Univ. Press, 1985.

Fielding, Sarah. *The Adventures of David Simple.* 1744. Reprint, Oxford: Oxford Univ. Press, 1969.

———. Preface to *The History of Countess Dellwyn.* London, 1759.

———. *The Lives of Cleopatra and Octavia.* 1757. Reprint, London: Scholartis Press, 1928.

———. *Remarks on Clarissa.* 1749. Reprint, Los Angeles: William Clark Memorial Library, no. 231, 1985.

Fleetwood, William. *The Relative Duties of Parents and Children, Husbands and Wives, Masters and Servants.* 1705. Reprint, New York: Garland, 1985.

Gally, Henry. *Some Considerations upon Clandestine Marriages.* London, 1729.

Gentleman's Magazine. Vols. 22–25. London, 1753–55.

Gisbourne, Thomas. *An Enquiry into the Duties of the Female Sex.* 1797. Reprint, New York: Garland, 1974.

Godwin, William. *Enquiry Concerning Political Justice.* 1793. Reprint, Oxford: Clarendon, 1971.

Gregory, John. *A Father's Legacy to His Daughters.* 1774. Reprint, New York: Garland, 1974.

Hamilton, Lady Mary. *Munster Village.* 1778. Reprint, London: Pandora, 1987.

Hanway, Mary Ann. *Ellinor; or the World as It Is.* 1798. Reprint, New York: Garland, 1974.

Hays, Mary. *Appeal to the Men of Great Britain in Behalf of Women.* 1798. Reprint, New York: Garland, 1974.

———. *Letters and Essays, Moral and Miscellaneous.* 1793. Reprint, New York: Garland, 1974.

———. *Memoirs of Emma Courtney.* 1796. Reprint, Oxford: Oxford Univ. Press, 1996.

———. *The Victim of Prejudice.* 1799. Reprint, Ontario: Broadview, 1994.

Haywood, Eliza. *The Female Spectator.* 4 vols. London, 1775.

———. *The History of Miss Betsy Thoughtless.* 1751. Reprint, Oxford: Oxford Univ. Press, 1996.

Home, Henry, Lord Kames. *Elements of Criticism.* 1763. Reprint, New York: Barnes, 1855.

Hume, David. *Essays Literary, Moral and Political.* London: Ward, Locke & Tyler, n.d.

Hutcheson, Francis. *Collected Works.* Hildesheim, Germany: Georg Olms Facsimile Edition, 1969.

Inchbald, Elizabeth. *Nature and Art.* 1796. Reprint, Oxford: Woodstock Books, 1994.

———. *A Simple Story.* 1791. Reprint, London: Pandora, 1987.

Johnson, Samuel. *Dictionary.* Corrected and revised. 8th ed. London, 1799.

———. *The Rambler,* no. 4. London, 1751.

Knox, Vicissimus. *Essays, Moral and Literary.* 2 vols. 1792. Reprint, New York: Garland, 1972.

Lennox, Charlotte. *Sophia.* 1762. Reprint, New York: Garland, 1974.

Letter to the Public containing the Substance of what hath been offered in late Debates upon the Subject of the Act of Parliament for the better preventing of Clandestine Marriages. London, 1753.

Locke, John. *Essay Concerning Human Understanding.* London: Everyman, 1947.

———. "Some Thoughts Concerning Education." In *The Educational Writings of John Locke.* Ed. James L. Laxwell. Cambridge: Cambridge Univ. Press, 1968.

———. *Two Treatises on Government.* Ed. and Intro. Peter Laslett. Cambridge: Cambridge Univ. Press, 1967.

Macauley, Catherine. *Letters on Education.* 1790. Reprint, New York: Garland, 1974.

Makin, Bathsua. *An Essay to revive the Antient Education of Gentlewomen in Religion, Manners, Arts and Tongues.* London, 1673.

Malthus, Thomas Robert. *First Essay on Population.* 1798. Reprint, New York: Reprints of Economic Classics, 1965.

Mandeville, Bernard. *Fable of the Bees; or Private Vices, Publick Benefits.* 1714. Oxford: Clarendon, 1924.

Manley, Mary Delariviere. *The Secret History of Queen Zarah and the Zarazians.* London, 1705.

———. "The Wife's Resentment." In *The Meridian Anthology of Early Women Writers: British Literary Women from Aphra Behn to Maria Edgeworth, 1660–1800.* Ed. Katharine M. Rogers and William McCarthy. New York: St. Martin's, 1964.

Masham, Lady Damaris. *Occasional Thoughts in Reference to a Vertuous or Christian Life.* London, 1705.

Mill, John Stuart. *The Subjection of Women.* 1869. Reprint, London: Virago, 1983.

Montesquieu, Charles de Secondat, Baron de. *De L'Esprit des Lois.* 6 vols. Paris, 1834.

More, Hannah. *Works.* 12 vols. London, 1818.

Oldmixon, John. *An Essay on Criticism.* 1728. Reprint, Los Angeles: Augustan Reprint Society, no. 107, 1964.

Opie, Amelia. *Adeline Mowbray, or The Mother and Daughter.* 1804. Reprint, London: Pandora, 1986.

Paley, William. *Paley's Moral Philosophy.* Annotated by Richard Whateley. London: Parker & Son, 1859.

Philogamus. *The Present State of Matrimony.* 1739. Reprint, New York: Garland, 1985.

Pope, Alexander. "Eloisa to Abelard." In *The Poems of Alexander Pope.* Ed. John Butt. 1717. London: Methuen, 1963.

Radcliffe, Ann. *The Romance of the Forest.* 1791. Reprint, Oxford: Oxford Univ. Press, 1986.

Radcliffe, Mary Ann. *The Female Advocate; or an Attempt to Recover the Rights of Women from Male Usurpation.* 1788. Reprint, New York: Garland, 1974.

Ramsey, William. *Conjugium Conjurgium.* 1673. Reprint, New York: Garland, 1976.

Reeve, Clara. *Plans of Education, with Remarks on the Systems of other Writers.* 1792. Reprint, New York: Garland, 1974.

——. *The Progress of Romance.* 1785. Reprint, New York: Facsimile Editions, 1974.

Rousseau, Jean-Jacques. *Du Contrat Social.* Paris: Editions Sociales, 1955.

——. *Emilius and Sophia; or, an Essay on Education by John James Rousseau, Citizen of Geneva.* Trans. William Kendrick. Dublin, 1775.

——. *First and Second Discourses.* Ed. Roger D. Masters. New York: St. Martin's, 1964.

——. *Julia; or the New Eloisa. A Series of Original Letters Collected and Published by J. J. Rousseau.* 3 vols. Trans. William Kendrick. Edinburgh, 1794.

Salmon, Thomas. *A Critical Essay Concerning Marriage.* 1724. Reprint, New York: Garland, 1985.

Scott, Sarah. *The History of Cornelia.* 1750. Reprint, New York: Garland, 1976.

——. *The History of Sir George Ellison.* 1766. Reprint, Lexington: Univ. Press of Kentucky, 1996.

——. *Millenium Hall* 1762. Reprint, Ontario: Broadview, 1994.

Seymour, William. *Marriage Asserted: In Answer to a Book Entitled Conjugium Conjurgium.* 1674. Reprint, New York: Garland, 1976.

Sheridan, Frances. *Memoirs of Miss Sidney Bidulph.* 1761. Reprint, Oxford: Oxford Univ. Press, 1996.

Smith, Adam. *An Inquiry into the Nature and Causes of the Wealth of Nations.* 1776. New York: Modern Library, 1937.

——. *The Theory of Moral Sentiments.* 1759. Ed. Raphel Macfie. Oxford: Clarendon, 1979.

Smith, Charlotte. *Desmond.* 1792. Reprint, New York: Garland, 1974.

———. *Emmeline: The Orphan of the Castle.* 1788. Reprint, Oxford: Oxford Univ. Press, 1971.

———. *Marchmont.* 1796. Reprint, New York: Scholars Facsimiles, 1989.

———. *Montalbert.* 1795. Reprint, New York: Scholars Facsimiles, 1989.

———. *The Old Manor House.* 1793. Reprint, London: Pandora, 1987.

———. *The Young Philosopher.* 1798. Reprint, Lexington: Univ. Press of Kentucky, 1999.

Stanhope, Philip Dormer, Lord Chesterfield. *Letters to His Son.* 2nd ed. London, 1775.

Stebbing, Henry. *A Dissertation on the Power of States to Deny Civil Protection to the Marriages of Minors made without the Consent of their Parents or Guardians.* London, 1754.

———. *An Inquiry into the Force and Operation of the Annulling Clauses of a Late Act for the better preventing of Clandestine Marriages.* London, 1753.

Steuart, James. *An Inquiry into the Principles of Political Economy.* 1767; revised 1780. Edinburgh: Oliver & Boyd, 1966.

Wakefield, Priscilla. *Reflections on the Present Condition of the Female Sex.* 1798. Reprint, New York: Garland, 1974.

West, Jane. *Letters to a Young Lady in which the Duties and Characters of Women are Considered.* 3 vols. 2nd ed. of 1806. Reprint, New York: Garland, 1974.

———. *A Gossip's Story.* 1797. Reprint, New York: Garland, 1974.

Williams, Helen Maria. *Julia.* 1790. Reprint, New York: Garland, 1974.

Williams, Ioan, ed. *Novel and Romance, 1700–1800: A Documentary History.* New York: Barnes & Noble, 1970.

Wollstonecraft, Mary. *Mary and the Wrongs of Woman.* 1788; 1798. Reprint, Oxford: Oxford Univ. Press, 1976.

———. *A Vindication of the Rights of Man.* Edited by Sylvana Tomaselli. 1790. Reprint, Cambridge: Cambridge Univ. Press: 1995.

———. *A Vindication of the Rights of Woman, with Strictures on Moral and Political Subjects.* Ed. Ulrich H. Hardt. 1792. Reprint, New York: Whitston, 1982.

Secondary Texts

Abbott, Mary. *Family Ties: English Families, 1540–1920.* New York: Routledge, 1993.

Abbott, Pamela, and Claire Wallace. *The Family and the New Right.* London: Pluto, 1992.

Ackley, Katherine Anne. "Violence against Women in the Novels of Early British

Women Writers." In *Living by the Pen: Early British Women Writers,* ed. Dale Spender. New York: Teachers' College Press, 1992.

Amos, Flora Ross. *Early Theories of Translation.* New York: Columbia Univ. Press, 1920.

Amussen, Susan Dwyer. *An Ordered Society: Gender and Class in Early Modern England.* Oxford: Blackwell, 1988.

Anderson, Michael. "The Social Implications of Demographic Change." In *The Cambridge Social History of Britain, 1750–1950,* ed. F. M. L. Thompson. Cambridge: Cambridge Univ. Press, 1990.

Armstrong, Nancy. *Desire and Domestic Fiction: A Political History of the Novel.* Oxford: Oxford Univ. Press, 1987.

Armstrong, Nancy, and Leonard Tennenhouse. *The Imaginary Puritan: Literature, Intellectual Labour, and the Origins of Personal Life.* Berkeley: Univ. of California Press, 1992.

Ashcraft, Richard. *Revolutionary Politics and Locke's "Two Treatises on Government".* Princeton, N.J.: Princeton Univ. Press, 1986.

Bacchi, Carol Lee. *Same Difference: Feminism and Sexual Difference.* Sydney: Allen & Unwin, 1990.

Bannet, Eve Tavor. "Analogy as Translation: Derrida, Wittgenstein, and the Law of Language." *New Literary History* 28, no. 4 (Fall 1997): 655–72.

——. *Postcultural Theory: Critical Theory after the Marxist Paradigm.* London: Macmillan, 1993.

——. "The Scene of Translation: After Jakobson, Benjamin, Derrida, and De Man." *New Literary History* 24, no. 3 (August 1993): 577–95.

[Bannet], Eve Tavor. *Scepticism, Society, and the Eighteenth-Century Novel.* London: Macmillan, 1987; New York: St. Martin's, 1987.

Barthes, Roland. *Sollers Ecrivain.* Paris: Seuil, 1979.

Baumann, Zygmunt. *Legislators and Interpreters.* Cambridge: Polity Press, 1987.

Benn, S. I., and G. F. Ganz. *Public and Private in Social Life.* New York: St. Martin's, 1983.

Bowers, Toni. *The Politics of Motherhood: British Writing and Culture, 1680–1760.* Cambridge: Cambridge Univ. Press, 1996.

Bowstead, Diana. "Charlotte Smith's *Desmond:* The Epistolary Novel as Ideological Argument." In *Fetter'd or Free? British Women Novelists, 1670–1815.* Ed. Mary Anne Schofield and Cecilia Macheski, 237–63. Athens: Ohio Univ. Press, 1986.

Brennan, Teresa, and Carole Pateman. "Mere Auxiliaries of the Commonwealth: Women and the Origins of Liberalism." *Political Studies* 27, no. 2 (June 1979): 183–200.

Brown, Roger Lee. "The Rise and Fall of Fleet Marriages." In *Marriage and Society: Studies in the Social History of Marriage,* ed. R. B. Outhwaite. New York: St. Martin's, 1981.

Browne, Alice. *The Eighteenth-Century Feminist Mind.* Detroit: Wayne State Univ. Press, 1987.

Buchanan, Constance H. *Choosing to Lead: Women and the Crisis of American Values.* Boston: Beacon, 1996.

Butler, Marilyn. "Edgeworth's Stern Father: Escaping Thomas Day 1795–1801." In *Tradition in Transition: Women Writers, Marginal Texts, and the Eighteenth-Century Canon,* ed. Alvar Ribeiro and James G. Basker. Oxford: Clarendon, 1996.

——. *Jane Austen and the War of Ideas.* Oxford: Clarendon, 1975.

——. "Revolving in Deep Time: The French Revolution as Narrative." In *Revolution and English Romanticism: Politics and Rhetoric,* ed. Keith Hanley and Raman Selden. New York: St. Martin's, 1990.

——, ed. *Burke, Paine, Godwin, and the Revolutionary Conspiracy.* Cambridge: Cambridge Univ. Press, 1984.

Butler, Melissa. "Early Liberal Roots of Feminism: John Locke and the Attack on Patriarchy." *American Political Science Review* 72 (1978): 135–50.

Cannon, John. *Aristocratic Century: The Peerage in Eighteenth-Century England.* Cambridge: Cambridge Univ. Press, 1984.

Castle, Terry. *Masquerade and Civilization: The Carnivalesque in Eighteenth-Century English Culture and Fiction.* Stanford, Calif.: Stanford Univ. Press, 1986.

Clark, Alice. *Working Life of Women in the Seventeenth Century.* London: Routledge, 1919.

Clark, J. C. D. *English Society, 1688–1832: Ideology, Social Structure, and Political Practice during the Ancien Régime.* Cambridge: Cambridge Univ. Press, 1985.

Colley, Linda. *Britons: Forging the Nation, 1707–1837.* New Haven: Yale Univ. Press, 1992.

Conger, Syndy McMillen. "The Sorrows of Young Charlotte: Werther's English Sisters." *Goethe Yearbook* 3 (1986): 21–56.

Copeland, Edward. *Women Writing about Money: Women's Fiction in England, 1790–1820.* Cambridge: Cambridge Univ. Press, 1995.

Coward, Rosalind. *Our Treacherous Hearts.* London: Faber & Faber, 1992.

Curtis, S. J. and M. E. A. Boultwood. *An Introductory History of English Education since 1800.* London: University Tutorial Press, 1960.

Cutting-Gray, Joanne. *Woman as "Nobody:" The Novels of Fanny Burney.* Gainsville: Univ. Press of Florida, 1992.

Davidoff, Leonore. "The Family in Britain." In *The Cambridge Social History of*

Britain, 1750–1950, ed. F. M. L. Thompson. Cambridge: Cambridge Univ. Press, 1990.

Davidoff, Leonore, and Catherine Hall. *Family Fortunes: Men and Women of the English Middle Class, 1780–1850.* Chicago: Chicago Univ. Press, 1987.

Davis, Lennard J. *Factual Fictions: The Origins of the English Novel.* New York: Columbia Univ. Press, 1983.

Deane, Seamus. *The French Revolution and the Enlightenment in England, 1789–1832.* Cambridge: Cambridge Univ. Press, 1988.

Derrida, Jacques. *The Ear of the Other: Otobiography, Transference, Translation.* New York: Schocken, 1982.

——. "Les Langues et les Institutions de la Philosophie," *Texte* 4 (1985).

——. "Des Tours de Babel." In *Psyche: Invention de l'Autre.* Paris: Seuil, 1987.

Donzelot, Jacques. *The Policing of Families.* New York: Pantheon, 1979.

Doody, Margaret Ann. "Frances Sheridan: Morality and Annihilated Time." In *Fetter'd or Free? British Women Novelists, 1670–1815,* ed. Mary Anne Schofield and Cecilia Macheschi, 324–58. Athens: Ohio Univ. Press, 1986.

Duffy, Edward. *Rousseau in England: The Context of Shelley's Critique of the Enlightenment.* Berkeley: Univ. of California Press, 1979.

Durston, Christopher. *The Family in the English Revolution.* Oxford: Blackwell, 1989.

Eisenstein, Zillah. *The Radical Future of Liberal Feminism.* New York: Longman, 1981.

Elliott, Pat. "Charlotte Smith's Feminism." In *Living by the Pen: Early British Women Writers,* ed. Dale Spender, 91–112. New York: Teacher's College Press, 1992.

Ellis, Kate Ferguson. *The Contested Castle: Gothic Novels and the Subversion of Domestic Ideology.* Champaign: Univ. of Illinois Press, 1989.

Elshtain, Jean Bethke. *Private Woman and Public Man: Women in Social and Political Thought.* Princeton, N.J.: Princeton Univ. Press, 1981.

——, ed. *The Family in Political Thought.* Amherst: Univ. of Massachussetts Press, 1982.

Epstein, Julia. *The Iron Pen: Frances Burney and the Politics of Women's Writing.* Madison: Univ. of Wisconsin Press, 1989.

Evans, Judith. *Feminist Theory Today: An Introduction to Second-Wave Feminism.* London: Sage, 1995.

Ezell, Margaret J. *The Patriarch's Wife.* Chapel Hill: Univ. of North Carolina Press, 1987.

——. *Writing Women's Literary History.* Baltimore: Johns Hopkins University Press, 1993.

Fairchild, Cissie. "Female Sexual Attitudes and the Rise of Illegitimacy: A Case Study." *Journal of Interdisciplinary History* 8, no. 4 (Spring 1978): 627–67.

Ferguson, Moira. *Subject to Others: British Women Writers and Colonial Slavery, 1670–1834.* New York: Routledge, 1992.

Flandrin, Jean Louis. *Families in Former Times: Kinship, Household, and Sexuality.* Cambridge: Cambridge Univ. Press, 1976.

Fletcher, Anthony. *Gender, Sex, and Subordination in England, 1500–1800.* New Haven, Conn.: Yale Univ. Press, 1995.

Friedan, Betty. *Beyond Gender.* Washington D.C.: Woodrow Wilson Center Press, 1997.

Fry, Carroll L. *Charlotte Smith.* New York: Twayne, 1996.

Furniss, Tom. "Gender in Revolution: Edmund Burke and Mary Wollstonecraft." In *Revolution in Writing: British Literary Responses to the French Revolution,* ed. Kevin Everest. Buckingham, England: Open Univ. Press, 1991.

Gallagher, Catherine. *Nobody's Story: The Vanishing Acts of Women Writers in the Market Place, 1670–1820.* Berkeley: Univ. of California Press, 1994.

Gatens, Moira. *Feminism and Philosophy.* Bloomington: Indiana Univ. Press, 1991.

Gilligan, Carol. *In a Different Voice: Psychological Theory and Women's Development.* Cambridge: Harvard Univ. Press, 1982.

Gillis, John. *For Better or Worse: British Marriages, 1600 to the Present.* Oxford: Oxford Univ. Press, 1985.

Gobetti, Daniela. *Private and Public: Individuals, Households, and the Body Politic in Locke and Hutcheson.* New York: Routledge, 1992.

Gonda, Caroline. *Reading Daughters' Fictions, 1709–1834.* Cambridge: Cambridge Univ. Press, 1996.

Green, Katherine Sobba. *The Courtship Novel, 1740–1820.* Lexington: Univ. Press of Kentucky, 1991.

Greenblatt, Stephen. *Renaissance Self-Fashioning from More to Shakespeare.* Chicago: Univ. of Chicago Press, 1980.

Griffin, Dustin. *Literary Patronage in England, 1650–1800.* Cambridge: Cambridge Univ. Press, 1996.

Grimshaw, Jean. *Philosophy and Feminist Thinking.* Minneapolis: Univ. of Minnesota Press, 1986.

Gross, Elizabeth. "Sexual Difference and the Problem of Essentialism." In *The Essential Difference,* ed. Naomi Shor and Elizabeth Weed. Bloomington: Indiana Univ. Press, 1994.

Guest, Harriet. "The Wanton Muse: Politics and Gender in Gothic Theory after 1760." In *Beyond Romanticism: New Approaches to Texts and Contexts,* ed. Stephen Copley and John Whale. London: Routledge, 1992.

Hampton, Timothy. *Writing from History: The Rhetoric of Exemplarity in Renaissance Literature.* Ithaca, N.Y.: Cornell Univ. Press, 1990.

Hill, Bridget. "A Refuge from Man: The Idea of a Protestant Nunnery." *Past and Present* 117 (1987): 107–30.

———. *The Republican Virago: The Life and Times of Catherine Macauley.* Oxford: Clarendon, 1992.

———. *Women, Work, and Sexual Politics in Eighteenth-Century England.* Oxford: Blackwell, 1989.

Hinds, Hilary. *God's Englishwoman: Seventeenth-Century Radical Sectarian Writing and Feminist Criticism.* Manchester: Manchester Univ. Press, 1996.

Hirsch, Mariane, and Evelyn Fox Keller, eds. *Conflicts in Feminism.* New York: Routledge, 1990.

Hobby, Elaine. *Virtue of Necessity: English Women's Writing, 1646–1688.* London: Virago, 1988.

Hoeveler, Diane Long. *Gothic Feminism: The Professionalization of Gender from Charlotte Smith to the Brontës.* University Park: Pennsylvania State Univ. Press, 1995.

Houlbrooke, Ralph. A. *The English Family, 1450–1700.* New York: Longman, 1984.

Howard, George Elliot. *A History of Matrimonial Institutions.* 2 vols. Chicago: Univ. of Chicago Press, 1904.

Hufton, Olwen H. *Women and the Limits of Citizenship in the French Revolution.* Toronto: Univ. of Toronto Press, 1992.

Hunt, Lynn. *The Family Romance of the French Revolution.* Berkeley: Univ. of California Press, 1992.

Hurst, Michael. *Maria Edgeworth and the Public Scene: Intellect, Fine Feeling, and Landlordism in the Age of Reform.* Coral Gables, Fla.: Univ. of Miami Press, 1969.

Ingram, Martin. "The Reform of Popular Culture? Sex and Marriage in Early Modern England." In *Popular Culture in Seventeenth-Century England,* ed. Barry Reay. New York: St. Martin's, 1985.

Johnson, Claudia. *Equivocal Beings: Politics, Gender, and Sentimentality in th 1790s: Wollstonecraft, Radcliffe, Burney, Austen.* Chicago: Univ. of Chicago Press, 1995.

Kamuf, Peggy. *Fictions of Feminine Desire: Disclosures of Heloise.* Lincoln: Univ. of Nebraska Press, 1982.

Kelly, Gary. *Revolutionary Feminism: The Life and Career of Mary Wollstonecraft.* New York: St. Martin's, 1992.

———. *Women, Writing, and Revolution.* Oxford: Clarendon, 1993.

Kennedy, Ellen, and Susan Mendus, eds. *Women in Western Philosophy: Kant to Nietzsche.* New York: St. Martin's, 1987.

Kenny, Virginia C. *The Country-House Ethos in English Literature, 1688–1750.* Sussex: Harvester, 1984.

Kinnaird, Joan K. 1979. "Astell and the Conservative Contribution to English Feminism." *Journal of British Studies* 19, no. 1 (1979): 53–75.

Korskin, Paul K. *Typologies in England, 1650–1820.* Princeton, N.J.: Princeton Univ. Press, 1982.

Kowalski-Wallace, Elizabeth. *Their Fathers' Daughters: Hannah More, Maria Edgeworth and Patriarchal Complicity.* Oxford: Oxford Univ. Press, 1991.

Laclau, Ernesto, and Chantal Mouffe. *Hegemony and Socialist Strategy: Towards a Radical Democratic Politics.* London: Verso, 1985.

Langford, Paul. *Public Life and the Propertied Englishman, 1689–1798.* Oxford: Clarendon, 1991.

Langland, Elizabeth. *Nobody's Angels: Middle-Class Women and Domestic Ideology in Victorian Culture.* Ithaca, N.Y.: Cornell Univ. Press, 1995.

Laslett, Peter. *Family Life and Illicit Love in Earlier Generations.* Cambridge: Cambridge Univ. Press, 1977.

Laslett, Peter, and Richard Wall, eds. *Household and Family in Past Time.* Cambridge: Cambridge Univ. Press, 1972.

Leneman, Leah, and Rosalind Mitchison. "Clandestine Marriage in the Scottish Cities, 1660–1780." *Journal of Social History* 24, no. 4 (1993): 845–61.

Lewis, Judith Schneid. *In the Family Way: Childbearing in the British Aristocracy, 1760–1860.* New Brunswick, N.J.: Rutgers Univ. Press, 1986.

Lloyd, Genevieve. *The Man of Reason: Male and Female in Western Philosophy.* London: Methuen, 1984.

London, April. "Jane West and the Politics of Reading." In *Tradition in Transition: Women Writers, Marginal Texts, and the Eighteenth-Century Canon,* ed. Alvaro Ribeiro and James G. Basker, 56–74. Oxford: Clarendon, 1996.

Lyons, John D. *Exemplum: The Rhetoric of Example in Early Modern France and Italy.* Princeton, N.J.: Princeton Univ. Press, 1989.

Madoff, Mark. "The Useful Myth of Gothic Ancestry." *Studies in Eighteenth-Century Culture* 8 (1979): 337–50.

McKeon, Michael. *The Origins of the English Novel, 1600–1740.* Baltimore: Johns Hopkins University Press, 1987.

McMullen, Lorraine. *An Odd Attempt in a Woman: The Literary Life of Frances Brooke.* Vancouver: Univ. of British Columbia Press, 1983.

Mellor, Anne. "'Am I not a Woman and a Sister?' Slavery, Romanticism and Gender." In *Romanticism, Race and Imperial Culture, 1780–1834,* ed. Alan Richardson and Sonio Hofkosh. Bloomington: Indiana Univ. Press, 1996.

———. *Romanticism and Gender.* New York: Routledge, 1993.

Messer-Davidow, Ellen. "'For Softeness She': Gender Ideology and Esthetics in Eighteenth-Century England." In *Eighteenth-Century Women and the Arts,* ed. Frederick M. Keener and Susan E. Lorsch. New York: Greenwood, 1988.

Meteyard, Belinda. "Illegitimacy and Marriage in Eighteenth-Century England." *Journal of Interdisciplinary History* 10 (1980): 479–89.

Miles, Robert. *Gothic Writing, 1750–1820: A Genealogy.* New York: Routledge, 1993.

Morgenstern, Mira. *Rousseau and the Politics of Ambiguity: Self, Culture, and Society.* University Park: Pennsylvania State Univ. Press, 1996.

Myers, Mitzi. "Daddy's Girl as Motherless Child: Maria Edgeworth and Maternal Romance; an Essay in Reassessment." In *Living by the Pen: Early British Women Writers,* ed. Dale Spender, 137–59. New York: Teachers' College Press, 1992.

———. "Hannah More's Tracts for the Times: Social Fiction and Female Ideology." In *Fetter'd or Free? British Women Novelists, 1670–1815,* ed. Mary Anne Schofield and Cecilia Macheski, 264–84. Athens: Ohio Univ. Press, 1986.

Myers, Sylvia Harcstark. *The Bluestocking Circle: Women, Friendship, and the Life of the Mind in Eighteenth-Century England.* Oxford: Clarendon, 1990.

Nicholas, Joseph. "Revolutions Compared: The English Civil War as Political Touchstone in Romantic Literature." In *Revolution and English Romanticism: Politics and Rhetoric,* ed. Keith Hanley and Raman Selden, 261–76. New York: St. Martin's, 1990.

Nicholson, Linda J. *Gender and History: The Limits of Social Theory in the Age of the Family.* New York: Columbia Univ. Press, 1986.

Nussbaum, Felicity A. *The Brink of All We Hate.* Lexington: Kentucky Univ. Press, 1984.

———. *Torrid Zones: Maternity, Sexuality, and Empire in Eighteenth-Century English Narratives.* Baltimore: Johns Hopkins Univ. Press, 1995.

Pateman, Carol. "Feminist Critiques of the Public/Private Dichotomy." In *Public and Private in Social Life,* ed. S. I. Benn and G. F. Ganz. New York: St. Martin's, 1983.

———. *The Social Contract.* Stanford, Calif.: Stanford Univ. Press, 1988.

Paulson, Ronald. *Representations of Revolution, 1789–1820.* New Haven, Conn.: Yale Univ. Press, 1983.

Perkin, Harold. *The Origins of Modern English Society, 1780–1880.* London: Routledge, 1969.

Perry, Ruth. *The Celebrated Mary Astell: An Early English Feminist.* Chicago: Univ. of Chicago Press, 1986.

Phillips, Anne. *Democracy and Difference.* University Park: Penn State Univ. Press, 1993.

Phillips, Roderick. *Putting Asunder: A History of Divorce in Western Society*. Cambridge: Cambridge Univ. Press, 1988.

Pinchbeck, Ivy. *Women Workers and the Industrial Revolution*. London: Routledge, 1930.

Pinchbeck, Ivy, and Margaret Hewitt. *Children in English Society: From Tudor Times to the Eighteenth Century*. 2 vols. London: Routledge, 1969.

Pocock, J. G. A. *The Ancient Constitution and the Feudal Law*. New York: Cambridge Univ. Press, 1987.

——. *Virtue, Commerce, and History*. Cambridge: Cambridge Univ. Press, 1985.

Pollock, Sir Frederick, and Maitland Pollock. *A History of English Law*. Cambridge: Cambridge Univ. Press, 1898.

Poovey, Mary. *The Proper Lady and the Woman Writer: Ideology and Style in the Works of Mary Wollstonecraft, Mary Shelley, and Jane Austen*. Chicago: Univ. of Chicago Press, 1984.

Prickett, Stephen, ed. *England and the French Revolution*. London: Macmillan, 1989.

Ray, William. *Story and History: Narrative Authority and Social Identity in the Eighteenth-Century French and English Novel*. Oxford: Blackwell, 1990.

Rendall, Jane. *The Origins of Modern Feminism, 1780–1860*. Chicago: Lyceum, 1985.

Rhode, Deborah L. *Theoretical Perspectives on Sexual Difference*. New Haven, Conn.: Yale Univ. Press, 1990.

Rich, Adrienne. *Of Woman Born: Motherhood as Experience and Institution*. New York: Norton, 1976.

Richter, David H. *The Progress of Romance: Literary Historiography and the Gothic Novel*. Columbus: Ohio State Univ. Press, 1996.

Rizzo, Betty. *Companions without Vows: Relations among Eighteenth-Century British Women*. Athens: Univ. of Georgia Press, 1994.

Robbins, Caroline. *The Eighteenth-Century Commonwealthsman*. Cambridge: Harvard Univ. Press, 1959.

Roddier, Henri. *Jean-Jacques Rousseau en Angleterre au dix-huitième Siècle*. Paris: Boivin, 1950.

Rogers, Deborah, ed. *The Critical Response to Ann Radcliffe*. Westport, Conn.: Greenwood, 1994.

Rogers, Katharine. 1992. "Elizabeth Inchbald: Not Such a Simple Story." In *Living by the Pen: Early British Women Writers*, ed. Dale Spender, 82–90. New York: Teachers' College Press, 1992.

——. *Feminism in Eighteenth-Century England*. Champaign: Univ. of Illinois Press, 1982.

———. *Frances Burney: The World of Female Difficulties.* New York: Harvester Wheatsheaf, 1990.

Rotberg, R. I., and Theodore K. Rabb, eds. *Marriage and Fertility.* Princeton, N.J.: Princeton Univ. Press, 1980.

Sack, James J. *From Jacobite to Conservative: Reaction and Orthodoxy in Britain, 1760–1832.* Cambridge: Cambridge Univ. Press, 1993.

Schellekens, Jona. "Courtship, the Clandestine Marriage Act, and Fertility in England." *Journal of Interdisciplinary History* 25, no. 3 (Winter 1995): 433–44.

Schnorrenberg, Barbara. "A Paradise Like Eve's: Three Eighteenth-Century British Utopias." *Women's Studies* 9, no. 3 (1982): 263–73.

Schochet, Gordon J. *Patriarchalism in Political Thought.* Oxford: Blackwell, 1975.

Schofield, Mary Anne. *Masking and Unmasking the Female Mind: Disguising Romances in Feminine Fiction, 1713–1799.* Newark: Univ. of Delaware Press, 1990.

Schor, Naomi, and Elizabeth Weed, eds. *The Essential Difference.* Bloomington: Indiana Univ. Press, 1994.

Shanley, Mary Lyndon. "Marriage Contract and Social Contract in Seventeenth-Century English Political Thought." *American Political Science Review* 32 (1979): 79–91.

Sharp, Andrew, ed. *Political Ideas of the English Civil Wars, 1641–1649.* London: Longman, 1983.

Sheriff, John K. *The Good-Natured Man: The Evolution of a Moral Ideal, 1660–1800.* Tuscaloosa: Univ. of Alabama Press, 1982.

Shoemaker, Robert B. *Gender and English Society, 1650–1850.* London: Longman, 1998.

Siskin, Clifford. *The Work of Writing: Literature and Social Change in Britain, 1700–1830.* Baltimore: Johns Hopkins Univ. Press, 1998.

Smith, Hilda. *Reason's Disciples: Seventeenth-Century English Feminists.* Urbana: Univ. of Illinois Press, 1982.

Spacks, Patricia Myer. *Desire and Truth: Functions of Plot in Eighteenth-Century English Novels.* Chicago: Univ. of Chicago Press, 1990.

———. "Sisters." In *Fetter'd or Free: British Women Novelists, 1670–1815,* ed. Mary Ann Schofield and Cecilia Macheschi. Athens: Ohio Univ. Press, 1986: 136–51.

Spencer, Jane. *The Rise of the Woman Novelist: From Aphra Behn to Jane Austen.* Oxford: Blackwell, 1986.

———. "The Use of Her Daughter: Maternal Authority in Early Women Novelists." In *Living by the Pen: Early British Women Writers,* ed. Dale Spender. New York: Teachers' College Press, 1992.

Spender, Dale. *Mothers of the Novel: 100 Good Women Writers before Jane Austen.* London: Pandora, 1986.

Stanton, Judith Phillips. "Statistical Profile of Women Writing in English from 1660 to 1800." In *Eighteenth-Century Women and the Arts,* ed. Frederick M. Keener and Susan E. Korsch. New York: Greenwood, 1988.

Staves, Susan. *Married Women's Separate Property in England, 1660–1833.* Cambridge: Harvard Univ. Press, 1990.

Stone, Lawrence. *The Family, Sex, and Marriage in England, 1500–1800.* New York: Harper & Row, 1977.

———. *The Road to Divorce: England 1530–1987.* Oxford: Oxford Univ. Press, 1992.

Straub, Kristina. *Divided Fictions: Fanny Burney and Feminine Strategy.* Lexington: Univ. Press of Kentucky, 1987.

Streeter, Harold Wade. *The English Novel in French Translation.* New York: Institute of French Studies, 1936.

Suleiman, Susan. *Authoritarian Fictions: The Ideological Novel as a Literary Genre.* New York: Columbia Univ. Press, 1983.

Sutherland, Katherine. "Hannah More's Counter-Revolutionary Feminism." In *Revolution in Writing: British Literary Responses to the French Revolution,* ed. Kevin Everest. Buckingham: Open Univ. Press, 1991.

Tavor [Bannet], Eve. *Scepticism, Society, and the Eighteenth-Century Novel.* London: Macmillan, 1987; New York: St. Martin's, 1987.

Taylor, Barbara. *Eve and the New Jerusalem: Socialism and Feminism in the Nineteenth Century.* New York: Pantheon, 1983.

Texte, Joseph. *Jean-Jacques Rousseau and the Cosmopolitan Spirit in Literature.* New York: G. E. Stechert, 1899.

Thompson, James. *Models of Value: Eighteenth-Century Political Economy and the Novel.* Durham: Duke Univ. Press, 1996.

Thompson, Martyn P. *Ideas of Contract in English Political Thought in the Age of John Locke.* New York: Garland, 1987.

Tilly, Louise, and Joan Scott. *Women, Work, and Family.* New York: Methuen, 1978.

Tobin, Beth Fowkes. *Superintending the Poor: Charitable Ladies and Paternal Landlords in British Fiction, 1770–1860.* New Haven, Conn.: Yale Univ. Press, 1993.

Todd, Janet. *Sensibility: An Introduction.* London: Methuen, 1986.

———. *The Sign of Angellica: Women, Writing, and Fiction, 1660–1800.* New York: Columbia Univ. Press, 1989.

———. *Women's Friendship in Literature.* New York: Columbia Univ. Press, 1980.

Tompkins, J. M. S. *The Popular Novel in England, 1770–1800.* Lincoln: Univ. of Nebraska Press, 1961.

Trill, Suzanne. "Religion and the Construction of Femininity." In *Women and Literature in Britain, 1500–1700,* ed. Helen Wilcox. Cambridge: Cambridge Univ. Press, 1996.

Trumbach, Randolph. *The Rise of the Egalitarian Family: Aristocratic Kinship and Domestic Relations in Eighteenth-Century England* New York: Academic Press, 1978.

Turner, Cheryl. *Living by the Pen: Women Writers in the Eighteenth Century.* London: Routledge, 1992.

Ty, Eleonor. *Unsexed Revolutionaries: Five Women Novelists of the 1790s* Toronto: Univ. of Toronto Press, 1993.

Venuti, Lawrence. *The Translator's Invisibility: A History of Translation.* New York: Routledge, 1995.

Vickery, Amanda. "Golden Age to Separate Spheres; a Review of the Categories and Chronology of English Women's History." *The Historical Journal* 36, no. 2 (1993): 383–414.

Voisine, Jacques. *Jean-Jacques Rousseau en Angleterre.* Paris: Didier, 1956.

Watson, Nicola. *Revolution and the Form of the British Novel. 1790–1825.* Oxford: Clarendon, 1994.

Weeks, Jeffrey. *Sex, Politics, and Society.* London: Longman, 1989.

Williams, Anne. *Art of Darkness: A Poetics of Gothic.* Chicago: Univ. of Chicago Press, 1995.

Woodward, Carolyn. "Sarah Fielding's Self-Destructive Utopia: The Adventures of David Simple." In *Living by the Pen: Early British Women Writers,* ed. Dale Spender. New York: Teachers' College Press, 1992.

Wright, Julia. "'I am ill-fitted': Conflicts of Genre in Eliza Fenwick's *Secresy.*" In *Romanticism, History, and the Possibilities of Genre: Reforming Literature, 1789–1837,* ed. Tilottama Rajan and Julia M. Wright. Cambridge: Cambridge Univ. Press, 1998.

Wrigley, E. A. *People, Cities, and Wealth: The Transformation of Traditional Society.* Oxford: Blackwell, 1987.

Yeazell, Ruth Bernard. *Fictions of Modesty: Women and Courtship in the English Novel.* Chicago: Univ. of Chicago Press, 1991.

INDEX

· Library of Congress Cataloging-in-Publication Data

Bannet, Eve Tavor, 1947–
  The domestic revolution : Enlightenment feminisms and the novel /
Eve Tavor Bannet
    p. cm.
Includes bibliographical references (p.   ) and index.
  ISBN 0-8018-6416-x (alk. paper)
  ISBN 0-8018-6417-8 (pbk : alk. paper)
1. English fiction — 18th century — History and criticism. 2. Feminism
and literature — Great Britain — History — 18th century. 3. English
prose literature — Women authors — History and criticism. 4. English
prose literature — 18th century — History and criticism. 5. Politics and
literature — Great Britain — History — 18th century. 6. Literature and
society — Great Britain — History — 18th century. 7. Women and literature — Great Britain — History — 18th century. 8. English fiction
— Women authors — History and criticism. 9. Domestic fiction, English — History and criticism. 10. Feminist fiction, English — History
and criticism. 11. Family in literature. 12. Enlightenment. I. Title.
PR858.F45 T38 2000
828'.508099287—dc21   99-051004